Copyright © 2018 Latashia Holmes

All rights reserved. This book or any portion thereof
may not be reproduced or used in any manner whatsoever
without the express written permission of the publisher
except for the use of brief quotations in a book review.

ISBN-978-0-9989026-1-6

First Printing, 2019
Printed in the United States of America

Author, Latashia M. Holmes
Editor, Latasha Johnson
Contributor Shannon Holmes

Contact @frxshinc for book covers

So Inspired Publishing Co.

www.soinspiredpublishingco.com

Acknowledgements

First given honor to God I cannot Thank you enough for all you continue to do for me. Your Grace and Mercy Is Sufficient I love You.
This book is dedicated to my late father Charles Holmes Sr. Rip You taught me the true definition of being yourself and that it doesn't matter what anyone thinks about how you live your life as long as you're happy with yourself. You said what you felt at all times even if it hurt someone feelings, you did what you wanted to do regardless of how anyone felt, and you kept a smile on your face and you made everyone around you laugh. You encouraged me to take the leap of faith in life and that I could do whatever It was I wanted to do (right or wrong) Smh and you gave me the strength to believe I could be whatever it was I wanted to be. Thank you again for being the person you were you inspired me to write this book given a character your personality (Bianca) bringing this book to life. May your infectious energy and vibe live on forever I love you daddy.
Special shout out to a few people who ride for me No matter what!! Sometimes in life you get tested by situations and don't know where to turn to. Well in my case God gave me a few people that proven time and time again the true definition of loyalty and support with no limits. I'm humbly grateful for my friends and family that never made me question where I stand in their lives.

My two favorite gals my grandmother Ms. Lee Ester Moore and My Mom the love of my life.

Latasha Johnson whew child I could write a book about you maybe one day I will. You're my BFF but your more than that to me. You're my Everything and I do mean everything literally!! Man, I can't even say what I really want to say without breaking down. If I was you, I would have been stop dealing with me years ago but nope you keep staying by my side No matter what cheering, motivating and encouraging me even helping me up every time I fall. I know God exist in my life because he gave me you. My own personal Angel I love you so much it hurts. Your blessings is coming this our year let's Go!!!

Jerrilynn Vinson Ha thought I wasn't going to mention you huh? Surprise my sweet soul. Your Amazing. Never switched up from day one. Always a phone call away. And such a giving spirit. I owe you everything and some. The world is yours my friend God had a blessing with your name on it. I love you.

Sam Bracy my favorite cousin. You're so beautiful and kind I'm grateful to have you in my life. You're my shoulder to lean on and an ear to listen when I vent. Your generosity doesn't go unnoticed I appreciate all you do for me. I love you

To my children Tamia you're the best daughter anyone could dream of your perfect. I'm obsessed with you, I love everything about you seriously your amazing. Love you daughter

Damarko, I'm so proud of the man that you've become. You keep surprising me with your growth God has something up his sleeve for you. I can't wait to witness it. I love you so much son

Zion you're a dreamer like your mom. Hold on tight to that part of you because dreams become reality!! Look at me I once dreamed of becoming an author and here I am on book two. Keep trusting God and he's going to open doors no man can shut and move mountains and bless you in the presence of your enemies. Trust me I know I love you so much kiddo and hopefully one day you'll understand that. Love mom

Special Thanks to Shannon Holmes for your continued support and guidance meant a lot to me love you bro

To my family that supports me Thank You I love you

And to all my supporters and Thank you so much for coming on this journey with me called life. It's an amazing time to be alive. I'm excited for each and every one of you'll. And I couldn't do what I love to do write stories without you. So, thank you so very much for supporting what I do. I can't wait to support each and everyone on your successful journey. Go be great this year let nothing, or no one hold you back. Godless Everyone and Enjoy I love you Latashia Holmes.

Chapter

1 Till death do us part Chapter

2 Say it isn't so Chapter

3 Side chick chronicles Chapter

4 Handling business Chapter

5 When Reality Hits Chapter

6 Smh Chapter

7 Is This The End

The cold crisp air made the temperature in New York City feel a lot colder than it was. When Amir and Royalty stepped out of the Uber black car, they were greeted by the harsh New York winter once again. Being from Cali they never were quite accustomed to the brutal east coast winters, still the matching lavish grey Chinchilla full length
fur coats and hats had adequately insulated them from the cold.
"Bae, grab them all them bags. We might be a minute. Ain't no sense in having this Uber wait for us when we can just call another one."
Royalty suggested.

Yeah, knowin' you this might take a while." Amir replied, ducking his upper body back into the car to retrieve their belongings. Shopping sprees in various cities across the country was normal for them. In all actuality their lives were anything but normal. Royalty laughed at the comment. Flashing a hint of her pearly white veneers. Royalty knew damn well it was true. Royalty wasn't leaving fifth avenue until she got everything she had come for. Including the knee high Christian Louboutin leather boots that she had been searching for all day.

Standing five foot two inches, Royalty's bold demeanor more than made up for her small stature. The way she carried herself gave
off the air of superiority like she was hood royalty. That's what her husband Amir always said.
A lot of times Amir just like to let her talk; Royalty mouthpiece was wicked. Royalty knew how to handle people. Royalty could talk her way out of trouble or talk way into a come up. Whatever the case maybe. Amir knew that Royalty was a strong woman more than capable of holding
him down. Royalty grind hard to become the woman that she was. For the last few hours the couple had been on a whirlwind shopping spree in high end retail stores up and down Manhattan's famous fifth avenue. They hit flagship stores like Saks fifth avenue, Apple, Louis Vuitton, Tiffany's and Prada to name a few. Currently Royalty had her eyes set on Bergdorf Goodman.

This the last store." Amir told her. "You should be tired of spending money by now.

Money don't have no owners only spenders. So, stop complaining' Amir. We're makin' money as we speak." Royalty explained.

Amir knew that Royalty had a very valid point. Still he wasn't about to let the truth sway his decision. Enough was enough. Amir was just about tired of shopping. You heard what I said." Amir stated. "Don't get cute." Royalty didn't bother to reply. Royalty bite her tongue, choosing not to make a smart ass comment. This wasn't the time to go back and forth with Amir. Royalty couldn't bear the thought of getting him in his feelings and him taking back everything they just bought. Amir could be trifling like that whenever Royalty attacked his manhood. Whether it was deliberate disrespect or accidental Amir always reacted in the same manner, petty.

In an attempt to defuse the situation, Royalty placed her arm under Amir's as they crossed the busy Manhattan street. They darted across the street, jaywalking, something they wouldn't dream of doing back home in Cali. The couple ducked and dodged oncoming traffic, almost getting hit a few times, by multiple New York City yellow taxi cab that seemed to own the chilly city night. Once they reached the sidewalk safely, they laughed wholehearted.

Silly moments like these were fleeting for the couple. Now that they were dealing with large sums of money, everything in their lives seemed to take on a whole different meaning. Everything was suddenly so dead serious.

" ....Girl, you slow. If it wasn't for me that car would have ran ya ass over." Amir jokes.

"Not with you right next to me. You would have jumped right in front of it before that could happen." Royalty stated, scuffling at the notion. "Ain't nothing gonna happen to me if you can help." Although Royalty made the statement in jest, it was the god's honest truth. Amir wasn't a man's man. He wouldn't let no harm come to his lady or anyone else that he loved, if he could help it. Amir was a protector and a provider. It had been that way since they were kids. In his previous life Amir had made a living hurting people.

Truth be told, Royalty owed Amir her life. He had saved her on numerous occasions with the survival skills he learned on the streets of Cali a long time ago.

At that moment looking at her man, made Royalty feel so warm and fuzzy inside. She wanted to give him some pussy right there on the spot. After all these years it was amazing how much Royalty still was physically attracted to Amir. And vice versa. They had had their ups and downs but as a couple they were still down for each other. They stared into each others' eyes, long lustful looks, as if they were frozen in time. For a moment it was as if no one else existed on the bustling New York city streets. They were oblivious to the cars and the

other pedestrians. Amir lowered his face to Royalty's height, gazed in her eyes as if he could read her thoughts. Not now." Amir said, snapping her back into reality. "

What?" Royalty blushed.

Royalty I already know what you're thinking. I know you. Keep that same energy for when we get back home, behind closed doors. Amir told Royalty.

An outpouring of love was written all over her face.

Amir often wondered how had Royalty ever fallen in love with a man like him. She knew who he was and what he did. They shared some deep dark
secrets that they both vowed to take to the grave.

Laughing, Royalty shook her head. "C'mon boy. I can't fuck with you, you know me too well. I swear… Royalty desires had momentarily gotten the best of her. All day Royalty had been having sexual fantasies about what she wanted to do to Amir. Royalty decided to take Amir advice because at home they wouldn't be interrupted.

Royalty walked to the department store entrance and politely held the door for Amir to enter. He brushed passed Royalty with half dozen shopping bags that he held in each hand. The couple made their way through the department store, up the escalator. Royalty still feeling lovey dovey, leans in a gives Amir a deep, passionate kiss despite his
pervious plea for shows of public affection.

Suddenly out her peripheral vision Royalty spots some yellow chick, a few steps away, nonchalantly pointing in their direction. As soon as Royalty looks in her direction, she immediately turns away and
pretends to be pointing at something else. However, her act isn't good enough to fool, Royalty. Royalty already on to her. Royalty kinda already knows what this is about. It's some fans from Amir's social media page, Instagram. He's got over three hundred thousand followers, and

growing daily, from all over the country, New York to Cali. Because of the extravagant lifestyle that Amir has projected to the public, they always get a lot of attention. Usually Amir is oblivious to it, he's
use to it by now, while Royalty picks up on it almost immediately. 'Here we go again.' Royalty thought to herself. As she rolled her eyes at Amir's social media admirers. Royalty had such disdain for Amir's followers that Royalty treated everyone of them as a potential stalker. Since the other females were looking Royalty decided to put on a show. Royalty started by gently placing her head on Amir shoulder marking her territory. Before Amir knew what was happening Royalty was tongue kissing him passionately. They were making out right there on the escalator like two high school kids. As they kissed Royalty kept an eye on Amir's fans. Royalty wanted to make sure that they were watching. Royalty wanted to make sure that they knew that Amir was her man. Even as the escalator deposited them to the prescribed floor, Royalty and Amir were still lip locked.

Bae, c'mon now. That's enough. This our floor." Amir managed to say. After breaking their embrace, the couple stepped off the escalator and walked towards the woman's shoe department. Royalty monitored the women closely enough to see that that they also departed the escalator on the same floor, maintaining a safe distance between the two parties. They entered the woman's shoe department, and it was like stepping into another world. Royalty fucked with the shoe department on many levels, it wasn't just the shoes that attracted her. It was the luxurious, inviting decor. The expensive crystal chandelier that hung delicately from the ceiling illuminating the area. The warm bright colors painted on the walls seem to add to the ambiance. The foot mannequins were creative in the latest designer tends. All of this eye candy seemed to appeal to Royalty senses. It made Royalty comfortable with spending large amounts of money on shoes. Bergdorf and Goodman wasn't just selling Royalty designer shoes they were selling a luxurious lifestyle. And Royalty bought into it. Time and time again.

Amir was the first to take advantage of the coziness of the woman's shoe department, he flopped down in the first available seat, he saw, a soft suede chair, letting the bags he was carrying rest nearby on the floor. Relaxing, he pulled out one of his many phones and immediately jumped on a social media app and began taking selfies. As soon as Amir found the pose he liked, he wrote a dope caption and posted to Instagram. Within seconds his phone started going crazy from all the notifications of the likes from the photo. Meanwhile Royalty busied herself looking at expensive designer shoes. As she did, a saleswoman rushed over to assist in her search.

Hello, Ma'am. Is there anything in particular I could help you with today? The young white saleswoman politely said.

Royalty loved the customer service in these high end department stores. Yet she didn't know if the store reps were genuinely being helpful or were, they just performing some act of loss prevention. Whatever the case may have been, she didn't dwell on the thought too long. Royalty knew that she was there to spend cash money and not
steal.

"Yes." Royalty cheerfully exclaimed. Royalty knew exactly what she wanted. "I'm look for a pair of Louboutin boots."

The saleswoman replied, "Sure I could help you with that."

The two women immersed themselves in the latest shoe designs. The sales woman retrieved not only the designer boots that Royalty wanted but few other comparable, high priced DESIGNER BOOTS Impulsively Royalty begins to try on the all the shoes, starting with the most expensive one she requested. Clearly Royalty was excited at the thought of not only trying on the boots, but actually being seen wearing them.
"Amir, how these look on me Bae?" She calls out.

You good. Amir replied, not even bothering to look up from his phone.

You make me sick. You not even paying' me no mind. Royalty snapped. One day I'm delete all ya damn social media accounts. Amir was an internet whore, what else did she expect him to be doing during this down time accept engaging in his favorite past time.

You do that Royalty and we gone have a problem Amir said.

Then we just have a problem then." Royalty answered.

You don't want them type of problems Royalty. I swear you don't. Amir half joked.

Whatever Amir. Royalty declared as she walked over to the ceiling to floor mirror to better examine her potential purchase. For a few moments Royalty was totally engrossed in trying on the boots. Royalty positioned her foot in various positions, on the thick plush carpet, looking at the designer boot from every angle until every insecurity about the size of her feet slowly melted away. Comfortably was the final test, Royalty strutted around the shoe department trying to get a better feel for the boots. As soon as Royalty began to move around, Royalty spots the two stalkers again. This time they were headed directly towards Amir. Royalty was tiring of playing this cat and mouse game with them. Royalty immediately positioned herself on a chair next to Amir, preparing herself for a confrontation.
"Miss I'll take these." Royalty stated, taking off the boot and handed to her.

The saleswoman happily takes the item and places the shoe back in the box. "Will that be all Ma'am?"

Ummm, I'm not sure. Royalty stated, as she put back on her YSL boots. "Gimme a minute and I'll let you know."

No rush take your time." The saleswoman replied as she happily walked away.

On cue, the sales woman's departure seemed to coincide with the stalker's arrival. Royalty couldn't have planned it any better. She wanted the woman out of earshot in case she had to get ignorant. '

Millionaire Mir?" One woman called out affectionately.

Amir couldn't pull his head out of his smart phone fast enough to reply.

Yeah, bitch that's him!" Royalty cursed. "Who are you? You fuckin' groupies ain't got no respect. Can't you see he's out with his woman."

The woman rolled her eyes not choosing to respond directly to Royalty. She came over there to request a picture with someone she followed on the internet and not to get attacked like this. It took every ounce of her self resolve not to verbally attack Royalty back. She had dealt bitter bitches, overprotective girlfriends and wives, of celebrities, like this before. After all this was New York City, there wasn't a friendly soul in the entire town. She didn't care about Royalty or her nasty attitude. All she wanted was a picture with Amir for her Instagram page. She knew she'd be lit if she could accomplish that.

Amir ignored Royalty, he loved the attention he was receiving. Whenever and wherever his fans recognized him, it stroked his ego. Royalty believed all this Instagram fame was going to his head. Yeah that's me." Amir proudly announced. "What's good?

I'm sorry I don't mean to disturb ya'll...." She apologized.

Royalty cut her off. "You already did!"

Do you mind if I get a picture wit you for my gram?" She wondered aloud. Amir fan asked

Sure, no problem." Amir answered before Royalty could reject the idea.

Meanwhile, Royalty rolled her eyes in disgust. She felt like Amir wasn't supposed to acknowledge his followers, groupies or fans while in her presence. If Royalty told Amir once she told him a thousand times, 'When you out with me, you out with me. You're on my time. You deal wit ya lil groupies on ya time. Yet time and time again, Amir violated that agreement. Whenever Royalty pressed him for an explanation on his actions.

Amir always said, 'If I gotta explain it to you then you won't understand. We see the situation differently. You see it as flirting'. I see it as business. The real reason why Amir was so kind to his female followers was simple, Amir never knew which shorty he could add to his roster. So, all the admiration he received from females may has well been potential dollar signs.
The females were giddy that 'Millionaire Amir' agreed to take a photo with them. Meanwhile Royalty seethed with anger in the chair, while
watching the scene transpire. Feeling disrespected, she let her disapproval register across her lips in the form of a sinister snarl.
Amir ignored Royalty Amir would deal with Royalty later. Now Amir was in celebrity mode, totally feeling himself. Royalty just shook her head in disgust, while she waited for any one of the two females to do something inappropriate, a touch, a look, anything. She was looking for a reason to get up in their asses.

Who gone take the picture?" One girl asked. They seemed to debate amongst each other for a moment.

Bitch, you better not even look over in this direction." Royalty snapped.

She trippin' don't ask her." Amir whispered.

What?" Royalty roared. "I ain't hear you. Amir don't fuckin' play yaself.

Once again, they ignored Royalty. The woman solved the problem by alternating taking the picture and being in the picture with Amir. Soon as they were done, they rushed off, as quickly as they came, with their faces buried in their smartphone, trying to decide which picture with Amir they was going to upload first.
"
You sure know how to fuck up a wet dream. That couldn't been money right there, you never know. Amir said Laughing

So. Royalty replied flatly. I don't care.

You better." Amir fired back. It's bitches like them that pay for shopping sprees like this. Get out ya feelings and let's get to this bag. Amir bent down and grabbed the bags and proceeded to head over to the register to pay for Royalty's designer boots in light of that exchange Amir was really ready to go home. Royalty obediently followed behind him. Although Royalty was mad at Amir, she wasn't stupid enough to say or do anything to mess up this purchase. How much is that Ma'am? Amir asked the saleswoman.

That be two thousand eight hundred total sir. The saleswoman stated matter factly. Will that be cash or credit?

Cash. Amir responded confidently.
Amir removed a large wad of cash from his pants pocket. He began thumbing through the currency, silently counting the money. When Amir was done, he peeled off the sum and handed to the saleswoman. She counted the money, then recounted the money, all under the watchful eye of Amir. Assured that she had the correct amount, she proceeded to check the money for counterfeit bills with a brown marked. Satisfied that everything was in order, she placed the cash in the register and extracted Amir's change, handing over his receipt. Thank you for your purchase sir." The saleswoman smiled, as she handed over the boots.

No, thank you." Amir insisted before turning and walking away.

Once again, Royalty trailed closely behind Amir. Royalty began to quicken her pace as her anger faded away. Thank you, Bae. Royalty said as stubbornness turn to gratitude.

You welcome." Amir replied, too tired to continue to argue. "Call that Uber so we can get out of here."
Within a few minutes their ride arrived, a black Cadillac Escalade pulled smoothly to the curb. Before the driver could get out and extend his passengers the courtesy of opening the door, Amir and Royalty slipped out of the department store, temporarily braving the frigid New
York City winter and quickly entered the luxury vehicle sitting comfortably inside.

Good evening. The driver said to no one in particular.

Good evening. The couple seemed say in unison.
Royalty snuggled up against her man. Just that quickly all the drama that had transpired in the department store was forgotten. The close proximity of Amir and Royalty seemed to suggest it.

The driver drove through the rush hour traffic, quickly moving in and out of lanes, in an effort to beat the snarling traffic. Behind the tinted windows Royalty occupied her mind by taking in the sights and sounds of New York, marveling at the vast numbers of people going to and fro like a tourist. Though Royalty had witnessed them countless times it never ceased to amaze her. The hustle and bustle of the city excited, made her feel alive. If it wasn't for the extremely cold weather, New York was a place she could see herself residing forever. To Royalty the city was picturesque as a postcard.

Exhausted Amir just relaxed in his seat, zoning out to a Meek Mill song that played, at a moderate volume, on New York's Hot 97 fm. It was clear what Amir would be doing for the entirety of the ride, absolutely nothing.

Damn, Amir you must be hella tired. Royalty stated. You ain't even on ya phone checking the book or ig.

I am. Amir replied. That should tell you something right there. It ain't easy being your personal concierge. I'm tired as shit.
Aww. Royalty commented. You know when we get home, I got you. Royalty smiled seductively at Amir, letting her sexually charged innuendo hang in the air. For his part, Amir played it cool. Silently he marinated on thoughts of sex. Soon they both returned to their previous train of thoughts, Royalty sightseeing and Amir relaxing. The ride up the West highway signaled to that they were well on their way home. Bright lights from skyscrapers loomed behind the car, while green lights that illuminated the outline of the George
Washington Bridge awaited them ahead. The blackness of the Hudson river was all that separated the occupants of the car from New York City and their condo in Edgewater, New Jersey. On this side of the George Washington Bridge trouble seemed a million miles away.

Royalty was a little hornier than even she thought. Without warning she started unzipping Amir's jeans, grabbing a handful of his manhood, Royalty removed it, exposing his penis. Royalty then proceeded to go down on Amir. Within seconds Amir was rock hard from the wetness and warmth of her mouth. Amir sank lower and lower into car's leather seats. Soft moans began to escape Amir's mouth as Royalty orally pleased Amir. The noises from the back seat, alerted the uber driver to the sexual favor that was transpiring in the vehicle. Every so often he stole looks in his rearview mirror, in an attempt to get a good look at
the action.

Everything alright back there. The Uber driver sarcastically said.

We hella good. Amir moaned. Just drive my guy.

The uber driver laughed, then did as he was instructed, turning his attention back to the road.

Up and down Royalty's head steadily boobed, while Amir closed his eyes and enjoyed every second of it. Instinctively, he grabbed the back of Royalty head, driving her mouth further and further down his dick. Royalty deep throated him like a champ. It gave her extreme pleasure to satisfy her man. Unable to contain himself, Amir began to squirm in his seat. Sucking his dick really turned Royalty on, but clearly, she was done.

Royalty stuck her free hand inside Amir's pants and began messaging Amir's balls, while jerking and sucking him off at the same time.
Giving Amir oral sex was making Royalty wet. She could feel the head of his dick swelling inside her mouth. Royalty increases her pace, feverishly she begins to boob her head, up and down. Suddenly loud slurping sounds fill the car, momentarily distracting the driver.

Bae you about to make me come. Amir whispers.

Royalty quickly removes her mouth from his penis. Come all in my mouth Amir. I wanna swallow. Almost on command, Amir exploded inside Royalty's mouth. Doubling her efforts, Royalty doubled locked her jaw shut around Amir dick. Royalty took a mouthful of the thick white body fluid, before making it quietly disappear down her throat. Once it was gone Royalty continued to give Amir head.

Stop! Stop!! Amir complained, unable to take it anymore. His words fall on deaf ears, as Royalty continues doing her thing. At this point Amir's penis was ultra sensitive, so he takes his hands and physically removes her from his manhood.

Oh, it's like that. Royalty laughs, reposition herself in the seat.

Amir ignores Royalty as he busies himself zipping up his pants and straightening out his clothes. When that's done, Amir places his arm around Royalty hugging her affectionately. In responses Royalty lays her head on his shoulder.

Damn bae, you the shit." Amir whispered into Royalty ear.

Royalty merely smiled ear to ear, signaling she was in agreement with what Amir said.

You know we gone have to tip ole boy a fat ass tip for turning his car into a tellie. Amir said Laughing

Handle that. Was all Royalty said.

Once inside their lavish condo Amir wastes no time telling Royalty to undress and backup all that teasing a nigga and shit, she was doing with her sexy ass.

Barely dropping all the bags, she was holding to the floor Royalty slips out her chinchilla and tosses it unto the sofa and faces Amir while unbuttoning her blouse one button at a time seductively sticking her tongue out.

Amir had already beat her to the punch and had removed all his clothing while coming in house. slamming the door with his foot then kicking his boots off and the rest of his clothing while in the foyer. Because Amir's dick had a mind of its on and being confined to his cargo pants wasn't an option especially when Amir was ready to take that pussy down like the Titanic Literally!! Amir was ready to get that pussy soaking wet and drown in it.

Licking his lips and rubbing his hands together admiring the striptease show Royalty was giving him was cool but Royalty time was up though. Take all that shit off except them boots Amir says to Royalty. Who was looking like a midnight snack.

The floor to ceiling windows in their living room which faced the Hudson River set the sexual ambience every time because it gave a ray of light off the water that lit up the room with the perfect lighting for fucking.

Bend over the couch and spread your legs so I can taste it. Amir says Pushing Royalty Over the plush velvet couch as if he was doing a felony search warrant.

Arching her back to oblige him and spreading her legs even more standing on her tiptoes Amir enters Royalty throbbing, wet pussy with his tongue while finger fucking her and giving her his head, finger combo which was Amir's specialty. Amir vigorously ate Royalty out like the last supper from behind while grabbing her ass driving Royalty insane.

Bay-beeee oh baby I'm coming Royalty screamed out in between moans while sucking on her own nipples of her titties not being able to contain herself from what was the best feeling Royalty had ever experienced. Making Royalty come with his tongue was a special talent Amir took very seriously and was only allowed for Royalty only!!Well maybe Amir shared his talents with a few other women on a way too much Hennessy night but that rarely happened and if a bitch caught him slipping, she deserved that. Was Amir's motto.

Wiping his mouth with his arm Amir gets up and grabs Royalty by her hand not giving her a chance to catch her breath and leads her to their bedroom and lays Royalty down on the king size bed with her back towards the headboard facing him. Amir climbs on top of Royalty putting both of her legs on top of his shoulders which placed their bodies together and Amir looked in Royalty eyes like you ready? As he slides the tip in and out teasing Royalty until she couldn't take it anymore and begs Amir to put it in. Amir still teasing Royalty tells Royalty to say Pretty Please before entering her completely. Once Royalty obliged Amir commands Amir puts his whole entire dick inside Royalty drenching wet pussy and every nerve in Amir's dick rejoiced. Amir commences to beat that pussy up while Royalty's gripping his head for dear life throwing that pussy back at Him pound for pound matching his rhythm. It's felt so good to both of them that unbearable feeling and sensation that they could hardly contain themselves. They're sloppy tongue kissing when Amir grabs Royalty by her throat squeezing for dear life until he comes inside her hoping this time Royalty gets pregnant. Upon releasing her throat Amir is thinking why do niggas be creeping when their bitch has good ass pussy? Laughing at himself for the thought.

Massaging her Adam's apple Royalty says you're going to kill me one day Amir with that freaky S&M shit laughing but seriously speaking.

After taking a few deep breaths Amir says" but did you die tho?" Slipping out of Royalty and putting her legs down. Sighing laying his head back on one of the many throw pillows on their bed taking it all in. Royalty never disappointed Him in the bedroom. Her pussy felt like a Golden glove. Royalty made Amir nut every mother fucking time they got busy Amir thinking to himself. Almost 10 minutes later Amir looked over at Royalty who was knocked the fuck out like she got hit by the heavyweight champ. Her arms were flung over her head and her hair was a hot mess looking like 4 packs of Brazilian body wave bundles, but it was all hers. Poor baby Royalty never can hang Amir was thinking She's always dead tired after getting that pussy beat the fuck up. Round two could never happen until Royalty had her power nap. But Amir knew how to wake that ass up if he really wanted to. But Amir was tired himself from running around with Royalty in all them damn stores plus he busted two nuts in one day within a few hours. That drained his whole soul. Time to recharge Is the last thing Amir was thinking before falling asleep himself.

A few hours later Amir's bladder was full to capacity and needed to be released plus his mouth was hella dry and Amir was thirsty so getting up was the only option for him at this time of the morning. Looking at his iPhone it read 3:30 am stretching his arms while yawning and placing his feet on the hardwood floor getting out the bed Amir almost tripped over Royalty boot, she must have took off and tossed it on his side. Amir thinking, he should hit her in the head with it and wake her ass up but knowing Royalty she would wake up swinging and shit. Naw we can't have that it's too damn early to be play fighting with her ass.
Because I'll be playing, and she'll be fighting Amir was thinking just let sleeping beauty rest Amir says to himself walking into the bathroom. After releasing what felt like a pint of urine into the toilet Amir walks back into the room and starts picking shit up off the floor and neatly puts everything where they belong. Amir was a neat freak at its finest he hated for shit to be outta place. Their house was neatly decorated and everything in order. Amir hated when he messed around with a chick with a dirty house too. That irritated his soul like bitch why is it so damn hard to clean up a project? It's only so big and if a girl had a nice apartment but it wasn't clean, he would think why even get a fucking apartment for? You should stay the fuck in the hood bitch same thing with a homeowner bitch with a nasty house. Amir actualy told one girl like hey Sis you wasted your hard earned money buying this Mother Fucker house and this shit ain't even clean. I've been by here on three different occasions and each time it always looks the same dirty as fuck. A nigga scared he might catch some sort of bacterial infection or something if he takes his shoes off. I'm cool walking to the front door. A nigga ain't even turned on no more. You cute and all but Cleanliness is next to Godliness in my book ma and your house looks like you going straight to hell my nigga. And Amir walked out and never answered Another call from her nasty ass. See Royalty wasn't as clean as Amir was, but Royalty knew not to even play with Amir a little bit when it came to cleaning up. That's why they had a housekeeper that came in 4 times a week even though they only lived there half the year it was money well spent in Amir's Book. Fuck that nasty shit It Made Amir's stomach hurt, and he instantly got a headache seeing people's house dirty especially a bitch with kids. What happened if the kid put something in their mouth off the nasty floor and died is what Amir always thought. He didn't want no scrubs around him None period. Growing up in the projects made Amir realize how he wanted to live when he got older and it wasn't in no small compact tuna box, low income housing community. That's why Amir hustled the way he did to make sure that wouldn't happen plus he didn't have any good memories about living in the jets anyways. Shit wasn't cool for Amir and Royalty growing up they both had two crack heads, prostitution mothers living in a two bedroom jet with hella people in it. Walking in the kitchen Trying to shake this memory opening the refrigerator door looking inside at the selection of drinks. Amir grabs a Pepsi his favorite knowing he shouldn't be drinking no soda but shit he did everything else that was wrong so why not. Amir had been catching felonies since he was 10 years old his first body, he was 12. Because sometimes a mother fucker will provoke you to do some foul shit and you have to let them know you ain't playing with they asses.

Leaning back on the marble island in the kitchen swallowing his soda and burping hella loud. This shit is Good Amir says to himself before hearing someone knocking at his front door. Who the fuck at the door at 3 something in the morning he was thinking. This shit better be good and about some money and I hope it ain't a nigga drunk and needing a place to crash because I'm slamming my door in that nigga face period for disrespecting my sleep. Even tho a nigga ain't sleep tho it's still disrespectful he's thinking. Walking thru the foyer and turning the alarm off he opens the door

Boom Boom two shots to Amir's head before he could say anything. His body falls back hitting the floor Hard. Bam cracking his skull open upon impact from the blunt force trauma the 44 Magnum had caused to his head.

Hearing a noise wakes Royalty up from her sleep she feels for Amir but realizes he's not on his side of the bed. She calls out his name but no answer. He's probably on the patio getting high Royalty thinking getting out the bed going to the bathroom. Looking in the mirror at her Hair that was all over the place putting it in a messy ponytail and grabbing her robe from behind the bathroom door to cover up her naked body plus for some reason the house was cold. Royalty Walks towards the dark living room wanting to hit the weed she believed Amir was smoking on the patio calling Amir's name again but nothing. Then she notices the front door is wide open and looks down and starts running and screaming Noooooooo!!! Reaching Amir's Lifeless body Royalty Slips in Amir's blood falling to the floor directly next to him. Hugging his body crying hysterically the room started spinning and unfolded a murder scene that would haunt Royalty dreams for a lifetime.
Not realizing how much time had passed or even when the police had arrived Royalty was no longer the women she was before this heinous crime occurred. It took three uniformed police officers and a homicide detective to remove Royalty from Amir's body and place her on a 24hr psychiatric observation hold which is the equivalent of suicide watch. Royalty couldn't contain her composure, she released her bladder without knowing and her screaming could wake the dead. So, for her safety and protection the lead homicide detective Mr. Maceo Black decided it was best that Royalty be watched overnight or until she could grasp reality and give him a full testimony of what he believed had taken place and caused Amir's demise. Looking around the extravagant, posh condo looking for clues and evidence that could tell the story of why someone would want Amir dead everything detective Maceo saw said Jealousy and Envy which is a deadly combination.
The following day pulling up at the hospital Detective Maceo looks towards the rusty gray brick building with chicken wire over the windows thinking this hospital looks depressing and detective Maceo seen it too many times and he was over it already. Detective Maceo parks in the spot reserved for police officers with the big blue and white sign like a disabled space but with the writing saying Police Officers Parking Only. People saw this park and stayed far away from it. Nobody really cared for the police especially a Detective but detective Maceo didn't really care one way or another because he didn't care for too many people himself but Detective Maceo was doing the job he took an oath for and he took it pretty seriously. Detective Maceo Black was contemplating on just how he was going to approach the young, distraught young women who was mourning the death of her lover and was considered a victim of a violent crime. Without seeming too pushy or aggressive and shutting her down from giving him what Detective Maceo had came for Answers. And If what Detective Maceo believed about Royalty was
true this wasn't going to be an easy task. Most young women with boyfriends who Detective Maceo assumed to be drug dealers always give Detective Maceo a hard Time when questioning them. With that around the way girl attitude smacking their lips while pooping their gum and swinging their hands around saying we don't fuck with no police sounding real ghetto and uneducated. But hopefully this wasn't the case with Miss Royalty. Detective Maceo hoped Royalty would prove him wrong this time. Not be a statistic but a rare case but deep down inside Detective Maceo knew he was right. He always was right. Detective Maceo had been down this road so many times before detective Maceo could write a book about all the shit he had experienced in his 12 plus years as a homicide detective. When detective Maceo retired he probably would consider writing one and it would be a bestseller he thinks to himself smirking... Stepping out the car in the freezing cold weather that you can see your breath in front of you when you breathe because it froze up. This that type of weather we're you could appreciate a Coogi sweater and timberlands boots. Making sure his

Louis Vuitton scarf was securing his neck properly and buttoning his trench coat Detective Maceo darted towards the hospital entrance to escape the cold.

While entering the hospital walking down the long dreadful hallways looking downward at the blood splatter on the floor and over stepping it seeing a sick child who's coughing repeatedly while the mother drags the child by his little hand to help the kid keep up. This is the worst repetitive cycle Detective Maceo wished wasn't apart of the job that he loved. Approaching the locked facility that housed the people labeled crazy or mental illnesses Detective Maceo pressed the buzzer and waited for the intake clerk to ask his credentials and buzz him in. Officer Maceo Black he says as the locked iron door opens slowly squeaking in desperate need of some maintenance. Walking in one door to welcome Another locked door with a huge glass window with security and nursing staff behind it. Seeing Det Maceo face for the hundred time was all the clearance they needed to allow him enter in. Buzzing him through yet another security door smiling from ear to ear. Hey, Det Black, looking good as usual the front desk clerk Betty says.

Thanks Betty, how are you? Being cordial but detective Maceo hated the clerk Betty flirtatious gestures every time he had to come and interview a patient. But Betty was harmless. Betty what room is Royalty Ocampo in? looking around at the rooms and noticing a man handcuffed to a bed in a hallway who had wet on himself and his clothes were filthy dirty, and he was screaming obscenities to anyone who was paying attention. Taking a deep breath turning his attention back to Betty who was rolling her eyes before she spoke again.

Oh, her the cute little girl who killed her boyfriend Betty says tilting her head and displaying duck lips.

Wait wait wait waving his hands like No Det Mateo says who told you that? She didn't kill her boyfriend detective Maceo says in Royalty defense. While smacking her lips Betty says killing her boyfriend, seeing her boyfriend get killed same thing.

No, it isn't Miss Betty Det Maceo says it's a tremendous difference and you should Never judge a person based on what you read in their chart plus what happened to patient confidentiality? Det Maceo says looking at her disappointed. You're not supposed to even discuss anyone's charges or symptoms.

You've been working here since Adam and Eve days you know better Miss Betty feeling offended. Which room is Royalty in? Raising his voice Detective Maceo asks.

Miss Betty pointed down the hallway before finally saying room 5 rolling her eyes again.

Not sure how Betty kept her job for so long especially being so unprofessional and rude Det Maceo shakes his head at the thought of Miss Betty while walking to room 5. When Det Maceo reaches the room, Miss Betty buzzes the room door and Detective Maceo opens the door. Royalty was sitting on the twin iron bed with the dingy gray covers still made up like she haven't slept all night. Royalty was sitting Indian style rocking and crying. The matching gray brick wall room was freezing cold also Detective Maceo couldn't imagine spending a night there the room alone would make a person go crazy. Royalty looked up and saw the Detective and asked When was she able to go home she hadn't done anything wrong. Detective Maceo just stared at her for a moment before replying we need to talk. Royalty was so overwhelmed she stood up and ran over to the detective and hugged him and cried on his shoulder. The detective didn't know how to respond but gently wrapped his arms around Royalty and said it would be ok but before he could finish his sentence Royalty disarmed his holster and grab Detective Maceo gun and was pointing it at him. Putting his hands up like he was the criminal pleading with Royalty. Look Royalty you really don't want to do this. I am a police officer and you can get into a lot of trouble for this. Put the gun down and we can work this out. I promise I just want to help you get through this.

Shut up and get me the fuck outta here cocking the gun. Royalty said.

Look Royalty we can't just leave this is a locked facility plus in about 3 minutes three big, black gorilla looking security guards are going to come bum rush you with no questions asked if you don't put that gun down. There's cameras all throughout this facility their watching us right now. Trying to stay calm and talk his way through this situation. Let me help you I know your experiencing Post Traumatic Stress Disorder. Trying to plead with Royalty. If you put the gun down now, you'll still have a chance for me to get you outta here and help you, but I can't help you if you don't put the gun down Royalty.

Looking perplexed not knowing if Detective Maceo was telling the truth or not Royalty slowly put the gun down and kicked it towards the Detective because Royalty didn't have the strength for no gun battle plus Royalty wanted to see Amir's body and make the funeral arrangements plus Royalty knew if she kidnapped a police officer, she would never see daylight again. Royalty wasn't thinking rationally maybe she was suffering from Post Traumatic disorder. He'll the way her life was set up Royalty should've been suffering from hella Traumatic disorders. Royalty was starting to think maybe this was the place she did need to be after all shaking her head.

After securing his gun and placing it back in the holster detective Maceo Grabs Royalty arm and tells her to turn around and do what he says handcuffing Royalty and leaning in close to her kicking her legs apart and do as I say whispering in her ear, I promise I'll get you out of here safely. Sure, enough three linebacker looking men came running in. Thanks, gentlemen, for coming 10 minutes after I would have been shot to death shaking his head brushing pass them out the room holding Royalty arm detective Maceo says.

We had another emergency on the other side of the hospital before we got this call Detective our bad shrugging his shoulders one officer said. You don't want us to detain her and take her to the medication room?

Turning around to answer the officer that was standing in formation with the other two alongside the hallway wall. No, I'm taking her to jail she doesn't need medication she's needs solitary confinement turning back around walking towards the front desk to sign Royalty out the facility. Stepping up to the front desk Miss Betty and now two other psychiatric staff members were there waiting for an explanation as to why Detective Maceo was taking Royalty out of the facility especially after she just drew down on him. I'm not no killer but don't push me Miss Betty was singing looking at Royalty as they approached the desk.
Really Miss Betty are you really singing Tupac? Detective Maceo said. You're the rudest person I've ever encountered seriously. Let me sign Royalty Ocampo Out please I'm transferring her, and I need her belongings also.

She didn't have any belongings Detective Miss Betty says sarcastically still looking at Royalty, but Royalty wasn't paying her no attention.

Signing all the appropriate papers needed for release Detective Maceo walks Royalty to the door and waits to be buzzed out not looking back in fear he would be turned into stone. This facility was used to crazy, deranged individuals especially the homeless community and mental illness patients they welcomed them. They had a little special medication room for those people. They would medicate a person or body shock them probably both depending on who was working and how aggressive the person was. Word on the street was you didn't want to be admitted to this psych ward under no circumstances because if you didn't come in crazy you was for sure leaving crazy guaranteed. The staff made sure their jobs were secured by any means necessary. And No one ever got charged with any negligence because they all stuck together, and nobody talked to anyone outside work about work they had each other's back. Their loyalty to each other was like a small gang.

Royalty was grateful Detective Maceo took her home to grab some things and took her to a hotel because Royalty couldn't stay at the condo it was to traumatizing for Royalty. Walking around the living room in her black lace panty and bra set on hair curly from getting wet while in the shower and freshly brushed to the back because Royalty didn't feel like being bothered with her hair today and for what Royalty was just relaxing today plus it was Sunday. You're supposed to relax on Sunday's to get yourself prepared for the following week. And Royalty wasn't ready for Monday anyways. Tomorrow Royalty needed to go officially identify Amir's body and make arrangements for his body to be shipped back home so Royalty could plan Amir's funeral service. Royalty had already booked her flight to return home to California due to Amir's death that forced her to return sooner than planned. Royalty and Amir wasn't supposed to go back to Cali until March but damn interrupting her thought a knock on her hotel suite door. Getting up off the couch grabbing her gun off the coffee table and cocking it pointing it straight ahead like it was guiding her in the direction she should go. Looking in the peephole and squinting her eyes to focus. Oh, it's Detective Maceo relaxing a bit putting her gun back on safety and unlocking the door and letting him in not even tripping she wasn't dressed appropriately.

I wasn't expecting to see Royalty dressed like this Detective Maceo thinking walking in. Is this a bad time he asks Royalty? Looking around not expecting to see her suite as lavishly decorated as it was either. Damn her suite looked like something for a President. Well duh it was the presidential suite Detective Maceo said to himself. Looking around at the oil painting on the wall and the baby grand piano and the marble fireplace that was burning and that had the living room feeling real cozy. The bay windows were beautiful also you could see the Empire State Building from Royalty suite. But detective Maceo didn't know what else he should have expected Royalty was on the 51st floor. It didn't get no better than this.

Looking at his amazement Royalty chuckled a little this your first time at the Four Season?

Still admiring the decor Instead of answering Detective Maceo shook his head yes. He never had been a man of lost words this had been a first for him. Royalty had taken him by surprise in more ways than one Detective Maceo kinda grew a new level of respect for Royalty at that moment. Clearing his throat, he finally spoke. This is really nice must have cost my whole months' pay laughing but seriously speaking.

What's your monthly pay? Royalty asked looking him right in his green eyes. Detective Maceo tried to look away but Royalty walked up on him. Clearing his throat again. Umm I see you like Mary J Blige was his response. Royalty had Mary J playing in the background her first cd My Life on repeat.

Smiling at Detective Maceo Royalty replies yes, she's my favorite singer I love her music especially her old stuff walking pass Detective Maceo making Him step back so her ass wouldn't rub against him while passing him out of respect. Damn she's sexy Detective Maceo thinking as Royalty walks into the kitchen making him turn his head in the direction, she was walking like he was hypnotized watching her voluptuous body move like a goddess.

It's bad enough Royalty badd as fuck favoring the actress Lauren London but Royalty body was even badder Royalty was built like a supermodel but a short one kinda thin but not too thin but with a nice ass, stomach snatched, and her titties sat up by themselves. And Royalty had the audacity to smell hella good. Ok keep your composure Detective Maceo keep telling himself but detective Maceo couldn't turn away until Royalty was out of his sight completely.
Royalty yells from the kitchen asking Detective Maceo did he want something to drink. Detective Maceo replies yes whatever your drinking. Turning his attention back to the lavish living room. Detective Maceo thinking it smells really good in here then he notices the scented candles everywhere and then he notices Royalty gun on the coffee table and wondered if Royalty had a license for it. Then Royalty comes walking back into the living room and hands him a glass of wine noticing Detective Maceo was looking at her gun.

Yes, I do have a license for that lying. Royalty says but it didn't matter Royalty knew Detective Maceo wouldn't ask to see it. Quickly changing the subject. Detective Maceo you're not supposed to be drinking on the job and Royalty knew it bending over retrieving her gun placing her ass all in Detective Maceo face. I'll just put this away because I know i'm safe with you here looking over her shoulder giving Detective Maceo a glance like, am I?

Detective Maceo opens his coat to show her that he was strapped and winked. But what Detective Maceo didn't show Royalty was his backup gun on his ankle underneath his jeans or the 9mm behind his back. No need to reveal all the goodies at once.

Smiling Royalty says ok showing her dimples that Detective Maceo never noticed until now.

Royalty really does look like Lauren London Detective Maceo was thinking damn they say we all have a twin in the world Royalty was really hers. Royalty definitely could be her stunt double sipping his glass of wine. Watching Royalty walk away and disappear again into the bedroom Detective Maceo thinking Amir was a lucky man. Which brings him to the point of his visit. When Royalty came back out, she had on a plush white hotel robe with Four Season engraved on it Royalty sat down in front of the fireplace and lit up a joint and blew a cloud of smoke before asking Detective Maceo did he smoke weed.

Turning his body around facing her Detective Maceo says No I don't but go ahead it doesn't bother me at all is all he could say because Royalty was already smoking it anyways.

I have to relax to answer your questions I'm not ready to come to terms with this Royalty says. In my mind Amir going to walk through the door at any minute looking towards the door.

Detective Maceo looked at the door also. I understand this is still fresh. It won't be easy but just take your time and do the best you can. I only have a few questions for you. Adjusting his body on the couch to face Royalty sitting on the floor in front of the fireplace sipping her wine and hitting her weed bouncing her head to Mary J. So, Royalty how long have you known Amir? And why do you think someone wanted him dead? Did Amir have any problems with anyone in particular? Do you think it was over money? And I know this is a very insensitive question, but I have to ask you. Do you think this may have been over Another women? Looking at Royalty facial expression change. Hitting her weed long and hard this time before answering.

Amir came home every night but that doesn't mean he was loyal during the day. Not looking at Detective Maceo but looking at her nails then looking out the bay windows in the living room that was floor to ceiling. Amir was still a young man with a lot of money plus Amir was very popular in the streets. So, anything's possible I suppose. Hitting her weed again then taking a sip of her wine before continuing to speak. Amir didn't have any enemies that I knew of lying to Detective Maceo again. Royalty didn't feel the need to put Amir's business in the streets and especially to no cop. No matter how cool he seemed. Amir was a standup guy that Royalty loved her whole entire life. We grew up together before we became a couple Royalty replies before downing her drink. Looking at Detective Maceo now is there anything else you want to ask me? Royalty asks.

Detective Maceo thinking there's a lot he wanted to ask Royalty, but he'll wait. No, I think that's it for now Detective Maceo responded. Oh, there is one more question taking the last sip of his wine feeling a little buzz. How did Amir make his money did he have a job?

Taking a deep breath hum the million dollar question huh? The question everyone in the world waving her hands in the air in a circle drawing the world wants to know. No Amir didn't work no traditional job. He was a business owner. Amir owned several barber shops throughout the Bay Area and record label in Los Angeles Amir also has a trucking company. Royalty said lying about some of Amir's business but that wasn't her job to tell everything Royalty would let the police do their job finding out. We bought our condo here in New York because because Amir was looking into starting a business out here.

Detective Maceo knew immediately that Amir was a drug dealer and a very successful one. Because the first thing drug dealers did when they wanted to start a business is open up a bootleg record label with a few drug dealer wannabe rappers and that old-school buy a barbershop to clean the money business is the oldest trick in the drug dealer book of Hard Knox. Ha Detective Maceo was hip to all the tricks but these new school drug dealers were up to new tricks or, so they thought. Buying their main girl, a hair salon was the new front and opening up these little boutiques. But what they failed to realize is that when the Feds whenever they got caught up wants to know where did you get that money to begin with to start these businesses. Detective Maceo wouldn't press Royalty now he knows she's grieving but he will question her later on as he came across some new developments. Well thank you for your hospitality Royalty and for answering my questions I appreciate that under the circumstances. I'll be in touch if I have any other questions. I'm going to leave you my business card with all my contact information and I believe I have all your information he stated.

Royalty was planning on going back to California to prepare for Amir's Funeral she said solemnly speaking. It doesn't even feel right saying that. Then Royalty Started to tear up. Sorry Royalty says. Wiping her eyes. I'll write my contact information down where you can reach me in case you need me walking into the bedroom. Detective Maceo stands up to stretch his legs. When Royalty reappears with a business card of her own and hands it to him. All my information on there plus I wrote my personal cell number on the back.

Looking at the card then back at Royalty Detective Maceo asks Royalty so you own a hair salon? Reading the card, she handed him that read The Royalty Treatment Salon and Spa.

Yes, I own a chain of hair salons Royalty replies.

Impressive Detective Maceo thinking. Amir was balling. They're not even 30 yrs. old yet he's thinking must be nice. Well nice while it lasted for him. Too bad he had to go out like that thinking to himself. Ok Royalty handing her his empty glass. Walking to the door but before he opened it and he turned and said Sorry for your loss and have a safe trip. Then he opened up the door and walked out thinking Amir probably got killed because of a drug deal that went horribly wrong. Or It probably was a cartel hit. At that point he started thinking Royalty needs to be very careful her life could be in jeopardy while pushing the elevator button to go down.

Finally, she could stop pretending to be so innocent and acting like she didn't know shit. Amir had prepared Royalty for everything except how to prepare for his death. Placing her head back on the front door and rubbing her hands through her hair Royalty said out loud. Good riddance you noisy mother fucker referring to Detective Maceo. As the tears started pouring down her face. She slid down the door with her ass crying uncontrollably landing on the floor with her legs open and her upper body laid out arms spread apart banging her fist on the ground. Screaming Amir why you leave me like this? This shit ain't fair. Screaming over and over.

Yo Bianca I'm not sure I'm going to be able to do this. Royalty said sitting on the toilet not wanting to get up not sure if she could get up. Royalty had the diarrhea. Shit wouldn't stop, and neither would the tears. I'm over here fucked up feeling like shit literally Royalty said thru the bathroom door. Today was the day Royalty was to lay Amir to rest. But Royalty hadn't rested one bit since Amir's died. And last night was the worse since Amir's death. Royalty and her best friend Bianca was up drinking and smoking and reminiscing about Amir all night.

Since Bianca picked Royalty up from the airport a week ago Bianca hasn't left Royalty side and that wasn't a good sign. Bianca was a bad influence over Royalty and always have been since third grade when her government name was Arthur Santiago the third. Royalty and Bianca had been through everything together and supported each other right or wrong. Royalty had been right there by Bianca side when Bianca went through her transition to women hood when they were 15 years old. The hormone shots, the facial hair removal treatments, the breast augmentation, and the ass shots and finally when Bianca surgery got approved for her sexual reassignment to become a female with a vagina Royalty was right there the whole entire time also. Royalty took care of Bianca aftercare, so you know Bianca was going to be right there for Royalty no matter how long it took for Royalty to get through this.

Royalty open the fucking door Bianca said bamming on the bathroom door like she was the police. Let me in so I can help you babe. Feeling sorry for her best friend.

I'm scared to get up Royalty replied. Plus, Royalty couldn't stop shitting wiping her nose from the snot and tears mixed together. What time is it anyway? Royalty asks.

Almost 9am and the car service arrives at 10 Bianca says looking at her Bezel out Rolex that Bianca had played Jimmy out of smiling. Try babe to hobble to the door even if you shit all over the floor Ol well bitch I'll clean it up Bianca said solemnly speaking. I need to get you together Royalty come on open the door bitch. Still bamming in it like that would make it magically open.

Ok ok trying to get up Royalty says hopping to the bathroom door taking a chance. When Royalty reached the bathroom door to open it sure enough her bowels released and right there on the bathroom floor Royalty went.

Bianca was so quick to come inside the bathroom she pushed the door open while Royalty was unlocking it and walked right into the shit. It was so runny she lost her balance like slipping on water and fell all in the shit and took Royalty down with her in the process. Bianca Versace heel buckled in the watery runny diarrhea on the floor taking her down having Bianca to slide right into it and getting all over her wide leg, high waisted Versace jeans. Bianca tried to break her fall using her hands but instead she broke two nails on the sink going down. Now Bianca and Royalty were both on the floor looking at each other crazy. Bianca looked at her hands scraped up with two broken nails and full of shit.

And Royalty was sitting on the floor next to her trying not to laugh because she knew Bianca was mad as fuck, she always had that don't look at me face when she got pissed and Bianca was displaying that look now. Lips poked out with Beddie eyes blinking uncontrollably.

But instead of Bianca getting mad she burst out laughing. And said your full of shit Bish this is so not how our morning was supposed to start.

Royalty burst out laughing too. And said Sorry bitch! And after laughing Royalty instantly felt better.

Right Bish Bianca responded but my main concern right now is that we make it on time to Amir's funeral and getting you together. Royalty what you want to look like? A centerfold or the main page Bish we got about 30 mins to make this magic happen looking seriously at Royalty getting up off the floor carefully then reaching for Royalty hand helping her up before washing her hands.
Bianca was the hottest makeup artist in town and was always thinking about her craft. Bianca never settled for nothing but perfection so of course Royalty face had to beat to the Gods for Amir funeral. While Royalty was taking a shower, Bianca undressed and wrapped a towel around her heading to the guest bathroom when Bianca heard the doorbell rang. Forgetting they had a black car coming she opened the door in shock and so was the driver seeing Bianca dressed like that. I'm so sorry Bianca says to the driver looking like a clean ass Muslim. We're no way near ready can you please come back in an hour?

Looking perplexed the driver nodded yes in agreement and hurried away not needing a explanation because he got a whiff of something smelling like shit thinking this Bitch better wash her ass before getting in my car plus she's too cute for those hygiene games getting back in his car reaching for his air freshener spraying the his car repeatedly trying to remove the smell that was stuck in his nostrils.

After showering and dressing Royalty and Bianca gets clean to go put Amir away. Royalty was dressed like Amir something they had talked about jokingly before while getting high. They joked about hella shit like that saying they would dress alike if one of them was to die not knowing this day would really come to pass. Royalty went from laughing to crying thinking about what was about to occur in a few moments. Royalty was about to actually bury her man Royalty still couldn't believe Amir was actually gone. And the fact that they had matching outfits already also was a little ironic. Amir had brought himself a Gucci signature black tie with matching cufflinks and a tailored black suit with white Givenchy red collar tip dress shirt to wear to his cousin all black wedding next month that he wouldn't obviously be attending so in reality he had chosen his own funeral attire without even knowing it even though Amir was having a close casket because sadly the funeral home couldn't remake his face to look like himself because most of his face was gone. Amir also had brought Royalty matching outfit to match his fly her attire was a black leather fitted skirt with a black and white and red signature Gucci satin blouse with the big bow and the oversized Gucci buckle belt, Black Gucci tights with black 6mm Christian Louboutin's. Amir loved to see Royalty kill shit walking into a room. Amir had a bad habit of surprising Royalty with designer outfits. Royalty sure was going to miss Amir. Royalty Sat down at her custom made all glass vanity set so Bianca could beat her face.

Hunny boom let's get this show on the road baby your hella late emphasizing hella to your man's funeral but that's ok because bitch you're going to walk in there fierce. Patting Royalty face with setting power. The tears had begun making it hard for Bianca to work her magic. But Bianca was good no great at what she does and that's making women look bomb even through tears. Kissing Royalty on the forehead I know babe I know reaching for some tissue wiping the corners of Royalty eyes and placing her mascara on and finishing her eyeliner. Even through the tears Bianca had Royalty faced on beat down mode. With a smokey Eye and mink glamour lashes added some Rihanna Trophy wife bronzer Bianca had Royalty looking like a model on the runway. Yess bitch yess!!! you serving all kinds of Bad Bitch Aroma today clapping her hands in excitement all you need now is that red lipstick fumbling through her makeup bag trying to find the right shade of red lipstick and bam securing Royalty lips in red Mac lipstick and adding a little gloss. Bitch you just shut the whole mother fucker down admiring her work.

Not feeling like smiling Royalty just smirked a bit. Yes, bitch keep that attitude with that beat down Bianca said feeling like she just conquered the world from her work having no empathy for Royalty and her situation at hand getting ready to bury Amir.
Just as Bianca was finishing up re touching her makeup the black Car returned. Right on time Bianca thinking. Taking another look in the mirror. Bitch you badd Bianca said to herself. And yes, Bianca was beyond conceited. Bianca had every right to be Bianca was absolutely stunning. No one could tell she was born a male. Bianca was Puerto Rican with the spicy attitude but her looks is what stood out the most. Bianca was small in height and Bianca had a body like she had it done in the Dominican island, but Bianca looked more like Miss Jackson, Nelly's girlfriend her face was as flawless as they came. Cocoa butter skin tone, high cheekbones, almond shaped eyes which were hazel with naturally dirty blonde hair. You couldn't tell Bianca she wasn't bad. And anyone who tried got shut down for being a hater. Today Bianca was wearing a fitted off the shoulder black lace dress with a strapless black bra and panties no slip. Her Ysl open toe pumps made it an easy kill. Putting one side of her perfectly even bob behind her ear and licking her lips thinking Go best friend that's my best friend. Ready to walk out and give the world life. Yelling into the other room were Royalty was at retrieving their Mink coats. You ready babe let's Go! Walking into the all white living room looking at a portrait of Amir and Royalty that was like 10 years old. Then it hit Bianca like a ton of bricks like damn my best friend about to bury her man getting chills in her body.

Handing Bianca her coat you cute you ready B? Royalty asks looking Bianca up and down.

Instead of answering Bianca grabs Royalty and gives her a big hug whispering in her ear I love you girl. Meaning every word. I'm so sorry about Amir grabbing Royalty by both arms looking Royalty dead in the eyes. Starting to tear up. I'm going to support you to the end.

Royalty getting emotional also mouthed I know grabbing Bianca hand leading her to the door and they both walked out the house and got into the black car that was waiting for them.
Pulling up at the church seeing all the cars parked and the people lined up to get inside the church. Royalty had mixed emotions. Royalty knew flying Amir's body back home to Los Angeles was the

only option for him to Rest In Peace. After all they were both raised in La they fell in love in La and La was home for them. Plus, all Amir's friends and foes were here. And looking at the turn out Royalty absolutely made the right decision. Looking over at Bianca who had just popped a Molly and was taking a sip of Hennessy to calm her nerves and placed her oversized Dolce and Gabbana crystal glasses on. Royalty felt a little queasy again. Royalty stomach was in knots and she felt like she couldn't breathe. I'm not sure I can do this Royalty said to Bianca.

You can do this friend and I'm here to help you. Opening her YSL clutch. Bianca reaches inside and pulls out a blue pill out of a small container and hands it to Royalty. Here drink this and hands Royalty a flask. Bianca watched Royalty making sure Royalty did exactly what she's told to do.

Damn bitch Royalty says after taking a sip what the fuck is that you gave me? That shit is Hella strong that's not Hennessy. Frowning up her face holding her burning chest.

Giggling no bitch, it ain't it's a concoction I made Bianca says fixing Royalty Hair and double checking her makeup. It's Henny, Remy, and French vanilla Cîroc I call it Hot tamale laughing.

Well you should call it suicide by way of Alcohol poisoning rolling her eyes. Bitch you trying to send me to my maker Royalty says. I do miss Amir but damn. Putting her bling out Gucci shades on and Stepping out the car grabbing the driver's hand who had been patiently waiting holding the car door open. The moment Royalty foot hit the ground she realized she was high as fuck, but she felt good.

Bianca gets out the car and hands the driver her clutch to hold without even asking his permission, so she could put her mink coat on. Once Bianca puts on her black on black floor length mink coat that wasn't even cold enough outside to be wearing anyways but of course Bianca and Royalty had to be extra. Bianca retrieved her clutch from the driver without thanking him and grabs Royalty hand and they proceeded to walk into the church. Now mind you this church is a mega church with 10,000 members. And it was full to capacity for Amir's funeral. Mostly spectators but never the less Amir brought the city out as usual. Anything with Amir's name attached the people came out in droves. Walking inside Royalty felt like all eyes were on her and she had every reason to feel like that because they were. It was like Royalty was walking in slow motion on clouds turning her head from left to right acknowledging everyone who said their condolences along the way. The long walk way to the front pew seemed like a country mile to reach. The choir started singing Well done by Dietrick Haddon the gospel singer hitting all those high notes sending the crowd in a frenzy. Broads I suppose a few of Amir's side chicks started screaming and falling out. Bianca stop dead in her tracks and turned around and started videotaping with her phone. Circling the room videotaping anyone who was screaming and acting out of order. All while Royalty made it to the front pew and sat down next to one of Amir's cousin who was crying blowing her nose in some tissue shaking her head in denial. Royalty was sitting there surveying the room feeling like she was in a sci fi movie. Royalty couldn't believe how many people was in one room to say their goodbyes to Amir.

Bianca finally came and squeezed in to sit next to Royalty elbowing Amir's cousin for space. Bianca thought she was whispering to Royalty, but everyone could hear her. You see this shit Bianca said forgetting she was in a church. These hoes in here doing way too much forgetting they were side bitches Hell some these hoes was side bitches to the side bitch saying angrily smacking her lips and rolling her eyes. I have a few bitch before she could finish saying Bitch someone sitting behind Bianca shushed Bianca saying this is a church have some respect.

But before Royalty could tell Bianca to chill plus Royalty was so high Royalty wasn't responding in a timely manner anyways. Bianca turned around and took her glasses off and handed them to Royalty and respond to the lady by saying loudly I know you ain't shushing me hoe with your eyebrows looking like McDonald's arch I hope since your repping the brand you're getting paid for it homie the clown. The whole church had gotten quiet and you could see people with their hands over their mouths in disbelief. What turning back around looking at Royalty for an answer. Royalty couldn't believe it either. Royalty knew Bianca had absolutely no filter but, in a church, really. But Royalty didn't say anything Royalty actually wanted to laugh but Royalty was too embarrassed.

The pastor came to the podium holding the obituary saying ok now if there is anyone who has some remarks about Brother Amir please come forward and let's please keep our remarks to a minimum of 2 mins Thank you and returned to his seat praying these remarks didn't spark a backlash. The line filled up quickly. Several girls pushed pass people to get up and tell about their memories of Amir. A few guys were in line also. The first two girls Royalty and Bianca knew they grew up with them and they were sweet girls who had good memories of Amir as a young boy. Royalty keep looking at Amir's gold casket and the twenty eight flower arrangements she ordered for the number of years of his life. The picture Royalty chose for display of Amir had her thinking maybe she should have chosen a different one. But this one was a black and white and the event planners wanted a professional photo for the funeral. Yes, Royalty had hired an event planner for the funeral arrangements and repass. Royalty didn't want to have to deal with any of the details.
Royalty was reminiscing on her and Amir how they hooked up for the first time and when Amir had saved her life and how life was going to be so hard without him.

Then a woman gets up to give her remarks and says Hello my name is Mercedes and me and Amir had a special relationship I'm going to really miss him.

Bianca looked at Royalty and interrupted her thoughts asking Royalty who that girl was? And Royalty looked from the casket to Bianca like I don't know who she is? then Royalty looked towards the altar at Mercedes to pay attention to what she was saying.

Mercedes continued saying. Amir was such a great guy he was always there when she needed him to be. Royalty forehead started to wrinkle up like what? Royalty was sitting there a little uncomfortable but held her composure only because she was high as a kite.

Mercedes continued saying she meet Amir a few years ago at a restaurant with her girlfriends and they didn't have enough for their bill and Amir overheard them going back and forth on who had what and Amir walked over to their table and handed her a stack of hundred dollar bills and said don't ruin You'll friendship over no money. And started to walk away but Mercedes chased him down and asked for his phone number. And from then on, they had a special relationship. And Mercedes was really going to miss Amir.

Ok Bianca thinking this chick is delusional and disrespectful getting up taking off her mink throwing it towards Royalty. Cutting the line to give her 2mins remark because she was pissed off at this point. Royalty was light way feeling the same way as Bianca, but Royalty wasn't about to get up and go head up with this chick not today, not here Royalty was sure they would bump into each other and when that day came it would be on site out of respect well in this case disrespect. But Bianca couldn't wait that long. Bianca wasn't a fighter at all Bianca was too cute for that, but you would never know that with that mouth Bianca had. It was something terrible. Bianca would put the fear of death in a person. Bianca could send you straight to Hell with her wrath.

Royalty just shook her head because Royalty already knew how this was about to go down. Even if Royalty wanted to stop what was about to happen from actually happening Royalty couldn't because Royalty was too high. All Royalty knew was this was going to be the most talked about funeral ever thanks to her BFF Bianca and to never take another pill or drink after Bianca ever!

Grabbing the microphone tapping it like Bianca didn't already have everybody's attention by wearing a see through lace dress to a funeral Bianca started in on her speech. First given honor to God and Amir Rest In Peace Brother we love you and you will be missed dearly solemnly speaking.

But. here she goes Royalty thinking putting her head down in her lap holding her head because Royalty couldn't take what Bianca was about to dish out.

I want to start off saying a lot of you hoes in here are thirsty super thirsty like you'll need that extra large big gulp for you'll thirsty ass throats. The whole church starting Oh my goshin.

The Pastor stood up and put his hand up like it's ok and asked everyone please calm down she's obviously upset over the loss of her brother please let her speak her peace. But he also ask Bianca to be respectful of the church and he quickly sat back down.

Bianca looked back at the pastor and smiled but didn't respond and turned back around to the congregation and said A lot of you Broads pointing her finger at the crowd. Better be glad we're in a church and the Pastor asked me to be respectful cause I would tear a new hole inside some of you'll about my sis over there pointing at Royalty who still had her head down from embarrassment. All you broads know that Royalty was Amir's wife coming up in here crying and falling out like You'll was in a real relationship with Amir getting mad all over again starting to cry. I just want to let all you lil thirsty broads pointing at the congregation All y'all niggas is on my hit list so don't act surprised when it happens because it is going to happen, you'll mark my words and a few of you'll it already happen saying it with a smirk on her face. Yeah and Mercedes clapping her hands saying her name talking about a special relationship What is a special relationship suppose to mean Boo boo? Speaking rhetorically pausing a minute knowing Mercedes wasn't going to answer before continuing on. I'm saying you Hella fowl my nigga. Plus, you don't look like no Mercedes to me. You look more like a Hyundai or a Kia. The whole church feel out laughing. You don't look like nothing foreign to me turning up her lip with a smirk. Wearing that fake Gucci headband. That spells Cucci not Gucci The Fuck!! I guess you're walking around here self advertising the product your selling. Bianca started Laughing to herself. That's your brand huh? Fake ass. you know the rest I'm being respectful but Don't You Ever!! Pausing for a minute looking straight at Mercedes and her friends who was sitting there devastated with Mercedes come for my sis like that! And to all you side chicks in here pointing across the congregation again. Stay in your place underneath them rocks you'll all come from damn Trolls because we really about that life throwing a gang signs dropping the mic and Bianca started walking down the steps saying Gang Gang over here !! scanning the whole congregation like what. The whole church was in disbelief of what just occurred. The choir started singing I'm going up a Yonder to be with my lord which was a welcoming distraction to what had just happened. Sitting down grabbing her coat and rolling her eyes. Bianca whispered something to Royalty who had lifted her head back up shaking it after Bianca Lil speech plus Royalty was fix stated on Amir's casket again. Still in denial of the current situation.

Royalty briefly looked over at Bianca and said what? softly then looked right back at the casket.

Bianca laid her head on Royalty shoulder for support the support Bianca was supposed to be giving to Royalty and said I love you sis I had to let them heffas know don't even think about all that slick dissing.

Turning around kissing Bianca on the forehead Royalty said I get it. They knew Royalty was vulnerable right now and it was all good though. Looking back at Amir's casket Royalty thinking you got all these broads in here thinking they can disrespect me now that you're gone but baby, they should think twice about that closing her eyes going into deep thought not even paying attention to the eulogy the pastor was given about Amir.
Royalty was so glad the funeral was over, and she was ready to lay Amir's body to rest. The white horse and carriage was outside waiting to carry Amir's body to his final resting place. The spectators was standing all around the carriage taking selfies and having photo shoots. People will do anything for social media Royalty thinking not believing her eyes. So much had transpired today it was just draining Royalty or maybe it was the combo of the pills and drink. But whatever it was Royalty felt exhausted. Walking out the church hugging Bianca walking fast not wanting to talk to anyone praying their black car service would be outside in front waiting for them because Amir's service went on way longer than expected. Nothing is on time when it comes to black people.

After the six pallbearers carried Amir's casket out and Royalty was ready to get in her car this young woman walks up to Royalty and taps Royalty lightly on Royalty shoulder and says this may not be the best time to say this but …Royalty started looking at the women who was very pretty with Caramel complexion and good hair looking mixed like Royalty but just a little thicker and she had nice teeth but everything else about her screamed cheap. Her outfit was cheap her shoes was cheap pleather and her knock off bag even looked cheap, but she was well put together, nevertheless.

Royalty was sizing the women up then Royalty said excuse me what you just say?

And the women repeated I'm pregnant by Amir I'm sorry.

It felt like a bomb just exploded because all Royalty could hear was a loud explosion and ringing in her ears, I'm pregnant by Amir over and over again. Royalty grabbed her ears to silence the noise but to no avail it was still there. Royalty was staring at this woman but couldn't say a word no words would come out Royalty mouth and Royalty felt dizzy. Then the unexpected happened Royalty passed out and everybody came running to her aid. When Royalty awaken, she was sitting inside an ambulance getting her blood pressure taken and given some Iv fluids for dehydration looking around like what the fuck was she doing in an ambulance.

Are you ok Miss one of the paramedics asks Royalty?

Yes, I'm fine what happened Royalty asks Him?

You passed out and before Royalty could respond Royalty looked around and she's the bitch who claims to be pregnant by Amir standing at the ambulance door crying asking was Royalty going to be ok.

Trying to get up the paramedics tell Royalty Ma'am Wait a minute we need to make sure you're ok.

I'm Fine please just let me go I feel better thank you Royalty says still trying to get up and leave to go check this bitch who had the audacity to try and disrespect her man's funeral and disrespect her while she was grieving. The situation started to look like a scene from a hood rat movie. The paramedic check Royalty vitals again and said Royalty was ok to leave the ambulance if she chose to but he recommended that Royalty go to the hospital to get further evaluation from a doctor. Of course, Royalty declined. Removing the mask off Royalty face that Royalty had halfway taking off anyways and taking out the iv Royalty gets out the ambulance truck and approaches Amir's so called baby momma screaming you thought Amir was the nigga that you have a baby by and you become a millionaire huh? Well that's 50 and he stiffed you bitch. You punk ass bitches always got some proof that you'll fucking somebody's husband or man but never have no real proof of you'll income!! Always trying to come up off a nigga. Ol keep a nigga baby to get a check ass bitch!! Ready to take off on the pregnant girl but one of Amir's partner Slim grabs Royalty before Royalty could hit the girl.

Yelling Royalty stop the girls pregnant plus this isn't the place for that you need to put Amir's body to rest. Trying to get Royalty away from the girl.

Yanking her arm away from Slim still looking at the pregnant girl crazy Royalty said this isn't over you hear me? Today's your lucky day meaning every word she said. You get a pass but as soon as you drop that baby bitch, I mean the very second the head pops out I'm on your helmet at the hospital bitch. You're going to be in the right place because I'm going to Fuck you up you disrespectful ass bitch! Royalty spits out ready to kill her and bury her with Amir. Yanking her arm completely away from Slims grip walking into the crowd of spectators standing around getting the tea on their phones to put Royalty business on Instagram and Twitter faster than a celebrity that got caught sucking dick for dope.

Bianca runs through the crowd of spectators because Bianca was in the cuts talking to this little dude she been eyeing for some time and Bianca finally got his attention but when she saw Royalty walking out the ambulance truck Bianca told ol boy she'll holler at him later and ran to get Royalty and grabs her arm and whisks Royalty into their black Car and tells their driver to take off. People were talking pictures on their phones and videos like they just saw Rihanna or something. They were like a small mob outside the scenery was mad crazy.
After Amir's body was put into the wall and the final prayer was said Royalty told Amir's friends and family, she'll meet them at the repass. The 100 or so people that was invited to the burial because Royalty wanted Amir's burial service private for family and close friends only. Royalty didn't want to share Amir's last moments with everybody Royalty only wanted people that loved and cared about Amir present plus Royalty wanted Amir's homecoming to be sacred and Royalty wanted something for herself she didn't have to share with the public. After giving hugs and kisses to everyone they all said their goodbyes and left the cemetery. Once back in the car Royalty broke down uncontrollably laying down on the backseat in fetal position asking God why did this have to happen to her? Bianca started crying also because her high was coming down and reality was sinking in shit was about to get real. Rubbing Royalty shoulder trying to console her best friend to no avail. Arriving at the repass that was being held in downtown Los Angeles at a luxury warehouse that Royalty hired a party planner to host for Amir. Bianca saw the all white balloon banner that spelled Amir's name out front with all white roses aligning the entrance walkway and the crowd of people standing outside conversing even though it was freezing cold and getting dark outside. Thank God it wasn't raining

today but looking at the sky that was dark gray and smokey looking Bianca knew it was about to rain at any second. Tapping Royalty who had fallen asleep Bianca wakes her to inform Royalty they were at their destination.

Sitting up seeing the crowd of people laughing and talking Royalty looked at Bianca and said I can't and laid back down and closed her eyes.

At that moment Bianca realizes Royalty had no more fight in her and instructed the driver to take them home. Once they got to Royalty house and settled in, they changed into their pajamas and Bianca made them some drinks. They sat up and talked, cried, and laughed about Amir throughout most of the night. Reminiscing on the good times and how they grew up in the projects and somehow made it out on top. Both of them falling asleep on the oversized black velvet couches with the fireplace keeping them warm while they hugged up underneath one another both passed out drunk and wore out from all of today's activities. Hoping that tomorrow would be a better day. Landing in Oakland, CA Royalty was glad that her flight was short and sweet. Only 45 mins from Los Angeles to Oakland and thank God there was no turbulence or screaming babies on the plane plus Royalty was still a tired from yesterday events and all of Bianca shenanigans at the funeral. Yawing grabbing her Louie travel tote from underneath the seat. Royalty was traveling light because she was only staying for one day looked around at the plane Thankful, she was in first class and didn't have to wait in line to get off this full flight. Placing her Gucci glasses on and putting on her Louis Vuitton scarf because the Bay Area weather was no joke in January. Royalty said her goodbyes to the stewardess and exited the plane and headed to the bus shuttle to take her to pick up her rental car. Royalty loved Hertz rental car because being a loyal customer meant no waiting in line for her. All Royalty had to do was go get into the Lincoln town car that was awaiting her and drive off. Royalty reservation was complete and paid for prior to arriving as usual. Easy breezy exactly how Royalty liked it. But driving this trip alone was going to be hard because normally Royalty and Amir drove to this destination together. This whole experience was going to be difficult without Amir being there. Life as Royalty knew it was going to be very challenging. Because Royalty whole life revolved around Amir. The only good thing about it was Royalty knew women who men left them or they broke up or whatever the case may have been and Royalty knew of at least one person whose boyfriend got killed and the life style they had while with their man changed dramatically because when the men left the women didn't have their own money and relied on them (man) for everything.

Royalty knew one girl name Liza who went from living in the suburbs gated community in a 3500 square foot house with a pool in the backyard to back to the projects to live with her family with her two kids and losing her Benz that was paid for because she winded up needing the money after a couple months. She went from bad and boujee to broke and stripping real quick. And the sad part about it was all the years she was fucking with her balling ass man she was stuck up and didn't even really fuck with her family like that. Her kids didn't know her family at all. Her dude Tommy had her cooped up in the burbs isolated from everyone even his side chick who winded up keeping all her shit she got from his ass. The difference in the two women was Liza didn't want no more than he gave her ass Just as long as he brought her all the name brand bags and shoes and made sure her, and the kids had a nice roof over their heads was enough for her. Liza act like it didn't bother her that he only came home a couple days out of the week and that he only gave her enough money to cover the bills and a few extra dollars here and there plus Liza didn't even have life insurance on the nigga or was she stacking her bread saving some for a rainy day like today. It started raining as soon as Royalty got to Hertz rental car lot. But Liza man Tommy side chick Latrice had a good job, her own place in her name and she did take out a life insurance policy on that nigga because she knew what type of nigga she was dealing with. Plus, she knew that being in the game there is no guaranteed security. She also knew that it's not how you start but how you finish in the game that matters. No nigga ever got remembered by being a big Time drug dealer from back in the day unless you was a drug lord. Which most niggas don't even close to being. Selling a few kilos here and there won't get you no television movie. Royalty thinking driving down hwy 580 thanking God she was 23 yrs. old and had her own business and had her own money. Royalty did have life insurance on Amir that he had taken out not her, but she didn't need it. Because she had the money to bury him if she needed to. Royalty was thankful she didn't have to do a go fund me or sell dinners to get her man put away nicely. Shit even if Royalty didn't have her own anything Amir had enough money that was now her money that she would be straight anyways. Amir Made sure Royalty had access to all his belongings. Royalty knew where all his money was at. All his accounts, his safe house and had keys to all his cars. And both properties was in both their names. The only thing Royalty didn't know about was the bitch that was pregnant, and Royalty was positive Amir was going to tell her about that before she found out through the streets. Coming across the San Rafael Point Richmond bridge headed towards Corte Madera Royalty turns up the volume on the steering wheel listening to Monica still standing album #3 Everything to me on repeat. Thinking damn Amir this shit is fucked up. Pulling up in the gravel parking lot taking a deep breath. Looking around like Royalty always did when they came here once a month. Reading the sign Department of Corrections California State Prison San Quentin. Warden Ronald Davis next to the black 7ft iron gate with three guards with guns. Taking it all in and preparing herself for the monthly visit to Amir's brother Jaheem that was serving a Life sentence without the possibility of parole for doing a drive by in La for killing 9 people on two blocks within 7 hours for retaliation of his homeboy that was killed in front of his wife and daughter at a fast food restaurant. Jaheem was the finest inmate at San Quentin hands down. Jaheem was so fine and manipulative that this nigga got three women prison guards pregnant at the same time and the women all had to get transferred and eventually lost their jobs, but they all got settlements for sexual harassment by an inmate and got paid six figures to keep quiet. The prison didn't want no more bad press than it already had. Especially since it was the only prison that housed the most inmates on death row. 750 to be exact. And the prison housed 3700 inmates total. Sounds like a lot and most of them was there for capital murder. Also, this is the prison well known for its lethal execution of Tookie Williams.

Lining up at the gate with the rest of the visitors waiting to see their love one that's doing time. Getting ready to go through this long, horrendous procedure again Royalty tells herself while letting out a sigh." This is your life, and this is what it's always looked like so suck it up." Royalty had to call beforehand to make an appointment for a visit that's how the rules was set up. Then there was the strict dress code. No clothing that resembled the prisoners no blue jeans, no blue shirts, no orange shirts, no clothing resembling the officers also. No green shirts or tan pants or no camouflage. Also, there was no skirts or dresses or shorts and see thru clothing or anything that showed cleavage and absolutely no tight clothing. No wigs unless medically necessary. So, all these bitches wearing wigs nowadays.

You won't be getting in here to see no nigga no matter what. And you can't wear no underwire bras because you have to go thru the metal detectors several times before visiting. Standing there waiting for her rental car to pass the search of the drug sniffing dogs and pass on to the next phase Royalty couldn't stop thinking that Amir was supposed to be standing next to her suffering throughout this ordeal just to get a visit. Dressed warmly because this wasn't her first rodeo. Royalty knew how this went down. But Royalty felt sorry for some of the women in line who came there trying to look too cute but standing out there freezing. Looking over the crowd of women Royalty could always tell who was there for the first time by their attire. But Royalty came prepared. Hot pink YSL turtleneck and black wool pants. Black Gucci loafers with the fur. With her clear Chanel clutch with her I'd and car key and 50 dollars in ones which is the max you can bring for a visit for snacks from the vending machine and photos if you wanted any. Finally, the deputies start letting the line in the building for processing for their visits. This is the worst part of the visiting thus far. Everyone had to be searched for contraband that meant being damn near strip searched removing clothing and shoes then going thru the metal detector and have your belt and shoes go through the X-ray machine and then you had to have Your I'd checked for warrants every time just in case you got caught up within the last time you visited and then you had to fill out a visiting pass with all your information even though they had all that information to approve you for visiting in the first place. And you had to get your visiting pass stamped contact or no contact, so they could separate you into groups. And once that's established you have to wait in your designated visiting area and wait for your love one to be brought down. Not to mention your being watched like a hawk by the prison guards and surveillance cameras everywhere. And those cold stainless steel table and chair sets that are freezing in the winter are hella uncomfortable. And if you're there visiting your man, he'll they only allow you to kiss the beginning and ending of the visit. And that's doesn't mean no tongue kisses either. And it's absolutely no touching whatsoever. You can try that shit if you want to and get yourself banned permanently. But all this is worth it to see my big brother every time. No matter how much Royalty complained Royalty wouldn't change a thing because Royalty loved seeing her brother and if being uncomfortable for a few hours was what it took so be it. 30 minutes later this 6'2, 250pds, dark chocolate smooth skin looking like he got weekly facials, with one deep dimple on his left cheek with long neatly done dreads that hung to his butt that he got twisted every two weeks since he's been incarcerated for 13 years by who Royalty didn't know because she never bothered to ask. Jaheem came walking in like looking like a whole damn meal. Cartier shades on and Yeezy sneakers on his feet wearing his heavy starched baby blues gifted by the Department of Corrections with the initials CDC on huge display on the front of his shirt and the back. Oh, and let's not forget the iced out cross and chain Jaheem got arrested wearing and was allowed to keep because religious reasons. Jaheem was a Muslim and always had been. Even before he was incarcerated Jaheem started practicing being a Muslim as a young boy. A lot of his big homies were Muslim and turned him on to the religion. Despite whatever went down in the streets Jaheem praised Allah. What's good little Sis? Jaheem says grabbing Royalty face giving her a kiss on both cheeks then sitting down next to her. Looking at Jaheem seeing the resemblance of Him and Amir broke Royalty heart.

Sensing her pain Jaheem says. You're going to have to let it out Sis and come to terms with Amir's death. It's not going to be easy and every day will bring out different emotions. But you have to trust Ali that you will get through this eventually and be able to move on with your life because you have a whole life ahead of you. I know you can't see it now, but this too shall pass, and you won't feel the hurt anymore just the loss of a love one. Wiping a tear from Royalty eyes.

Royalty looked Jaheem in the eyes and heard what he said but her heart wasn't ready yet to believe him.

Grabbing Royalty giving her a big bear hug while the paid off guards looked the other way and whispering in Royalty ear. Now with that being said Lil sis you know that I have all my people all over this. Amir was my baby brother them fools gotta die who did this it's an Eye for an Eye and I won't rest until his murder is revenged. That shit cut deep with me when I got that call and the thought that you were there and could have been harmed also just don't sit well with me. Whoever did this to my baby brother might as well take their own life and the life of their family. Because what I'm going to have done to them will make shit in the theater that was considered rated R look like a Pg movie when I'm done with them fools. Seriously speaking. I put a million dollar bounty on the heads of them fools and their families and their family pets. Kissing Royalty cheek and releasing her. You hungry sis? Jaheem asks. I know you haven't eaten this morning looking at Royalty like I'm not asking you to eat something I'm telling you to eat something.

Turning around looking at the vending machine that Royalty had memorized since she saw it on every visit for the past six years of visiting here. Royalty knew everything that was in the machine. Getting up to get a breakfast sandwich and ginger ale and a cranberry juice for Jaheem because that was his favorite. Before sitting back down Royalty gives Jaheem a kiss on the cheek and hands him his juice. I don't know what I'm going to do without Amir. Royalty says you and Amir was all the family I have. Royalty Started tearing up again.

Look Lil Sis crying is for the weak you know that Jaheem says. You know we're not built like that. I want you to grieve but you also know that the aftershock is going to be tremendous. So, save your tears for when you need them. Today's not the day for sadness. It's a celebration of life. We all have a date Royalty. And it's sad when people think they can plan their own departures the way they choose but they can't. If that was the case everyone would be changing the date. Laughing to himself finding that humorous. Some people's departure may be peaceful, and some may be brutal, but the end result is we all have a date to leave here permanently without our consent. I hate it when I hear people say why now or why him or her? My response to that is why not Him or her? It's the same amount of pain for everyone who is left behind. Some people live to be 100 some die at birth. But regardless if you die in a car accident or if your shot in a drive by or you die in your sleep. No one is exempt from death not you or me. That's what we all as humans have in common baby girl. But what we don't have in common is our relationship with Ali or whoever it is that people worship. We all have to answer to a higher power and face accountability for the way we have lived. Some of us will have more to discuss with Ali than others. And I just happen to be one of them people with a not so honorable past. But Honor means something different to everyone also. To me Honor is what I live by and what I stand for but to others my code of honor is a crime. But to me there's a reaction for every action. That's just the way life is set up. I didn't make the rules I'm just a messenger. Holding Royalty attention like he always did during their visits. I love you baby girl always have you're my little sister and it's my responsibility to protect you now that Amir is gone. So, with that being said. I need for you to take a trip for at least a month until I put some things into action. I hear Dubai is real nice place. And when you return, I want you to move back into the hood just temporarily. You can live at the condo plus you don't need to be living in no big ass house by yourself.

Chiming in Royalty says I've always wanted to visit Dubai me and Amir planned on going there this summer. I guess I'll be going by myself. Thinking about how the dynamic of her family changed overnight.

Well at least you can go do some shopping Jaheem says your favorite thing to do smiling at Royalty displaying his perfectly pearly whites with a gold crown at the top right side. That should distract you for a minute trying say something to cheer Royalty up. And getting away Always is a mood enhancer despite whatever a person may be going through. Shit look at me sis I can't escape and go anywhere shrugging his shoulder like what. But I can't be mad at nobody but myself I put myself here and I have to deal with this right here pointing at the prison door referring to being in prison. Reality is a Mother Fucker!! Sometimes we let what people do or say provoke us to do the unthinkable. Don't let that be you Royalty getting up from the table bending over Royalty giving her a kiss on the forehead then heading to the door to end the visit. But before Jaheem leaves, he says to Royalty I'll be in touch baby girl enjoy your trip, Asa Lam a Lakem with a wink of the eye. Then Jaheem tells the guards to take him back to his cell. When a guard unlocks the door, Jaheem exits the visiting room leaving the other visitors thinking visiting hours were over when in actuality they still had two more hours to go feeling relieved once they were informed. Royalty was allowed to leave the visit early also because that's how the arrangement was set up from the beginning since Jaheem had been incarcerated there. He ran the prison plus he paid his way to be a boss. And if he wanted to leave a visit early, he was allowed to. But for other inmates it had to be a medical emergency to leave early. Well I guess you could consider the death of his baby brother a medical emergency if you looked at it that way.

Bianca Chronicles

Today's going to be a good day Bianca says to herself removing the lock off the door to her shop getting ready to open up for business Bianca was fully booked and had plans on going to look at another property later for expanding her business to a second location. Bianca couldn't believe that she was getting the bag like she was without any help. Her first property her parents gifted her when she graduated from high school, they knew Bianca always wanted to open a salon that's all Bianca talked about growing up. Plus, Bianca mom had owned a hair salon every since Bianca was young. Bianca dad owned several barbershops and a liquor store and recently open a deluxe car detailing shop. Bianca family oozed with money. Bianca dad was one of the biggest drug lords in Los Angeles in the 80s he probably would have still been a drug lord but the feds shut him down when he got into a shootout with police and killed one and fought and beat a murder case on a technicality because the police had been framing him and setting him up and it got revealed by an informant that was working for the police. But Bianca dad knew the police wouldn't allow him to stay in the game after killing one of their own, so he went legit or, so the police thought because Bianca patents were still the plug. Shit they made millions in the game her dad beat a murder case and owned hella business, so it still was a win on his part. You have to know when to walk away and cut your losses he always told Bianca growing up. Now Bianca was buying her second property all on her own no cosigner, no investors, she didn't even need no man to help. This was all her and it felt so good Bianca was thinking as her first client Anna comes speed walking in outta breath.

Oh, hey Bianca Anna says you still talk to Black right?

Bianca looks her up and down for one because her outfit was not on point, she had on a Gap hoodie I didn't even know Gap still existed and two Anna was hella messy. Yeah why bitch what's good? Bianca asks.

Oh, I just saw him pass by here with some bitch in his car. He drives that money green 500sl right? Knowing damn well what he drove.

Now Bianca was hot thinking it probably was her messy ass he had in the car dropping her bitch ass off. Bianca knew Anna had always been feeling him. Bianca started thinking I dressed down for a reason. But Bianca dress down wasn't really dress down to most people. Bianca had on a brown Fendi signature fitted dress with a Fendi baseball cap over her 24 inches of Indian raw bone straight weave and tights on with Ugg boots to be comfortable because she knew she would be on her feet all day. Plus, Bianca was a label whore at least one thing she wore daily had to be some kinda designer. Sitting Anna down in her white leather swivel chair turning her around facing the floor to ceiling mirror and placing her signature drape I'm Stuck Up the name of her salon over Anna

clothing so no Makeup would get on her clothing and wiping her face clean before proceeding to give her a famous sought after Bianca beat.
Bianca started reminiscing about last night when her and Black was at her condo in bed eating Steak and lobster and sipping on Roscato Bianca favorite red wine when Black said they needed a break. After sipping her glass of wine Bianca laughed and said a break nigga what I'm wearing you out huh? Laughing Bianca thought Black meant a break from fucking. They had been going at it like dogs in heat lately. But now Bianca sees this nigga had ulterior motives all along. Having Bianca mind racing Bianca couldn't even focus on her work. Bianca didn't give a fuck if Anna looked like a fucking clown. Because that's how she felt about her at that moment. Bianca just keep thinking I'm going to have to show this nigga what my interpretation of a break means. Finishing Anna face Bianca knew she could have done better Work, but fuck Anna Bianca was thinking.

Thanks Anna said dryly knowing it wasn't Bianca Best Work, but Anna felt kinda bad about bringing Bianca bad news. Kinda.

Bianca had zoned out so badly that she forgot to turn off the alarm next door at Royalty Hair salon Pretty Please. Bianca was the manager over the salon and was the only one who knew the code besides Royalty. They set it up this way because Royalty traveled a lot so since Bianca shop was directly next door to Royalty on Rodeo drive. It just made sense plus they were best friends who else could Royalty trust with her lifeline. Bianca parents owned several properties on the block and when Royalty wanted to open up a Hair salon Bianca parents sold the property that was a vacant an ice cream polar to Amir who gifted it to Royalty for her 21st birthday. Royalty owns Two more Hair salons one in the Bay Area that her cousin ran and another one in Atlanta that Royalty had a business manager there running for her. Royalty keep expanding every year. Pretty Please is one of the high class salon to service a few celebrities. Royalty stylist can slay the shit out of some heads. And Pretty Please has won several awards and been featured in numerous magazines and blogs. Royalty definitely handled her business when it came to her businesses. And Bianca couldn't wait for her best friend to return from Dubai, so they couldn't get off the hook together. Bianca was hoping that Royalty would loosen up a bit now that she was single again even though it was by a tragedy. Bianca had big plans for them this upcoming summer. They were about to be so lit, but Royalty wasn't aware of it yet.
Bianca couldn't wait until her last client was done. Six faces, six different conversations and six long hours couldn't stop Bianca from thinking about Black and the fact that he totally disrespected her and her place of business. Bianca also was heated because she hasn't heard from Black all day either. No call, no texts. This mother fucker was really trying her patience. Black had Bianca so fucked Up Bianca couldn't even eat. Bianca just keep sipping champagne with clients fake smiling and not paying attention to shit they were talking about and keep looking at her Rolex counting down until she was able to show her ass and let this nigga know she wasn't to be fucked with period point blank. Bianca just keep thinking this nigga just don't know what I'm capable of. Planning her revenge thinking who could she call to have her back but decided she really didn't need anyone because Bianca didn't want nobody all up in her business like that. Looking at her finished product Bianca waited for her client to pay and schedule another appointment and then Bianca was out. Bianca didn't even put her makeup in cases and place them in the makeup drawers. Bianca just left everything were it was she'll take care of it tomorrow. Locking up the salon turning on the alarm then Bianca was out. Damn near running to her Range Rover hitting the alarm getting in slamming the car door Bianca went inside the glove compartment and took her stash out and lit up a blunt. Exhaling real slow leaning her head back. Thinking she was so glad this day was finally over. Looking at her phone still no text from this nigga getting madder by the minute. Ok it's on Bianca

thinking Black asked for it. To justify the actions Bianca was about to commit. Taking a deep breath talking to herself. "Ok Bitch you can do this go to this nigga momma house and fuck his car up." Hitting the blunt again looking for her Mary J Blige cd. Bingo smiling once she finds it. Turning on I'm not gonna cry playing it on repeat driving to Watts to fuck some shit up. Pulling up on Black momma block it's barely getting dark outside and it's starting to drizzle so nobody's really outside. I'll wait a minute to see if this nigga comes out Bianca thinking. Parked up the street from Black momma's house but close enough to see the house and Black car in the driveway. Firing up another blunt to calm her nerves Bianca gets her confidence to go fuck Black Car up. Looking around the street that's pretty much clear is a sign Bianca thinks saying go do it!! But in reality, Bianca should know it's never a good idea to go to anyone house starting shit under no circumstances but in her mind a clear street is a sign. That's the way crazy people think but whatever we've all been crazy in love before right.? So, Bianca gets out her truck and grabs a bat she keeps in her trunk and a crow bar also that's in the trunk also and her mase just in case the nigga come running out the house trying to fuck her up. Looking around one more time Bianca slams her trunk and looks inside her driver's side window to make sure her phone was on the passenger seat, so she wouldn't bring it by accident and drop it in case she had to run. It was sitting on the seat, so Bianca was cool. And Bianca left her truck running so she can make a speedy escape. Bianca walks quickly down the street with her double D's bouncing up and down nervous ass fuck but thinking oh well. When Bianca reaches the house Bianca quietly opens the gate and tiptoes into the yard and stares at Black Benz then bam hits the back window of his Benz shattering it now her adrenaline kicking in. Then bam the driver's window, then Bianca hit the front window several times before it shattered, and the car alarm finally goes off. But nobody came out the house. So, Bianca then did the unthinkable. She ran up to the front of the house and threw the bat into the bay window and watched it break. Then Bianca took off running in the rain like Flo jo not looking back. When Bianca reached her truck, Bianca got in and ducked down and locked her car doors why Bianca didn't know. But when Bianca came up seconds later the coast was clear then Bianca drove off feeling accomplished. Bianca felt like Angela Bassett in waiting to exhale when she set his car on fire smoking a cigarette walking away. Nobody can really know how that feels unless you been provoked to tearing somebody's shit up. Like nigga don't play with me.
Once Bianca was safely in her hotel room at the Marriott by the airport because Bianca was too scared to go home so Bianca felt safe at a hotel. Closing her hotel room door and closing the blinds Bianca lays across the bed and started laughing. That's what that fuck nigga get Bianca thinking Take that!! Laughing hysterically. Then when her phone starts ringing Bianca jumped. Oh, shit looking at her phone it's him. Thinking should she answer it or not. Bianca let Black go to voicemail. Then Black called again. Sitting up now on the few pillows getting nerves Bianca didn't know why because Black wasn't no were near her was, he? Bianca mind started playing tricks on her.

Then Black text her. Bitch you better call me back ASAP or else!!!

Oh, shit Bianca thinking what now damn. Contemplating on if she should or shouldn't Bianca wished she could hit her blunt right now. But all hotels are non-smoking facility fuck Bianca said to herself. Getting up and pacing the floor Bianca calls Black back getting smart when he answered. That's what the fuck you get you punk ass nigga driving bitches by my place of business nigga. What you trying to do show bitches how to level the fuck up or something? How to be a business owner nigga laughing.

Shaking his head hitting a blunt. Black says you're a dumb ass bitch seriously not fazed by Bianca comments at all. First of all, bitch the girl in my car was my little sister who I picked up from the airport she just flew in from college not that I have to explain shit to your punk ass bitch. Second of all I hate when bitches run, they fuckin mouth not knowing what the fuck they be talking about with that bullshit. Also putting a 10 on shit. Messy ass bitches. And I know exactly who told you that bull shit too because I saw that messy bitch at the bus stop and hit my horn and said what's up. Yeah, I'm going to chin check her ass too. Hitting his blunt again blowing out smoke pausing before he started talking again. But why do you weak bitches always listen to another mother fucker about your nigga tho? Seriously asking a rhetorical question. Not even realizing that the next bitch probably hating, mad she single not getting no dick ain't got no nigga to post as her MCM every Monday and you weak bitches always believe them. Your dumb ass bitch. Plus, I don't do crazy bitches. I don't fuck with crazy bitches at all. It only takes me one time to become a believer you'll never kill me in my sleep bitch. Laughing. Plus, bitch we only been fucking around for about two months, right? You don't even know me like that to be going all crazy and shit. And why you bust out my momma house window tho? You better be glad nobody was home because you would have got shot bitch. My whole family about that life even my lil sister in college laughing again. Plus, a nigga got his own crib bitch, but you wouldn't know that because you didn't make it to the next phase yet because you on that bullshit you own. You didn't even know I had a little sister laughing laying his head back on his couch hitting his blunt blowing smoke into the phone, so Bianca could hear him. Yeah bitch but it's good tho but check it. Bitch you better have 5 racks for a nigga by Friday and I don't accept checks either bitch laughing. And don't think about playing a nigga or I'm going to show you what a break really means and with that said Black hangs up in Bianca face laughing. While the bitch Anna that started all this shit was sucking his dick thinking mission accomplished. But what she didn't know was Black was going to give her ass the business too when she was done sucking his dick. Because Black was recording her, and he had went live on Instagram displaying her deep throating skills on him and Black had hella views Black also went on Snapchat showcasing her skills. And now he was about to post the video and tag her in it and his caption was going to say "You got a big mouth! #literally #keepyourmouthclosed laughing at himself. Bitches always provoking a nigga to do the unthinkable.

Standing on the corner looking at the street sign that read Zamora Ave confirmed that Royalty was officially back in Los Angeles from her 30 day much needed vacation and was back in her hood. The projects where it all began at in Nickerson gardens. Royalty hated this place but also loved it at the same time. Royalty knew that sometimes you're not so happy beginnings makes for your happy ending. It's not how you start but how you finish that matters. These projects is were Bianca and Amir grew up as kids playing outside until the late hours running around with dirty clothes on and shoes with holes in them. Were they couldn't wait to receive their government cheese box with Cheerios on the first of the month? This is where they first meet first kissed became brother and sister as kids and Amir became her protector because Bianca didn't have any biological siblings Royalty was the only child to Teresita Santiago the only Filipino crackhead in her projets. The memory of that alone made Royalty stomach hurt. But Royalty was glad that she came from humble beginnings because that what made Bianca the person she was today. Royalty actually envied people who didn't start out in the struggle. Because how else are you supposed to build your character if you don't know what it's like to go without having certain things in life. Like not having enough food for the month or worrying about how you're going to pay your light bill or cable bill, or which one is more important? Because some months you can't pay both. And if your sugar daddy didn't come around that month you were in trouble. And I'm not talking about the hood drug dealer that gave you a few dollars here or there. I'm talking about the real sugar daddy that licked his thumb before peeling off a few hundred dollars to your momma making sure you'll was ok for the month. Plus growing in the hood, you develop clarity on life. Life is black or white there is no gray areas. Also, the hood will make you or break you. Plus, pressure makes diamonds if you know anything about that. You either want out of the jets or your either all in repping your hood. From the hood Royalty was from the Nickerson Gardens most women become medical assistants and nurses pushing themselves forward and most men become drug dealers to push themselves forward. Then there's that rare few individuals that has big dreams and aspirations to make it out the projects completely with no looking back. Like your ballplayers and actors but like I stated it's very rare. Plus, you can take the person out the hood, but the hood is still going to be in them and that was Royalty and Amir case. Walking up to her old brick building 93 staring at clothes line in front brought back so many memories of her and Amir swinging from this clothesline falling down scraping her knee and kicking over the trash cans that was full to capacity and seeing the rats run from the trash and Amir shooting at them with his B.B. gun. and them laughing hysterically. Hearing the other kids' mom yell out the windows at their children saying it's getting dark outside its time to come inside. But never hearing Teresita voice being concerned about Bianca or the time or even Bianca whereabouts. But what bothered Royalty the most is so many parents don't realize that Loving and nurturing your children molds them into the adults they will one day become. But Teresita didn't know anything about that nor did she care. Looking up at building 93 apt 49 brought back so many memories that brought chills through Royalty body. Without warning Royalty started crying thinking that no child should have to go through life without a parent loving them or caring about their children wellbeing, but we all know there are parents out there that behave in this manner and worse. And in Royalty book they should all be placed on a deserted island and set that bitch on fire. Good morning sleepyhead Jinx says bringing Royalty breakfast in bed and sitting down at the foot of the bed smiling at Royalty. You slept a long time sweetie everything ok? Looking Royalty in the face waiting for an answer she never got.

Sitting up propping herself up on the pillows getting comfortable. Taking a bite of her scrambled eggs and sipping her orange juice making gulping sounds while swallowing. Thanks Royalty says for making me breakfast and letting me stay at your place until i figure out what's next in my life looking over the plate of homemade waffles, scrambled eggs, apple chicken sausage with a fruit platter and fresh squeezed orange juice. I appreciate your hospitality Jinx brushing her hair out her face and cutting her waffles.

Royalty you know it's always a pleasure hun. I love when you visit you can stay as long as you like. And Jaheem said for me to try to talk you into moving in for a while laughing. Jaheem called this morning, but you were sleep he said he'll talk to you later.

Smiling at Jinx Royalty likes Jinx more than she liked Jaheem other two baby mamas. Plus, Jinx wasn't with that Bullshit the other two was on. Jaheem had all three of them set up nice being it was his fault they all lost their jobs as Correctional Officers for fucking with him and getting pregnant even though they were all paid a nice payout for sexual harassment by an inmate. Jinx owned this condo on Prairie Ave in Inglewood before she started messing with Jaheem and even though he brought her a big house in the hills Jinx stays here at the condo because Jinx says she scared to be in that big ass house by herself. Jinx and Jaheem son Jaheem Jr. JJ for short doesn't live here for the most part. Jj never here he stays with Jinx parents in Pasadena and he goes to school out there and comes home on the weekends when he feels like it. He's thirteen and you know how teenagers can be. He looks exactly like his dad also same complexion dark with that skin like butter, dimple, with pretty eyes and wavy hair and he's really tall like Jinx. Jinx is a six ft tall woman but she's hella beautiful like she's from some island or something. The color of chocolate with hazel eyes and naturally short curly hair. She looks like a model tall a little thick with a nice ass but it's her demeanor that keep her winning. Jinx is the humblest person you would ever meet with the softest voice. Very religious and very intelligent. Jinx has two degrees and Jinx finished head of her class in the Police academy. It's a shame Jinx got caught up with Jaheem ass but sometimes love will make you do some unethical things. Plus, I believe Jinx was Jaheem favorite out of the three and they were all beautiful women. But the other two baby mamas Jaheem had smuggling in drugs but not Jinx. Also, the other two told their stories to the tabloids and got paid when their story was hot off the press. Everybody wanted to be on TMZ but not Jinx. Jinx never said a word. And Jinx been loyal to Jaheem since she started messing with him thirteen years ago. The other two baby mama's been fell off. Jinx evens gets Jaheem girls sometimes on the weekends from his other baby mamas they also look exactly like Jaheem and all his kids were born months apart their all thirteen years old. Jinx treats them all as her own. Jinx more involved in the girl's life more than their own trifling mothers are. Jinx was also banned from visiting Jaheem for about five years. But Jinx challenged the courts and won visitation and her and Jaheem got married two months later and Jinx has been visiting about three times a month for 8 yrs. now and brings all the kids. Plus, Jaheem has it set up with the guards for a hefty fee, but Jaheem isn't tripping because he got it. On regular visits Jaheem and Jinx goes goes into the bathroom and get it in for a about 30 minutes every visit. That's what the guards are paid for to not interrupt them at all. Royalty couldn't imagine what their relationship was like, but it works for them. Jinx owned a yoga studio and became a yoga instructor since she could never work in law enforcement again. Jinx doesn't have to ever work again if she chose not to like the other two lazy baby mamas' that didn't do shit all day but fuck with hella niggas and ride around in new cars messing with niggas that's looking at them like a go fund me account. Some broads are really pitiful in real life. Don't won't nothing and not going to have nothing but what you give them. Can't make shit happen on their own. That's why you see so many women that fucked with a baller or athlete and was walking around with their nose in the air like her shit don't stink. Looking down on mother fuckers then bam the nigga leave her ass and she's right back to her humbling beginnings riding the mother fucking bus with designer clothes on and an expensive bag. Chasing the next baller that want give her the time of day. Laughing at the thought.

What you laughing at Jinx asks Royalty?

Oh, I was just thinking how life has a way of humbling you without warning Royalty says finishing her food, so she could get this day over with.
Bitch you ready Bianca asks Royalty?

Looking at her phone Royalty wasn't sure if she wanted to cancel or just wait until the baby comes. Today Royalty was meeting with Amir allegedly baby mama to get a clear understanding of the situation at hand. But now Royalty starting to reconsider because Royalty was getting butterflies in her stomach. Royalty wasn't never one to back down but today Royalty felt like just maybe this wasn't her fight to be fighting. But the whole time Royalty was on her trip in Dubai Royalty keep thinking about that girl and when she said she was pregnant by Amir. Royalty couldn't understand why this girl haunted her thoughts and Royalty needed answers.

Yes, Bianca I'm getting ready come pick me up in an hour I'll be waiting outside. And Royalty hung up without saying goodbye. Yelling Jinx name Jinx please come here!

Running in the room from her room across the hall. What's wrong? Jinx asks looking nervous.

Sorry it's nothing serious I just wanted to ask you your opinion on something Royalty says.

Letting out a sigh of relief Jinx sits down at the edge of the bed while Royalty went thru her luggage looking for something to put on.

What's up honey how can I be of assistance? Jinx inquired.

Ok I know you know about the chick who is pregnant by Amir? Pausing waiting for Jinx reaction.

Putting her head down Jinx said yes Jaheem told me about that. I wanted to wait until you were comfortable with talking about it.

Well I'm going to meet her today to get some answers because it's not sitting well with me. My man hasn't been dead but a month and I'm meeting some side chick that's pregnant by Him. This isn't fair. But like Amir would say. You can't be a crybaby about shit. It is what it is. And I have to man up and accept what life throws at me and hit a Home room with that shit. But this isn't easy you know. This hurt.

Standing up hugging Royalty. I know sweetheart, but you know what will hurt you more is if you wouldn't be a woman about the situation and would have just washed your hands and said you didn't want no parts of the baby. And just knowing Amir had a baby out there and you weren't apart of the baby life. This is what Amir would have wanted regardless of how the baby was conceived that baby is innocent. Kissing Royalty cheek.

I know crying and that's why I wanted to talk with her it's not the baby's fault. And since Amir's gone, I feel like it's my responsibility you know. Wiping her eyes. I'm so tired of crying Jinx. Holding Jinx hands.

This too shall pass sweetheart I promise. The clouds don't stay gray forever. The sun comes out eventually. And I'm here for you no matter what. And I understand your pain. I was pregnant with two other women at the same time by a man doing a life sentence and lost my career starting to cry herself. I didn't see a way out the situation. My parents who are both in the legal profession gave up on me I embarrassed my family and myself. But you know what keep me going. My baby. I told myself God wouldn't have given me this innocent baby if he didn't have a plan. And you know what 16 years later holding Royalty face that was drenched with tears. God didn't let me down. He blessed me with the greatest gift ever Jaheem Jr. even though he can't stand being with me laughing. My parents finally came around and forgave me when I was 6 months pregnant and my so called friends who talked about me behind my back. Well let's just say they weren't real friends and exposed themselves and God removed them. I found my true purpose in life and lived happily ever after. Kissing Royalty. And you will to. It will all make sense one day. Death has its way of bringing clarity thru its pain. We might not understand it but there's always a reason for everything. And we don't know but maybe if Amir had not been murdered this baby would have separated, you'll permanently and that's like a death sentence sometimes to lose your life partner when they're still living and their loving someone else. So, we don't know why, and we shouldn't question it. Just know once again this too shall pass my dear, I love you. Hugging Royalty tight then releasing her walking out the room back into her bedroom closing the door getting on her knees to pray for Royalty meeting with Amir's baby mama.

Honking the horn just as ghetto as she wanted to be. Bianca wouldn't let up on the horn. Stepping out the shower Royalty grabs her towel and shakes her head.

Knocking on the bathroom door Jinx says Bianca outside laughing.

Yeah, I heard her. Can you please tell her to give me 20 mins Royalty says as she gets ready quickly putting her hair in a quick bun and throwing on a Givenchy sweat suit and Balenciaga sneakers and no makeup bare face but still cute. Giving Jinx a hug walking out the door.

Jinx says you got this with a wink.

Royalty felt so much better than earlier Royalty feels like she can take on the world now after her talk with Jinx.

Getting in the car Bianca says you ready giving Royalty the look over. I'm feeling that bag bitch Bianca says eyeing Royalty Hermès crocodile bag.

Yeah, I love it too. Amir brought this last Christmas. Most my good shit Amir brought. Touching her bag remembering when she opened this gift and the expression on Amir's face. Amir always got excited at Christmas time. Amir loved buying Royalty gifts. Even if it wasn't Christmas or her birthday. Amir just wanted to see Royalty happy.

You getting all fancy to go see this Lil bitch huh? Laughing Bianca says.

I beg your pardon? twisting up her face. You the one driving a Bentley to the hood bitch now that's fancy laughing.

Yeah bitch I have to show these mother fuckers what I'm working with. Just in case one of them want to holler at a bitch Bianca says. They better have they shit together and be on my level. Bianca said. See I don't care how the mother fucker gets his bag just as long as he's chasing that mother fucker feel me? Hitting her blunt. Preferably that mother fucking crocodile Hermès bag chase that bag laughing. Plus, the Range needs a tune up and oil change Laughing Bianca said.

You so silly Royalty says laughing also. Turn that shit up snapping her fingers bobbing her head to Migos Stir fry which makes Royalty feel like twerking every time it comes on. Turning into the Jungle I still can't believe Amir was fucking with some hood rat that lives in these projects. But nothing should have surprised Royalty when it came to Amir.

Looking for the address Bianca says these the projects Training Day was filmed in, right?

Yes, Royalty replies still looking for the address.

King Kong ain't got shit on me Bianca yells out laughing. That was my favorite part of the movie besides ol boy being handcuffed in the bathtub scared to death still laughing.

But Royalty didn't find anything amusing especially right now since Royalty was looking for Amir's side bitch address.

Right there Bianca says finding a Park right in front pulling in directly in front of the girl's house. Which was on the third level.

Hella kids was outside playing even though it was cold outside, and some didn't even have on jackets not surprisingly to Royalty though. Royalty was once one of these kids a straight hood baby.

You ready to go interrogate this bitch? Bianca asks seriously.

I guess Royalty replies then give me some Bianca says raising her hand for a high five that Royalty slaps in response. Let's do this getting out the car stepping into the chilly air looking around because some dudes had come outside now probably to see who was driving a Cocaine white Bentley in their hood. And of course, Bianca wouldn't be Bianca without doing the extra. Bianca steps out the driver's seat wearing a green bling out Gucci sweat suit with a Gucci Ny baseball cap, face beat up blinking her mink lashes and wearing a pair of red bottom boots with a Gucci crossbody with her gun a 22 semi automatic neatly tucked nicely inside in case somebody wanted some smoke. Because Bianca didn't have hands like Royalty did. But Bianca wasn't running from no fight either Plus coming to any hood you just never knew what might pop off. Hitting the car alarm Smiling at the dudes waving hi the dudes nodded what's up with their heads. Bianca flirted everywhere she went. Didn't matter if it was at the grocery store. And what made matters worse Bianca was bad ass fuck. A straight 10 in every area and Bianca knew it. Bianca kept bitches mad and she loved it. Walking up the three flights of stairs because the elevator smelled so pissy like a public bathroom unfortunately Royalty thinking this is ridiculous rolling her eyes. But Bianca didn't mind it at all as long as she had somebody watching her like the dudes that were standing on the block is all that mattered.

Finally reaching apt 313 Royalty knocks on the wooden door that was chipped up and looked like it had a bullet hole in it. Opening the door, the women with the cute face that Royalty wanted to slap the shit out of smiled and invited them in. Looking around at the beige brick walls and the extra small kitchen, the cheap beige carpet throughout the apt with hella spots because even getting it shampooed couldn't help clean it and the furnace attached to the wall brought back memories. Plus, the girl needed to clean this mother fucker up. It was shit everywhere. Clothes on the floor, toys everywhere plates sitting on the living room table that you can tell been sitting there for a couple days. Empty Capri sun pouches and the garbage can was full to capacity. But at least her black leather couches look pretty clean. She probably wiped them down because she knew Royalty was coming. The little flat screen tv was about a 40 inch if that the brand was an Apex you know the flat screen tv people be fighting over at Walmart during Christmas time for $199 you always see on the news it was one of those. She had the tv sitting on a milk crate the kind that be in the schools using it as a tv stand. And she forgot to clean the rest of the house. Royalty took a mental note to tell her about this place at a later date. But Royalty wanted to get to the task at hand that brought her there her man.
Extending her hand to Royalty the woman says we haven't been formally introduced my name is Liberty Mae but call me Liberty shaking Royalty hand like she was at a job interview.

But Royalty was thinking why this bitch got an old lady name to be so young. Her momma must have been old ass fuck when she had her. Sitting across on the opposite couch from Royalty and Bianca who were sitting next to each other on one couch. That only could fit two people comfortably, but the way Bianca was sitting so uncomfortable holding her purse tightly and legs bent up looking around like she hope there's no roaches or bugs were in the apt was priceless.

Liberty said I know you have lots of questions for me looking at Royalty not believing Amir wife was really sitting in her living room right now because all Liberty ever heard from Amir was horror stories about Royalty.

Yes, I do have hella questions for you Royalty says. First off where did you meet Amir at?

Putting her head down momentarily Liberty says at Its Lit the strip club the night they had the after party for summer jam.

Thinking back Royalty says I was there! Looking at Bianca who was scared to move a muscle because Bianca thought something was going to bite her. We was there that night remember Bianca that's the night me and Amir wasn't speaking we had a fight two days before summer jam and I put him out for a couple days and that night at Its Lit we were standing at the bar and he came up behind me and whispered in my ear.

Babe let's see who can get the most numbers tonight without getting mad. Let's just act like we don't know each other, and Amir walked away.

And when I turned around Amir was laughing smoking a cigar walking towards the VIP and I rolled my eyes. Like this bitch got me fucked all the way up. Reminiscing Waiting for Bianca to respond.

Bianca just shook her head yes.

Royalty wanted to bust out laughing and videotape Bianca ass since Bianca always caught Royalty off guard doing shit. But Royalty couldn't do her like that. Bianca was about that life until she really got to the hood. See Royalty was raised in the projects nothing surprised her. But Bianca silver spoon feed ass wasn't. Bianca always lived in a house with the white picket fence. Bianca didn't know what the fuck to think right now. Bianca was in shock. Turning back to back Liberty Royalty said. That night was bananas. Me and Amir was light way beefing and I hadn't spoken to him for a couple days. Me and Bianca went to the summer jam and decided to go to the after party I knew I would see Amir there, but I didn't care. I wanted to irate him. I even had on a tee shirt that read I Cheat Back!! Just in case I ran into his ass. Laughing thinking about it.

Liberty says that's crazy. Me and my girlfriend meet him when we walked by Amir table and he told us to sit down. Amir ordered us some drinks. And Amir said you remind me of my wife. Your beautiful just like her. Same kind of hair and body. And I was like what? Then Amir points towards a group of girls and says that's my wife right there the one with the Tee shirt on that says I cheat back laughing. That's crazy you brought that up. And all I remember saying was yeah, she's cute.

Royalty was looking at Liberty like we're not really having this conversation, are we?
Liberty was looking like yeah unfortunately we are. A slight pause then a knock on the door when Liberty gets up and opens the door and a little girl jumps in her arms yelling mommy, mommy I drew you a picture at school today. Kissing Liberty and putting her head down on her mommy shoulders. All Royalty could see was the long ponytails that hung down her back. Thanking the older woman at the door Liberty closed the door behind her and walked back into the living room with the most beautiful little girl Royalty had ever seen. This kid had a face of a little goddess. She was dark complexion like she was Ethiopian with the prettiest eyes with long eyelashes looking like hi.

When Liberty sat back down on the couch the little girl sat beside her mom smiling. Pointing at Royalty she said who's that mommy? she's pretty.

Bianca had been put her head down on her lap and checked out mentally this was too much for her brain to digest. Bianca had been just sitting there rolling her eyes the whole entire time every time Liberty said something Bianca rolled her eyes like bitch please.

It's not polite to point Angel you know that. Her name is Royalty.

Hi, miss Royalty my name is Angel I'm three and my birthday is coming soon I'll be four holding up 4 Fingers smiling real big.

Hi Angel, you're such a beautiful little girl when is your birthday? Royalty asks.

Looking at her mommy Liberty says tell her when your birthday is Angel? You know when it is.

My birthday is June 14 Miss Royalty and I'm going to have a mermaid party you want to come? Still smiling real big.

If you invite me, I'll come. Royalty replies smiling back at Angel cute self.

Angel jumps off the couch and hugs Royalty. Thank you miss Royalty I like you your sooo pretty like my mommy. Then Angel jumps on Bianca lap and Bianca almost had a major heart attack.

Screaming Whoa whoa little girl what you doing? throwing her hands in the air.

Angel pulls at Bianca hat. I like your hat your pretty too what's your name? You Miss Royalty Sister? Looking Bianca dead in the eyes.
Bianca didn't know what to do or say. She just keep looking back and forth at Royalty then at Liberty like get her please.

Liberty says to Angel baby girl get off of Bianca please that's rude. Laughing but Bianca didn't find nothing funny. Bianca didn't know them and planned on keeping it that way. Getting off Bianca Angel runs and jumps on the couch next to her mom and gives her a kiss. I like them mommy Angel says smiling. Royalty is Papa Amir wife remember he told you about his wife named Royalty Angel?

Royalty looking like Poppa Amir really.

And Bianca thinking" Royalty better go off on this bitch I don't care how cute her daughter is calling her man Big Papa is doing too much

Angel said yes mommy Papa Amir said I look like his wife when she was a little girl smiling. Papa Amir said his wife was so pretty with long hair just like mine when she was little like me. But Papa Amir said she was bad when she was a little girl holding her mouth like she said something wrong laughing.

Laughing too Royalty says I wasn't bad Angel. Papa Amir was just playing.

Ok Angel go to your room, so I can talk to Miss Royalty I'll be in there in a minute ok.

Ok mommy bye miss Royalty and Miss Royalty sister waving bye running to her room.

So why did Angel call Amir Papa? Royalty asks Who idea was that?

Taking a deep breath Liberty says Angel really taking a liking to Amir and Amir liked Angel too. I guess Angel liked him because Amir was nice to Angel and Angel hasn't really seen me with a man. Angel father died when she was six months old.

(Royalty thinking like damn both her baby daddies dead damn she's 0 for 2 This girl is a black widow)

And one time Angel asked would Amir be her daddy and Amir said I'm not your daddy your daddy's in heaven, but I can be your Papa ok? And Angel was ok with that. Amir was really nice to Angel she liked him a lot. Even though Angel didn't see a lot of Amir but when Angel did see Amir, he always gave her money for the ice cream truck and brought her new sneakers when he came by. They kinda bonded immediately. Looking at Royalty demeanor Liberty could tell Royalty was uncomfortable hearing her talk about Amir. But Royalty asked so Liberty told her the truth.
Ok ok enough of this bullshit with this make believe we good and it's all good in the hood shit waving her hands in the air. You broke the code on being a side chick Bianca says finally speaking up from holding her peace. Royalty and Liberty were both looking like what the fuck you talking about? But let Bianca finish with her rant. There's a side chick commandment you're supposed to follow when dealing with someone else's man Bianca said Raising her eyebrow like pay attention. Liberty was looking like huh? But Royalty was laughing inside because Royalty couldn't believe Bianca was going there. They made up the side chick Commandments when all these side chicks started coming together believing they were entitled to some respect. No ma'am Royalty and Bianca said. You gets no respect over here. When they got drunk one night and sat on Royalty living room floor laughing and listening to music Amir came in and crashed the no boys allowed party and joined them and helped form the Side Chick Commandments and he's the one who made the last two commandments that carry the most weight. Bianca goes on to say Miss Liberty pay attention but don't worry sweetie I'm going to get you a plaque made so you won't forget winking her eye. Royalty asks Liberty does she have any wine.

Liberty says yes, she'll get her a glass and got up and walked into the kitchen.

But Royalty says no please just bring me the bottle, but you might need to get you a glass tho after hearing these commandments Royalty says to Liberty shaking her head. Royalty looks at Bianca like you ain't shit. but didn't dare say it.

And Bianca looked back at Royalty frowning her face up like bitch be nice for what?

When Liberty returns, she is holding a bottle of white zinfandel in one hand and gives it to Royalty who instantly turns the bottle up and downs it. And Liberty had a glass of wine for herself in the other hand. She figured one glass wouldn't hurt plus Liberty knew after Bianca read her rights, she would need one as she sat down taking a sip preparing herself for the lesson of a lifetime.

Bianca stood up like she was about to do a motivational speech in front of a crowd of people. Making sure she had their attention. Starting off saying these commandments shall go down as law for all the side bitches. I'm getting it copyrighted and getting Tee shirts made. Thinking she had to do it ASAP because she knew it was going to go viral. But she also wanted to prove her point that side chicks should respect the main chick and stay in their lane period.
Bitches need to stop playing and abide by the rules of the game and respect the side chick commandments Bianca said if you want to be creeping with a nigga with a woman at home. Here are the SIDE CHICK COMMANDMENTS

1: You (sidechick) shall not purposely try to get pregnant by another woman's man!! But if you do

2: You (sidechick) shall Not name your baby after the father (junior) if it's a boy that right is reserved for his women

3: You (sidechick) shall not harass or covet the main women

4: You (sidechick) shall stay in your lane no pivoting in the fast lane where you don't belong

5: You (sidechick) Shall Not try to break up a happy home when you catch feelings your bad sis

6: You (sidechick) shall not try to be a copycat of the main women no same hairstyle, dressing similar etc

7: You (sidechick) shall not comment on any photos on the man the side chick on his social media pages leaving kisses or hearts and absolutely No tagging!!! That can and will get you a beat down on sight guaranteed

8: You (sidechick) shall never, never ever call, text, Skype, dm, facetime, email, podcast or any form of communication with someone else man just because you'll so called fucking!!!!!!!!

9: You: (sidechick) Shall not invite the alleged baby daddy to the baby shower if it comes to that point because he most definitely will not show up so save yourself the embarrassment

10: You (sidechick) should know this may be the final commandment but the most important one. Thou shall expect my man to help me fight you when I finally find out about the side chick situation just know that we are going to jump you!! So, fuck with my man at your own risk !!
After reciting the side chick commandments Bianca says to Liberty. No disrespect but you gets no respect for being a baby mama sitting down. You knew Amir had a woman at home and you still choose to keep your baby why? Throwing it out there. You could tell Liberty was embarrassed because Liberty didn't answer right away like she had to think about how exactly to respond. You know like Drake and Meek mill diss record everyone was waiting for the response. We needed answers like wtf? But then Liberty broke her silence.

Well for starters I grew up in foster care Liberty says sadly. And I don't have any family. So, my kids are all I have. Plus, I don't believe in abortions. I'm a product from a rape and my mother gave me up because if it. I believe I was born for a reason almost crying. I haven't figured the reason out yet, but I know I have a purpose. And maybe my purpose is to be mother I don't know.
Wow is all Royalty could say.

But Bianca on the other hand had plenty to say. When you and Amir first hooked up did Amir take you out? Or was it just a fuck what?

Bianca looking at Liberty like a kid on the first day of school sitting at their desk taking it all in. Just waiting for the teacher to speak.

Looking embarrassed Liberty says. I left with him that night after Its lit. We were both drunk and he bet me $1000 I wouldn't leave with him after the party especially after Amir told me he had a wife. And Amir said he bet I wouldn't take his money also. So, I told Amir I bet him I would. Amir keep ordering me and my girls drinks all night. Then Amir told me to meet him down the street at the liquor store and I did, and you know the rest.

So, your saying clapping her hand. You let Amir hit the night he meet you over a bet? Bianca said looking puzzled. Shaking her head yes is how Liberty responded.

So, Liberty tell me what Car was Amir driving that night? Bianca asks

I think it was Bentley truck Liberty says

Umm hum Bianca says so Amir was in his brand new Bentley truck huh? slightly laughing. Yeah If I was you, I wouldn't believe in abortions either. Especially if I got a band and a ride in a Bentley truck from a nigga, I just meet either. Being Hella sarcastic.

Royalty couldn't believe what she was hearing. Damn sometimes you really don't know people like how you thought you did. And Royalty and Amir had known each other their whole entire life. But Royalty never knew Amir to be this careless and irresponsible. There was a lot Royalty didn't know about Amir apparently. A knock on the door made everyone jump looking towards the door like who the fuck was knocking.

Getting up saying excuse me while passing Over Royalty liberty answers the door nervously Liberty didn't know why she was nervous though.

You good Lil Sis the guy at the door asks peeking in to make sure everything was ok.

Yes, I'm fine Rob thanks for checking in on me. Come in opening the door widely for his entrance. This is Royalty Amir's wife and her friend Bianca. Who was staring at Rob up and down especially at his dick print that was budging through his gray sweatpants imagining what he looked like undressed. Bianca couldn't believe a man this fine was checking in on Liberty.

Where's Angel Rob inquired?

Oh, she's in her room probably watching tv or on her iPad Laughing.

Ok I was just making sure you'll was straight in here looking at Royalty and Bianca like don't fuck with Liberty or else.

Nice meeting you Bianca said as Rob was walking away and out the door without even responding. Who the fuck he is? Bianca asks.

He's like my play brother. We were in foster care together once. He's a little over protective of me and Angel Liberty says laughing.

He wasn't over protected of your friendly ass when you were over here fucking someone else man unprotected Bianca thinking but didn't say out loud. Standing up Looking down at Royalty you ready I have an appointment lying but ready to go Bianca had heard enough for one day.

Liberty calls out to Angel to come say goodbye to Royalty and Bianca.

Running in the living room yes mommy I was playing my game.

Ok baby I just wanted you to come say goodbye to the ladies Liberty says smiling at her daughter.

Saying and waving goodbye Angel tells Royalty and Bianca bye and asks are you coming back running up and giving Royalty a big hug around her waist. Royalty reaches down and hugs her back and says yes, I'll come back to visit you.

You promise Miss Royalty I'll teach you how to play my game next time. Poppa Amir use to come play with me.

Smiling Royalty says I promise.

Angel then turns and hugs Bianca who doesn't reciprocate. Then Angel runs back to her room skipping.

Well it's been a pleasure Liberty says getting up you're welcome to visit anytime she says to Royalty.

Royalty replies I'll be in touch take care and turns and walks to the door following Bianca. Walking to the car Bianca notices a note that was left on her windshield. Removing it and reading it Bianca immediately started smiling forgetting that she was about to talk a gang of shit about Liberty home wrecking ass while getting in the car.

What you cheesing about Royalty asks? What did the note say?
Handing the note to Royalty to read still smiling contemplating what tonight could be like. Royalty grabs the note and started reading it out loud.

I see ya ma you fine or whatever. We have the same taste in cars but mine is black. I would love to meet you tonight at Mr. Chows for a drink at 8pm. If you don't show up, I'll understand. Sincerely your secret admirer.

Looking at Bianca crazy while Bianca rolled up her blunt. You're not going are you? Knowing deep down inside Bianca was going.

Hitting her weed Bianca replies what you think?

What I think is that you could be getting set up to be robbed bitch Royalty says.

Blowing smoke in Royalty face driving off Bianca says the only thing that nigga gone take is this pussy winking her eye. Turning up Gucci Mane "I get the bag "on full blast with her mood turning savage feeling like she had a semiautomatic in the car and was about to go hit a lick on some dope boys while vibing to the beat.

Royalty didn't know what was more disgusting at this moment the fact that Bianca just left a bitch apt that was pregnant by her recently deceased man or the fact that his side chick daughter called her man Poppa or the fact that her best friend was geeked about an anonymous man she was going on a blind date with just because he left a little note on her car like they were in junior high school or the fact that her best friend was a true sex addict and will take a nigga down like the Titanic. All of it just made Royalty sick. And exhaling looking out the car window Royalty was mentally exhausted and missed Amir like crazy.

Royalty didn't get out of bed for a couple days only getting up to use the bathroom Royalty didn't even feel like eating. Knocking on the guest room door Jinx waits to hear Royalty say come in but Royalty never did. Jinx places her ear to the door to see if she could hear anything but heard nothing so Jinx quietly opens the door and scans the room which is pitch black, but Jinx could see Royalty was emerged under the covers with only her hair showing. Turning on the light Jinx says loudly Get up right now!! In an Authoritative voice. Royalty doesn't move so Jinx goes over to the bed and snatches the covers off Royalty. Looking at Jinx like what you do that for? Royalty sits up yawning looking a mess. Sitting on the edge of the bed Jinx says get up and get in the shower you smell like a homeless person with athlete's feet and wash your hair it looks like it's about to start dreading up at any second giving Royalty a final look over and opening up the bedroom window and walking out the room leaving the door open. Royalty didn't feel like moving but Royalty knew Jinx was right. Royalty did need to get up and stop feeling sorry for herself. Plus, Royalty doesn't even remember what day of the week it was. After a lengthy hot shower which Royalty needed and washing her hair which was hella tangled Jinx wasn't lying about that. Royalty felt like a new woman. Royalty felt better than she had since Amir's passing a few months ago. Moussing her hair so the curls would lock in and putting on a Nike workout top and bottoms with Fendi slides Royalty walks into the lavish kitchen. Jinx whole house had recently been remodeled and her kitchen looked like it had won Hella awards and should be featured in a magazine. And to Royalty surprise Bianca was there feeding her greedy face.

I'm so glad you decided to join us Jinx says smiling. Smiling back Royalty pulls out a glass stool and sits at the breakfast nook to join the two.

What's up taking a bite out of her homemade waffle Bianca says. You never returned any of my calls bitch. I thought you went to be with Amir or something taking a bite out of her chicken like she just didn't even say something offensive as that.

Royalty just shook it off because Royalty knew she had to rebuke them bad vibes before they even started.
Walking over handing Royalty a plate of smoking hot chicken and waffles with a fresh glass of orange juice and a bottle of Moët Jinx says eat up. Making a glass of mimosa Bianca starts going in.

Bitch that nigga that left the note on my car was a full fledged gang banger you hear me. That fool came dressed in Dickies from head to toe with a pair of chucks on. Fresh braids to the back with the scarf wrap around his head. I thought he was going to ask me to join his gang he was so fucking hard core. Bianca says laughing

That made Royalty laugh and Jinx too. That's what your hot pussy ass get still laughing in between sipping on her mimosa Royalty says. I told you it was a bad idea from the beginning. Did he really have a Bentley?

Girlllll wait a minute. Bianca said. Yes, he was driving a Bentley but was he the owner was the real question. When I asked him where he brought his car at, he didn't know. Laughing.

Huh what you mean he didn't know? Royalty asks.

The nigga had the audacity to tell me that he couldn't read or write and that his momma brought the car.

Spitting her drink out Royalty started cracking up. He can't what? Laughing so hard.

Jinx said. I hope you walked out on that preschooler and didn't look back laughing. He should have learned how to read and write by now and how did he leave a note on your car if he can't write anyway?

Jinx you're not going to believe me when I tell you. The nigga has a paid handwriting guy that he keeps with him 24-7 dying laughing. Throwing her hands in the air like whatever Jinx says I'm done and sits and pours herself a drink.

No fucking way Bianca Royalty says only you shaking her head only you. You always get the good ones cutting into her waffle not believing that bullshit she just heard. I guess that nigga really been hustling his whole entire life literally laughing again.

Yes, bitch he's the epitome of a real hustler baby Bianca says laughing. I excused myself and went to the bathroom and l paid a staffer 200 dollars to let me leave out the employee entrance in the back. The fuck don't nobody got time for that Bull shit in 2018. They all started laughing in agreement. Finishing all her breakfast Royalty was hungrier than she thought. Bianca finished telling them about her worst date in history story and they all got a big laugh out of it. So, Royalty did you tell Jinx about our visit at the gold digging baby mamma house?

But before Royalty could answer Jinx says. When Royalty ready to talk about it we can and if Royalty chooses not to talk about it it's ok. All this is going to take some time. And I'm going to support you Royalty whatever decision you make.

Royalty laughter subsided, and Royalty started looking sad again. I really don't want to talk about that right now I still can't wrap my mind around the fact that Amir is having a baby with another woman let alone his death. These last 30 something days has been the worst days of my life. I still can't believe Amir's gone. Like Amir taught me everything about life everything except how to live without him. It's hard to keep going strong after this. Then some random women says she's pregnant. It's almost too much for one person to handle alone.

You're not alone Royalty you have me always and Jaheem Jinx says. And me too Bianca says.

I know that, but you'll know what I mean. Royalty replies. When I was in Dubai, I didn't tell you'll I never came out my room except maybe a couple times. I just ordered room service and cried for hours starting to cry not believing Amir was gone and the way Amir went crying harder. Consoling Royalty Bianca and Jinx gives her a group hug.

I know it isn't fair Royalty, but life is cruel to all at some point in time. Unfortunately. You're a very strong individual and with time you'll become even stronger. God gives his strongest assignments to his strongest soldiers. He doesn't give us anything he knows we can't bare. You just have to take things one day at a time. Rubbing Royalty Head Jinx says.

I know it just hurts so bad I lost my best friend me and Amir have been through so much together I thought we would grow old together and laugh at our memories you know. But now I have nothing but memories of him. I loved Amir so much way more than he ever loved me Amir was my whole entire life. Royalty says saddened

I know sweetie but your still here and have to live even if it's with a broken heart. Don't try and rush the grieving process. It takes time Jinx says solemnly.

Looking up with tear filled eyes Royalty says. I wish they would have killed me too. They don't even realize that they did actually kill me emotionally but let me still continue to let me breath. Putting her head back down crying hysterically. There wasn't anything anyone could say to soothe Royalty pain that she was experiencing.

They were all crying at this point holding one Another when Jinx lifts her head up and says. Enough of these tears wiping her eyes. We're going shopping and spending some Benjamin's ladies.

Getting Bianca attention right away who stopped crying instantly like she was acting for a star role and the director said cut. But Royalty was a little apprehensive and wasn't sure if she wanted to go.

I'm tired maybe I'll just lay back down Royalty says.

Oh, hell No Jinx says you're going no rebuttal Royalty go get your coat I'll drive Jinx says walking out the kitchen into her room, so she could change and get dressed to go.

Bitch if you don't snap out of it and live a little Bianca says. I know your hurting, I know you lost your man and I know nobody knows what you're going through. But what I do know is when I was transitioning into who I am today you wouldn't allow me to get depressed or think I was going crazy. You were my biggest cheerleader and support system besides my parents. I would be ashamed of myself if I didn't stand by you and help you get through this ordeal. And with that being said Bitch you need to stop feeling sorry for yourself and be Royalty for a moment. The Royalty that laughs at all my jokes, that's always smiling and happy. That loves to go shopping and loves to turn the fuck up. I want that Royalty back if it's only for one day. Giving Royalty a big bear hug kissing her cheek then tickling her stomach making her laugh a little.

Ok ok I'll go shopping but don't think I'll be happy about it. I don't have anyone to dress up for anymore looking at the floor.

Yes, you do bitch. You have yourself and your fans. All these mad ass bitches who want to see you lose it all. Yourself and your mind. But that's why you got me snapping her fingers and moving her neck around to snap you the fuck out of it and keep you being the bad bitch that you are!! Bitches like us don't fold we bend. Winking her eye sashay walking out the kitchen grabbing Royalty hand like a rag doll dragging her along.

Riding down Melrose Ave in West Hollywood on a Chilly Saturday morning the temperature was only 65 at its best on a fall March day. But that didn't stop the wealthy crowd that was walking up and down the street frequenting the various boutiques on the famous street known for housing a store that the Kardashian's clan owns. Finding a park down the street from Jinx favorite boutique that was black owned. Jinx couldn't find a closer parking space. Jinx parks her big body Benz and looks Royalty straight in the eyes and says. Look fresh air is good for you also doing things you love to do, and shopping is a stress reliever for all women. So, don't hold back get whatever it is you want. This shopping spree is on me and Jaheem our little gift to you and we won't take No for an answer. Grabbing Royalty face giving her a kiss then getting out the car.

Bianca getting out the back looking like a celebrity as usual says what about me with her hands in the air like what laughing slamming the car door.

Jinx looks at Bianca with her hand on her hip and says. Girl your little shopping spree is going to be spent on my car door the way you just slammed it.

Oh, my bad Bianca says still laughing grabbing Royalty hand like she was her daughter or something following Jinx walking down the street heading to her favorite boutique.

I got you too Bianca, but you can't get whatever you want turning around looking at Bianca and Royalty who had been quiet most of the car ride and still was. Your limit is 5,000 which is ok in this boutique. Jacques has a lot of nice pieces. Some of them are one of kind pieces. Jacques my go to plus I support my peoples whenever I can. Walking into the boutique that's semi crowded then this little short black lady with silver dreads that was neatly braided in two big braids comes up to Jinx and gives her a hug.

Glad you came back to see me Jacques is going to be happy to see you smiling.

Smiling back at the seasoned lady Jinx says Ms. Peta -gay which means Blessings from Heaven in Jamaica. This is Royalty my sister in law Royalty I told you about and her good friend Bianca. Introducing them.

It's a pleasure to meet you both I'm Jacques mother I help out on the weekend. Reaching for Royalty hand placing it with hers. I'm truly sorry for your lost. My God bless you and give you strength.

Thank you, you're so beautiful Royalty says. Ms. Peta- gay was Haitian with silver dreads past her butt. She was only 4'11 but a little thick. Ms. Gay had the most beautiful chocolate, round face with the cutest accent. She made you feel welcome immediately.

Jacques had walked up after finishing up with another customer. Jacques gave Jinx a hug and said Thank you for stopping by it's always good to see you. Looking at Royalty and Bianca greeting them. Welcome Beautiful ladies you care for a glass of champagne?

Royalty and Bianca looked at each other and both of them says yes Bianca even shaking her head yes.

Ok I'll be right back Jacques says look around and if you see anything you like my assistant is here to help walking away looking like a whole snack. Bianca thinking.

He's fineee!! Bianca says to Jinx. Is that you?

Laughing Jinx replies I'm happily married Bianca, but he is all that huh? Plus, Jacques is a little too young for me laughing Jacques only about 30 I think that's what his mom told me. He's a young entrepreneur doing his thang I also believe he's married but I think his wife lives in Jamaica.

Royalty had started looking around the high end boutique wondering why she never knew about this store. It was fabulous. All high end designers and some vintage pieces with high price tags on them. Royalty was in love. Sitting down on a stitched black leather ottoman Royalty removed her sneaker to try on a pair of over the knee boots that Royalty knew she had to have. They were crushed velvet deep purple with a silver spike heel admiring the boot Jacques comes over and hands Royalty a glass of champagne.

You'll look lovely in those they're a jaw dropping coveted boot of the elite. I only had three pair and those are my last pair. I hope there your size. Looking up from the boot at Jacques Royalty really looked at Jacques features. Dark chocolate with perfect white teeth a neatly groomed beard like he was from Philly but with a Jamaican accent, but his eyes was what got Royalty attention. They were colored but Royalty didn't know what color they were. Royalty believed they were bluish-green. Now what is a black ass man doing with green eyes Royalty was thinking.

But before Royalty could even ask Jacques says. I know what you're thinking I get that look all the time smiling. And yes, there Real I was born with them. I think my mom was creeping with the mailman Jacques says jokingly.

That made Royalty laugh. Wow there Beautiful is what came out Royalty mouth.

Thank you. Beautiful just like you. Jacques replies before taking a sip of champagne from a flute he had on a tray with several glasses of champagne.
Him and Royalty locked eyes for a moment frozen in time until Bianca walks up to them and snaps them both out of their trance.

Laughing a little Royalty asks Bianca what she thought about the boot.

Oh, it's so you Bish if you don't want them, I do seriously speaking.

What size do you where Jacques asks Royalty?

Um a size 71/2 Royalty replies smiling.

Well there from Italy so there European 38.5 which is a Us 8 but I'm sure you can fit them try them on kneeling down to assist Royalty placing her foot inside the boot assisting her with standing up and retrieving her empty champagne glass placing it on the tray he sat down next to the ottoman. They look fabulous on you. Walk around you want the other boot?

Yes, please but this one feels really good Royalty says walking towards the mirror.

I'm glad you like them smiling going to get the mate of the boot.

What was that all about Bish? Bianca asks Royalty. I saw how you'll was looking at each other. I've never seen you look at nobody like that not even no Bitch which is your favorite past time smirking. Royalty and Amir had threesome quite a bit per Royalty request Royalty mostly picked the women also. That's why Royalty couldn't understand why Amir kept his baby mama a secret from her.

Girl I don't know what you're talking about he's nice that's all. Royalty replies Jacques just has superb customer service still smiling. Royalty didn't know what the fuck was happening to her at that moment but what Royalty did know was that Jacques gave her pussy a fast heartbeat that she hadn't felt since Amir. But with everything that had been happening lately Royalty wasn't that surprised. Not wanting to admit how she was feeling at that moment because Royalty didn't even know what she was feeling. Royalty even felt kinda bad about letting some man she just meet 5 mins ago get her pussy moist. But it had been almost 90 days since Amir's death. When Jacques returns with the other boot and another glass of champagne Royalty already knew she wanted the boots. Before Jacques could hand Royalty, the boot Royalty says I'll take these reaching for the champagne flute.

Ok I thought you liked them you still want to look around and maybe find something to go with the boots? Jacques says Looking Royalty in the eyes again smiling sending chills down Royalty's body. Jacques was a well dressed man wearing dark denim jeans with a blue and white striped dress shirt that was slightly opened displaying his thick gold chain with an iced out cross on his hairy chest. His shirt was neatly tucked into his pants with a tailored dark blue cashmere blazer with a brown leather Hermès belt and brown leather Christian Louboutin's boots. But it's the cologne Jacques was wearing that was driving Royalty in sane even though Royalty didn't even know what it was he was wearing. How could a mystery man change her mood from depressed to obsessed so quickly Royalty thinking to herself but what Royalty did know was she had to have Jacques in the worst way even if it was for only one night. But how was a mystery to her also. It didn't matter though Royalty felt some type of way and she wanted to continue to feel like this. Royalty knew people said one Day you'll just feel a little better and want to go on with life. Well Royalty believed that day has finally come.
After their little shopping spree getting in the car Royalty was all smiles. Buckling her seat belt Royalty Thanks Jinx and says I appreciate you taking me out today and especially for the shopping spree I definitely needed that and my new boots baby I can't wait to rock them cheesing Hard. Your welcome babe I knew this is exactly what you needed. You'll hungry? Jinx asks because I'm starving let's go to Roscoe's I'm craving some fried chicken and macaroni and cheese.

No yelling from the back there's no bar there. Let's go to Nas chicken spot Sweet chick I hear its really good Bianca says hungry ass fuck and wanted a strong alcohol beverage to wash her food down with.

Oh yeah, I've heard about that place I hear it's doing well. Jinx replies ok let's go there what's the address, so I can put it in my GPS Bianca gives her the address reading it off of google from her phone. Pulling out the parking spot listening to Tupac Toss it up with everyone in the car bobbing their heads. Turning on Fairfax securing a park directly in front of the restaurant Sweet chick.

How sweet was that getting a park right in front of sweet chick Bianca said jokingly but nobody laughed but her.
Your so corny Royalty tells her, but Bianca ignores Royalty all together but asks Royalty before even letting one bloody shoe hit the ground to take her picture across the street in front of Pink dolphin store.

I love their hoodies and hats Amir had a couple things from this store Royalty says while making sure she got the right angles snapping pictures of Bianca posing in various positions gotta do it for the gram ass. Ok, ok that's enough Royalty complains frowning up her face I'm hungry. Looking across the street at the restaurant like it would magically pull her inside and sit her down and have a plate ready smoking hot., You and all these damn pictures I'm over it bish let's go eat already. Turning walking away leaving Bianca running behind her in the street still looking at her phone. Once inside Jinx had already ordered everyone drinks her favorite lemon drop and was reading over the menu. Thanks, sis, for everything again Royalty says sitting down sipping her drink waiting on the waitress who appeared like she had read Royalty mind.

Hi ladies you ready to order? The cute waitress says nicely.

Chicken and waffles and side order of macaroni and cheese please Royalty says already knowing what she wanted. She had looked at the menu on her phone in the car heading to the restaurant. Same here Bianca says and me too Jinx says all ordering the same meal they heard was popping and wanted to see for themselves, and another round of drinks says Royalty who was lightweight tipsy already. After eating every bit of food placed on the table and downing their drinks. Royalty, Bianca and Jinx was all sleepy and needed to lay their game down.

That shit was popping Bianca says laying down in the back seat of the car hella tired now.

I know right Nas restaurant is the bomb I'm proud of him. I'm glad he opened a restaurant on the west coast and didn't act stingy keeping all the love in New York Royalty says.

I know that food was excellent Jinx chimes in I respects his hustle. Bringing a restaurant to La was good business sense a lot of celebrities are living in La now including him I think I heard that. I should open up a restaurant myself, but I need a targeted location with a lot of foot traffic.

I'll help you Jinx I can be a waitress Bianca says lying. I've always wanted to be a sluty waitress laughing.

That's a good idea Bianca I could name it The Sultry Affair bar and grill laughing.

You sleepy Royalty says laughing both you'll sleepy.

I'm hella tired Bianca says but I want to go out tonight you down Royalty and Jinx? She asks kicking back with her legs crossed wiggling one foot.

Oh no once I hit my bed that's it Jinx says stopping at a red light looking back at Bianca who was sprawled out on her backseat with her feet on her red leather seats with her red bottom heels on disrespecting her car. But Jinx didn't say a word she just shook her head.

What about you Miss smiling at a nigga because he had colored eyes you down after you take your power nap? Bianca asks Royalty.

Royalty wanted so badly to say no but she didn't want to hear Bianca mouth, so she agreed to go but only for a few hours that's it. Bianca closed her eyes excited because her best friend was slowly returning to being herself.
Everybody was sluggish getting out the car like three big fat bitches after running on a treadmill. Barely able to walk and out of breath walking into the condo. Bianca and Royalty feel down on the couch and Jinx went into her bedroom and shut the door. Them all being tired and full was an understatement. Royalty woke up first and glanced at the grandfather clock that was facing her in the living room that said 9:00 pm. Damn we been sleep for 5 hours Royalty was thinking Looking over at Bianca who had one leg on the couch and one on the floor legs spreaded wide open like she was ready to get fucked but then again Bianca did have her arms covering her face so I guess not. Royalty started to take a picture of Bianca but decided otherwise. Instead Royalty kicked Bianca foot and Bianca jumped up while Royalty stood there with her arms crossed. I should have let your drunk ass sleep and said fuck going out.

No, the fuck you shouldn't have Bish because I would have woke up and beat your ass looking like you don't want these problems. Bianca thinking

Girl bye laughing releasing her arm Royalty said waving Bianca off. You hella funny walking into the bathroom to get ready. Peeking her head out the bathroom door Royalty says start getting ready or I'm not going then shutting the door.

Bianca just sat there for a moment getting her thoughts together thinking about what to wear. Bianca only packed a work out outfit thinking her, and Royalty was going to go walking. Bianca was thinking maybe she could keep on what she was wearing shit Bianca was already dressed for the club laughing at herself. Looking at her own attire. Versace printed button up blouse tied in a knot at the waist with matching leggings and red bottoms. Rolling her eyes and releasing a deep breath. Bianca thought fuck it I'll wear my work out outfit with heels and still kill shit smiling getting up yawning and stretching ready to go turn up.

Getting out the shower Royalty standing naked in the guest room looking in the full length mirror behind the door admiring her own body. Royalty was bad. Her titties sat up just right, small waist and nice ass turning around to get a better look at it was perfect Ok Royalty don't freak out tonight just go have fun it's only for a few hours. Royalty keep telling herself trying to figure out what to throw on. Looking thru her travel bag Royalty located the perfect outfit. Red Lace lingerie bodysuit with black slim fit jeans with the red shingles on the side that fit her like a glove with her YSL black signature heels and she put her hair up in a bun after she got out the shower, so she could show off her tone arms and shoulders that she moisturized with Vaseline cocoa butter gel and gold body shimmer. All Royalty needed now was a Bianca face beat then it was game over for these hoes. Royalty sprayed on some Tom Ford and changed her clutch then got dressed and waited for slow poke ass Bianca.

Bianca was in the other guest bathroom finishing up her shower doing her makeup listening to Kashdoll and Big Sean So Good through her phone vibing.

Hurry up Royalty walks in and says plus I need my face done.

After Bianca gives Royalty a smokey eye and perfect red lips Bianca gets dressed and beats her own face flawless. Bianca looked like a goddess. Bianca knew her hands should be registered as lethal weapons Bianca was just that good.

Bitch you rocking that sweat suit making it look like your fresh off fashion week in NYC Royalty says to Bianca looking her up and down.

Acting like she's modeling Bianca does a few poses laughing. You like Bianca says twirling showing off her white Nike just do it sports bra and matching jogging pants that buttoned on the side but she had the buttons open all the way to the thigh and the pants leg were flared Bianca was also wearing a white Nike baseball cap with black stitching that read Just do it with some blonde clip in for length that went to her waist bone straight. But Bianca body was body goals for real. Bianca double D's we're sitting real pretty, and her stomach looked like a surfboard and let's not talk about that ass of hers which was elephant in the room literally.

Yeah, I thought we were going to go walking this morning Bianca said so I was going to wear this jogging outfit. Knowing she looked cute. Bianca put back on her black red bottoms because those were the only heels, she brought with her plus they were comfortable even though she had been walking in them all day. But Bianca wasn't like most women she's been practicing wearing heels since she was about 5 or 6 yrs. old. It was nothing to her.
Look at all these mother fucking foreign cars Bish pulling up to the club it's lit!! Bianca says parking. How you feeling over there looking at Royalty? Who was in the mirror looking at her hair and makeup.

Flipping the sun visor back up Royalty looks at Bianca and smiles and says let's go get em B!! Winking her eye.

Hitting the steering wheel yelling my Bish is back Yesssssss! Accidentally hitting the horn and some people walking by jumped from being startled. Grabbing Royalty by the neck kissing her cheek.

Stop Bish get off me Royalty said pushing Bianca off her laughing. I'm not on pussy tonight.

Whatever checking her makeup now Bianca replies. Let's go start some shit and give these bitches migraines laughing. Getting out her Bentley like I'm the bitch you love to hate hitting the alarm and throwing the keys at Royalty. Bitch keep my car keys just in case I get some work tonight. I may leave early laughing and that means you have to drive home alone. Still laughing. But hopefully you get some work too winking this time also handing her phone to Royalty take her picture again for the hundred time today. But this time using the boomerang app while she kept shaking her ass up and down next to her car and Bianca hadn't even had a drink yet. Royalty thinking. Making sure she got the angles right again. Getting in the club was a breeze because Bianca was a VIP member which meant she never had to wait in line and Bianca had a standing table in the VIP area whenever Bianca came there.

What's up Royalty how have you been? You look good the bouncer asks.

Thanks Bubba I'm good thanks for asking Royalty replies.

You want an escort to your table? He asks.

Naw we good walking past the red velvet robe into the loud club where you couldn't even hear your cell phone ringing. The club was packed like sardines and it was only 11:00 p.m. Royalty started thinking maybe she did need a fucking escort before somebody tried to test her gangster. Plus, Royalty was dripping in bling. Royalty brought out some of her best jewels tonight. Royalty was rocking her Patek Philippe nautilus watch and her Cartier bracelet and her Blue Nile 10 carat diamond tennis bracelet. Not to mention her 4 carat diamond earrings and one of Amir's iced out diamond chain and cross. Shit Royalty jewelry alone was someone retirement fund. But Royalty wasn't too worried because inside her YSL clutch was her most valued gift that Amir had ever given Royalty her 9mm and Royalty considered herself a Navy seal when it came to shooting her nine. Royalty never missed a mark. So, no matter what Royalty knew they was good. After giving a few hugs and small talk with a few people Royalty and Bianca made it to their table where a few other cats were already sitting. The music was so lit Bianca never sat down Bianca poured herself a drink that was the dudes that was already sitting at the table without even asking if it was ok and shook her ass in their faces. Royalty just sat there vibing to the music. When Drake Nice For What came on Bianca went off putting one foot on the table and twerking sticking her tongue out letting a few niggas smack her ass feeling it. Royalty was feeling it to dancing in her seat pointing her finger in the air singing every word. The bottle service had arrived for Bianca and Royalty with the 4 girls carrying sparkles and booty shorts with Its lit half top tees on displaying their flat stomachs smiling and clapping like it was their birthday or something. This probably would have excited most bitches, but Royalty and Bianca were used to it whenever they came out this was how it looked. It was even worse when Amir was alive Royalty started thinking. Damn I wish Amir was here. But before Royalty could finish her thoughts Bianca was taping Royalty on the shoulder pointing at the entrance door.

Bitch look who just walked in with an entourage. Jacques Royalty couldn't believe it. Jacques looked totally different. Jacques had on a Gucci sweatsuit with the matching cap and Gucci fur loafers smoking a cigar looking like a million bucks. If Royalty didn't know better Royalty would have thought Jacques ass was a rapper. The women was going wild trying to get next to him. But Jacques was removing girls hands off him left and right walking towards Vip. Walking up the stairs to Vip Jacques notices Royalty and started smiling walking right up to her.

What's up Royalty kissing her cheek then stepping back taking a look at Royalty from head to toe shaking his head blowing smoke from his cigar. Then Jacques grabs Royalty hand and tells Royalty to come sit with him at his table.

Oh, and what's up Bianca Jacques says and says what's up to the dudes at the table with his head before walking away to his table. Sitting down Jaques puts his arm around Royalty and put his leg up on the table like a boss smoking on his Cuban cigar feeling the music and Royalty at the same time. Leaning in close whispering in Royalty ear Damn you look hot I love your makeup Jacques said making Royalty blush.

Royalty whispered back but first Royalty stuck her tongue in and out Jacques ear then said you look like a rapper. And they both bust up laughing. When the bottle service came Jacques poured Royalty a drink. Their table had bottles of Moët and shots of Hennessy. Jacques was drinking out the bottle and feeling himself. Especially when Royalty started giving him a lap dance when Cardi B I like came on. Bianca had come over and hyped Royalty up. Fuck it up best friend, that's my best friend clapping and bouncing. Royalty was feeling It when her part came on singing every word on point.

Royalty was grinding on Jaques giving him a lap dance Doing her duck lips looking back at him rubbing his head after she slapped his hat off. Bianca was feeling like a proud parent watching Royalty at that moment. Bianca got in Royalty face singing her part rubbing on her own body grinding. Hot tamale snapping her fingers Pointing at the bitches staring at her and Royalty raising her hands in the air pumped. When the song went off Royalty and Bianca felt like strippers all the twerking and grinding, they done. Slapping high five Bianca said yes Sis were the baddest bitches up in here. And Bianca was right no two other bitches could see them about nothing tonight. Every nigga in the club was checking for them. They had drinks coming to them faster than they could keep up. This one dude even had the audacity to sneak in the vip area and approach Royalty while she was leaning over pouring herself another drink and say. Oh, excuse me Beautiful I hope I'm not interrupting you cheesing hella hard. Royalty looked up entertained Royalty wanted to see where this was going and what type of reaction, she would get out of Jaques. Who was sitting there like the boss that he was just chilling. Because Royalty knew if this was Amir things would have went in two different ways. Not good or really Not Good. There was No in between with Amir. He went from 0-100 Real quick. Not wanting to laugh Royalty says what's up how may I help you?

Well I was just wondering if I could buy you a drink and possibly get your number? The bold dude says Looking like he was about to get a DUI when he left the club because he was way past the legal limit.

Looking him up and down Royalty notices he had on the what looks like the very first pair of Jordan's that was ever created and not the ones that was considered to be very valuable and rare with some khakis and an all white tee. Royalty was the thinking maybe he just got out of jail or something. I'm flattered honestly but... I don't think so we're not on the same level sorry, plus you don't want these problems Royalty says in between sipping on her drink.

What you mean not on the same level? getting mad. He responded.

But Royalty held her composure because what Royalty really wanted to do was to bust out laughing. But before Royalty could even reply here comes Bianca walking up in the dude's face because Bianca had been standing right there waiting for dude to say some slick shit so they could get it Poppin anyways plus Bianca was fuck up at this point.

Sipping on her drink Bianca says look partner do we really look like we entertain suckers like you?

Oh lord he Bianca go Royalty thinking.

Bitch what? Who you calling a sucker? You don't know me like that pointing in Bianca face. You better watch your mouth and stay in a child's place he retorted angrily.

You pussy ass nigga poking the dude in his chest. Do my bitch pointing at Royalty look like a Go fund me account my nigga? Laughing Waiting for him to answer? Briefly pausing still sipping on her 5 or 6 drink. Now like she said you ain't on her level now bounce on outta her in them Heelys turning her back on him walking away.

Did Bianca just call his shoes some Heelys? Royalty thinking dying laughing damn near spitting out her drink. (Those are the tennis shoes all the kids are wearing that has wheels on them that turns the shoe into roller skates)

The vip area erupted with laughter until that nigga grabbed Bianca hair and yanked her towards him.

But before he had a chance to do whatever he thought he was going to do to Bianca Royalty had pulled out her 9 and cocked it and had it pointed at the niggas head. You not getting my number ain't worth you dying over and becoming a statistic my nigga Royalty said ready to tag toe his ass in front of a crowd of witnesses.

Jacques was thinking these bitches are gangster as fuck and he loved it. That shit gave him a hard on. Calm down shorty Jacques said still chillin like a boss with his leg up on the table holding his cigar Not worried because if shit got real his hitters to his left and to his right had them uzi's ready lock and loaded because that's how he rolled. No need to catch a body up in this mother fucker babe referring to Royalty. Plus, dude you're just embarrassed laughing. Real men snatch panties off not weaves my nigga Jacques said to the bitter man still laughing all men get turned down at some point in time my Nigga we all get a turn. So, keep cool there's plenty fine bitches up in here pointing around the room that's on your level my nigga still laughing. But this one pointing at Royalty is in a totally different tax bracket.

Royalty lowered her gun and the dude let Bianca Hair go from his tight grip. By then the lights in the club had come on and the music had stopped. The club was like it was in the twilight zone. People was stuck in the positions they were in before the incident occurred and now, they were frozen. Looking like hella mannequin challenges going on. Waiting on the outcome. Looking like do we run in a frenzy screaming somebody got a gun or do we watch and see what's going to happen? Because you'll know that black people are the noisiest people on earth. Most white people would have ran as soon as they saw a gun well not all of them. But black people we staying for the finale we can tell you who did what and when. That's why niggas always be on the first 48 because they see and know every fucking thing. We not even going to talk about the noisy black people sitting on their porches until bedtime in the summer in the projects that see all the drive by shooting and break ins that occur. They know who stole your fucking new flat screen tv off the 6 floor they just not saying shit, but they know. Royalty thinking laughing to herself.

Bianca snapped everyone back to normal when she screamed loud as fuck. You bitch ass nigga don't ever touch my mother fucking hair!! This weave cost me more than your fucking Lil school uniform you got on. The whole club started laughing. The dude was so embarrassed he walked out of Vip and out the club all together. The music came back on and shit went right back to how it was. Super lit in the club. Security had come to check on Royalty and Bianca but other than that it was back to business. One monkey don't stop no show I guess was their motto.
Royalty sat back down next to Jacques Hella irritated. That dude had killed her vibe and Royalty was ready to go.

Sensing her frustration Jacques pours Royalty another drink and whispers in Royalty ear. You coming with me tonight and I'm not taking no for an answer rubbing on Royalty thigh.

Looking into Jacques green eyes Royalty knew Jacques meant business. And Royalty was thinking fuck it why not. I like a man that can take control. Grabbing Jacques head and sticking her tongue in Jacques mouth. Royalty started kissing Jacques like her life depending on the air from his lungs. Jacques obliged and tongued Royalty back. Pulling away after a few moments of going at it Royalty still looking in Jacques eyes says, and you better not disappoint me!!

Reaching in Jacques pants grabbing his dick. Royalty boldness had Jacques rock hard. Jacques felt like fucking Royalty right there in a room full of people, but Jacques respected Royalty enough to wait.

Feels like somebody is a big boy Royalty whispers in Jacques ear turning him the fuck on. Massaging his balls and playing with the head of his dick until the pre-cum came running out. Royalty keep stroking Jacques dick up and down faster and faster until Jacques was about to cum. Just when Jacques was about to bust. Royalty takes a shot of Hennessy with her free hand not missing a beat stroking his dick then Royalty ducks underneath the table and puts Jacques dick in her mouth giving Jacques a few strokes of her tongue then sucks the tip of Jacques dick extracting a set of twins from Jacques dick. Jacques turned up a bottle of Moët but what Jacques really wanted to do was scream in ecstasy because that shit felt so good. The music was loud the lights were dim and the whole euphoria had Jacques and Royalty on one. When Royalty lifted her head from underneath the table like nothing never happened. Royalty excused herself to go to the bathroom. When passing by Jacques to get up to leave Jacques slaps Royalty on her ass to thank her for her exceptional service.

Going to the bathroom Royalty walk up to Bianca table and grabs Bianca by the hand and says excuse me to her all boys party Bianca was crashing. Bianca always did know how to enjoy herself wherever she went. It didn't bother Bianca one bit that she was the only woman at the table of five men. That's basically how Bianca preferred it anyways because Bianca hated bitches. We need to go to the lady's room now yanking Bianca arm.

Ok ok no need to be all aggressive bitch I'm coming Bianca says slurring.

Bitch you too drunk to be sitting at a table alone with five niggas let's get you some water. Walking towards the bar. Royalty wasn't scared for Bianca Royalty was more scared for the niggas for what Bianca would do to them. Fucking multiple men was Bianca speciality and Bianca fucked their heads up right along with the good time. Bianca once had three partnas stalking her at the same time turning them niggas against one another. Bianca was a beast and Bianca knew it. Her young ass was definitely living her best life. After getting Bianca to jug down several glasses of water which Royalty drunk several glasses herself. One to cleanse her mouth from prior engagements even though Royalty had a shot of Hennessy afterwards and we all know that alcohol kills all germs, right? and second to bring her own high down a little.

I have to pee Bianca said wiggling around holding her private area. Walking into the bathroom there was a line about 5 women who was waiting. Bianca walked pass all them and as soon as this one woman was coming out a stall Bianca rushed right in.

Sorry Royalty said trying to soften the blow. She wasn't raised right shrugging she doesn't have any manners laughing underneath her breath. Royalty had done it herself so many times before and overheard Bianca say the same exact thing. It was their go to speech when one of them cut the line. Royalty could hear Bianca throwing up in the stall, so Royalty started knocking on the bathroom door. You ok in there? let me in so I can help you Royalty said shaking the door. Bianca let Royalty in the tiny bathroom stall flushing the toilet and wiping her mouth scouting side ways to accommodate her and Royalty being in the small area. You good Royalty asks?

Yes, I stuck my finger down my throat to get that alcohol out my stomach and to get you in here because I know you have to pee laughing.

Laughing with Bianca pulling her pants down kneeling over the toilet peeing. Thanks, boo I would have waited though Royalty says but you always got my back flushing the toilet with her feet. Walking out the stall Royalty notices the line was much longer than before. And the five women who was previously waiting for the bathroom was still in line waiting and rolled their eyes in disgust. Washing their hands Royalty was glancing in the mirror at a few of their facial expression and Royalty could tell they were hot. But Royalty didn't care how they felt as long as they didn't express it verbally.
Approaching the Vip area Royalty saw a few new faces and bodies assuming they were groupies because of the way they were acting rubbing all over them niggas in vip area. Dancing Bending over showing their assets and of course indulging in the free drinks looking hella thirsty like 7-Eleven big gulp thirsty. Let me say my goodbyes to Jacques then we out Royalty says to Bianca changing her mind about staying with Jacques tonight. Bianca was standing at the stairs to the Vip area gripping it for dear life. Bianca was in agreeance to go because Bianca was hella tired.

Walking over to to Jaques table three new bitches were sitting at the table acting like they couldn't move to let Royalty by and Jacques told them to excuse themselves for a moment. They didn't move fast enough for him, so Jacques stood up and waved his hand saying you'll deaf? Get the fuck away from my table ASAP with authority.

Royalty started laughing at them hoes shaking her head. Thanks Royalty said to Jacques hugging him. Look I have to give you a rain check for tonight. My girl is white girl wasted and I'm her designated driver you do understand right? Looking at him in those puppy dog eyes.

Of course, shorty I understand I was going to ask you if she was cool, I saw her downing shit over there like a she was going to be admitted to alcoholic anonymous tomorrow Laughing.

Yeah, I know right. She's a real party girl laughing Royalty said.

Reaching down giving Royalty a kiss Jacques says those magic lips with a wink. Text me and let me know when you make it home safely hitting Royalty on her ass while she walked away smiling. Bianca guy friends she was partying with in Vip offered to help Royalty with assisting Bianca to her car. Thank you, Royalty, said to the two guys holding Bianca up as they walked out the club into the cold air. Shivering A bit Royalty wishes she would have at least brought her shawl. The car parked across the street pointing straight ahead in the parking lot Royalty says as the three follows behind her. Walking kinda fast to get out the cold and not get hit by the ongoing traffic Royalty jaywalks and crosses the street leaving Bianca and the guys behind her waiting until the coast was clear to cross. Wrapping her hands around her own shoulders for a little warmth looking at Bianca who kept slumping over drunk Royalty thinking throwing up and drinking water did nothing for Bianca. Poor thing slightly laughing. Out of nowhere a red Jeep pulls up and slightly stops right in front on the club and starts shooting. Bam, bam, bam, bam and drives off before Royalty could even get her 9mm out her purse. When Royalty realizes what just happened Royalty grabs her gun and runs in the middle of the street after the Jeep and start bussing. Royalty was able to shoot out the back window of the Jeep but whoever was driving the Jeep was still was able to get away. Royalty wasn't sure if she hit anybody or not. Turning back Royalty could see from a distance Bianca on the ground and one of the guys that had been holding Bianca up and the other dude hovering over them. Running back Royalty adrenaline had taken over and Royalty breathing became rapid. The club had let out and people were outside screaming and panicking. Royalty could hear sirens in the background sounding like they were close by but not close enough. Royalty also felt like she was moving in slow motion. When Royalty finally reaches Bianca, Royalty realizes Bianca had been shot but the guy helping Bianca was shot in the head and neck but was still alive he feel on top of Bianca who was passed out probably from hitting her head on the ground.

Jacques grabs Royalty gun out her hand and passes it to one of his boys and gives Royalty a handkerchief and pulls Royalty up and grabs Royalty by both shoulders looking her in her eyes and says. Let's Go your coming with me will meet Bianca at the hospital but I have to get you outta here now. Looking down at Bianca lying on the ground Royalty started tearing up and didn't want to leave Bianca but the fire department had arrived, and Royalty knew they would take care of Bianca. Let's go grabbing Royalty Jacques says pulling her into his Lamborghini that his boy had pulled up in throwing Royalty in the seat. Drive Royalty to my house so Royalty can change her clothes and get that gun residue off her hands because I'm sure the police is going to want to holler at her for pulling the strap in the club. Some noisy mutherfucker is going to mention it I'm sure. But let's clean Royalty up a bit before taking Royalty to Martin Luther King Hospital you know that's where they bring everybody to that gets shot. Running all lights doing almost a buck fifteen in that thing feeling like a spaceship getting them the fuck outta there that wasn't really considered fast because the Lambo could reach two seventeen with no problem. Turning around looking at Royalty Jacques says to her. My dear did you forget you were a pistol packin mama inside the club in front of Hella witnesses and you want to stay at the scene of a crime? Looking at her like duh! Royalty didn't say anything Royalty just hoped and prayed Bianca was ok. Jacques turned back around because Jacques understood Royalty nonverbal language.
Still distraught Royalty mood swiftly changes when this nigga pulls up to a gated community with a live guard.
Good evening Mr McKenzie opening the gate will there be any more cars accompanying you tonight the gate keeper asks? Speaking through the driver's side with Jacques looking at him responding from the passenger seat.

No Fredric that's it have a good night and be safe then Jacques driver pulls off.

Where are we? Royalty asks dumbfounded.

We're still in La laughing were in Bel Air Jacques says. You're not from La I take it?

No, I am born and raised in the projects on the east side, but I've never been up here looking at all the beautiful mansions in amazement. It was Beautiful even at night. How much does property start at up here? Royalty asks.

Umm I'm not too sure I think probably around 5 Mill but I'm not positive it's been a minute since I checked the property value. Pulling into what seemed like a castle the driver pulls into a garage that housed about 15 cars. They parked directly next to a Bugatti Royalty knew what it was because Amir keep saying he wanted one, but Amir also keep saying it costs about 20 racks just for an oil change on that bitch.

Looking at Royalty expression Jacques started laughing. You like that Car woman he asks? With his strong Jamaican accent.

Yes, it's nice Royalty says still looking at the massive Car collection. Who lives here? Royalty ask wanting to know seriously was this Jacques Home.

Still laughing at Royalty walking into what Royalty thought was a living room which ended up being a mud room Royalty was so confused but whatever. Taking Royalty into the bathroom Jacques tells Royalty to sit on the toilet like she was using the restroom. Looking puzzled Royalty was like why?

Listen my dear I'm from Jamaica we do everything by old folk's tales no modern day stuff that doesn't work. Stick both your hands in the toilet and I'm going to urinate on them.

Looking like what type of freaky shit was this nigga really into. Royalty thinking but boldly said What that going to do?

Urine erases the gunpowder off your hands Jacques says you never heard of that? Asking seriously.

No shaking her head no I've never heard that Royalty says.

Yeah it figures you Americans watch too much tv laughing. You'll should read more and learn about other cultures. Jacques pulled his dick out and peed all over Royalty hands even shaking his dick and letting the drips fall on them. Leaning over Royalty Jacques flushed the toilet for Royalty and told Royalty to shake the wetness off into the toilet. Jacques then went underneath the faucet and grabbed a huge bottle of vinegar. Come over here Jacques demanded. Stick your hands out over the sink. Once Royalty stuck her arms out Jacques poured Vinegar all over Royalty hands and arms as well. I know it might smell but it works giving Royalty a kiss. Google it Laughing. It saved a lot of people I fuck with from a lot of trouble trust me because I associate with some bad characters at times that don't like to play fair in these streets. Handing Royalty a dry off towel. And to answer your question I live here with my mom's you know the older lady you meet at my boutique with the dreads. My parents owned this house every since I was a little boy. My father was an investment broker he owned an investment firm in Jamaica and also, he inherited a Sugar and Rum plantation from His father. Most of the cars you saw in the garage belong to my father. He had a thing for very expensive cars smiling though his pain. My father lost his fight to cancer last year surrounded with our whole family at our home in Montego Bay, Jamaica. So, it's just me and my mom now. I have a little sister who's in college in Europe obtaining her PhD.

So, are you some kind of prince or something Royalty asks not knowing what the exact title should be called?

Laughing again No I wish I'm just a typical nigga from the hood baby. Laughing again.

There's nothing typical about all this waving her stinky arms and hands around in a circle. Royalty says.

Well maybe not typical but it's regular to me. Plus, I didn't grow up here I grew up in Jamaica. Nothing fancy just a way of life. This is God's Blessings for many years of hard work from both my parents. I'm just blessed to have the parents God choose for me humbly speaking.

You sure are Blessed looking around. Highly favored Royalty thinking.

Ok strip down Jacques says interrupting Royalty thoughts. Huh? Strip Royalty responded.

No, no not like that we're burning Your clothes.

Wait why? I've done nothing wrong here. You act like I've killed someone or something getting frustrated. Royalty didn't understand any of Jacques tactics.

Listen Miss Royalty let me explain something to you. In your county you're really not innocent until proven guilty. So hypothetically speaking once you get up to the hospital and the police are there and they want to question you about the shooting you're the number one suspect because a few hundred people saw you pull a gun out on a man and they really don't know what actually occurred. The music was loud, they were drinking and for all they know that guy that got shot could be the guy you were arguing with even though he wasn't. Nobody going to remember the guy you got into with but their most definitely going to remember the cute girl holding the gun. You following me? Looking at Royalty like pay attention you might learn something. Then after your brought in for questioning and even if you ask for your attorney. Your clothes is evidence and their allowed to test your hands for gun residue. That's like a drunk driver. They can refuse to take a breathalyzer test, but the police can still do a blood test on them especially if someone gets killed. The rules change depending on the circumstances my dear. So, with that being said. You shot your gun of course my good friend got rid of it for you and your welcome by the way. I'll get you another one no problem now we have to get rid of the clothes you're wearing they have gunpowder on them also from you firing the gun. Technology is a mother fucker nowadays. That's why people get caught up for not covering all bases. They forget to dot their eyes and cross their T's which ends up with lengthy sentences which could have been beat on a technicality for lack of evidence that's needed for dismissal like gun powder on clothes and hands winking at Royalty. So once again strip down to save yourself the trouble so we can go to the hospital to check on your friend. And I just got a text. Oh boy just died on the surgery table. So, murder is the case that they gave you!! If you don't do what I say. And hurry up Jaques says going into a drawer pulling out a brown paper bag.

Taking Royalty clothes and shoes off Royalty thinking why this rich ass nigga has all the necessities to cover up a murder in this bathroom. Looking over at Jacques who had put on some rubber gloves and was putting her clothes in a brown paper bag.

Should I remove my underwear? Royalty asks turning around looking Royalty up and down Jacques grabs his dick which was getting hard looking at her perfect body. And replies only if you want to get fucked tonight and I do mean Fucked!!!smirking. Licking his lips Jacques continues. There's no way in hell I could just fuck you once I know once won't suffice for me. Once isn't going to satisfy my sexual appetite I have for you. The moment I laid my eyes on you I knew I had to have you in the worse way baby. And I always get what I want. At any cost smiling. I'm not being arrogant either I'm just stating facts winking at Royalty.

Damn Jacques felt the same way as me that's crazy Royalty thinking. This whole day had been a freaking movie.

Now it's up to you to take off your cute little lace undies or leave them on. The balls are in your court laughing at his own joke.

Did this nigga say balls? Royalty thinking laughing. Jacques I already gave you a rain check Boo I need to go check on Bianca. Grabbing her jewelry, she had taken off when coming into the bathroom.

Looking at Royalty like she made the right decision because Jacques was ready to fuck the shit out of Royalty all night and the night after that also. Jacques knew from the club encounter that he had finally meet his match. And Royalty wasn't into him for his money.

Opening a closet door in the bathroom Jacques pulls out a one piece cargo romper and hands it to Royalty. Here put this on you should be able to fit this Jacques says.

Taking the romper putting it over her legs Royalty asks why do you have women clothes in a closet in your bathroom? Royalty was so confused.

Well I do own a boutique woman, and these were clothes from a photo shoot I had at the house a while ago. I just never brought them to the store. Plus, there some exclusive pieces from Italy that I hadn't put out yet. I'll send you your bill later Laughing.

Jacques was something else Royalty was thinking damn, and he's married? Maybe these were his wife clothes. But whatever this romper is cute and it's mine now zipping it up. What about shoes? I need shoes remember you took mine.

No, you can have your shoes back but if you like I have hundreds of boxes of Uggs boots, so you can be comfortable. I have them in a few colors and sizes. I just haven't brought them to the boutique yet. Shrugging. Opening another closet door full to capacity with boxes of ugg boots. What size you wear? Jacques asks Royalty.

You don't remember Royalty replies.

Laughing oh yeah 7 1/2. You know how many women feet I service every day at the boutique? It's sometimes hard to remember everyone size. But I promise from now on I'll remember reaching down grabbing three boxes of black, brown and an orange suede pair of boots handing the boxes to Royalty. Just a little something to remember me by smiling.

Awe thank you, but I'll prefer the Bugatti please Laughing.

Not the Bugatti Baby laughing You don't want no smoke with her she deadly Ma. She so strong and will give you a run for your money Laughing. But I tell you what. Whenever you think you're ready for her she's all yours for however long you want her touching Royalty noise. You gotta be for sure you're ready!!

Royalty didn't know what the hell Jacques was talking about she wasn't ready. But they'll soon find out.

Ok we're in here laughing and joking when an innocent man just died. Jacques says walking towards the door holding the brown paper bag in hand. Royalty was right on his heels with her three new pair of uggs. Walking back into the garage Jacques hits the alarm for a Ferrari and tells Royalty to get in while he hands the bag paper bag to the previous driver and says something to him that wasn't within ears reach then gives him dap. Getting in the Ferrari Jacques asks Royalty you ready to fly? Looking at her buckling his seatbelt. Buckle up woman I'm about to get you to the hospital in 2.5

seconds Laughing revving up the engine and upon turning on the car Nas cd started playing sounding like a club inside the car. Turning the music down Jacques apologizes for the music being so loud. I like my music loud in my cars, so I can block everything out backing out. Hold on the kick if fire switching gears on the clutch. Driving down the freeway Royalty didn't feel anything underneath her. It felt like she was riding in an invisible car. The ride was amazing. And despite all the talking her and Jacques did at his house they didn't say a word to one another on the ride. And Jacques wasn't lying they did fly to the hospital. Pulling into Mlk Jr Community hospital parking lot you could see hella cars and people standing outside crying consoling each other. Royalty almost didn't want to get out the car, but Royalty knew she had to. Looking over at Jacques who was hitting a blunt.

I didn't know you smoked Royalty said.

Yes, way too much I'm from Jamaica remember laughing. But how would you know that we've only known each other for about 5 mins and some change laughing hitting his blunt. There's a lot we don't know about each other my dear but that's the fun part isn't it cutie? Winking. Let's go in and check on your girl Jacques says turning the car off getting out blowing smoke.

How did Jacques know that I was about to ask him was he coming in. Royalty thinking. This the second time this has happened getting out the car. There's way too many coincidences with this dude. We just ate at Nas restaurant and when I get in his car, he's blasting Nas cd. And everything I'm thinking he's saying. This shit is crazy. Royalty said to herself.
Walking into the hospital all you could hear was screaming and people falling out and hugging each other. One man was hitting the wall screaming No!! Royalty didn't know what to do. The atmosphere was gloomy. Royalty saw Bianca parents standing next to the nurse's station and walked over to them. Tapping Bianca mom on the shoulder this little Puerto Rican women turns around and gives Royalty a tight hug. We've been calling you where have you been? We were worried about you looking relieved holding her tight.

I'm fine Royalty says feeling smothered.

Letting Royalty go but keeping her hands on Royalty shoulders Bianca mom Liza says what happened? Someone died, and the police were here asking for you and what happened to Bianca she has a concussion and she was grazed by a bullet in her shoulder. What the hell happen? Looking frightened.

Cutting in the the conversation Hi my name Jacques extending his hand. I'm Royalty and Bianca friend I was with them tonight I think it's best if we spoke outside where it's more intimate and quieter.

Looking Jacques up and down Liza finally says your Jamaican?

Laughing Yes, I am Ma'am Jacques says walking out the hospital and Bianca parents and Royalty following behind him. Hitting the alarm on his car

Bianca father Louis another spicy Puerto Rican says we all can't fit in this car let's sit in my car. Now leading the pack walking to their car which was parked directly in front of the Emergency entrance.

Nice Jacques was thinking to himself the RR Phantom with peanut butter leather interior. Opening the back door for Royalty to get in then following in behind Royalty closing the door behind him.

Getting in passenger seat turning around looking at Royalty Liza says ok Royalty what the fuck happened tonight? Waiting to hear the whole entire draining story. Taking a deep breath Royalty tells Bianca parents everything that happen except the part about going to Jacques house because that part was irrelevant at this point.

I don't know when you two will stay out of fuckin trouble Louis says. We've have been dealing with this shit since they were 10 years old looking and talking to Jacques in frustration. All we can do is make sure Bianca life insurance is paid every damn month. And Royalty stop pulling out your piece on these busters unless you're going to take them out. You know these niggas ain't cool. I tell you'll this all the damn time. They either hungry and broke or jealous which boils down to niggas ain't cool and they running around here mad at the world thinking somebody owe them something. And they use any excuse to take their frustration out on anyone especially women. I tell you two hard headed mother fuckers that all the time. Shaking his head. You'll gonna be the death of me I swear. Seriously speaking. Ok who is the dude you'll got into it with. You know him?

Royalty Shaking her head no.

That's ok my guy owns the club so getting the tape is easy. Plus, we need it before the police gets it especially since you acting like Scarface all on tape and shit. You should have been a boy instead of Bianca.

Huh? Bianca a boy!! Wait a minute Bianca bad as fuck I mean he damn what the fuck. Jacques is thinking. What the fuck is really going on. Needing some air now. Excuse me I'm going to step out and hit my blunt. It was a pleasure meeting you'll I'm sorry it's under these circumstances though extending his hand again Jacques says getting out the car in a hurry.

It's nice meeting you also Liza says. He's handsome Royalty you sure know how to pick em Liza says before Jacques gets out the car.

Shutting the door Jacques walks over to his car and hits his blunt in complete shock of tonight's revelations.

I have Bianca car keys you want them Royalty asks Liza?

He'll no you keep them since you're going to be the one picking Bianca hot ass up in the morning. As long as we know Bianca good, I'm not fucking with her hot headed ass. Tell Bianca to call me when she gets home. Shit woke us up for this bullshit. You'll need to keep you'll hot asses out the damn club. It's always something with you two bitches. And I see your doing ok not depressed no more looking over at Jacques. He's cute but take it slow you just buried Amir we don't need no more funerals hunny. Looking at Royalty like be careful. Now get out our car so I can go home and try and get some damn sleep. Good night Royalty meaning get out their car.

Getting out walking over to Jacques who was high as fuck laughing at Royalty when she walked up. Oh, you laughing at Liza and Louis crazy asses Royalty asks?

Naw cutie I'm laughing at you. Jacques replies.

Me pointing at herself Royalty says why? What I do now.

You didn't do anything cutie. It's just like what you said earlier we really don't know shit about each other still laughing. I wouldn't have known ol girl was really oh boy laughing. And her parents was hilarious. They seem hella cool.

Yeah, they are the double L's that's what we've always called them every since I was a little girl. And Bianca is all female trust me always has been. There's nothing male about Bianca besides the dick she rides occasionally seriously speaking. Bianca had her complete surgery when we were in high school but even before then Bianca looked and dressed as a girl. He moms always gave her ponytails and Bianca always loved wearing dresses. The double Ls just let her be who she wanted to be even as a little kid. I think that's one of the reasons Bianca so damn confident with herself. She's always been Bianca since day one.

That's cool Jacques says. But does Bianca tell people? Like dudes I mean.

Yes and no but it doesn't even really matter niggas fuck with her regardless. Bianca is that bitch stating facts. Royalty proclaims.

Bianca looks 100 percent better than most of these real hoes that got their bodies done. And Bianca has that girly face can't even tell at all. Everything about her is feminine. Jacques says still in awe about Bianca.

Can we sit in your car I'm cold standing out here Royalty asks?

Hitting the door unlock get in Jacques says opening the car door for Royalty. Looking at Royalty ass thinking he wanted to bite it. As Royalty bending down getting inside the Ferrari that sat low to the ground. Jacques was glad that him and Royalty could converse so freely Jacques felt comfortable with Royalty. It was something about Royalty that felt authentic. But Jacques also knew how women could be. The beginning always start off lovely then bam. hell, doors open up and you're now dating a demon. Jacques hoped this wasn't the case with Royalty. Jacques wanted to get to know Royalty better. You cold I can warm up the seats and you can talk to the car it talks back laughing but seriously speaking. Tell the car what music you want to hear, and it will play it. She's kinda like Siri but sexier don't be scared!!

Both Royalty and Jacques were tired as fuck and wanted to lay down. But Royalty was not letting Jacques sleep in her and Amir's bed that was out of the question. Grabbing Jacques hand leading him to her plush guest bedroom on the lower level was exactly were Jacques would sleep. After all Jacques was a guest in her home.

Royalty pulled back the comforter for Jacques being courteous Jacques says. Are you going to tuck me in also? smiling

Yep if that what's you want with your sexy ass winking Royalty replies. Taking his shirt off Royalty couldn't stop staring. The boy was fine. Chocolate like Royalty liked it and sexy as a mother fucker not to mention his accent. And Jacques knew it. Jacques stood there shirtless for a moment giving

Royalty a show. His hairy chest had a tattoo of his county on it and his bling out chain and cross all diamonds made him look even more sexier and Jacques had fat diamonds in both ears like Royalty liked it also. Royalty loved a man that wore his wealth appropriately and confidently. Jacques had a tattoo on his forearm with a date on it. What's the date about Royalty asked curiously?

The date my father passed. I was going to get his date of birth but to me the date of passing going to be with the lord is more significant. It signifies your integrity as a person to me. My father lived a long, prosperous, honorable life. He was well respected globally. Taking off his pants displaying his Versace briefs with the perfect budging print. Folding his clothes up neatly setting them on the ottoman reminded Royalty of Amir. A lot about Jacques reminded Royalty of Amir. They both had the same mannerisms. Clean cut, handsome and chocolate and rich. And despite trying to be respectful to Amir Royalty wanted to ride Jacques dick in the worst way. Royalty liked everything about Jacques especially the fact that Jacques had nice pedicured feet for a man. Royalty had a foot fetish.

Getting in the bed Jacques thanks Royalty for her hospitality. Thanks, love I appreciate you for allowing a perfect stranger in your home.

Perfect is the right word. Royalty thinking but how perfect is your death stroke? Contemplating fucking him.

Royalty, Royalty Jacques said trying to get her attention.

Oh huh? Sorry I'm so tired I wasn't paying attention Royalty said lying.

Good night go get some rest sweetheart smiling. Jacques says.

Lord help me Royalty thinking walking out the room turning off the light saying Goodnight closing the door.

Damn I wish I could hold her Jacques was thinking turning trying to get comfortable.

Walking up the steps to her bedroom Royalty thinking shit I should turn around and go fuck the shit out of him. You already sucked his dick. Hella backwards and ratchet Royalty thinking laughing to herself. Walking in her room looking around Royalty felt a cold breeze that gave her a chill. Amir if that's you I'm sorry. Checking to see if her bedroom window was open but it wasn't. Getting a little frightened Royalty thinking maybe she should go downstairs and sleep on the couch then Royalty felt the cold breeze again. It's like it touched her face gently and Royalty wasn't scared but felt like maybe Amir was saying it was ok. Royalty thinking, I must be tired as fuck I'm hallucinating. The chill came back and seemed like it surrounded Royalty completely, but it was extremely gentle breeze then it left completely. I don't know what that is or means but he'll naw I'm not sleeping up here by myself Royalty thinking walking really fast down the staircase. Opening up the guest room door Jacques was knocked out. Royalty tip toed over to the other side of the bed and removed all her clothes except her underwear and got inside the bed turning her back towards Jacques.

Royalty getting in the bed woke Jacques up and he wrapped his arms around Royalty pulling her close to him and whispered in her ear. Changed your mind huh?

Turning over facing Jacques Royalty noise was touching Jacques said I got scared a cold breeze felt like it was touching me gently then it left.

Smiling Jacques says to Royalty. Not you the baddest chick in LA, the only woman I ever meet that will bring the noise to any nigga without backing down. Not Royalty you to gangster to be scared of ghosts. Grabbing Royalty tight hugging her and started tickling her. Stop Jacques acting like she wanted him to stop but really was enjoying his touch. Jacques started kissing Royalty seductively undoing her ponytail then unbuckling her bra and Royalty didn't object. Jacques starts massaging Royalty titties rubbing them and circling her nipples pinching them until Royalty let out a soft moan getting excited. Jacques started kissing on Royalty titties taking them both in his mouth licking on her nipples then sucking on them until Royalty nipples got hard. Jacques starting kissing Royalty neck while pulling her hair dry humping her in a grinding motion as if they were fucking sucking on Royalty earlobes then kissing Royalty sticking his tongue in her mouth. Royalty was on fire wanting him inside her grabbing at Jacques boxers trying to get them off.

Wait a minute baby Jacques whispered in Royalty ear. Let me taste you first sucking on her ear sticking his tongue inside it. Pulling off her panties spreading her legs like airplanes wings Jacques licks Royalty pussy like an ice cream cone. Baby your so wet. You want this dick huh baby? Jacques asks Royalty who could barely breathe.

Yes, Royalty said barely audible.

That's all Jacques needed to hear. Before diving in Royalty pussy with a vengeance. He stuck his tongue as far as it would go inside her wetness and pushed his face as deep as could in and out with his tongue while licking and sucking like he was sucking on a Jamaican oxtail grabbing her ass squeezing it tight.

Oooh awe ooh oh my god Jacques grabbing Jacques head for dear life. Ooh awe Jacques I'm coming busting a nut and flowing like a raving river gushing in Jacques mouth quenching his thirst. While Jacques continued sucking and licking driving Royalty in sane.

Jacques wiped his mouth and turned Royalty over in all four. Jacques started biting on Royalty ass cheeks and slapping her ass then Jacques spread Royalty legs apart and entered her soaking wet pussy almost making him cum instantly. Keeping his composure Teasing Royalty going in and out slowly until Royalty couldn't take it anymore and started throwing that pussy on Jacques like she was in a twerk contest. Turned the fuck on Jacques started eating Royalty ass. Spreading Royalty ass cheeks and sticking his tongue in there and sucking Royalty ass hole while pumping in and out her pussy. Royalty thought she died and went to heaven the shit felt so damn good. Royalty moaning turned Jacques the fuck on to where Jacques lost control. Take this dick ramming his dick into Royalty soul, It feels good don't it baby? Jacques asks.

Yes, Royalty screams louder, Yessssss ohh Jacques yes it feels soooo good moaning loud enough to wake the dead.

Jacques started kissing Royalty ass literally. Then Jacques pulled out and flipped Royalty up on top of him while he laid on his back. Royalty now on top rode Jacques dick from the back gripping the quilted headboard squeezing all her pussy muscles on his dick. Damn baby this some good tight pussy Jacques says feeling the buildup about to cum.

Moaning baby damn you about to make me cum Royalty says Stroking Jacques faster with Jacques help by holding Royalty waist.

I'm coming too Jacques says and the two come together. Breathing fast, sweaty and hella sticky they were both trying to get their equilibrium intact. Jacques just lays back with his eyes closed until he gets soft and his dick slides out. And Royalty was resting on the headboard trying to catch her breath.

Jacques finally says I need a toothbrush and a wet towel laughing and Royalty started laughing too looking at the window seeing the sunrise.
Damn we did an all nighter laughing. Fucking with you a nigga will never get no sleep. Jacques says seriously speaking. He couldn't wait until round two after he took a nap first though.
Jacques and Royalty cell phones were both ringing off the hook continuously waking Jacques up. Looking at his Rolex it read 11am. Then Jacques looked over at Royalty who was still knocked out cold. Laughing to himself poor baby had a long night. Grabbing his phone getting out of bed putting on his boxers Jacques quietly walks out the room slightly closing the door. Stretching while walking into the all white marble kitchen. Jacques admired Royalty taste in her decor. Royalty whole house was mainly all white with Marble everywhere. And it was sparking clean and smelled good. Jacques was real big on cleanliness. And Jacques couldn't stand a woman who had a dirty microwave. That shit irked Jacques last nerve. That put you on Jacques liability list couldn't be an asset with no dirty house. It was a No for Jacques immediately thinking well Royalty passed that test and the most important test of all. Royalty was a freak in the bed. All that I don't fuck on the first date and No I don't suck dick and especially that holier than thou I'm waiting until I get married stuff is what kept side bitches winning all 2018 Jacques thinking laughing to himself opening up the French door refrigerator with the touch screen built in computer on it that Jacques had to get now that Jacques saw Royalty. This nice Jacques thinking I'll tell my assistant to order one. Making a mental note. Looks like Royalty doesn't eat to healthy from the contents of her refrigerator. Royalty had a lot of snacks and Pepsi sodas. But Royalty had all the right ingredients for a fulfilling breakfast. Having to pee Jacques walks out the kitchen into the guest bathroom that was decorated with the Tiffany store colors. Washing his hands looking in the cabinet Jacques finds a pack of new toothbrushes Jacques assumed was for the guest. It was a guest bathroom. Also finding towels Jacques grabs one and washes his face and brushes his teeth and heads back into the kitchen and makes a quick breakfast. Grits and eggs, hash brown and wheat toast with a tall glass of orange juice. Placing all the pots in the dishwasher and starting it. Jacques makes Royalty plate and brings it in the room to her. Opening the door, she's still sleep? Wow laughing this dick will definitely drain the soul out of a mother fucker looking at Royalty who was beautiful even in her sleep.

Sleeping beauty shaking Royalty a few times until Royalty opened her eyes looking up at Jacques Smiling. Placing the breakfast tray on Royalty lap as Royalty sat up in bed grabbing a piece of toast.

Thank you Jacques I wasn't expecting this biting her toast. Royalty says

Your welcome it's nothing. I woke up famished and it wouldn't be right to just make myself breakfast in your home and not make the hostess breakfast smiling. Jacques says.

Damn this nigga cook too? Royalty thinking. What time is it Royalty asks?

Looking at his Rolex Jacques says almost noon.

Noon Oh Hell naw I have to get to the hospital Bianca going to kill me reaching for her phone that was on the nightstand next to her. Three missed calls shaking her head already knowing this wasn't going to be good. Let me call this girl back before Bianca have a fucking heart attack hitting the call back button. Hello Bianca.

Bitch where you at? I'm shot the fuck Up and you ain't even here? Bianca yelling through the phone.

Royalty looking at the phone mouthing she crazy to Jacques who was standing there laughing to himself. Girl calm down first of all you ain't even been shot and secondly, I'm in my way I wanted you to get your rest.

Well hurry the fuck up Bianca says I have to go get another X-ray then the doctor said he'll discharge me. I'll see you when you get up here hanging up in Royalty face.

Letting out a sigh Royalty says I have a little time relieved eating her breakfast.

Putting his clothes on Jacques tells Royalty he had a great time with her last night despite all the bullshit. And Jacques knew Royalty was going to stay with her girl for a couple days. But Jacques really wanted to hang out with Royalty again as soon as Royalty was ready. Sitting on the bed next to Royalty putting his socks and shoes on.

Royalty looked into Jacques green eyes and said man I will fuck your whole life up I'm nothing but bad luck solemnly speaking. We had a good time, but I don't know Royalty says not sure seeing Jacques again was a good idea.

Grabbing Royalty face placing and his face directly in next front of hers Jacques responded Well Fuck it up then!! Giving Royalty a kiss on her lips standing up looking Royalty straight in her eyes. Ain't nobody scared of you! They both bust out laughing. Royalty knew then she about to fuck Jacques whole entire life up at that point.
Driving Home Jacques was thinking about last night and how all that shit went down at the club. They didn't really know who actually did that drive by they assumed it was ol boy because Royalty and Bianca got into it with him at the club. But what if that hit wasn't him. He didn't strike Jacques of being the type to come back and try and shoot up a club. But niggas do be butt hurt in they feelings acting like bitches sometimes. But just to be on the safe side Jacques would have to put some money in the streets to see what was being said and have the person handled. After all the person didn't even care about shooting women. I guess those days when women and children were off limits came and went. Everybody can get that smoke nowadays seems like. Hitting his blunt turning up Nipsey Hussle Last time that I checked flying down the 405 Highway with his speedometer reading 120 switching lanes.

Pulling up at the hospital Royalty keep flashing back to last night events. With all the people standing in front of the hospital crying, angry, and sad because they just lost a loved one and thinking that could have her or Bianca. Royalty hadn't even gave it any thought until now. Damn first Amir and then last night that could have been me. Maybe somebody was trying to finish the job. Naw Royalty you tripping she's thinking. They would have been got at you. Royalty thinking. You were hella vulnerable when Amir first passed. Looking inside her Chanel bag Royalty had

Amir's gun tucked away nicely in there. Especially since hers got confiscated by the help last night, I was slipping I got to be more careful and be on my game Royalty thinking no more mishaps like last night. Walking into the hospital cold as fuck outside looking dreary and looking like it was about to rain. Royalty was glad she went home so she could dress appropriately for this weather. Wearing her new pair of Uggs courtesy of Jacques Looking at her new cute boots made Royalty smile. And these ugg boots matched perfectly with Royalty green Montclair puff jacket and hat. Walking up to the information booth Royalty asks the clerk which room Bianca Santiago in. was

Who are you? And how are you related? This young, black girl with a terrible weave popping her gum asked Royalty Looking like (bitch I ain't giving you no information) with her arms crossed.

Royalty was thinking I should slap the shit out this little disrespectful bitch but today she's going to get a pass plus it's Sunday and I just said I wasn't doing no more reckless shit unless it's called for. Smiling at the girl Royalty says as politely as possible I'm her sister my name is.

I didn't ask your name the information clerk says rudely.

Ok Royalty count to 10 before speaking.

I asked how was you related to the patient all the extra I don't need to know looking at her computer screen for the room number. Writing the room number on a piece of paper handing it to Royalty rolling her eyes.

Walking away Royalty says Thank you you little bitch.

What you call me the information clerk says.

But Royalty keep walking laughing to herself. These ghetto hospitals be a trip getting into the elevator pushing 4. Walking into Bianca hospital room Royalty walks right into an ambush of police officers questioning Bianca who was cussing them out.

I ain't saying shit without my lawyers you'll ain't slick thinking I'm medicated and going to talk to you mother fuckers. Get the fuck out my room Bianca says before I sue, you'll for harassment pointing her finger towards the door. The police turn to leave and spot Royalty.

Miss Royalty one Officer says.

Un Un shaking her head. No before the police could even finish what they were about to say. The same thing Bianca just said. I'm not talking without my attorney and a warrant shrugging her shoulders. Royalty said. The two police officers leave out without incident.

Bitch what took you so long? Bianca says sitting up waiting on the nurse to come remove her IV and release her.

Did you have your xray done yet Royalty asks?

Yes, and I'm ready to get the fuck out of here. I want to go home and take a shower and smoke my weed. Bitch I almost died last night.

Looking at Bianca Royalty thinking she couldn't take another death or funeral of the two people she loved the most Royalty would definitely lose her mind. Changing the subject Royalty says. Bitch guess what I did?

Fucked that fine ass nigga last night and this morning that's why you're late and can't stop smiling laughing. Bitch how was it? Was that nigga the truth or weak as fuck? But from the look of that smile on your cute ass face that nigga broke your back Sis.

I hate you Royalty says laughing. I hate you know me so well.

Yeah, I do and I'm happy for you. Shit it's been over 90 days. You strong sis Bianca says trying to get comfortable but couldn't.

Strong girl I just buried my man if anything I'm scandalous.

Why you scandalous bitch? Amir has a whole ass baby on the way looking at Royalty like stupid bitch. Shit if anything you should have made you a baby last night Bianca says Laughing.

Ok bitch you got jokes on this good Sunday I see Royalty says. They done gave your smart mouth ass too much morphine hoe laughing. But shit it felt like we went half on a baby though laughing.

Word Bianca says like that.

It was everything smiling Royalty says reminiscing.

I knew that nigga had dick how Jacques walks around all arrogant and shit Bianca says. Ain't no low self esteem with that nigga that's for sure. Straight confident laughing.

You always diagnosing somebody Royalty says. You should be the fucking doctor bitch instead of the patient Laughing. Oh, and the double L's came up here last night.

I know I spoke to they asses this morning that's how it know you was with Jacques last night. My messy ass momma told me laughing.

I should have known Royalty says rolling her eyes in her head.

Yeah talking bout Royalty was with some green-eyed Jamaican that was fine ass fuck, but damn Royalty could at least waited until Amir was settled in his grave. You know I had to give her the business right.

I said what you mean settled? Girl you sound like them hating ass bitches that be group chatting about people they jealous of. Always got something to say negative instead of being happy for you and that you ain't somewhere crazy or on dope. Then I told her oh I forgot you want everybody on dope since you and your husband are the biggest dope dealers in La. and I could hear my daddy in the background saying hang up on that bitch before I go up there to the hospital and finish the job the shooter couldn't do. Then my momma hung up.

Royalty was looking like yeah, they all needed medication and a Social security check. Shaking her head.

Finally, the nurse walks in with Bianca release papers and has Bianca sign them and takes Bianca IV out and Bianca was good to go. The doctor gave Bianca a prescription for Norcos and Bianca was juiced. A bitch about to be super lit Bianca keep saying.

Calm down Air force one referring to Bianca being high Royalty says. Get dressed so we can get out of this nasty ass, ghetto hospital. You want to stay at my house for a couple days Royalty asks Bianca?

No bitch your house probably smell like you been getting fucked all night laughing. You come stay with me plus all my weed and shit at the house. I don't feel like packing all my shit to come to your whore house laughing.

Fuck you bitch Royalty says.

No correction He fucked you not me Bianca says laughing. Once Bianca got dressed, they left hand and hand talking about last night. Bianca said she was going to send some flowers to the funeral home for the guy that got killed because he saved her life. And Bianca said she found out he was married but didn't have any kids so she would send his wife a nice donation also that was the least Bianca could do out of respect for him since he lost his life saving her life. Bianca didn't have proof that the shooter was after her but either way Bianca could respect it.

The last past couple of days has been hilarious, sad and refreshing for Royalty and Bianca. The whole entire time Bianca got high and talked shit about everybody and everything. Royalty and Bianca stayed up all night talking about everything that was going on in their lives at this moment and what their plans were for the future. Well bitch I'm expanding my shop I'm getting it remolded giving it a face lift. You know that's what I'm good at beating faces right? Hitting her blunt. I'm going to freak the fuck out the shop. High level shit only baby. I'm also looking at a couple other properties to open another shop like a sister store that sells makeup along with the beat. And I'm going to give tutorials on certain days and specials. And I'm thinking about naming it And the Beat Goes On singing it. It has a ring to it huh? Asking Royalty who was in her own world thinking about Amir.

Huh what you say? Royalty says

I said I'm opening up another spot naming it And the Beat Goes On. Bianca repeated.

Yeah, I like that B the grand opening is going to be bananas getting siked. Royalty says.

I know I'm about to make these maddies kill themselves Bianca says laughing. You know if they can't take me owning one business like a boss bitch image me owning two throwing up the deuces.

Yes!! I can't wait I'm so happy for you best friend my face gone stay beat up the Royalty way by my sis laughing.

Hey, Hey Bianca says. We leveling up baby getting up of the couch twerking.

I miss Amir so much Bianca I don't think I will ever get over this. Royalty says having a moment.

Sitting back down next to Royalty. I know baby I miss his mean ass too laughing. Bianca says.

Amir wasn't mean bitch Royalty says. Amir just knew you was a hoe trying to pimp me out laughing.

I know Sis remember that time I came to You'll crib crying over that nigga Jordan.

Hell, yeah Sis Amir was like if you really want to get that nigga back fuck his brother and your stupid ass did just that. Listening to Amir no good ass laughing.

Sis the cold part is the brother was the total package tho. Fine, Big dick, balling that nigga didn't even have no kids but his downfall was the nigga was a straight powder head tho.

Damn he was fine as fuck too. Have you seen him lately Royalty asks?

Fuck No! And if I did, I wouldn't speak to his dopefiend ass fuck him and his brother.

You did Sis laughing. Royalty says.

Oh, my bad I did laughing right along with Royalty.

I need a drink going into Bianca kitchen to get some wine. Royalty loved Bianca house it was brand new and everything in it was brand new. The TVs, the furniture everything but Bianca had went all out with custom pieces throughout the house. Everywhere you looked it was bling. The kitchen was full of crystal pieces that looked like diamonds sparkling throughout. Bianca house looked like something in a magazine the shit was on another level. And the color coordination was exquisite also. Bianca whole house was money green, black and silver. But it was her plush money green leather sectional couch that was everything. The shit was so large it could only fit inside a house it was too large for an apartment. And When it got delivered, they had to bring it in through the window. So, if Bianca decides to ever move. Whoever buys this place has to buy it already decorated. That's when and if Bianca ever decides to move out. Plus, Bianca lives in Baldwin Hills an elite community. So, it takes a certain type of person to want to live in this area. The bad and boujee type. Bianca had this large picture on the wall over the couch with a million dollars in a chrome briefcase that was so dope that Royalty loved, so whenever Bianca decided to move out Royalty was claiming dibs on that picture. Opening up the wine cooler that housed sixty bottles Royalty grabs a bottle of red wine because that is her favorite. Skipping the wine glass Royalty was in the mood for drinking straight from the bottle.

Why every time you come over here you drink out the damn bottle bitch? I do have fancy wine glasses Laughing Bianca says.

Waving Bianca off sitting Indian style on the floor Royalty says why waste a fancy glass that you have to rinse off and put in the dishwasher when I can just drink it like this turning up the bottle like a wino.

I should throw your ole ghetto ass out, but I need you to make sure I don't overdose laughing. Bianca says laughing with Royalty.

Who you calling ghetto bitch? For real Laughing. You the one who was twerking in a church crushing on the pastor. So, I think that you win the most ghetto- ish person in the world contest dying Laughing. Royalty says sipping out of her wine bottle.

Ghetto- Ish bitch forreal? That's not even a word. You tried it hoe. Bianca says laughing standing up twerking demonstrating how she was twerking in church that one time disrespecting the congregation while walking out. Let's order some Chinese food Bianca says.

Let's not oh that reminds me I forgot to tell you Jacques ate my ass the night we fucked. Royalty says nonchalantly.

HE DID WHAT?? Bianca screams please tell me more getting excited. How could you forget to tell Me pointing to herself the most important part? I hope you didn't poot in the nigga face asking seriously.

Laughing no I didn't. Royalty says.

Because you know it tickles Bianca says but hey shit happens laughing.

Why you gotta say shit turning her nose up Royalty replies.

My bad Bianca says laughing. So, do tell how'd you like it?

I've had it done before. Amir was an ass nigga you know that. Why you think my ass is this perfect poking it out at Bianca laughing. All these bitches including you paying for an ass like mine when you can get ass like this for free just by getting some dick in the asshole seriously speaking.

Well Ms Perfect ass Royalty everybody's not into taking dick from the dark side like you and me bitch. The shit does hurt at first Bianca says. But it does get your ass looking right smiling. So that fine ass nigga is an ass eater huh? Who would have known laughing?

That nigga can fuck too had me Waking the dead and shit laughing. Royalty says

Well as long as it wasn't Amir you cool Bianca says.

You always gotta say something to kill my damn vibe bitch getting up walking into the kitchen to throw away her empty wine bottle away. Walking back into the living room Royalty says three nights of being with your ass is enough I'm going home. Walking into the guest room to get her shit so she could go.

Following behind Royalty, Bianca says I'm sorry Sis plus you can't drink and drive trying to persuade Royalty to stay. Grabbing her bag and putting on her coat on Royalty walks pass Bianca to the front door and turns around and tells Bianca Fuck you bitch. And walks out slamming the door behind her.

Waking up in her own bed in her own house alone was somewhat liberating to Royalty this morning. Looking around her bedroom Royalty knew that her past life was now over, and new beginnings had to begin to move forward. Ok Royalty it's time that get back to business and handle your business Royalty tells herself getting out of bed heading to the bathroom. Getting in the shower letting the hot water hit her to fully wake her up. After lathering up and washing her hair Royalty Steps out the shower thinking what to put on for her business meeting for one of Amir's business later. Royalty wanted to be comfortable but cute. So, Royalty Decided on hot pink blazer and matching slacks with a white ruffle shirt pinning her black Chanel pendant on her blazer with her black Chanel clutch and black fedora. And Royalty knew she would be running around all day, so she put on her Chanel sneakers but had her So Kate black Louboutins in her briefcase.

Going in the garage Royalty looked at her G5 wagon that needed to be washed and decided to drive it, so she could get it detailed at some point and time today. Plus, Royalty hadn't driven it in a while and Royalty actually really loved her truck. Amir brought it for her for Valentine's Day a few years back. Amir brought Royalty the best gifts sometimes just because. These were the few little things Royalty was going to miss about Amir was Amir's thoughtfulness towards her. Going thru the drive thru at Starbucks ordering her favorite grande Caramel Macchiato with whip cream and a blueberry muffin Royalty was ready to start her day. Pulling up at Amir's trucking Co looking around Royalty was still in awe at the way Amir constructed this once small Black business into an empire. Amir started this business with his money from hustling with just one truck delivering cars for people moving from coast to coast. Amir first truck could ship 10 cars total which wasn't bad for starters. But now Amir's Company has a fleet of trucks shipping cars for car dealers and car lots and business executives to athletes across the country Not bad for a man that grew up in the projects in La's worse side of the ghetto. Walking into the building everyone gave Royalty a warm welcome and their condolences except one person who was kinda standoffish a little but didn't think Royalty noticed it, but Royalty did. That was Amir assistant who has worked with him from the beginning. Jessica was Amir's and Royalty neighbor growing up in the hood they all went way back as kids. Let's talk in Amir's office Royalty says to Jessica whispering in her ear then heading into Amir's office switching her ass like what. Amirs office had pictures of the monopoly game everywhere in Big gold frames. The monopoly old bald head man with the beard holding a sack of money was one picture, Monopoly money was another picture and Park place and the chrome car was another. And Amir's desk was the image of the monopoly game board on top of a cherry wood desk. To say Amir was obsessed with the monopoly game was an understatement.

Sitting down at Amir's desk Royalty tells Jessica to close the door and have a seat.

Getting a little nerves Jessica didn't understand why Royalty was there and why now? Jessica had taken care of Amir's business for almost 7 years and never recalled seeing Royalty but maybe once and Royalty didn't even come into the building when she did come Royalty sat in Amir's Car on her phone the whole entire time.The business was doing well and Jessica felt like she was handing business exceptionally well so what could Royalty want with her Jessica thinking and it showed in her demeanor. Jessica kinda displayed a get the fuck outta here this is not your territory attitude.

Hello Jessica, it's been a minute since we saw each other, how are you? Royalty asks trying to feel Jessica out.

I'm good, real good. Business is doing great we're expanding soon and I'm thinking about taking the company global smiling.

Smiling back at Jessica Royalty says oh is that right and who did you talk to about making that kinda move with? Royalty wanted to know.

Well saying it sarcastically Amir put me in charge of running his business and gave me the authority to make the day to day decisions Jessica says.

Ok Amir's no longer with us Jessica why haven't you reached out to me? Royalty asks

I didn't think I had to Jessica blatantly says. Amir told me in the event that anything ever happened to him that I would take over his business.

This business? Royalty asks.

Yes, this business Jessica responded.

Kinda laughing Royalty says now why would you think that Amir would just give you pointing at Jessica his business that's worth millions of dollars I'm curious?

Well I did start this business with Amir from the beginning and Amir Appreciated that plus Amir said he wanted to make sure I was compensated for my years of service and being loyal to the company Jessica says almost in tears.

Well Jessica did Amir put that in writing? Or did you two just have this conversation.

No Amir didn't put it in writing, but Amir told me that several times so that means something I know.

Looking at Jessica like bitch please Royalty says. What's the name of this company Jessica?

The Royalty Express Jessica says looking down at her feet.

Jessica I'm up here pointing at herself Royalty says. What's the name of this company again?

The Royalty Express Company Jessica says again agitated.

Ok so why the fuck would you Jessica think Amir would give you standing up now pointing at Jessica raising her voice where the whole office outside the office could hear now. A company named after me? It doesn't make any sense plus sweetie you didn't start shit with Amir you worked for Amir that's a big Fucking difference!! You got a check every two weeks like every other employee that works here does. You may have had a bonus every now and then but. Oh, and speaking of Fucking. I know for a fact you was fucking on Amir for years. Looking Jessica straight in her face. You want to know how I know that Jessica because I saw all your texts messages sweetie. Amir showed them all to me while we laughed at them together. The I love you Amir please call me back I'm sorry. The text when you claim to be pregnant and Amir gave you a grand for your fake ass abortion. Because you never was pregnant bitch, I found that out later. And how you begged Amir to leave me for your dumb ass really bitch look at you and look at me Royalty said being sarcastic. And then you insisted on being Amir's only side bitch and demanding that Amir didn't fuck with anyone else besides you like your somebody to want to settle down with bitch. Your one of those ugly bitches that wants people to know they're are pregnant and had an abortion to prove you getting some dick. Calm the fuck down Lil ugly. Jessica was a really sweet girl but ugly as fuck. You know how those girls be shaped like a cornerback football player. Real big at the top with a big back and tiny with no ass at the bottom that was Jessica with a midnight black face, long weave with pink lipstick on. Amir really should have been ashamed of himself, but he wasn't Amir thought it was funny when Amir told Royalty about it and how Jessica so called raped him one late night they were working late, and Amir was high and drunk and Jessica took advantage of him. Royalty replied well if that Big black gorilla looking bitch raped you doing her fingers like hypothetically speaking press charges on her ass then. Rape is still considered a serious crime Amir and have her returned to wildlife. Amir buckled over with laughter because Amir thought that what Royalty said was hella funny. Whatever was Royalty comeback at the time. You going to make that Bugga Bear commit suicide Amir is all Royalty could say while Amir continued laughing. Those were the type of conversations Royalty and Amir had all the time regarding Amir's shenanigans. Royalty was waiting for Jessica to say something smart in response, so she could beat her ass in Amir's office, but Jessica didn't Jessica sat there in shock and was looking like she was ready to cry. Yeah bitch I know it all. The only fucking reason your dumbass is still working here is because Amir said you had some good pussy and he felt sorry for your snake ass but that's as far as it went. But me Royalty says patting her chest. I could give two fucks about you or whatever it is you think you bring to this company. As of looking at her Rolex watch 10:08 am Bitch you are No longer employed for The Royalty Express Company Period!! Royalty yells at Jessica. Now get the fuck out my man's office. Bitches is getting the business today and Not getting a business today!!! Still yelling. The fuck!! still mad at the thought that Jessica even believed Royalty was just going to hand over Amir's business to her. Getting up crying uncontrollably Jessica friend comes into the office to console her. Oh, and by the way whatever the fuck your name is Royalty says to Jessica friend YOU'RE FIRED TOO!! Now both you bitches get the fuck out and shut the office door behind you. Oh, and you'll service pay will be mailed to you and you'll can use the company as a reference Laughing Royalty says. Walking out Amir's office a few moments after Jessica Royalty says to the whole office team. Everyone's doing a great job lunch is on me today I'll order it and have it delivered and waved bye and walks out. While waiting for her truck to finish getting detailed Royalty makes some business calls, orders lunch for Amir's Company and manages to pay a couple bills and cancels all Jessica company credit cards. Bitch won't shop off me Royalty thinking. As Royalty truck pulls up looking brand new Thank you Royalty says handing the worker a $100 tip because he deserved it. Royalty G5 wagon was looking on point. You could tell that is was Royal blue and not black now. Driving to Jacques boutique Royalty was in luck and found a park right in front. Yes, Royalty thinking now I can put on my heels without all that walking and look cute looking in the mirror applying some lipstick and checking her curls. That was the benefit of being of mixed descent was having curly hair. Royalty stepped out her truck and double checked her attire that was still looking bomb. Royalty slacks hugged her body perfectly and made her ass look bigger than it actually was. And Royalty loved the color against her caramel skin tone.

As the buzzer went off in the store as Royalty walked in Jacques looked up from behind the counter and started smiling. You busy Royalty asked.

I'm never busy when it comes to you still smiling. Looking Royalty up and down. You look hot babygirl that business look suits you well. I love a woman who can do both. Jacques says smiling.

Referring to handing her business and being hood Royalty was thinking.

Give me some love hugging Royalty grabbing her ass. Ohh and you smell good too still smiling Jacques says. Stepping back looking Royalty over again. I thought you dumped me since I hadn't heard from you. Trying to get a reaction out of Royalty. How's your girl doing? Jacques asks

Oh, Bianca fine, I guess. When I left her house last night Bianca was good. You look nice yourself Royalty tells Jacques with your Armani stripe suit on with a pink button up shirt and I'm feeling the Louie tennis shoes to dress it down. That's a look.

You like Jacques says opening up his blazer spinning around laughing. A lil something something. You hungry? Jacques asks I'm starving.

I am a little hungry Royalty says but it has to be quick I have a meeting in a few hours.

Ok bet what you have a taste for Beautiful? Jacques asks

Umm I don't know. But wherever we go I need a drink it's been a long day already. Royalty replies

Bet same here smiling. You're my kinda girl Jacques says. Walking to Royalty truck with Jacques right behind her. Jacques says this is a nice truck getting in. I've always wanted one of these but never purchased one. I hear they're really good Suvs.

Yes, they are I love mine I've had it for a little over two years. I'll take this car over any of my other ones any day. Where to Royalty asks Jacques.

Oh, ok let's go to the Four Seasons Hotel on Wilshire Beverly Hills. Everything else is closed until 4:30. Heading in that direction Royalty says if I didn't know any better, I would think you was trying to fuck me again giving Jacques the side eye.

Looking at Royalty laughing. You do look like a snack, but you're pressed for time. Unless you want a quickie smirking back at Royalty who bust out laughing. What's so funny Jacques asks.

A quickie are you serious right now Royalty asks.

Yes, I'm dead serious Jacques says.

Get a room then and let's see how serious you are winking. Royalty said

Not sure if Royalty was serious or not Jacques booked a room and was thinking they could order room service. Valet parking Royalty and Jacques gets out and goes check in at the Four Season

I love this hotel Royalty says getting on the elevator.

Humm you come here often? Being sarcastic Jacques replies.

Playfully Punching Jacques softly Royalty says boy quit playing you know I'm a call girl laughing.

Hitting Royalty back getting her face Jacques says you know "SHIT GOES DOWN WHEN THERE'S A BILLION DOLLARS IN THE ELEVATOR "laughing but Jacques meant it literally kissing Royalty cheek.

Royalty started laughing too thinking this fool probably is really worth a billion dollars I have to google him. Getting off the elevator on 14 floor entering the penthouse suite Royalty tells Jacques to strip down butt naked. Doing as he was told Royalty does the same and grabs Jacques hand and leads him to the bathroom. While turning on the bathtub Royalty turns Jacques on also putting his whole dick in her mouth like a popsicle then licked it up and down teasing Jacques then stopped. Sticking her foot in the water to test it. Perfect. Getting in pulling Jacques in with her. Jacques sits back on the bathtub pillow and Royalty sits on top of Jacques kissing and biting on Jacques lips. I bet you never got fucked in a bathtub before Royalty says in Jacques ear while sucking on his earlobe.

Nope never Jacques says getting aroused.

Continuing sucking on Jacques ear then sucking on his neck Royalty makes her way down grabbing Jacques dick out the water putting it in her mouth while sitting on her knees in the bathtub Royalty goes to work making Jacques squirm. Just when Jacques was about to cum Royalty stopped and said now you can't be selfish smiling getting on top of Jacques sliding down on his dick while the water splashed around her ass. Holding on to the tub Royalty started speeding up her strokes tilting her head back while Jacques sucked on her titties. The water moving around them and the splashing sounds plus the moaning was too much for the both of them Jacques grabbed Royalty by the back of her head bringing her face to his kissing Royalty and sucking on Royalty lips and face while Royalty was stroking up and down on his dick going faster and faster massaging Jacques head and scratching his back.

I'm coming baby Jacques says grabbing Royalty ass diving himself all the way into Royalty making the water splash all over the floor.

I'm COMING TOOOOO!! Royalty moans coming right behind Jacques. Laying her head on Jacques chest breathing heavy.

After a couple minutes Jacques says to Royalty. You're a man eater with all this disrespectful sex.

Royalty responds You think so? It's your fault tho your too damn sexy. Not opening her eyes just laying there on Jacques chest masking in their love making knowing she was falling hard for this dude. Jacques had provoked Royalty to believe that she could possibly be happy again. Royalty and Jacques laid in the tub until the water got cold. Then they both got out the tub and climb into the king size bed and made love all over again until they both fell asleep in each other's arms.
Oh my God it's 5:00 pm I missed my freaking meeting looking at the clock on the desk in the room then at Jacques who was still kinda sleep.

Huh? Jacques says sitting up pulling the covers over himself to hide is nakedness.

It's all your fault yelling at Jacques Royalty says.

Rubbing his eyes Jacques starts laughing. Ok but you're the one who started all this freaky shit. Hell, I didn't even get a chance to put the sign in the window at the boutique that says I was out to lunch and wouldn't be returning laughing.

Taking a deep breath Royalty says your right it's my fault. I don't know what's coming over me lately but it's your fault for making me act this way getting up out the bed getting her phone.

Laughing to himself Jacques says got her! Laying back with his hands behind his head admiring Royalty handle her business on the phone.

Mr Reiss I apologize my phone died and I was stuck in traffic and I forgot my blackberry. Today has been one heck of a day I tell you. Looking over at Jacques holding her fist up. Yes, I can absolutely make it next Monday at 11am. I'll even show up early Laughing. Yes, and I have all the paperwork and my attorney will be joining us I'm excited about the merger. Thank you Mr. Reiss I look forward to our meeting. Have a great week goodbye. Sighing. Thank God that worked out walking back climbing into bed. Remind me Not to fuck with you before I have a business meeting. I almost blew that deal.

Staring at Royalty and how beautiful Royalty was and handling her business turned Jacques on. Damn baby you Hella sexy doing your boss lady shit. Pushing her back tonguing her down.

Grabbing Jacques erect manhood Royalty puts Jacques inside her lifting her legs and ass up and starts grinding slowly. Take your time with me baby Royalty whispered in Jacques ear while matching Jacques strokes until Royalty couldn't take it anymore and threw that pussy at Jacques full throttle. Making Jacques cum instantly.

Falling over on his back Jacques says you gone have me taken some viagra fucking with you laughing.

Naw your good Royalty says getting up to order room service. Looking over the menu Royalty asks Jacques what he wanted to order.

No babe let's get dressed and go downstairs to the bar like we originally planned just give me a minute to catch my breath Jacques says closing his eyes for a second.

Ok I'm getting in the shower you care to join me Royalty says laughing.

Opening his eyes wide Jacques replies you know what women whatever you're on I need some of that because I most definitely can't hang with you laughing. I'm going to sit this one out coach I'm tired. Jacques says closing his eyes again.

While taking a shower Royalty contemplates whether she should tell Jacques that he's the second man she's ever been with sexually. Amir was her first and only man Royalty ever loved. Royalty owed her whole entire life to Amir and now that Amir was gone Royalty thinking all these women coming out of the wood works must have provoked her into really digging Jacques. Royalty didn't think she would ever be into another man and especially so quickly. Royalty thought that she would probably have a girlfriend before a man because Royalty was into Beautiful, feminine women.

Royalty and Amir often had threesome per Royalty request. Royalty reminiscenced on the first time her and Amir brought someone home. They were in a club and Royalty saw a girl she couldn't keep her eyes off of and Amir noticed it but didn't say anything right away. Amir went to the bar and ordered the young lady a drink and pointed to their table and invited her to join them if she wanted to and walked away. A few moments later the girl Royalty was admiring came to their vip area with a friend.

Hi, my name is Lisa extending her hand to Royalty your friend invited me to join You'll for drinks.

Moving over to make room for her and her friend Royalty lets Lisa in and asked Lisa what was she drinking.

I like dark drinks the girl Lisa said.

Well we're drinking Moët you ever had Moët before? Royalty asks Lisa.

No, I haven't Lisa replied.

Pouring Lisa, a glass and handing it to her Royalty says try it. The whole time Amir was admiring Royalty pimping. Amir knew Royalty always did have a thing for girls, but Amir never saw Royalty in action. The shit got Amir horny as fuck. Amir was sitting back watching Royalty cheering Royalty on like get her babe. Royalty and Lisa drank and small talked for about 20 mins when Royalty told Lisa she found her attractive. That's my man the one buying you these drinks but I'm the one whose feeling you. Your fucking gorgeous. Lisa didn't know what to say because she thought Royalty was gorgeous also and also Amir. Can I kiss you? Royalty asks but before Lisa couldn't even respond Royalty just started kissing her and Lisa kissed Royalty back. Amir couldn't believe what he was seeing Royalty just had knocked her first bitch in the club. After making out in the club Royalty asked Lisa to come home with her and Amir and that they would make it worth Lisa wild.

But I came here with my friend Lisa said what do I tell her? Looking puzzled.

Royalty opens her Chanel bag and pulls out a stack of hundreds and hands them to Lisa. Give her this and tell her you'll see her tomorrow.

Looking at the money then back at Royalty Lisa says I don't want to give her all this. Wanting to keep some for herself.

Looking Lisa in the eyes Royalty says we got you, your good it's just a little something for her troubles winking. If Lisa had any second thoughts before Royalty was sure they were gone now. Leaving the club getting into Amir's Benz Lisa felt like she was among a few celebrities. It's funny how bitches get geeked off of a car a nigga driving that might not even be the person that's driving it actual car. But in this case, it was. Royalty was thinking at the time. When Amir pulled up to their house you could tell Lisa was so amazed.

You'll live here Lisa kept asking.

Laughing Royalty keep saying yes. Walking in Royalty gives Lisa a tour of the house and asks Lisa would she like another drink. Lisa said no but was it ok if she smoked her weed. Once Amir found out Lisa smoked Amir brought out his best stash and got Lisa super fuck up in the backyard standing by the pool overlooking the quiet night of Los Angeles. Amir followed Royalty lead once they got Lisa in the bedroom. Royalty wasted no time taking Lisa down. Playing in Lisa hair and rubbing on her face Royalty keep thinking this girl is beautiful while climbing on top of lisa kissing her pulling Lisa hair grinding their bodies together. Then Royalty moves down and sucks on Lisa titties. Amir was videotaping them as much as he could while beating his own meat with excitement. Royalty wasn't playing no games sucking and licking in between Lisa legs that was in the air spread as wide as they could go. Lisa moans sounded like they were bouncing off the walls to Amir's ears. Amir wanted to jump in like tag your it's your turn. And like on que Royalty turns Lisa over doggy style and gets up and let's Amir hit it from the back laying on the bed rubbing on Lisa titties and tongue kissing Amir. Royalty gets up off the bed and watches Amir drill that ass egging Amir on. Get it Daddy, Yes!!! Lisa who had cum multiple times was through Lisa couldn't handle no more. But Amir and Royalty on the other hand showers then they had they own party. The following morning. Amir's gives Lisa five grand and a ride home. Lisa became Royalty and Amir girlfriend for almost 2 years until Lisa started catching feelings and wanted more out of the relationship than they were willing to offer. But there were many more girlfriends after Lisa and they were all compensated generously. Royalty believe in paying her dues and Royalty was a big tipper.

You ok in there? Jacques yells out to Royalty.

Turning off the shower and drying off walking into the bedroom suite smiling. Yes, I was just in my feelings washing away some sins.

Oh, ok I hope you left some hot water for a nigga because you ever tried to shower in cold water? Shit feels like being tortured. I'll take a hoe bath before showering in cold water Jacques says laughing.

That's why I like you Jacques you keep me laughing Royalty says throwing her towel at Jacques who caught the towel and flicked it at Royalty ass laughing.

That's what I'm here for its my calling to bring laughter to the world Jacques says getting out the bed getting in the shower.

Royalty started plotting on how she could introduce a threesome to Jacques. Royalty knew Jacques was with it after all this nigga eats ass. Royalty thinking, she was a snack to Jacques, but Jacques was ready for an entree with some sides.
After a long night fooling around with Jacques Royalty was well rested and energized now and was ready to start her day. Royalty had a long list of errands she needed to do but her first stop would be at Donut Snob to grab a box of their decorative donuts that are so good especially when there hot. After picking up two dozen donuts Royalty heads to her salon to surprise the ladies who Royalty hadn't seen in months.

Walking into the salon her employees started screaming like they saw a celebrity. Royalty!!! Omg where have you been leaving their clients hanging running up to Royalty giving her hugs.

I'm happy to see you'll too trying to get out the bear hug. I can't breathe let me go Royalty says breaking free. I brought donuts for the you guys and the clients. Walking over to to clients opening the box of donuts for each client to get one out.

Thank you, girl one client says how, have you been Royalty? Asking sincerely. She was a faithful client who had been coming to the shop since it first opened.

I'm good Tootie thanks for asking Royalty says continuing passing around donuts to everyone. I have my days, but I still have to live Royalty replies.

Well you look hella good girl I'm praying for you. Tootie says

Thanks, I need all the prayers I can get Royalty says sitting the box of donuts at the reception desk.

Looking around the shop that was immaculate. Amir had chosen the color scheme saying he wanted it to be an upscale prestigious salon not a hood salon. Well so much for that. There had been several fights that jumped off in this salon behind somebody's man cheating and the side woman came up in the salon when the main woman was there. Royalty remembered that one incident a fight jumped off in the shop that Royalty couldn't forget because it was herself fighting some broad over Amir who came in the shop talking shit not realizing Royalty was the owner and was in the back in her office. Royalty came out the office and it was on sight with them two and of course Bianca jumped in because Bianca was at the shop arguing with the girl who was talking shit. And that's what brought Royalty out her office because Royalty heard the commotion. And Yes, there was plenty of other Hair salons in La that was nice, but Royalty had the top three hairstylists in the city hands down. Pretty Please was the most talked about salon around. There was a lot of buzz about the shop and its hairstylist. The three hairstylists were all bad as fuck. Top notch bad bodies and all three were single with no kids. So, to say they were popping was an understatement. Every nigga from ball players to entertainers was checking for these hot commodities. All three stylists had a huge social media following and they all lived their best lives with a profitable clientele. Royalty stylist even had a few celebrities' clients at Pretty Please despite the shenanigans that occurred sometimes.

> The salon was beautifully decorated also and by looking at the decor you would never suspect that it was a hood salon. The walls were bomb silver glitter with chandeliers over every station and floor to ceiling mirrors at every station. The white wooden pergo floors went throughout the salon with silver flakes with a touch of bling. Custom white leather swivel chairs at each station. Black and white Vintage Chanel photos were on the walls and the stylists each had floating glass storage closets at their stations for their client's coats and belongings. The closest also housed a small personal safe inside for the stylist security because everybody wasn't as loyal as they portrayed to be. But the entrance was the elephant in the room. The glass French doors that spelled Pretty Please in crystal writing opened up to a red carpet that lead clients to the lounge area that had two black velvet couches and three matching chairs. There was two flat screen tvs opposite each other on the walls and a jukebox and a photo booth personalized for Pretty Please that uploaded pictures taken to all social media handles. Most clients flicked it up after they finished getting their hair laid. But the highlight of the shop was the philanthropy services the hairstylist gave one Monday every first Monday of the month. Pretty Please opened up the shop every First Monday and serviced homeless women and men with free hair washing and styling and men haircuts. Pretty please also feed the homeless. Pretty Please had a decorated hall in the back of the shop that Royalty rents out per request. But on first Monday's of the month Pretty please caters food for the homeless community in the hall. Royalty and Amir felt it was their duty to give back and this was just one way of doing it. Royalty knew what it felt like to have

nothing and be hopeless. Growing up Royalty wasn't homeless but in her little mind Royalty was. There were plenty of days Royalty barley ate from lack of food in the house. So, homelessness and abused children was a weakness for Royalty.

Look what the wind blew in. Kiki one of Royalty stylists says as Bianca struts in looking like she was auditioning for a modeling job. One foot crosses over the other sashaying.

Oh, bitch you not returning calls now? Looking at Royalty like what's up.

I didn't get any calls from you Royalty says lying.

Bitch stop lying to my face Bianca yells.

Look there's clients in here respect my salon Royalty says to Bianca.

Fuck your salon and you to bitch acting all bougie and shit. Bianca says seriously.

Look Bianca once again calm down this is a place of business. I don't come next door yelling and cussing when you have clients Royalty says seriously.

Miss me with all that Royalty we need to talk walking towards Royalty office like come on let's talk now!!

Following behind Bianca shaking her head and putting her hand to her head like it was a gun like just kill me already. Royalty does as she was told.

Sitting down in Royalty chair at Royalty desk spinning around like a big ass kid leaving the client chair for Royalty to sit in or the couch that was in the office.

Royalty sits on the couch because Royalty didn't want to be that close to Bianca Just in case some shit popped off. Bianca starts to go in on Royalty.

Look bitch I don't know if it's that time of the month or that you need some dick but whatever it is you need to handle that and lose the fucking attitude with me. I'm your only family besides Jaheem fine ass you got left. I'm your sister bitch. And sisters may fight or whatever, but they get over it and move on. But not you miss goodie two shoes, fucking cry baby ass bitch.

Royalty was just sitting there looking at her nails thinking she had to go get them done this week it was time. Not really paying any attention to Bianca who went off on Royalty at least once a week for the same reason. So, Royalty was used to this.

Look Bianca I'm about to go I have Hella shit to do today but I'll call you later getting up to leave unless I forget or get too busy walking out leaving the door open Laughing. Royalty says

Don't walk out on me you bitch Bianca says going through Royalty drawers on her desk being nosy finding some old pictures of Amir and Royalty from their vacation in Mexico from a few years ago and how happy they looked. Then Bianca started to feel bad for being so selfish and not being more supportive to her best friend who was grieving the loss of her man.

I'm going to holler at you'll later Royalty says giving her stylists hugs before leaving.

Don't be no stranger Kiki says we love ya girl.

I love you too Kiki I'll be back in a couple days plus I have to update you on a few things. Referring to Jacques.

Ok bet plus I forgot to tell you I'm seeing this ball player now smiling Kiki says he plays for the Lakers, so you already know what it is right snapping her fingers. Hardwood floors all basketball season bitch laughing. We about to be basketball wives in that bitch giving hoes life in the Staple center.

Is that right Royalty says? Congratulations boo don't fuck this one up like you did the last one Laughing Royalty says.

Crossing her chest like pray for me Kiki says Girl you already know. Hopefully he don't say something to make me snap. Because you know I don't care about how much money that nigga got. He can't try and play me. That's a No for me dawg. I ain't having it.

We know everyone said in unison in the shop laughing.

Well all I can say is I got bail money if you need it Kiki. Royalty says Laughing walking out waving bye. Getting in her car Royalty Phone started ringing but it was at the bottom of her purse, so Royalty missed the call. Driving off Royalty Phone rang again. Pulling up to the light Royalty looked at her phone and recognized the number and stared at the phone for a moment. The light changed from red to green, but Royalty was still looking at her phone until the cars behind Royalty started blowing at her snapping Royalty out her daze. Hello Royalty says softly.

Can I speak to Royalty?

This is Royalty.

Hi Royalty, this Detective Maceo how are you?

You find Amir's killer? Royalty asked frightened to hear the answer.

No not yet but I have a few leads that's why I'm calling you to let you know this case is far from being closed and I'm not going to let it get cold. Detective Maceo says. I spoke with another detective out there in Los Angeles they said they talk to you about a shooting at a nightclub and a murder that didn't have anything to do with Amir did it? Detective Maceo asks.

No that had nothing to do with Amir and I spoke with them briefly I couldn't help them with that case Royalty replies nervously.
Just hearing Detective Maceo voice gave Royalty the chills. It brought it all back up like it was happening again. Royalty had to pull over because Royalty was shaking. Seeing Amir on the floor covered in blood started flashing thru Royalty mind and Royalty started tearing up.

Royalty you still there? Detective Maceo says on the other end of the call.

Yes, I'm still here. Can I call you right back? Royalty asks looking at the phone seeing the 718-area code.

Yes, call me back at any time and take care of yourself Detective Maceo says before hanging up.

Grabbing the steering wheel squeezing it placing her head down on it. Royalty lets it all out crying hitting the steering wheel yelling no and then heads to the cemetery.
Pulling up on Florence turning into the Inglewood cemetery gave Royalty the chills. But Royalty needed to do this Royalty had to do this. It was way overdue. Parking going into the mausoleum Royalty started praying Lord let me be ok while walking slowly to Amir's resting place. Putting her hands on Amir's tomb Royalty touches every letter of Amir's name and softly says I miss you Amir I'm so sorry I haven't been to see you. I wasn't ready until today. Starting to cry. Shit I've been going crazy since you left. I couldn't eat or think correctly for months I barely just got myself together. I'm not totally all together still. You prepared me for everything but how to live without you. It's not fair you left me all alone like this. Crying harder now. I wish they would have taken me with you. They just don't understand that we're a team. There's no you without me. Falling down on the ground crying uncontrollably. I hella miss you babe sitting on the ground holding her knees to her chest rocking. Crying Amir over and over again.

The grounds men came inside checking the premises and saw Royalty sitting on the ground crying and walks over to Royalty and hands Royalty some Kleenex.

Taking the Kleenex and telling him Thank You and blowing her nose. Royalty stands up and looks at the groundskeeper with her eye's bloodshot red with tears in her eyes.

Sorry for your loss the groundskeeper says you have a little over an hour before I lock up, he says turning walking away feeling sorry for Royalty and all the other people he saw in this predicament for the last twenty years or so he had been working there.

Looking at Amir's tomb Royalty continues saying Amir I thought that it gets easier by the days, but it doesn't my days seem longer now if anything but I'm not crying myself to sleep anymore or thinking about ending my own life. Yes, I thought about it I didn't see any reason to live without you. I have no one that really matters you was all I had still crying. But somehow, I've been strong enough to make it this far it's been ninety days already. And I meet Liberty and Angel I don't know why you didn't tell me about her. Laughing a little wiping her nose. Well I do know why but anyways. You having a baby by someone else was not part of our plan. But I guess everything happens for a reason Amir because you know damn well, I didn't want to be nobody's momma. That mommy shit is overrated. I just wish you would have told me Amir we could have worked it out. I'm going to do right by your kid even though you probably would have hid him or her from me until they were 18 Laughing again. Oh, and I fired that bitch Jessica because you didn't have the balls to do it even though you said you were numerous of times but didn't. Well I did it for you. Also, I meet someone I think I like. I know what you're probably saying wow Royalty so fast. It just happened Amir and no I don't love him. He just makes me laugh. He reminds me a lot of you. Touching Amir's tomb. But nobody will ever replace you my first love. Kissing Amir tomb nobody. I'll be back real soon to visit you again tearing up again. I Hella miss you and I love you Amir. Please watch over me. Walking away looking back until Royalty couldn't see Amir's name on his plate any longer. It was getting dark outside and Royalty had one more person to visit while she was there.

Royalty never visited before not even once, but something led her to her mother's Teresita gravesite. Teresita was on the opposite side of the mausoleum from Amir. Royalty looked Teresita name up and found her gravesite directly under a tree. Reading Teresita tombstone Royalty laughed.

Teresita Gigante Loving Mother, Caring sister and beloved friend born 08-24-1966 - Departure to destiny 12-21-2000 Gone way too soon but you will never be forgotten.

Royalty just looked at the gravesite for about 20 minutes before saying a word. You're lucky that Amir cared about your trick ass to bury you correctly because if it was up to me you would have been buried as a John fucking doe. No plot, no nothing Royalty says talking to Teresita gravesite. This is all your fault I'm standing her today visiting Amir you know, that right? If it wasn't for you, we wouldn't even be in this situation I'm in. You ruined our lives. And it's because of you Amir had to go as hard as he went. Getting mad and having a meltdown. It's all your fucking fault you stupid ass bitch. You had one job and that was to be a Mother to me and you couldn't even do that correctly. No instead you chose to care only about your fucking self. That's why you're Buried 10 feet under now. Loving mother my ass it should have read that you loved crack and heroin and turning tricks with your trick ass . Them were the only three things you loved. You never loved me. What did I do to you to make you hate me so much ? Starting to cry? It's ok though because in the end look who's standing me and who ain't you. I would say Rest In Peace but that's not how I really feel when it comes to you. I hope you burn in hell you dopefiend crackhead. And remember you did this to yourself Teresita dead in your forties. Royalty said shaking her head walking away heading to her car feeling liberated from all the cleansing she just did at the cemetery.
After leaving the cemetery Royalty felt like she needed a drink and someone to talk to to lay all her burdens on. And the only person Royalty could think of was Bianca pulling into her driveway pulling next to a Baby Blue Benz Royalty never saw before. I wonder who Bianca has over here Royalty thinking while walking to the door. After ringing the doorbell a few times and no answer Royalty took out her keys Royalty had a spare key to Bianca's house plus Royalty wanted to be nosey. Letting herself in the House was dark but Royalty could hear the tv on in the living room. Royalty headed to the kitchen and makes herself a drink then goes in the living room scaring the shit out of Bianca and her friend startling them both while sitting down on the couch.

Bitch I could have shot you thinking you were a burglar bitch. Bianca said looking up at Royalty while sitting in between her guy friend legs on the floor.

Taking a sip of her Hennessy Royalty replies I doubt that you could shoot anybody with that lil ass Victoria Secret robe on with nothing under it. Where was you was to hide your gun at in your ass bitch? laughing.

What the fuck You doing here anyways bitch I thought we wasn't speaking? And what if I was in here sucking dick bitch? Making that what the fuck face Bianca says.

Downing her drink getting up to go pour another One Royalty says standing up getting ready to go back into the kitchen. Bitch Please it ain't like I haven't never seen you suck a dick before and I can say your pretty good at it lifting up her glass like giving her a toast laughing. Shit we've been in the same bed before while you was fucking. Really Bianca you ain't trying to go, there are you? Laughing at herself Royalty said walking into the kitchen.

What the fuck is your problem bitch? Bianca says coming into the kitchen right behind Royalty barefoot walking fast.

Looking down at Bianca feet Royalty says. I like that nail color on your toes what color is that? And your feet ain't cold on this marble floor? Oh, your floor must heat up pouring herself another drink Laughing.

What happened to you Royalty that got you come bargen in my house and getting drunk? What the fuck is going on?

You want a drink bitch Royalty asks Bianca.

Yeah pour me one I know I'm going to need it after talking with your ass laughing. Bianca says

Who's the dude he kinda cute. Not your type but… Royalty asks.

Shhh sis lower your voice damn. That's my new friend I meet at the hospital. Bianca replies

When you was just there? Royalty asks

Yeah, he works there he's a nurse bitch laughing.

A what? Shaking her head. Royalty says you a hoe bitch damn. You fucking the nurse now I guess the doctor next Laughing.

Bianca laughed too. Naw the bitch was a girl, but she was cute tho sipping her drink.

Damn I thought I was bad for fucking on Amir so fast but I ain't got shit on you bitch downing her second drink pouring another one.

Bitch you're going to burn your intestines up slow down on the Hennessy Bianca says.

Fuck you!! I went and visited Amir tonight. Oh, now I see what this is about.

Sorry sis how that go? Bianca says Handing Royalty her empty glass to refill it.

It was cool I guess I had a moment when I broke down but I'm glad I went. I also went to Teresita gravesite too. Royalty says

Bianca eyes got big and Bianca got quiet for a moment then walked into the storage closet and pulled out a bottle of Louis X111 and hands it to Royalty. Ok now this is better for the occasion because we need to get fucked Up Royalty since you went to see mom dukes what made you go visit Teresita? You've never done that before. You want me to tell ol boy to bounce? Bianca says seriously.

Naw it's cool Royalty says ask him does he want a drink though we're being hella rude opening the Louie ready to get fucked up. But shit we some rude bitches man Royalty says laughing.

Sitting down on the couch fucked up Royalty takes off her shoes and fold her legs and gets comfortable. Turn on some music Royalty says to Bianca who was trying to find a movie changing channels with the remote.

You want to listen to some music instead of watching tv? Bianca asks. Looking at her guy friend who hadn't said one word since Royalty came in and crashed the party. You good boo? Because we can go in my room, but my sister lost her man and she's went to visit him at the cemetery tonight and she's fucked Up literally.

Royalty had the whole bottle of Louie in her hand drinking straight from the bottle with her eyes closed nodding like a dopefiend. Royalty keep nodding off sitting up then instantly waking up talking and taking another drink.

Bianca boy toy looked at Royalty and finally said. Your girl wasted you need to tend to her. I'll check with you tomorrow or something getting up grabbing his jacket off the couch.

Ok thanks for understanding I'll walk you to the door Bianca says getting up fixing her robe that barely covered up her ass. Giving her friend a goodbye kiss Bianca tells him I'll make it up to you I promise grabbing his dick.

Smiling he says I know you will. Your girl already certified that head. I can't wait to see what that mouth do kissing Bianca back hitting her on the ass. Opening the door walking out he says make sure your girl take some Tylenol because she definitely going to need it in the morning Laughing leaving out shutting the door behind him.

Ok Royalty taking the bottle out Royalty hand let's get you in the bed helping Royalty up.

No no I'm going home slurring Royalty says.

You're at home Bianca says now let's get you in bed walking into her guest bedroom laying Royalty across the Queen canopy bed on her back with all her clothes on. Bianca gets a blanket out the closet and places it over Royalty who looked so beautiful to Bianca even while she slept. Bianca hated that her best friend was going through this, but Bianca also knew this wouldn't be the last time Royalty would need her for support. Going in the living room turning off the tv and the lights and checking all the locks and turning on the alarm. Bianca keep hearing a vibrating noise. What is that noise Bianca was thinking. The noise vibrated again, and Bianca could hear it was coming from the couch. Reaching into the couch Bianca found her friend Phone he must have forgotten it and he had it on vibrate. Damn he had Hella missed calls and texts. Then another text came thru while Bianca was holding the phone. Looking at the text thinking Bianca put his phone down you don't even know him like that. But also thinking fuck it he left his phone so read it. Of course, Bianca read the text message

(Babe why you ain't answering your phone?? I know your off work stop playing with me nigga)
(Babe answer my calls I've been calling you all day this some bullshit)

Typing a quick response.

(He's on his way bitch and tell him he left his phone and he can come get it tomorrow I'm going to bed now I'm tired and I'm not answering my phone tonight Goodnight with the kissy emoji) Send … Laughing. Fuck both them Bianca thinking laying the phone back on the couch going to bed. Wake up bitch shaking Royalty trying to wake Royalty up. Opening one Eye Royalty sees Bianca twerking to Rich sex by Nicki Minaj that was playing Hella loud throughout the house. Get up bitch let's go get some breakfast dancing like she was at the club or something.

Wiping her eyes Royalty says. Are you serious right now looking at her Rolex it's 8 am damn. Rich sex before 9am. Can I at least wash my face and brush my teeth before I listen to Nicki fine ass? Getting up heading to the bathroom. And why you let me sleep in my clothes? Royalty says before closing the bathroom door. Looking in the mirror Royalty said to herself girl get it together yawning still tired but starving. Bianca had the music on full blast and on repeat. Royalty took a quick shower and gets out and washes her face and brushes her teeth and places her hair in a bun. Walking into the living room where Bianca was straightening up at to tell Bianca she needed a sweatsuit to throw on.

What the fuck jumping Bianca yells. Bitch why you naked?

Laughing why not it's only you and me here right looking around Royalty says.

Yeah but damn looking at Royalty perfect natural body. Your body is bomb though to not have no work done. Bianca says

Royalty start poking her ass out shaking it with her hands in the air dancing off Rich sex naked. This is my shit though Nicki came hard with facts on this track snapping her fingers.

Let me go get your Adam and Eve looking ass something to wear Bianca says walking pass Royalty who was acting like she was on a nude beach or something.

Royalty went into the kitchen and got some orange juice and started drinking it from the carton.

What you doing bitch? Bianca says catching Royalty.

Almost spitting her juice out from laughing Royalty says it was almost empty anyways I was just finishing the last of it Laughing.

Sitting a sweatsuit down on the kitchen stool. This one of my favorite sweatsuits so you giving this one back. Bianca says. You always come over and spend the night and take my sweatsuits and never return them.

Ok damn you got a whole closet full of sweatsuits anyways why you trippin off this one? Royalty says putting on the Gucci sweatsuit with no panties or bra. This sweatsuit Hella cute too thanks boo. Royalty says zipping up the jacket to her boobs leaving her cleavage out.

Don't thanks boo me bitch I'm coming to your house and getting all my shit from your hoarding ass. I can't take shit of yours from your house without hearing No you can't take that Amir brought this or that. The fuck. But you always coming over here stealing shit. You got way more money than me go buy your own shit. Seriously speaking Bianca was tired of Royalty taking her shit and never returning it.

Ok ok cry baby I'll buy you That Chanel bag you wanted if you let me keep this sweatsuit Royalty says. Plus, I need some sneakers to wear too Laughing. Royalty and Bianca didn't wear the same size shoe Bianca foot was a whole shoe size bigger but with thick socks on Royalty could get away with it and Bianca had all the fly sneakers every pair damn near.

Nope you're not getting a pair of shoes. Wear the shoes you came with. Bitch what I look like Saks Fifth to you? Bianca says.

Well you kinda do now that you mention it Laughing Royalty says. Pointing at Bianca singing Rich Sex sticking her tongue out.

Ignoring Royalty Bianca says you know that nigga that was here last night left his phone.

Word damn I know he mad Royalty says.

Yeah real mad because his bitch keep texting him and I replied Bianca said.

What you say Royalty asked.

I texted back and said he left his phone over here and he can come pick it up today. And told that bitch to stop texting because I was tired and going to bed.

Shaking her head Royalty says only you laughing. I know he'll triple check from now on before leaving his phone anywhere else laughing. Where we going to eat at Royalty asks. I'm so hungry I could eat a horse right now.

Ugh you nasty you talking about eating pork Bianca says.

A horse isn't pork fool Royalty says laughing. Plus, I'm hypothetically speaking not literally but you wouldn't know the difference bitch you didn't pay attention in school we both know that. All you cared about was the boys Royalty says.

That's all I still care about Bianca says laughing.

True Royalty responds laughing also.

And bitch we going straight to the Chanel store after we eat breakfast too now that's facts and I don't want to hear no I left my credit cards at home or I don't got no money on me either. Because that's all bullshit. We both know you keep emergency cash on hand I know you got about 10 racks on you right now bitch. Don't make me rob your punk ass about my Chanel bag because I will Bianca says laughing but serious as a heart attack.
After eating at the Griddle Cafe and going to the Chanel store where Bianca had the nerve to want a 7,000 bag and Royalty had to set Bianca straight. First of all, bitch we ain't fucking pointing back and forth from herself and then Bianca. I said I'll get you a bag, but bitch don't try and play me, or you want get shit. Now get you a little 3,500 bag and be happy Royalty tells Bianca who head got

deflated because she really wanted that Big boy flap bag and didn't want to buy it herself because Bianca was so use to everybody doing shit for her ass. But not today Royalty thinking. 7,000 this bitch must be crazy. I'm not even getting myself No 7,000 bag. Getting a Chanel fanny pack for 2,500 for herself. Royalty wasn't used to buying herself bags anyways. Amir brought mostly all Royalty bags. Amir would come in the house and hand Royalty a Chanel black bag and say I brought you a thot bag today Laughing. Amir said all the thots was walking around with fake Chanel bags and he should have just brought Royalty one from the flea market and saved his money Laughing. Royalty laughed at that thought. Royalty really missed Amir. Handing the sales clerk her black card for her 8,000-total purchase for both Chanel bags Royalty felt like she did good even though Bianca still played Royalty and got an almost 5,000 bag and a headscarf. But Royalty wasn't tripping because Royalty loved seeing her friend happy even at her expense.

Thank you, sis, smiling from ear to ear Bianca says holding up her Chanel bag getting in her car blowing Royalty kisses.

Yeah yeah back at you Royalty replies. Call me later I'm going home and taking a nap I'm full and tired getting in her car turning up Teyana Taylor new cd to the max to keep her woke on the ride home. Royalty had the music so loud Royalty didn't even hear her phone ringing. Pulling into the garage getting her Chanel bag off the passenger seat Royalty picks up her phone and sees she had four missed calls from Jacques and Royalty started smiling. Damn four missed calls huh? What's so important Royalty thinking. Jacques likes me laughing to herself walking into the house. Sitting her stuff down on the kitchen counter Royalty was so tired she couldn't make it upstairs to her bedroom, so Royalty laid down in the guest bedroom and crashed for a couple hours. When Royalty woke up Royalty could smell Jacques cologne on the pillow and smiled thinking she needed to call him back. Royalty gets up goes upstairs into her bathroom and runs some bath water and lit some candles and turns on some music, so she could relax and soothe her mind. But before getting in the tub Royalty ran downstairs to grab a bottle of wine and noticed her phone was beeping about to go dead. Damn I was that tired I forgot to charge my phone grabbing it and her bottle of wine running back upstairs. Plugging in her phone it immediately started to ring. Hello

Why you couldn't answer none of my calls today Royalty I'm curious?

Jacques asks sounding like we were in a relationship and he was going to check me Royalty thinking laughing to herself. Huh? What you talking about boy I just woke up from a nap. Royalty says.

Who you calling a boy Lil girl scared of the dark and shit laughing. Jacques replies.

Whatever what's good tho? I'm sorry I didn't call you back earlier I did see you had called but I was so freaking tired. I got drunk with Bianca last night and spent the night at her house then this morning we went and ate breakfast then Bianca made me go to the Chanel store and buy her a purse.

You said all that without taking a breath damn girl Jacques says laughing again. And how Bianca make you buy her a Chanel bag? Now I'm really curious Jacques says wanting to know.

Well it's a long story but basically every time I stay at Bianca's house Bianca always gives me something to put on when I leave of hers, so Bianca says I owed her something and Bianca wanted a Chanel bag.

Oh, I get it now. Well you owe me too, I guess. You came to my place and needed something to wear also and you got three pair of shoes. So, I guess you owe me also laughing Jacques says.

I guess I do what you want? Royalty says smiling. I'm about to get in the tub if you were here you could join me Laughing.

Is that right. I'm close by I can swing by if you like leave the door unlock unless you scared Jacques says laughing.

I ain't never scared Royalty says I'll leave it unlocked for you hurry up before the water gets cold. Hanging up in Jacques face.

Royalty didn't know Jacques was closer than he admitted. When Royalty wasn't answering her phone, Jacques got a little worried about Royalty and decided to come by and check on Royalty. Jacques also wanted to make sure Royalty didn't have another nigga at her house too. Jacques didn't know what he would've done if Royalty did have someone else there Jacques was just glad that Royalty didn't so Jacques didn't have to even think about the outcome. But Jacques knew at that point he was starting to fall for Royalty and this had never happened to him before, but Jacques liked how it felt being spontaneous. Most women thought by giving their complete self to a man always got him but with Jacques it was the complete opposite. Royalty gave Jacques her body freely but everything else about Royalty was off limits to Jacques. And that's what turned Jacques on. It was something about a woman that held some things back that keeps a man coming back for more. Creeping up the stairs being very careful not to make a sound that would alert Royalty he was in the house Jacques wanted to scare the shit out of Royalty. But as loud as the music was playing Royalty couldn't hear Jacques anyways or anyone else for that matter. Entering Royalty bedroom all the lights were off, but a dim light came from the bathroom where Jacques stood by the bathroom door watching Royalty in the tub without Royalty even noticing that Jacques was standing there. Royalty had several Jo Malone scented candles lit surrounding the tub and on the counter with the bathroom light turned off with her head tilted back and her eyes closed laying on a tub pillow with her legs spread open playing with herself using two fingers. Enjoying the show Jacques just stood there and watched for a minute. As Royalty squeezed her own breast and fingered herself vigorously going in and out of her own pussy moaning enjoying the feeling she was receiving. Getting Hard grabbing his dick Jacques says Hummm clearing his throat. I didn't mean to crash the party smiling.

Opening her eyes and focusing on Jacques Royalty smiled back and said hi baby you look nice and comfortable you want to take over? Pulling her fingers out herself and licking them. I love the taste of clean pussy. Royalty says.

Me too Jacques says get out the tub and come give me a taste walking out the bathroom into Royalty room undressing.

When Royalty gets out the tub Royalty doesn't even dry off Royalty walks into the dark bedroom where she can see Jacques silhouette laying on the bed naked. Licking her lips Royalty waste no time putting him in her mouth sucking seductive on Jacques dick.

Rubbing his fingers through Royalty Hair Jacques says you trying make me fall in love with that mouth of yours.

Royalty stops sucking momentarily and looks up at Jacques and says softly" Try" I don't try to do anything I succeed at "Everything" I do winking putting Jacques dick back in her mouth slobbing on Jacques nob. After a few moments of pleasing Jacques Royalty comes up for air and says I want to feel you inside me crawling up Jacques body until Royalty reaches Jacques lips and kisses him and then whispers in Jacques ear. Now get on top and fuck me.

Obliging Royalty command Jacques does as he's told making Royalty come multiple times until Jacques came himself and feel asleep inside Royalty.

Waking up booed up Royalty stares at Jacques who was knocked the fuck out sleeping like a newborn and looking like one too with his smooth chocolate flawless skin. Royalty started thinking what the hell was she doing, was it too late to turn back now and Royalty wasn't sure she even wanted too. It felt so right and wrong all at the same time. Grief affects everyone differently and Royalty thought her grieving caused her to seek companionship in Jacques. Because Royalty didn't love Jacques, Royalty didn't believe she even really liked Jacques all like that, but Royalty did lust for Jacques touch and to hear his laughter and to see Jacques smile. Royalty keep telling herself don't get caught up with this dude. Amir just died give yourself some time to explore life. That's what Amir would have wanted. Date other people your officially single now don't get yourself into another committed relationship so fast. Your only twenty-four you have your whole life ahead of you plus this nigga married sliding from underneath Jacques climbing out of bed going into the bathroom to brush her teeth and put on a robe. Going downstairs Royalty opens all the windows in the house and turns on Janelle Monae I Like That cd and put it on repeat and made some breakfast.

When the biscuits were almost done Jacques comes walking into the kitchen just wearing his Balenciaga boxer shorts and says something smells good sitting on the glass kitchen stoll looking at Royalty like what's for breakfast.

You slept good? Royalty asks Jacques.

Smiling Jacques says yes thanks to you.

Your welcome Royalty replies turning back around at the stove making Jacques an omelette.

Fixing Jacques plate and pouring him some orange juice and placing a bowl of fruit in front of Him Jacques says, and you can cook too you're a keeper for sure Blessing his food.

Smiling Royalty thinking you are too it's almost like it's too good to be true. A keeper is that right Royalty replies. Laughing. What's that supposed to mean? sitting down across from Jacques at the breakfast nook with her plate.

In between bites Jacques says exactly what it means. You want me to look the definition up in the dictionary? laughing.

No but I do want you to tell me if you're really married or not. Royalty says sipping her tea.

Looking Royalty straight in her eyes Jacques says seriously. Ok ok let me get this straight Laughing. After sucking my dick in the club for starters, Me eating your ass, us fucking unprotected multiple times and me damn near saving you from a homicide charge you want to know if I'm married or not? You care more about my social media status more than your concerned about my HIV status Laughing. You never even asked me my Surname or my date of birth, but you want to know if I'm married? You kidding me right, now right? Taking a bite of his omelette. This breakfast good as fuck Jacques says washing his food down with his orange juice.

Royalty was stuck like she didn't have a rebuttal.

Don't get quiet now with your sexy ass Jacques says laughing. You should know that you never should ask a question you really don't want the answer too. Especially asking a Real man, real questions can hurt a girl feeling winking finishing the rest of his breakfast.

Damn did this nigga just get at me like that? Royalty thinking.

Eat your food sweetheart before it gets cold Jacques said with a smirk on his face. What's wrong? The cat got your tongue laughing. A minute a go You had 21 questions like fifty cent laughing Royalty laughed too.

Just answer the damn question Royalty says not letting Jacques win this battle she started.

Smiling Jacques says Yes, I'm happily married with three kids laughing.

Three kids are your serious right now Royalty says.

Naw are you serious right now? Jacques replies. I don't have no kids, but I am married. Is that a problem? Jacques asks

Royalty wasn't prepared for this conversation and didn't know why she even brought it up.

My wife lives in Jamaica and we're actually separated. She lived here but went back home a year ago. But we're still cool. We've been friends since childhood.

Oh, I see that's the same thing with me and Amir Royalty says. We grew up together also actually in the same house.

The same house Jacques asks.

Yes, it's a long story I'll tell you about it one day. It's complicated getting up from the breakfast nook taking both their plates emptying them placing them in the dishwasher.

Do you have a housekeeper? Jacques asks.

Yes, three days a week. But she's on vacation. Royalty says.

Speaking of vacations, you want to go on one for a couple days. I need a break from reality Jacques says. I want some sun I need to change the forecast laughing. You with it? Jacques asks.

Looking at Jacques like hell yeah, I'm with it!! But instead Royalty says I have to think about it. And check my schedule lying...

Driving home Jacques was thinking to himself that Royalty was starting to develop feelings for him smiling. Jacques knew whenever a woman started inquiring about you personally when she didn't inquire in the beginning she was starting to get in her feelings. Jacques also knew Royalty wasn't like your typical woman either. Jacques didn't have to teach Royalty the ropes Royalty had been taught already. Jacques didn't have to teach Royalty how to act around people with money because most women didn't really know how to conduct themselves around rich people. They always claim to be living their best life until they got around people that was actually living their best lives. Royalty was already in the millionaire club and had been there for quite some time. Jacques could be himself around Royalty Jacques didn't have to be cautious about what he said or did because some people took it as being cocky or showing off. Jacques had been labeled arrogant on more than one occasion. Because how Jacques liked to dress or because where Jacques liked to eat at even where Jacques shopped. But to Jacques it was normal it was his lifestyle. Jacques could afford to do whatever he wanted to do. Come and go as he please. And Jacques knew Royalty lived the same way. So, it was harder to impress Royalty also. Jacques peeped that earlier when Jacques asked Royalty if she wanted to go on a vacation and how Royalty brushed him off like she was hella busy. The thought made Jacques laugh. Women.

Taking a nice hot shower Royalty thinking I'm not fucking with no married man period. But Jacques did have a point. They had done everything under the sun so why stop now. Letting the water completely consume her from head to toe Royalty started feeling depressed again thinking about Amir. Does this pain ever go away? There wasn't a day that Royalty didn't think about Amir it seemed like the only time Royalty didn't really think about Amir was when she was with Jacques. And Royalty didn't know if that was a good or bad thing. But what Royalty did know was she was falling hard for Jacques and fast and Royalty needed to slow down. But why Royalty keep asking herself life was way too short for regrets as Royalty learned with losing Amir. Royalty was so confused and needed some real advice from someone who would not be judgemental and keep it one hundred. Looking at her phone going thru her call log. Dialing Jinx. Hello what's up sis you busy? Can you meet me for lunch today? Not for lunch oh ok when? Ok I'll be there at 5pm I'll see you there.

Going in her custom made closet that Amir designed and had built in the basement when they brought the house. The whole entire lower level was transformed into a closet with glass doors and glass chandeliers even the flooring was glass with white bear fur rugs there was absolutely no shoes allowed in this closet. One end of the closet housed a cedar closet for Royalty fur coats even though they lived in California Royalty and Amir frequent the west coast and always needed to be prepared. Royalty also had a closet for all her jewelry inside this closet. No need for a jewelry box when you had a closet allocated for that. Royalty put all of Amir's jewelry in there also to secure it because Royalty closet had a separate alarm and touch screen lock for entry. The closet also housed up to 1500 pairs of shoes with glass shelving and housed 1000 of Royalty designer bags on glass shelving also. Amir also had a glass vanity built for most of Royalty perfumes with a white fur ottoman. Amir called the closet Winter Wonderland. And Amir never went downstairs. It was Royalty little safe haven for herself plus it was the security room or bunker inside their home. So just in case someone broke into the house or whatever. Royalty closet once inside couldn't be opened from the outside. There was a separate secure phone line and WiFi in the closet and Amir had a gun dresser in there that was all crystal that was in the middle of the closet that had six drawers for Royalty accessories in the first three drawers and the next three drawers housed guns and magazines. The drawers were kept locked. Amir also had a gun closet inside their bedroom walk in closet in all their houses also. Walking into the closet Royalty looked around in amazement as Royalty did every time Royalty came into her closet at all the effort Amir put into getting her this closet built. It warmed Royalty heart that Amir loved her so much. No matter what they went through Amir always put Royalty first. Amir always made Royalty feel like Royalty. Coming downstairs was rare for Royalty also unless Royalty wanted to pull out her best pieces and get bad and boujee. And meeting Big Sis at Mastro's in Beverly Hills was one of them. Royalty was pulling out the big guns and showing out. It had been awhile since Royalty been to the restaurant and Royalty always came correct when she showed up. So, coming downstairs to the closet was a must. Looking around the closet Royalty was trying figure out how she wanted to look. Royalty had four rare Hermès Birkin bags Amir brought her for her 21st birthday that totaled $105,000 that Amir didn't think twice about how much they cost when Amir brought all the bags. Amir just wanted Royalty to have them. Amir also brought Royalty a S550 Benz and filled the backseat with 21 gifts from Tiffany, Chanel Gucci and Louis Vuitton and Surprised Royalty with a couple's massage during the day and a dinner on a yacht that night. Amir also surprised Royalty and flew them to Paris for the weekend of Royalty birthday. It was a birthday Royalty would never forget. Royalty really was going to miss all that Amir had done for her. Being so thoughtful and caring despite all Amir's cheating. Amir's desire of other women is what made him be so giving most of the time. Because Amir always felt bad about what he was doing to Royalty and Royalty remaining faithful and turning the other cheek.

Royalty was excited about tonight and couldn't wait to debut the hot pink crocodile bag. It was the perfect companion for a date. It was beautiful, classy and rich. Amir bought this bag when they were in Paris and Royalty had never wore this bag before. But tonight, Royalty was in the mood for pulling it out. It was the perfect bag with her Versace outfit and heels. Royalty loved going to Mastero's and dressing up. It made Royalty feel important and rich dining there. Royalty couldn't wait to see Jinx but more importantly Royalty couldn't wait to see who they might run into at the restaurant. Maybe Royalty could snag herself another baller and Royalty meant that literally. Arriving at Mastro's it was kinda crowded to be still early in the evening Royalty was thinking looking for Jinx car spotting her RR parked in the back. Pulling up Royalty asks valet could he park her car next to the Rolls Royce getting out looking and feeling like a million bucks. Walking in Royalty spots Jinx who was waving at her. Surveillancing the restaurant Royalty noticed what seemed like a lot of people who had appeared to be just getting off work. Because most individuals had on suit and tie and professional attire. Giving Jinx a hug Royalty sat down.

Jinx says aren't you just as cute as button. I love your satin Versace fit that's real cute. Looking Royalty over. Noticing Royalty Hermès bag grabbing it sitting it on the table. When you get this rubbing, it smiling.

Royalty laughs it was a gift from Amir for my 21st birthday.

This was the best gift ever. Jinx says admiring the bag.

Yes, it was. It was one of four Royalty replies smiling again.

Four No Amir didn't Jinx says laughing proud of Amir. Amir loved him some you Royalty. You can never replace him sincerely speaking. I miss my brother Jinx says sitting Royalty purse back down next to her.

I know that why I wanted to talk to you about that. I haven't been loyal to Amir since his death. Looking at Jinx seriously. You know ever since you introduced me to Jacques that day at his store, we've been kicking it.

Almost spitting out her water Jinx says. No, I didn't know that. Really?

Yes, it's been really consistent I think I like Jacques Royalty confesses. As on que the waitress arrives and takes their order and Royalty orders a drink that she desperately needed. Royalty nerves was bad at this point.

Well Royalty all I'm going to say is be careful and trust your gut. Jacques a very attractive man with a lot of money but Jacques is also married with a wife in Jamaica but while Jacques here in America Jacques acts like he's single.

Thank you, Royalty says to the waitress, who handed her drink while Royalty still was listening intensely to Jinx talk. I know Jinx Jacques told me he was married but said their separated Royalty says sipping her drink.

Well I don't know about that Royalty Jacques might be I mean Jacques here she's there who really knows what's really going on between them two. Doesn't really matter just don't get yourself caught up with him. Plus, you're still grieving placing her hand on Royalty hand. Take things slow don't get too involved ok. Sincerely speaking.

I know I know It's just that Jinx I think I like him Jacques makes me laugh and smile Jacques fun to be around. Royalty says sipping on her drink.

Looking shocked Jinx says it's only been like a couple weeks you already feel like that?

I don't know what I feel anymore Jinx my head is cloudy most of the time. But Jacques makes me feel good smiling. Getting up I'll be right back I'm going to the bar to get another drink Royalty says walking to the bar.

Jinx pulls out her phone and texts Jacques and tells him to meet her at her house around 9p Jinx wanted to talk to him about something important. Then puts her phone back in her purse thinking about what Royalty said about Jacques. Jinx didn't want Royalty to get hurt again Royalty was still hurting from the loss of Amir. Why two drinks Jinx asks Royalty as Royalty sat back down holding two drinks one in each hand.

Well one is a shot and the other is a chaser laughing Royalty says.

Ok little Miss Betty Ford Rehab you are driving Jinx says seriously.

I'm ok Jinx I'm good. Two drinks just makes me feel breezy not drunk. Throwing her drinks back like a real alcoholic Royalty says.

Whatever you say Royalty but please be careful. Jinx says, and Jaheem wants to know when you coming back to visit him he misses you.

I know I miss him too. Maybe next weekend Royalty says. Hearing her phone ringing a couple times then it stops. Getting her phone out her purses looking at it a missed call from an anonymous caller. Who the fuck could that be Royalty thinking. Then again Royalty Phone starts ringing anonymously. Hello who's this? Royalty answered with an attitude. Ok calm down what happened? Ok ok I'm on my way. Hanging up. Jinx I'm sorry but I have to go that was Bianca ass she's in jail and needs me to bail her out again. Royalty says shaking her head. I swear I'm going to buy some stock in the prisons and try and get some of my money back laughing Royalty says but serious as fuck.

What happened to Bianca? Jinx asks.

Who knows with her ass it's always something and its never Bianca fault Laughing and Bianca die if I leave her in there Royalty replies. Bianca just said she had a fight. That probably means Bianca was arguing with some niggas woman and if the person was with someone else Bianca felt threatened and maced them both laughing again. That's what Bianca does. Bianca not going to allow anyone to get too close to that pretty face laughing.

Bianca is Hella pretty though Jinx says laughing too shaking her head. That girl is a mess I'm going to pray for her. Standing up giving Royalty a hug goodbye. I'm going to wait for our food to come out since we ordered it. I'll just get it to go Jinx says. You want me to save yours and you come by and pick it up later? Jinx asks Royalty.

No, I don't know how long this might take but Thank you going in her wallet pulling out a hundred dollars handing it to Jinx dinner was on me remember. I love you I'll call you later Royalty says walking out waving bye. Waiting for valet to bring her car out Royalty notices a car full of dudes in a Range Rover with tinted windows pulling in wondering why all the tint. As the extra tall dudes get out the car Royalty realizes why the truck tint was so dark. They were a few celebrity basketball players going into the restaurant. Royalty started to get mad at Bianca for interfering with her flow, but Royalty knew if it was meant for her to meet any one of them, she'll see them again. Plus, they were too deep for Royalty to choose from at one time. Royalty needed them to be at least two at one time not the whole damn team. But the way Royalty sex drive was set up at this point Royalty probably could have taken them all down if Royalty wanted to with no remorse Royalty was thinking laughing to herself getting in her car driving off.

Waiting outside Lynwood county jail for this fool Bianca after having to post $10,000 bail Royalty was past irritated. Sitting in her car debating on if she should make Bianca take an Uber home or not Bianca knocks on the passenger door window. Rolling the window down just a little bit where Bianca could stick her eyes in.

Unlock the fucking car door Bitch I'm cold and quit playing let me in Bianca says angrily already mad she had to go to jail behind some bullshit again.

Why should I let you in Bianca? For the hundred time. You need to stop going to jail bitch it's not a good look. Royalty says seriously.

Fuck You Bianca says open the door yanking on the car door getting madder than she already was.

Unlocking the door Royalty says this is the last time I'm bailing you out looking at Bianca who looked like she was about to have a heart attack wow what happened? Royalty asks wanting to know all the details of what happened to get Bianca to this point again.

Drive off Bitch Bianca says before they come and rearrest my ass locking her door and leaning her seat back.

Why would they come and arrest you again what you do while you were in there? Royalty wanted to know.

Nothing bitch drive off. While Driving off Bianca starts telling Royalty the story. So, you know ole boy who was at the house the other night right? Bianca says reminding Royalty of the guy she had over at her house.

Yeah, the nurse guy? Royalty asks.

Yeah him anyways we were out eating at Benihana and his bitch comes in with two of her friends and says she has a tracker on his phone since he got caught cheating or whatever and she came to the restaurant. So, I'm drinking my drink minding my own business because that's your nigga take it up with him right. But this bitch friends keep looking at me crazy. So, I said what the fuck you looking at? To one of them standing there that was looking me up and down looking like a baby pitbull and we started arguing. Then the other ugly friend gone butt in and say. Bitches always fucking on somebody's else man, so I told her ugly ass. You'll bitches mad because you'll can't fuck on nobody's man, you'll ugly ass fuck. No real nigga would be caught dead in public with you dog face looking bitches. You better get out my face for I neuter you bitches. So, the lil Asian cook was setting up his lil area. And when one of those bitches tried to take off of me. I smashed that hoe face right on the hot ass grill and held it down until her skin started peeling off her face for fucking with me.

Bianca you better be glad you didn't get charged with attempted murder Royalty says Damn the other friend didn't help her?

By the time she tried I had grab one of the cook ginseng knives and was daring her to come near me.

Oh my God Bianca your about to go viral laughing. You know everyone in the restaurant probably recorded you on their phone. Your about to be on the Shade Room bitch on Instagram and all the blogs laughing. Royalty said

I know right Bianca says humiliated. Hella people did have their phones out thinking back. At least I'm hella cute Bianca says being conceited. Bianca did look cute though with Fendi signature sweater and jean Palazzo pants and her Fendi stocking with Fendi ankle boots and her long Nicki Minaj weave past her butt with China bangs. Bianca gave bitches a run for they money that's why they couldn't stand her ass. And the poor Benihana staff didn't know what to do Bianca said laughing they had no choice but to call the police.

Bitch that's not funny Bianca you can be in a whole lot of trouble Royalty says still in disbelief of what her crazy best friend just did.

Oh well Bianca says seriously. Bitches should stop trying me. I get a pass every time anyway because technically I'm certified crazy laughing.

Shaking her head Royalty says that story going to play out soon. Those judges going to get tired of seeing your ass in their courtrooms Laughing.

Bullshit. I'm fucking a few of them remember that one that was my sugar daddy I meet at the pub? So, I wish they would try me laughing.

You so nasty Royalty says laughing right along with Bianca. Damn shame fucking them old ass men to stay out of jail.

Shit a bitch got to do what she got to do Bianca says. Damn I need a blunt turning up the music.

Where am I dropping you off at? Royalty asks Bianca. Ready for her to get out her car.

The W hotel Bianca replies.

The what? Why you going to a hotel? Royalty wanted to know.

Because the nigga got us a room so after dinner, we could chill Bianca says laughing.

You mean to tell me bitch I bailed you out, so you can go right back to jail? Royalty says looking perplexed. You did say his woman had a tracker on his phone, didn't you?

Yeah but he dropped his phone in his drink when the bitch told him that. And when the police came, he told me to meet him at the spot when I got out Bianca says laughing.

So why didn't the nigga bail you out and instead of me? Royalty asked mad now.

Because I couldn't call him duh. But I'll make him pay you back tomorrow. Bianca says lying.

Pulling into the W hotel. Shaking her head once again. Royalty couldn't believe she feel for the bullshit again from Bianca.

Thanks sis leaning over her seat kissing Royalty cheek before getting out the car.

Rolling the passenger window down while Bianca skips her hot ass to the hotel entrance Royalty yells out the window. I'm turning my phone off bitch don't call me if them hoes come up here and jump you while you coming to chill laughing. Alright Bianca bitch you just might be chilling for real on some ice after they kill your hot ass. Rolling the window back up laughing while Bianca laughed and gave Royalty the finger going inside the hotel lobby smiling. Royalty didn't know what she was going to do with her best friend who lived her young life like everyday was her last.
Royalty was tired and just wanted to turn on her fireplace and lay down. Getting off the exit to the house Royalty gets a text message and is hesitatent to reply but plays along anyway knowing she should have left him on not read.

Jacques texts: (what's up babe you miss the D lol)

Royalty texts back: (No I don't miss the d lol)

Jacques: (babe it's a big D)

Royalty replies: (huh what are you talking about big D???)

Jacques: (you type lower case d instead of capitol D lol don't do that shit no more)

Royalty: (look Lil bow wow, Kevin Hart, Jermaine Dupri, all the short men who might seem like they have small d's but might actually have big D's I'm not interested in no d's I mean D) I'm tired.

Jacques: (why you comparing me to them niggas tho? I'm not short nor do I have a small D) Smh go to bed I'll talk to you tomorrow and remember it's a big "D"

Royalty: (come over so we can cuddle and remember no d I mean D lol)

Jacques: (I'm already at your house hurry up I'm tired too I had a long ass Day)

Royalty looked at the phone like Jacques had to be joking I know he's not at my house. But pulling into the driveway Jacques Porsche truck was parked in front. Smiling Royalty thinking damn Jacques going to be a hard one to get rid of. I guess good pussy will keep a nigga coming back for more letting up the garage pulling in.

Walking up besides Royalty Car Jacques says Hi baby opening the door for Royalty.

Hi Big D Royalty replies Laughing.

I'm glad you got your D's straight laughing with Royalty helping her out the car.

What brings you by Royalty asks Jacques.

I missed you plus I didn't want us to be on bad terms. When I left you this morning it was a little tension between us, I didn't want it to carry over for days. How was your dinner with Jinx?

Looking at Jacques like how the fuck Jacques know she had dinner with Jinx. Oh, so you following me now Royalty asked Jacques seriously walking into the house not sure if she should be bothered with his stalking ass or not.

You wish I was following you huh? Jacques says laughing. You thinking you got a nigga sprung huh? Looking Royalty in the eyes standing in front of her blocking her movement.

Well how did you know who I had dinner with then Royalty replies.

Maybe I talked to Jinx did that ever occur to you Miss I got this nigga sprung off my head game already and I'm the shit got him following me and shit!! Laughing.

Putting her head down in embarrassment Royalty chuckles. My bad.

Lifting Royalty chin up kissing her you do kinda got a nigga feeling you tho. Winking let's go cuddle grabbing Royalty hand leading her upstairs to her bedroom. Jacques gets in the shower and Royalty lights the fireplace in her bedroom and then gets in the shower with Jacques. They make love throughout most of the night, but they did cuddle until noon the following day. Jacques Phone was ringing off the hook when he reached over to grab it to see who he was going to have to cuss the fuck out. Looking at all the miss calls Jacques knew he had to take this call. Sliding from underneath Royalty kissing her back. Jacques whispers baby I have to make an emergency call I'll be right back. Getting out the bed naked walking into the bathroom closing the door or so he thought. Looking in the bathroom mirror rubbing his hand over his head. My spot got hit? How and when? For how much? Jacques was looking in the mirror at his perfectly white teeth trying to distract himself from the anger he was feeling. Listening to his boy tell him how his stash house just got hit. Dude listen that's enough I don't want to hear No more! Jacques says furious cutting the conversation short. Check this out. I need the shit to go down like the Purge my nigga tonight!! I want it to sound like the Fourth of July around this bitch. Straight fireworks light this Mother fucking city up my nigga. Then get back at me. Nigga what you mean why I didn't call you back earlier? I was chilling with my girl nigga that's why? Anything else you need to know nigga?

Did this fool just say he was chilling with his girl? Royalty thinking to herself eavesdropping on Jacques conversation not believing what she just heard him say. Did Jacques just put me in a relationship with him without my consent? And did this fool say he just got robbed and ordered a hit on whoever did it? Telling his boys to do a Purge. Royalty was so confused. Wondering if Jacques was referring to the movie. What the fuck did I get myself into Royalty thinking. This shit can't be really happening. Closing her eyes really tight and pulling the covers over her head hoping that this was some sort of a bad dream.

Continuing his conversation Jacques says to the caller and nigga don't call me back until it's done or else!! Jacques says before hanging up and turning on the sink to wash his face and brush his teeth. Walking out the bathroom Jacques walks over to Royalty and rubs on her ass saying wake up sleepyhead.

Royalty was playing sleep like she hadn't heard a thing that Jacques was just talking about. But Royalty was light way terrified of this man Royalty hardly knew judging from his conversation, but Royalty was feeling him at the same time. Royalty was thinking to herself her life was a fucking movie and she should sale her script to Paramount pictures or something it would be a blockbuster movie for damn sure.
Royalty body reacts to Jacques touch and Royalty pokes her ass out and Jacques pulls the comforter back and climbs on top of Royalty kissing her neck. Whispering in her ear babe you know morning sex gets you pregnant licking on Royalty ear lobe.

Is that right? taking a deep breath while Jacques slid inside her Royalty says smiling.

Stroking slow and passionate while kissing on Royalty neck while humping on her ass going in and out of Royalty Jacques says. I can't seem to get enough of you stroking faster. This pussy is driving me wild matching Royalty strokes that Royalty was throwing back on Jacques. The sound of Royalty moaning turned Jacques into a beast. Jacques pulled Royalty Hair bringing her face to his while lifting her ass ramming his dick inside her uncontrollably. Whose pussy is this Jacques asks pumping faster

Ohh baby it's yours Royalty yells out.

Say my name baby tell me who's pussy this is increasing his strokes.

Moaning because it felt so good. Royalty yells out Ohh Jacques baby this your pussy coming all over Jacques making him cum with her releasing her hair and falling on top of Royalty with his excessive breathing.

I just made a deposit of a set of twins inside you ma Jacques says breathing like he just ran a race.

Trying to catch her breath also. Royalty replies that was a set of triplet's babe laughing. But Please Get off me Jacques I can't breathe Royalty says seriously feeling like she needed an inhaler and she didn't even have asthma. They both feel back to sleep in each other's arms and didn't wake up until the sound of the doorbell woke Royalty and Jacques up looking at each other like what the fuck. Getting out of bed grabbing her robe Royalty heads downstairs to see who was at her door knocking like the police. Jacques goes into the bathroom to pee and got in the shower. Opening the door Bianca walks in Hella loud.

Bitch what's wrong with you? Looking at Royalty all strange. Who you got up in here looking around waiting for someone to appear.

Shh why you so loud damn. Royalty says fixing her robe.

Laughing at Royalty Bianca says. I know what you were doing tapping Royalty shoulder. Girl you was doing the nasty smiling. That nigga must got some good good bitch because you haven't gotten off that dick since you first rode it. Sitting her Gucci bag down on the kitchen counter walking into the kitchen going into the pantry looking for some snacks.

What do you want Bianca? sitting down Royalty says. I have company.

Looking back at Royalty Bianca says So! shrugging her shoulders. And what's that's supposed to mean? Bianca asks. You'll already disrespected my brother's house fucking in his bed. Grabbing some barbecue chips and getting a soda out the refrigerator and sitting down opposite of Royalty. Did you even change the sheets that you and Amir slept on bitch before you let that nigga hit? Bianca asks seriously.

Rolling her eyes Royalty says What do you want Bianca getting up getting herself a glass of water.

Babe you want to go out to eat? Jacques says walking down the stairs looking like a tall glass of chocolate milk.

Damn you Fine Bianca says staring at Jacques who didn't have a shirt or shoes on. Only his jeans, I almost forgot what you looked like. Bianca says lustfully.

Laughing Jacques replies. What's up Bianca how you feeling since your accident? Walking up behind Royalty kissing on her neck. Babe I know you hungry get dressed so we can grab something to eat. Jacques says in Royalty ear.

I'm going with You'll Bianca yells out. Jacques you know me, and Royalty are twins laughing.

Jacques turns Royalty around and looks her in her face and then turns to Bianca then says. Yes, I can see the resemblance laughing. Me and Royalty damn near made some twins this morning Laughing slapping Royalty on her ass while she walked away going up the stairs laughing also.

I'm going to take a shower I'll be ready in a few Royalty says. You'll kids play nicely running up the stairs Royalty says trying to be quick.

So, Jacques you feeling my girl I see eating her chips Bianca says.

Yeah, she cool peoples. I'm feeling her. And hopefully she's feeling me too. Jacques replies.

Are you serious right now? Bianca says about to run her mouth like diarrhea and tell all the business. You're the only man Royalty been with besides Amir. Royalty's really into women you know?

Jacques was looking at Bianca like is that right? Royalty forgot to mention that. I'll keep a mental note tho.

And my girl got you all in her dead niggas house and shit that's big for her. Royalty never lets anyone knows where she lives at. I'm her best friend and I barely came over this mother fucker when Amir was alive laughing. Shit the other spot I've never even been too. Royalty and Amir was hella secretive. I'm really surprised Royalty fucking with you like she is. So, I know Royalty must really like you. You must be really be putting it down on my girl looking Jacques up and down making him feel uncomfortable.

I'll be back Jacques says running up the stairs to get dressed. And get away from that Volture of a best friend of Royalty.

Coming out the bathroom with her towel wrapped around her hair Royalty jumps in surprise when Jacques comes in the room and closes the bedroom door. Oh, Jacques you scared me jumping Royalty says laughing.

No babe your friend scares me Jacques says laughing. What's up with all the questions like a detective babe? Laughing

Royalty says that's how Bianca is. She's Miss Little Sherlock Holmes babe laughing. Speaking of Sherlock Holmes Royalty was thinking she was going to put Bianca noisy ass on the case to get the 411 on Jacques ass. Royalty wanted to know all Jacques business and Bianca was the right person for the job. Bianca could find anything out about anyone she wanted to Bianca knew everybody's business.

You so fine baby Jacques says to Royalty checking out her nakedness. Royalty was a little brick house.

Thank you, Royalty says walking, into her closet switching her ass because Royalty knew Jacques was watching her.

Sitting on the bed putting his shirt and shoes on. Jacques thinking there's no way Royalty likes girls. Jacques couldn't be that lucky could he. Shit Royalty was a bonafide freak though. Good looks, good pussy had her own bag and Royalty went both ways. Jacques started counting his blessings and started feeling grateful.

Walking out the closet looking delicious Jacques could have stripped Royalty right out of her clothes Royalty just had put on Royalty looked so damn good to Jacques. Wearing Black Nike leggings that looked painted on her ass with a black nike wife beater black, Blue and white Jordan's with a Nike black cap with her hair curly underneath it. But it was her natural beauty that captivated Jacques. Even without any makeup on Royalty was beautiful. Royalty face was angelic to Jacques and Jacques really noticed that Royalty favored the actress Lauren London. Royalty looked like she could be her little sister. Jacques could see how Royalty could easily have a bunch of niggas because every nigga Jacques knew had a hard on for Lauren London fine ass.

Smiling at Jacques Royalty says you ok over there?

Smiling back at Royalty Jacques says yeah, I'm good baby. I like how you switch it up and still be on point. But I'm not sure I'm comfortable with you showing your ass off like that? Laughing but serious as fuck.

Royalty turns around and twerks a little laughing. Where we eating at, I'm starving? Royalty says hungry as hell.

Me too baby you make a nigga work up an appetite Laughing. Fucking with you a nigga will be hella big.

Your slim what you talking about Jacques. I'm the thick one in this relationship Royalty says laughing.

Oh, we in a relationship now? Jacques says. Let me know so I can let all my hoes go Laughing. Singing I got hoes in different area codes.

Laughing with Jacques Royalty says. You know what I meant boy. Thinking to herself how did she let that slip out that's not how she felt was it? Royalty was just having fun with Jacques that was it nothing more nothing less. Can we go to Ruth Chris I want some Lobster macaroni and cheese Royalty asks?

We can go wherever you want cutie. You want to go to the moon I'll take you there winking at Royalty Jacques says seriously.

I like that Royalty responds looking in the mirror giving herself a one over before leaving. Heading downstairs Royalty tells Jacques that they'll drive in separate cars because after going to the restaurant Royalty wanted to stop off at her Hair salon to catch up on some work she needed to do.

That's cool Jacques says I have some business to take care of later also walking to his car. I'll meet you'll there.

Can you drive? Royalty asks Bianca who was looking at her crazy walking to her car.

Bitch you don't know if I have plans or not why can't you drive?

Do you have plans Royalty asks Bianca?

No not at the moment but. Bianca says.

Well that settles it I'm riding with you Royalty says walking to Bianca Car laughing thinking this bitch thinks she's slick always trying to dip out after a free meal.

We're too Bianca says looking at Royalty crazy again.

Ruth Chris smiling Royalty says.

What you smiling about Bianca asks and why do I always have to drive?

Girl just drive and shut up turning up the music drowning Bianca out. Royalty wasn't in the mood for Bianca shenanigans tonight.

Arriving at the restaurant Bianca mood changes instantly from irritated to excited. Bitch this Car lineup in Valet parking ain't no joke chessing hella hard looking at all the foreign cars. Rolls Royce, Ferrari, Jaguars Bianca was in her Bentley and Jacques was in his Porsche Truck.

Shaking her head Royalty says to Bianca that's a damn shame you let this bullshit excite you. Most of these niggas are for everyone and have no substance Laughing.

Bitch who you talking too? looking around Bianca says like I know you're not talking to me? I don't give a fuck about none of that shit. I'm For Everybody to the fuck!! I just want a nigga with some money to spoil me, fuck me good and take me shopping. All that other shit is for the other mother fuckers he dealing with. He can do him because I'm definitely going to do me.

Rolling her eyes getting out the car Royalty just laughed to herself because Royalty knew Bianca meant every word she just said. Jacques was waiting for them at the restaurant entrance Jacques had gotten them a table and thank God Jacques had connections because the restaurant had no openings, they were completely full and to their capacity.

It's all in who you know Jacques says walking to the table. Ladies gesturing for Royalty and Bianca to sit down first.

Ordering their drinks having small talk Bianca spots a chick her and Royalty went to high school with sitting at a booth with a dude and two kids. Royalty isn't that Shannon who we went to school with sitting over there with that dude? he looks familiar Bianca asks.

Trying not to be too obvious Royalty turns around and looks over in her direction. As soon as Royalty looks over at Shannon, she spots Royalty and looks and then waves at Royalty. Royalty waves back and gives her a fake smile because they weren't really ever friends like that. Getting up walking towards Royalty. Shannon comes up to the table and greets everyone.

Hi Royalty, it's been years since we've seen each other how are you doing? Looking at everyone at the table.

I'm good and you Shannon, right? Royalty says.

Yes, girl you remember me. You and Hi Bianca turning to speak to Bianca who didn't speak back. You remember you and Bianca tried to jump me staring at Bianca.

No correction we did jump you Bianca says rolling her eyes.

Turning her attention back to Royalty Shannon says. Anyways girl it's good seeing you. You look good. That's my husband and two sons over there pointing to her family. My husband plays in the NFL for the Los Angeles Rams. Smiling like she was rubbing something in their faces.

That's nice, cute kids Royalty says.

So, I see some people do change Bianca interrupts Shannon and says.

Huh excuse me? Shannon says looking unsure of what Bianca was referring to.

Oh, your shocked huh? Me too Bianca says. I'm shocked somebody married your ass because you was the biggest toss up in high school you fucked everybody that's why me and Royalty jumped you. Over Freddie you remember now? Refreshing Shannon memory. Don't come over her trying to front on us bitch.

Calm down Bianca Royalty says laughing.

Shannon walked away flabbergasted.

You didn't have to bust her out like that Bianca Royalty says laughing.

Damn you'll two are beast Jacques says laughing. I hate to be on the receiving end of some beef with you two. Shaking his head.

Naw fuck that she asked for it Laughing Bianca says. Shit trying to come over here acting all prissy and shit. Bitch fucked the whole football team in high school. Now she's married to one. Imagine that. She's probably fucking his teammates too because them little boys don't look like her husband.

Royalty wanted to look over at Shannon table so bad, but Royalty didn't want to Look noisy. Let me know when Shannon gets up to leave so I can wave bye Royalty said then I can get a good look at her husband laughing to Bianca who was on her Phone googling Shannon husband.

When the waitress finally came to take the order Bianca Lil greedy self ordered the whole damn menu. Lamb chops, stuffed mushrooms crab meat, Spicy shrimp, grilled Asparagus, crab cakes, and lobster Mac and cheese. Jacques was looking like really this can't be happening. Looking at Bianca then back at Royalty in amazement. Royalty just shrugged her shoulders. Jacques ordered a steak and Royalty shared most of Bianca food with her since Bianca ordered so much.

Shannon husband got up to go to the restroom and not even five minutes later Bianca had to go to the restroom also. Your girl is going to be messy Jacques inquired.

Yep sure is Royalty says laughing. Bianca a hot ass mess. Bianca doesn't mean any harm most of the time Bianca just can't help herself, I guess.

A few minutes later sitting back down smiling Bianca says I'm ready to go I have other plans looking at Royalty like I'm going to leave you. Oh, and thank you for dinner Jacques the next meal is on me.

Never and your welcome Jacques says I was raised to treat women like queens. You'll never pay for anything when you're with me finishing his food.

Alrighty then Bianca says. I need to clone your ass laughing.

Jacques started laughing too. American men are different their values are different than my country. We don't even like our women to work in my country.

Well I need to live over there in your country Bianca says seriously.

I couldn't live there Royalty says I don't want to be controlled like that.

Who said anything about control? Bianca says.

Well if you rely on a man for everything, he controls you right or wrong? Royalty says.

Well in my county we take care of our women some do work but they don't have to Jacques interjected.

Still I don't want to have to ask nobody for nothing Royalty says, I want some independence. Does your wife have to ask you for money? Royalty asks Jacques.

Wait you have a wife? Bianca says curiously.

Yes, Bianca I have a wife in Jamaica we're separated though.

Yeah right you expect me to believe that Bianca says laughing you'll probably don't even have separation in your country. It's probably against the law to get a divorce there Laughing. Plus, can't you'll have as many wives as you like?

Jacques wasn't fazed by none of Bianca questions. He simply said. I have no reason to lie I'm a grown ass man. My word is my bond and to answer your question Royalty no she doesn't have the ask me for anything. She's very well taken care of. There's enough money in the bank for generations to come plus she comes from a wealthy family then Jacques continued eating his food.

Bianca and Royalty looked at each other but didn't say a word. This was the first nigga to leave them both speechless. Royalty was looking and feeling so dumbfounded that Royalty didn't even see Shannon and her family leave out.
Leaving out the restaurant saying their goodbyes Royalty gives Jacques a goodbye kiss hit me later Jacques says getting in his truck.

Sure, will Royalty replies getting in the car with Bianca who was rolling her weed.

Jacques phone started ringing from a blocked number and Jacques was thinking who the fuck is this answering it. What's up? Who this?

Nigga it's your worst nightmare the caller said. You pussy ass nigga laughing.

Pussy huh? Then nigga why you calling from a block number fool? Man, up and reveal your identity nigga. Let's link up Jacques says Pulling his gun out placing it on his lap just in case the nigga on the other end hiding was somewhere nearby.

I'm the nigga that's hitting your spots and I'm the nigga you should be worried about still laughing.

Looking at his phone Jacques was heated but calmly responded is that right? Well for one I'm never worried about the next man and what he has going on. And nigga if you have to try and take from me you obviously need it.

Try nigga I took!! Screaming in the phone at Jacques.

Calm down Lil telephone gangster what you took yelling back I make in a day. Now laughing.

Oh, nigga you think it's funny you soft ass nigga. The caller says irritated.

Ain't nothing soft about me nigga but my dick right now laughing Jacques says and you should have done a background check on me first before you decided to Try and rob me nigga. I changed my life nigga, so you could enjoy yours. But shit gone change in a few minutes. So, don't hold your breath or your miss out on your last minutes of breathing hanging up on the caller.
Grabbing his burner phone out the glove department Jacques calls his boy.

Hello, the person says on the other end.

Where you'll at? Jacques asks

At the spot? The caller replies

Ok bet there's a change of plans. I'm on my way. Put my gear together I'll be there in 5 mins Jacques says hanging up. When Jacques reaches the spot, the caravan was out front that let Jacques know everyone was ready. Jacques goes inside to change his clothes.

What you mean you gearing up? One of Jacques homeboy says as he walks in.

It means exactly what the fuck I said. Don't worry you niggas still getting paid for this hit but now it's a little personal Jacques says putting on his all black dickeys' uniform and bulletproof vest. I got some black timbs here don't I? Jacques asks no one in particular. Yep in the closet in the back someone blurts out.

Walking to the bedroom to retrieve his boots Jacques sees a few guns lying on the bed and grabs them also. Walking back into the den holding the guns up Jacques asks who left these lying on the bed?

High as fuck Black says nigga, I was tripping a nigga high as hell laughing.

So, you niggas know these fools are hitting my spots and you niggas leaving guns lying around it's bad enough these niggas taking candy from me and making me lose money at the same time. And you want to leave guns out too? Looking around at everybody. That's like giving niggas guns to kill your asses with. Looking disappointed.

My bad black says right before Jacques shoots him in the stomach.

My bad too my nigga Jacques says as Black falls to the ground screeching in pain.

Black cry's out nigga it was an accident holding his stomach.

I only want niggas around me I can trust Jacques says. Leaving guns out for my enemies can never be by accident. then Jacques shoots Black in the face that sealed the deal and walks out and tells one of his boys to set the house on fire.

Getting in the van Jacques asks his boy Fresh did he have eyes on them niggas and Fresh said yep at the pool hall on Crenshaw and Exposition Blvd.

Checking the clip Jacques gets prepared for the task at hand. It was something he had to do to redeem himself. Especially since this nigga wanted to call him a pussy ass nigga.

Well we'll just see about that Jacques was thinking pulling up to the spot. Park down the street and follow my que Jacques says let's go pulling his black ski mask over his face just in case. No innocent bystanders if we can help it Jacques says jumping out the van revved up let's go. Storming in the pool hall lighting shit up. Bam bam bam bodies started dropping everywhere. People was screaming and hollering hitting the floor for cover. These niggas didn't even see it coming. The shot caller or ring leader whatever title he went by tried to run out the back, but the gate was locked and he couldn't get too far. Running right behind him Jacques takes off his mask and says you going somewhere nigga laughing.

Look man can't we just work this out stuttering and pleading for his life.

Wait nigga just a minute ago you was talking all that hard shit niggas always playing games thinking they winning until a nigga like me put that shit on two players laughing. Talking all that boss shit nigga, you robbed me, I'm a pussy ass nigga blah, blah, blah. Jacques says sarcastically. Jacques three boys had came to join him in the back now that they cleaned house.

This that fool who robbed us? Fresh asks Jacques.

Yep that's him the head nigga in charge. He says we can work something out what you'll think about that? Looking around at his boys. They all removed their masks briefly and laughed.

Look I will give you all the money and dope I got put up in a safe house in Pasadena the nigga says for exchange for his life.

You mean your girls house on 590 Ellis Street? Oh, my boy already there and got that on lock my nigga. I told him to kill everything that moved Jacques replied.

Sweating and crying pleading please don't kill my girl she had nothing to do with this.

So now you calling me a liar to my face Jacques says? You know as well as I do that your bitch set all this up fucking with my boy Black and learning my moves and spots and then she reported back to you. Well buddie don't worry you'll be together soon. Jacques says seriously speaking. Bam one shot to the head and all his worries was over. Jacques boy Fresh shot him again in the chest just in case because believe it or not some people survive headshots. Placing his mask back on Jacques tells his boys get their keys to their cars and let's roll out. Within 7 mins of handing business police sirens and helicopters could be heard coming from everywhere. The van had been long gone. And Jacques and his boys was headed to them niggas hood to do a drive by in their cars so them other niggas wouldn't know what hit they asses. Jacques and his boys wasn't the type of niggas to be playing with. They set the city of Los Angeles on fire this night literally.

Going to the salon to do some paperwork and pay some bills Royalty sets down at her desk in her office and turns the tv on. Immediately there's breaking news. Five black men gunned down at a pool hall on Crenshaw tonight around 7pm looks like a targeted hit because several people were left unharmed but said they couldn't identify the shooters because they were told to lay down facing the ground with their eyes closed. The shooters came in and shoot and killed 5 men whose names have been withheld until the families are notified. Also breaking news, a drive by shooting in Inglewood projects that killed six men shooting dice and left one person injured and was taken to the hospital with life threatening injuries. Damn the world is so cruel Royalty thinking to herself about to cut the television off when another breaking news flash came across the screen. More breaking news firefighters are trying to put out a 7 alarm house fire in Pasadena that's believed to be a weed growing house police say they had been alerted to this property several times before because of electrical issues and electrical bills in the thousands that alone gave the tip to the electric company that someone was using more electricity than normal indicating some foul and abnormal behavior. The fire department suspects that a malfunction may have been the cause that set the house on fire. The fire department isn't sure if anyone was in the home at the time of the fire. Stay tuned for more details. That was enough Royalty couldn't take no more bad news. Jacques crossed Royalty mind, so Royalty decided to call and check up on Jacques Pulling her cell out and calling Jacques number.

Hello what's good cutie? you still working Jacques asks.

Yep Royalty replies just got to the shop fooling around with Bianca ratchet self had me on a wild goose chase with some nigga she met Laughing.

Is that right Jacques responds yawning? I just woke up. I was Hella tired and full after fooling with you babe laughing. You wore a nigga out.

Smiling Royalty says. Do you ever watch the news? Hella shit happened tonight. A drive by in Inglewood a killing at a pool hall and a weed house on fire in Pasadena.

Babe stop watching all that depressing shit ok. Jacques says laughing. The only people that watch the news are mad ass people laughing. I only watch the news when I want to get mad at some shit Jacques says laughing because I'm always happy.

Laughing with Jacques Royalty agrees forreal huh babe? That's crazy. I'm about to be here working for a few hours I got a lot of paperwork to catch up on.

Still yawning Jacques says. Bet. I'm about to take a quick shower and have a nightcap and go back to bed a nigga put in some work these past few days fucking around with you and now I need to catch up on my rest laughing again.

Whatever boy I'll talk to you tomorrow goodnight. Royalty says.

Same to you cutie and don't let Bianca get you fucked Up chilling with no other nigga laughing. Jacques says seriously.

Boy go to sleep you hella tired Royalty says laughing hanging up in Jacques face.

Walking into Royalty office scaring the shit out of her. Damn Bianca I be forgetting you got a key holding her chest. Bitch the news was lit tonight you saw it? Royalty asks Bianca.

Yes, bitch I had a client who wanted to watch the news before going out for her anniversary and after watching the news she changed her mind. She said they were doing their anniversary right at Home laughing with her Face beat and all.

That shit was crazy Royalty replies.

These fools ain't playing in these streets about they respect bitch. I'm going to have to stop talking so much shit to mother fuckers laughing. Bitch before a nigga kill my punk ass Bianca says seriously.

Looking at Bianca like this the realest shit Bianca ever said. Amen to that you do be talking hella crazy to people light way disrespectful ass fuck. Royalty says. Hitting the remote for the stereo turning on Nicki Minaj King Kong to change the mood.

Pour me a drink Bianca says to Royalty who was headed to the mini bar to pour herself one.

Turning around looking over her shoulder damn bitch do I have to do everything for you? Laughing. And don't be picky either you drinking what I'm drinking pouring two shots of Hennessy and grabbing two Red Bull's out the mini fridge. Here handing Bianca her drink. Let's toast to new beginnings and happiness bitch. Clicking glasses.

Taking their shots. Bianca replies I'll drink to that. I'll be back to get you in a few hours Bianca says setting her glass down on the mahogany wood desk and walks to the door and looks at Royalty. Bitch we all we got winking her eye. You my bitch for life twerking and laughing.

Royalty started twerking in her chair laughing too. Ok bitch I should be done in a few hours probably around midnight don't be late Royalty says pulling her gun out from her purse setting it on her desk just in case.

I won't walking out Bianca says.

Oh, and make sure you lock the doors behind you Royalty yells out. Looking over all the work she had to do that couldn't be put off any longer. Royalty hated this part of running a business, but Royalty didn't trust nobody with the books but herself especially when it came to getting to the money. Amir also told Royalty that she had to stay on top of handling business pertaining to the money. Because no matter how much money you may have someone will try you if you don't know how much money you have yourself. Having an accountant was cool but Amir always double checked everything before anything was paid out. Amir always said nobody was going to hustle him out of the money he was hustling for. Royalty started drinking her Red Bull because Royalty knew she was going to need it and then Royalty started taking care of the business that took care of her. Bills wasn't going to pay themselves plus it took Royalty mind off everything else Royalty had going on even if it was just temporarily. Doing normal shit Made Royalty feel better even if it was just for a few hours.
Waking up to a hard on Jacques instantly thinks about Royalty wishing Royalty was laying next to him to give him some of her bomb head that makes his stomach cave in like a Capri sun drink when you still sucking and it's nothing left in the pouch.

Royalty wakes up to Bianca cussing some nigga out telling telling him to get the fuck out her house and that his dick was so small Bianca felt like beating his bitch up for getting mad over him cheating on her when his bitch should have been the one actually doing all the cheating. Bianca told him he was a side chick too and Royalty bust up laughing when Royalty heard that and wish she would've followed her first mind and went home like she planned on doing. But no Bianca was so high and drunk Bianca needed Royalty once again to drive her and her new Lil Boo Home and be a third wheel as usual. Getting up going into the adjoining bathroom in the room. Thank goodness because Royalty didn't want any parts of Bianca love triangle this morning or any morning as a matter of fact. Royalty planned on freshening up and sneaking out. Calling an Uber when Royalty was ready but instead Jacques just text her good morning so Royalty thinking she'll have Jacques pick her up instead.

Reading Jacques text: Good Morning Beautiful I hope you slept well and dreamed about me!!!

Replying back Royalty text: Always Lol come pick me up Player I'm at Bianca and I'm sneaking out in 10 mins I need a ride pls can you come save me? Lol

Replying back Jacques texts: Absolutely I'm on my way forward your location.

Royalty text her location from google maps and tiptoe out the bedroom peeking around to make sure Bianca doesn't hear her leaving. But Bianca couldn't hear if her own house was getting robbed because Bianca and the dude was screaming profanities at each other over the loud music. Royalty was so glad to get out of there when she did because wasn't no telling what was about to jump off and Royalty didn't want to be an accessory to nobody bullshit. Closing the door behind her softly Royalty walks to the corner to wait for Jacques who pulled up within 20 mins. Damn that was quick you would think you lived right around the corner Royalty said getting in the car laughing.

I was already heading out to the boutique when I texted you, I was about to walk out the door. You know I drive jets baby Laughing Jacques says.

I see looking at his 2 seater Porsche. You drive a different car every day huh? Royalty asks.

But the truth was Jacques didn't want no one to ever recognize him for driving a certain kind of car. Jacques switched up cars often with multiple colors to confuse people. For all that they knew Jacques could be renting cars as much as Jacques changed them. Jacques learned that from his dad. His father never drove one Car twice in a week. He drove a different car everyday unless he got chauffeured. Jacques grew up seeing boss moves and emulated what he saw every day growing up including having multiple women whenever Jacques wanted too. But it was something about Royalty Jacques couldn't get enough of. Royalty was definitely different from all the rest Jacques had dealt with prior to her. Where to Beautiful Jacques asks Royalty?

Home I need to wash my ass laughing Royalty says.

Looking over at Royalty Jacques asks why what you do last night? Raising his eyebrow wanting to know.

Laughing Royalty says nothing fool hitting Jacques shoulder playfully. I just need to wash my ass and get dressed and start my day. I already brushed my teeth at Bianca I keep some toiletries there, but I couldn't get dressed because I had to leave out in a hurry before a 187 occurred Royalty says laughing.

Who was Bianca going to kill you? Jacques asks thinking he would have put Bianca on ice if it came down to it hopefully Royalty was kidding.

No fool laughing Royalty says Bianca had some dude she was fooling around with he spent the night and they got into it this morning.

Oh, ok I'm glad it didn't have anything to do with you Jacques says seriously speaking.

Royalty was starting to feel Jacques on another level. Royalty couldn't stop smiling and kept looking at Jacques while he drove. Pulling up to Royalty house before getting out Royalty says Thank you so much, I really appreciate all that you do.

Is that right Jacques replies prove it then laughing but was serious as fuck? Catching Royalty off guard.

Prove what Royalty asks?

That you appreciate me Jacques replies. Go on a mini vacation with me then. Jacques says waiting for Royalty to say no and make up hella excuses.

Ok when? Royalty asks. I'm ready when you are.

Really you ready? Jacques asks again. We're leaving tonight so be ready by 10pm leaning over his seat kissing Royalty. Oh, and pack lightly well shop when we get there. Just bring all your medication and shit laughing.

Wait what medication you talking about I don't take no meds Royalty says hella confused.

You know those crazy pills you need to be taking Laughing because your ass is crazy ass fuck.

Royalty started laughing too. Opening the car door. Fuck you I'll see you tonight and I'm not bringing no credit cards either so don't play yourself. Your bag better be heavy because my shopping habits can get a little wild winking her eye and popping her collar.

It ain't trickin if you got it winking back. Jacques says seriously Let me worry about my bag love trust me whatever you spend I can blow in a day it's nothing to a boss! Now close my car door and go get ready for this adventure blowing Royalty a kiss and Royalty caught it with her hand.

Waving bye walking backwards looking at Jacques drive off Royalty was like what has she gotten herself into she couldn't be that lucky. Walking into the house Royalty looked in the gigantic crystal mirror in her foyer that hung over a glass console table with fresh red roses sitting on it at herself and saw that smile Jacques kept on her face and told herself it was ok to love again.
Royalty put her keys down on the kitchen counter and made herself a mimosa and went and sat in the living room looking out the balcony at the blue clear sky thinking was she making the right decision and was she moving too fast with Jacques second guessing herself. Sipping her mimosa Royalty decided to call Bianca to get a second opinion even though Royalty knew Bianca never thought rationally. Speed dialing Bianca number Bianca picked up on the first ring.

Bitch you snuck outta here again with your punk ass Bianca said laughing.

Ain't shit funny hoe don't nobody want to be an accessory to murder bitch I'm trying to live my best life not end my life fucking around with your bullshit. Anyways is that Lil dick nigga gone?

Laughing Bianca says yes, he just left after he tried to beat this pussy up to try to prove he was packing some heat. But Bitch it was the same result the nigga came up short once again laughing.

Damn poor Him Royalty says somely. Anyways guess what?

What's up? Bianca responds you cool over there? You miss me?

No bitch I don't actually Royalty says but Jacques wants to take me shopping out the country.

Bitch where? Yelling in the phone. You lucky bitch I wish it was me, but I keep finding these scrubs the passenger and shit laughing.

You like homeless men bitch Royalty says to Bianca. You like fixing them up and having them need you for shit. Fuck all that. I like mine established already Laughing. I want the fucking CFO bitch not the janitor laughing.

Well bitch I like mines hood bitch and what's wrong with the janitor Bianca says.

Nothing wrong with the janitor if he's trying to become the CEO Royalty replies but a hood CEO laughing with Bianca.

So, when you'll leaving? Bianca asks

Tonight at 10 Royalty replies

Tonight!! Damn what that nigga rushing for he running from the police? Laughing Bianca asks

No bitch he's not. Jacques asked me to go away before, but I lied and said I was busy.

Why you lie? You scared or something? Bianca asks.

Well kinda it's so soon I mean what would people think?

Who is people and why do you even care what people think? You ain't fucking the people, are you? The people ain't taking you out the country shopping, are they? These people your referring to what bills they pay at your house? I'm curious because last time I checked the people worked for you bitch. Bianca said. You know I could care less what the people say about me. The people can suck my ass laughing.

That's why I love you best friend you always gas me up Royalty said feeling pumped. But I don't want nobody to know just yet like Jinx.

Fuck Jinx Bianca said. Who's going to tell her anyways I ain't. Shit that's your family not mine I don't owe Jinx ass no explanations about shit. Bianca says seriously. And truthfully you don't either. So, stop beating yourself up and live your best life bitch I'm happy for you. I was worried about you until you meet Jacques fine ass. You better be glad I didn't get him first because you know I would have been fake pregnant by now laughing.

Shaking her head Royalty laughs not the fake pregnancy your notorious for. Damn you ain't cool Bianca bitch. Royalty says laughing feeling better about her decision to go out of town with Jacques. Listen Bianca I need a huge favor though.

Anything for you what you need me to come beat your face before leaving? Bianca says

Oh yeah that too but I need you to do a background check on Jacques for me please. Royalty says seriously.

Laughing falling on the floor off the bed Bianca drops her phone.

Hello, hello bitch you still there Royalty yells in the phone.

Picking up her phone still laughing Bianca says bitch a background check why? You already fucked him, your about to go out of town with the nigga and you want a background check now. That's hella backwards. Why now you think he's a serial killer or something Laughing.

Look just see what they saying in the streets and text me damn. What if Jacques gets me out of town and kills me or something? Royalty says.

Then I just have to identify your body bitch. So, make sure your cute at all times. Because I'm going to be hella mad if you're wearing something ugly ass fuck and I have to identify your ass Laughing. Bianca said.

You ain't cool seriously laughing at Bianca Royalty says.

Ok ok still laughing not able to contain herself Bianca says I'll be over there by 6:30 with your scary ass. I don't even know why you even carry a gun for bitch. You think it makes you look cute or something but what happens when it comes time to shoot it you punk ass bitch still laughing. Bianca couldn't believe Royalty right now acting all nervous and shit for what. What could happen while they went out of town? Jacques seemed hella cool with a lot of dineros. Shit Bianca was thinking if it was her, she wouldn't give a fuck if that fine ass nigga was a serial killer or not Bianca would travel the world helping get rid of bodies on some real Bonnie and Clyde shit. Still laughing at Royalty seriously wanting a background check on that nigga. The only background check Royalty needed was the background noise that nigga Made why beating up that pussy. Bianca was thinking still laughing hanging up the phone.

Ten o'clock on the dot Jacques driver pulled up in a Maybach to pick Royalty up. Looking out the door Royalty really felt like Royalty at this moment. Jacques wasn't playing fair and Jacques was actually making it hard for the next man to even get one in if he tried to with Royalty. Stepping out the car and walking up to Royalty door to retrieve Royalty overnight bag Jacques looked hella good and Jacques smelled good also. Royalty legs started shaking Royalty didn't know why but they did. Jacques had on a Fendi sweater with black jeans and Fendi sneakers and Jacques was wearing a black Fedora with Cartier shades on and a thick gold chain. Looking like old money. Royalty couldn't keep her eyes off Jacques and Jacques knew it. It's something about a man with confidence that turned Royalty on. Strong men was an aphrodisiac to Royalty it was something about their swag that turned Royalty on. Handing Jacques her overnight bag they locked eyes for a brief moment and they both smiled at the same time. Royalty was getting excited all over again. Royalty felt like a kid at Christmas time anticipating opening their gifts. Jacques grabbed Royalty hand and led Royalty to the car and put her luggage in the trunk and then got in the back and sat right beside Royalty.
Damn you smell delicious Royalty said what are you wearing sniffing on Jacques neck nibbling on it.

Smiling real hard Jacques says. Oh, you like that huh? I smell good baby? It's my favorite cologne right now it's called Mojave Ghost staring at Royalty smiling. You look nice cutie I like your ensemble Jacques says still smiling looking Royalty over like Royalty was a steak dinner.

Kicking her leg up on Jacques lap to give him a better view of her thigh high suede black boot and Gucci stockings. I'm glad you like it just a little something something I put together lying. Because Bianca had picked out Royalty whole attire for tonight.

Bianca was all in Royalty closet pulling outfits out until Bianca found the perfect one saying you're wearing this one Sis, so you can fuck his head up when Jacques sees you excitedly. Bianca laid out a black velvet strapless corset with black leather shorts with Royalty Big buckle Gucci belt and a long black and red Gucci cardigan sweater and Royalty blinged out Gucci glasses with Royalty black suede Gucci bag. Bianca had Royalty Gucci down to her socks literally. Bianca even flat ironed Royalty long jet black Hair that hung to her ass with a part down the middle and did Royalty makeup flawless with red lips. Bianca even took hella pictures of Royalty and posted Royalty on the gram. With a caption that read (I'm Not Posting My Bish For The Likes Because You Hoes Don't Like Her Anyways But All You'll Niggas Do!!) And Bianca instantly got a few thousand likes and comments on Royalty picture. Bianca knew she would be receiving a few niggas sliding in her Dm inquiring about Royalty who barely even went on Instagram.

Pulling into the airport private security area Royalty knew they were about to get on a private plane. Where are you taking me? Royalty asked Jacques who just kept staring at Royalty.

You'll find out when we get there Jacques says not even giving Royalty a hint. When the car stops right in front of the private jet the driver opens the door for his two passengers to exit. Stepping out first Jacques takes Royalty hand and leads Royalty to the red carpet that lead to the stairwell of the plane. Walking up the six steps bending his head to enter the plane Jacques looks at Royalty and asks Royalty if she was ready to go to paradise.

And Royalty softly replies back yes as long as I'm going with you, I'm ready to go anywhere smiling from ear to ear boarding the plane which Jacques who had arranged to have a bottle of champagne on ice waiting and two dozen yellow roses because yellow meant happiness and success to Jacques and a box of turtle's chocolate candy which was Royalty favorite. At this moment all the anxiety Royalty had prior to boarding the jet Royalty left it back in the maybach all Royalty felt now was pure joy. Jacques knew exactly how to win Royalty over and this was just the beginning.
Royalty slept most of the 20-hour flight and when Royalty woke up Royalty was in Maldives in the middle of the Indian Ocean. When the jet landed, they still had to take a boat to their private island. Royalty just keep saying wow over and over again. This place looks exactly like what you see it on pictures and tv it's absolutely beautiful looking around in amazement. Royalty couldn't believe how turquoise Blue the ocean was or how clear it was you could look down at the water at actually see the fish swimming around you. This is what Royalty imagined Heaven to look like.

Royalty was so happy at this moment Royalty couldn't stop smiling. Arriving at their private island surrounded by nothing but white sand and large green trees Royalty looked in amazement at where they were going to stay for a week. Their hut was the size of a small mansion but was made out what looked like red wood with a straw roof top and it was completely open with no doors it was two story with an infinity pool with a slide attached from the second level that lead to the ocean. This island looked like a postcard it was unbelievable but true. Royalty had traveled to some beautiful places, but nothing compared to this place. Taking their shoes off walking on the white sand hand and handmade Royalty feel like anything was possible. Maldives empowered Royalty it awaken her inner spirit. Royalty felt alive.

Walking into the hut Royalty and Jacques was greeted by their personal butler and chef who would be at their beck and call for their whole entire stay. The staff introduced themselves and Jacques thanked them and said they wouldn't need them until supper time and they dismissed themselves back into the kitchen. Royalty looked at Jacques who was looking at Royalty smiling.
Jacques was happy that Royalty was happy. Thank you, Royalty, sincerely said I'm so amazed.

I see I'm glad you like it. But there's more to come cutie Jacques says smiling showing off his pearly white as usual.

This place is so beautiful looking around I could stay here forever Royalty says taking it all in.

We can if you want to Jacques says but It's really quiet and peaceful here you might get bored waiting to see Royalty reaction.

Never Royalty says I could get use to this. I love it already and I've only been here a few minutes laughing.

Ok I'm going to ask you that same question in a couple days and see if you have the same answer Jacques says grabbing their bags heading upstairs. Come on check out our master suite Jacques says going up the stairs.

Royalty stood there frozen for a moment in a daze until the butler came back into the living room and handed her a chilled glass of champagne and some fresh fruit. Royalty thanked the butler and went upstairs and once she reached the bedroom, she saw Jacques in the outside shower on the balcony of their room.

When Jacques noticed Royalty looking at him, he asked her did she want to join him.

Royalty mouth was wide open, but she didn't say a word. Jacques laughed because he knew he had outdone himself with this trip. He couldn't wait to see how Royalty was going to respond to all the other things he had planned for their weeklong vacation but one thing Jacques did know was that after this vacation he didn't have to worry about Royalty trying to fuck with no other nigga because they couldn't compare to him. They just couldn't keep up with his swag. It was impossible he won the minute they stepped foot on the island. His father taught him it's not what you do but how you do it. And Jacques took that very seriously at whatever it was he did.

Royalty felt like she was in some type of fairy tale movie. Royalty couldn't possibly be this happy and in love again this, quickly could she? Whatever was happening Royalty was here for it. Looking at Jacques in the outdoor shower turned Royalty on her body started to tingle with excitement. So, Royalty removed all her clothing and dropped them on the floor where she stood and joined Jacques outside on the balcony. Getting into the shower letting the chrome rainforest shower head consume her whole body Royalty couldn't contain herself from getting on her knees and putting Jacques manhood in her mouth. Jacques titled his head back letting the water hit his face placing his hand onto the the rock wall and gripping Royalty Head motioning her strokes with his other hand enjoying what that mouth did to his dick as Royalty was sucking on him. After a few sucks and slurps Jacques pulled Royalty up to Him kissing her. Thank you, baby, but I'm not ready to cum just yet smiling kissing Royalty again.

Let me wash you up grabbing the soap lathering Royalty whole body. Royalty turned her back to Jacques and moved her hair towards her breast, so Jacques could wash her back which he did but Jacques took it a step forward and also washed Royalty ass and cleaned her clit. After letting the water remove the suds Jacques went down on his knees and gave Royalty some head from the back while the shower soaked them both having Royalty grabbing the tree leaves and trying to grab hold of the rock shower area but wasn't able to even breaking a nail in the process. Holding on as best she could Royalty was screaming in ecstasy on her tippy toes trying to ride the wave out Jacques had taken her on cumming multiple times even after Jacques stop sucking. Standing up Jacques turned Royalty around and kissed her under the shower head until Jacques couldn't take it anymore grabbing Royalty hand leading her to the bed laying her wet body in top of the covers climbing on top of her. I want to make love to you staring in Royalty eyes anticipating how good she felt. Spreading her legs open Royalty pulled Jacques face to hers and stuck her whole entire tongue in his mouth sloppy tongue kissing him. Sliding in Royalty already wet pussy it was still a little tight. Jacques pushed with a little force and Royalty started to open up as Jacques starts to go deeper. Jacques slows it up a bit because he wanted to please Royalty. This pussy is so good baby damn you going to make a nigga cum too fast Jacques said trying to hold his composure, but the way Royalty was circling on his dick like a she was doing the hula hoop in slow motion had Jacques about to explode.

Ooh baby moaning this dick is soooo good Royalty says grabbing Jacques back pushing him into her soul then grabbing his head kissing him for dear life.

Jacques dug into Royalty speeding up his strokes and sucking on her neck damn near biting Royalty and grabbing Royalty Hair pulling it forcing Royalty to look at him while Jacques deep stroked Royalty a couple times before they both came together. Jacques and Royalty laid there basking in their love making falling asleep for a few hours. Jacques woke up first inhaling the fresh air and admiring the sun going down right before his eyes. Jacques just loved this place. Jacques had been to Maldives a couple times since buying the property that Him and Royalty was actually staying at. Jacques had his honeymoon here also. But Jacques wouldn't disclose any of this information to Royalty. Jacques wanted Royalty to enjoy her vacation that Jacques felt Royalty deserved plus this was Jacques alibi if needed because they were actually a day ahead of time back in the states. So, if anyone ever checked they had been there 24hrs before they actually arrived depending on how you asked the question. Getting out the bed Jacques just stared at Royalty who was in the fetal position knocked out admiring Royalty beauty and body thinking this is going to be a great seven days. Jacques couldn't wait to make love to Royalty all over the island. Jacques was ready to take it to the next level with Royalty because Jacques started to feel something for Royalty that he couldn't explain. Jacques knew he wanted her in his life permanently now that's why Jacques keep going raw like he was. If a nigga really want, you in his life permanently Jacques was thinking he'll definitely nut in you as much as he could without any regrets. And Jacques had no regrets whatsoever.
Royalty awaken to jazz music playing and a full moon overlooking a blue ocean with a glow in the dark beach thinking this is incredible. Jacques was sitting on the balcony smoking a Cuban cigar enjoying the tranquility of it all. Getting up and grabbing the satin white robe that was laid out for her Royalty walks towards Jacques and places her arms around his neck. Sleeping beauty finally awakes Jacques says blowing out smoke from his cigar. You were tired my dear I hope you got some good rest Jacques says pulling Royalty into his lap. Resting her head on Jacques chest Royalty shook her head yes in agreeance. You looked so beautiful resting I didn't want to disturb you plus I know you were tired from the long flight and getting dicked down laughing. Jacques says

Royalty started smiling but didn't respond.

Jacques brushed Royalty hair back off her face and stared at her for a moment and said you know your beautiful and I think I'm falling for you puffing on his cigar blowing smoke in Royalty face.

Lifting up a little coughing Royalty says why you do that?

My bad my love I thought you might like it laughing. You hungry Jacques asks?

A little Royalty says laying her head back on Jacques chest.

Ringing a bell for the butler Jacques says have a seat your food is on its way kissing Royalty forehead. Getting up and laying directly across from Jacques in a hammock chilling waiting on her food to arrive. The butler comes approximately 10 minutes after Jacques rung the bell with a full platter of food and a bottle of wine and sits it down in front of Royalty on a table and set up

Royalty eating utensils and pops the cork of the wine and pours Royalty a glass of wine and places the napkin across Royalty lap and tells Royalty to enjoy and walks away as fast as he came. Royalty looked at Jacques who wasn't fazed one bit. Jacques actually laughed at Royalty facial expression when the butler came and set everything up but especially how Royalty looked when the butler placed the napkin over Royalty lap like he was about to feed Royalty or something.

Stop looking at me and eat your food Laughing Jacques said. Babe it's ok to be treated like a queen every now and then laughing.

How did you know what I was thinking Royalty asks?

It's written all over your face still laughing now eat woman Jacques says laughing.

Royalty looked at all the food Grilled lobster, scallops and asparagus with white sauce, grilled shrimp a fancy salad and fresh fruit and of course red wine. Royalty just couldn't believe her eyes. This was way too much to take in all at one time. Royalty couldn't believe Jacques had went out of his way to please her. Royalty felt special at this moment and Jacques wanted to make sure Royalty always felt that way if he could help it.

Royalty and Jacques slept in most of the morning they were both exhausted from the flight and making love all day. After Royalty finished her dinner last night Royalty and Jacques headed to the beach and went for a night swim and sat on the beach talking until the sun came up. So technically they really didn't go to sleep until this morning. Jacques instructed the butler to wake them both up at 3:00 pm sharp. Jacques had something special planned for Royalty.

Lightly tapping Jacques on his shoulder to wake him the butler says. It's 3pm sharp sir you instructed me to wake you. I'll bring lunch out when you're ready.

Jacques thanked the Butler and told him that wouldn't be necessary. Looking over at Royalty who was sleeping like a baby Jacques hoped Royalty loved the surprise he had planned for her today. Jacques knew Royalty loved surprises. Shaking Royalty legs babe wake up we have to get ready to go Jacques said a couple times before Royalty actually fully woke up. I'll get in the shower first because if we get in together smiling you know what's going happen.

Smiling back still tired Royalty says ok. While Jacques was showering Royalty looked inside the closet where Jacques had so many outfits, he brought her for their vacation. Royalty didn't even know how Jacques knew her size but everything Royalty tried on fit perfectly. Jacques told Royalty last night to wear a swimming suit and a sun dress so that's what Royalty would put on after she showered. Jacques had brought Royalty over ten different designer swimsuits and a dozen summer dresses. Jacques also had purchased Royalty several Nike workout clothing with matching shoes. Jacques also made sure Royalty had every flip flop and sandal he could fine. Royalty didn't know how Jacques had done so much shopping in such a short time, but Jacques did that and also brought Royalty matching underwear sets and several pair of sunglasses. Jacques had turned into Royalty little personal shopper. And everything Jacques purchased was from different stores like Gucci, Louis Vuitton, Burberry, Nike just to name a few. Jacques was more materialistic than Royalty was everything Jacques wore was a name brand. As Jacques was getting out the shower Royalty got in. Jacques told Royalty she had approximately 30 mins to get out the shower before they had to leave. So, Royalty washed the most important parts of her body and got out and dressed in twenty minutes. How do I look Royalty said walking up behind Jacques with her Burberry swimming suit and matching head scarf and Givenchy slides?

Taking a second look Jacques says sternly you need to switch your shoes they don't match and turned back around and finished getting his cigars out that he was taking with them.

Looking down at her feet Royalty says you didn't buy me any Burberry sandals disappointed.

Not even turning around when he responded to Royalty Jacques says I just placed the orders online and had my driver to pick them up but I'm almost positive I ordered you Burberry sandals double check I'm trying to get my smoking supplies together and hurry up, so we can go.

Royalty rolled her eyes and went to look inside the closet for her matching shoes. Found them Royalty says changing her shoes to the Burberry slides that was underneath a bag in the closet that's why she didn't see them.

Ok good let's go we're late Jacques says grabbing his camera and weed. You look nice by the way Jacques says looking at Royalty shoes much better hitting Royalty on her ass as Royalty was walking down the stairs. I know what I be doing Jacques says laughing.

Boy hush you did alright Royalty replied walking outside in shock making her eyes bulge seeing a helicopter on the beach waiting to take them to wherever they were going that was a big surprise. The sun was beaming down on them and it felt so good, but you definitely needed shades on. Jacques had on his fly Gucci shades and a straw Gucci brim looking like Puffy in his younger years when he went by the name Puff Daddy. Also wearing a Gucci signature wife beater with matching Gucci stripe shorts and Gucci slides and had his Gucci man bag strapped across Him with his Gucci backpack on that had their beach towels inside and his camera and of course his weed and cigars. Royalty just shook her head at all the matchy match Jacques did but Jacques looked cute though.

Where are we going Royalty asked Jacques?

You'll see in a few minutes Jacques says chilling with his hands behind his head and his feet up on an unoccupied seat. A few minutes later the helicopter landed on a 100 ft luxury yacht that was absolutely Beautiful and the crew was standing in formation waiting for them to board. Jacques said "Surprise "smiling.

Damn you ain't playing you're going all out Royalty says exiting the helicopter taking the captain hand helping her board the yacht.

Welcome aboard the Serenity the captain says to Royalty enjoy.

Jacques follows behind Royalty without any assistance and shakes the captain hand. And says what's up to the crew.

Welcome back Senor Jacques the captain says how's your mom?

She's blessed, and highly favored Jacques says thanks for asking captain. Looking around the yacht Royalty couldn't believe her eyes. This ship looked like a 5-star hotel. Heading downstairs on the

spiral staircase. For one Royalty wasn't expecting that there would be a spiral staircase on a yacht and then the big glass chandelier overlooking the entire living room and the huge white leather sectional sofa with baby blue velvet throw pillows and Big flat screen tv mounted inside the wall and a full wet bar. The list goes on and on with this yacht and Royalty hadn't even made it to the bedroom yet. The flooring was white marble with a huge mungas Blue rug that looked like the ocean.
Staring out the glass patio door Royalty was outdone.

Walking up behind Royalty putting his arms around Royalty waist sticking his tongue in and out of Royalty ear then kissing her neck Jacques says you like that huh?

Royalty rubs her ass on Jacques dick while he was standing behind her starting to feel him getting hard. Yep I do why you stop? Royalty asks

Jacques released Royalty waist and turned her around facing him. Because we haven't even ate anything today looking Royalty right in her eyes seductively and I have something planned for you and I don't want you to be all tired squeezing Royalty titties.

Well stop fucking playing with me then Royalty says slapping Jacques hand away and pushing him aside, so she could get by.

Laughing Jacques says awe you so horney.
Come on let's go back upstairs so we can eat you little horney thing still laughing heading up the stairs with Royalty right on his heels laughing also even though Jacques did just make her horney for a minute. Jacques takes Royalty by the hand and leads her to an intimate table on the deck that was nicely set up for two. The sun was beaming on them and it was scorching hot Jacques was grateful their table had an umbrella to block the heat. Pulling Royalty chair out for her and placing her napkin on her lap Jacques says sorry about the tease baby but I got other plans for you today, but I promise tonight I'll make it up to you winking sitting opposite facing Royalty. The personal chef came out and brought oysters, shrimp salad, grilled shrimp and rigatoni with vodka sauce and poured them both a bottle of red wine.

After eating Royalty asks Jacques baby who helped you plan all this? Very curious because Royalty knew Jacques didn't plan all this by himself.

Laughing Jacques replies Helped? Baby, listen
woman aren't the only ones that knows how to plan events. I'm a good planner baby you'll be surprised at all the things I know how to do. I'm like a renaissance man baby I can do all things winking. Remember that. I wear many hats plus I was raised traveling the world I know a lot about different cultures and different continents I bet you didn't know I speak several different languages. I'm bilingual laughing.

Really no I didn't know that Royalty says interested. That's awesome what languages do you speak? Royalty asked Jacques.

Well let's see of course I speak English, I speak French, I speak Spanish and I also speak patois which is Jamaican creole my native language. I did learn to speak Chinese, but I forgot most of it because I never used it. But I can understand it sometimes if they don't talk too fast Jacques says laughing.

Royalty was in awe right now. She couldn't believe what she was hearing. This fool definitely wasn't from the projects. Because nobody from the projects even spoke a second language. Wow that's so dope Jacques I've never meet anyone who spoke several different languages. Growing up in the projects nobody spoke nothing but english. Even the Mexicans spoke English Hell I never even heard them speak Spanish laughing. And my mother was Filipino she never once spoke the Filipino language to me. All she even spoke was English I kinda forgot at times she was even Filipino she was so ghetto laughing.

Was your mom short? Because most Filipino women are very short Jacques asks.

Yeah she was she was 4'11 and skinny as fuck but I don't want to talk about her right now getting up from the table walking to the edge of the yacht looking at the water.

Jacques could seance something was wrong but didn't want to press the issue. Babe come here patting his lap. Come sit down a minute. Royalty cane and sat on Jacques lap hugging his neck and laid her head on his chest. Kissing Royalty forehead. You ready to get in the water? Looking up at Jacques Royalty said water what you mean? I mean you want to ride some jet skis and go do some snorkeling and swim with the sharks? Hello yeah jumping up excited Royalty says. Jacques gets up and says let's go get changed and then we racing I hope you can drive a jet ski babe because I'm going to smoke that ass literally, I'm not going to spare you laughing Jacques says heading downstairs to change into his swimming trunks and put on their life jackets. Boy I'm not knew to this Royalty adds I'm true to this jumping on Jacques back putting her arms around his neck. You lucky you're a buck ten or we'll both be in trouble going down these stairs carefully taking his time to not trip. That would be hella funny is we fell Royalty says laughing. It wouldn't be funny if you buss your ass not to mention your head. Girl we're way out in the ocean in the middle of who knows where we aren't near no hospitals. There's only so much I can do to save you babe. But if you get hurt, I'll do my best to save you ok putting her down laughing. Hitting him playfully Royalty says well hopefully nothing happens Doc Laughing. Ok take that off babe Jacques says to Royalty pointing at her clothes. What you want me to strip Royalty says with a raised eyebrow laughing. Looking at Royalty thinking he'll yes! I would love to see you naked on a jet ski titties and ass floopying everywhere getting wet. But Jacques says. No babe you know what I mean hitting Royalty on her ass hurry up let's go race you want to make a bet for some head tonight? Some head? Royalty says. Yes, some head whoever wins has to suck all night no breaks. For example, if I win which I will you have to suck my dick all night whenever I ask you too and vice versa. If you win, I have to do the same. So, if you wake up at 3:30 and want done head guess what? I turn into a head doctor. Or we can bet for money but babe my money way longer than yours I'll put you in the poor house Laughing. Boy please you don't know what I'm worth Royalty says seriously. No babe your right. But what I do know is that your few million dollars you are worth at least a million babe aren't you? Jacques asks laughing is pennies compared to me being cocky now. I didn't want to tell you babe but you fucking with a real one laughing. A real billionaire winking. Now hurry up Lil Millie let's go walking to the couch to get his backpack getting his swimming trunks out stripping down to his birthday suit looking better than ever now that Royalty knew he was papered up like he was. Getting dressed Jacques glances over at Royalty who was standing there staring at him and asked Royalty what you looking at babe? You've seen it, felt it and tasted it Laughing hurry up change into your swimming suit. Jacques says with some base in his throat because he was serious.

You must have forgot I'm wearing my swimsuit underneath my dress throwing her arms up like duh Royalty says waiting on Jacques to get ready because Royalty came prepared for whatever.

Ok then take that dress off and let's go Jacques says hella bossy. After Jacques changed into his swimming trunks and swim shoes Jacques was ready to roll. Babe come on let's get the show on the road grabbing Royalty hand pulling her towards the deck on the lower level. The captain and a few staffers was waiting to assist in the exiting of the yacht handing Jacques and Royalty life jackets and helping them get on the jet ski and making sure Royalty was completely comfortable which Royalty was and Royalty said it multiple times before Jacques was convinced. Ok babe if you have a problem or get nervous, I'm close by ok? Jacques said reassuring. We're going to go for a ride and when we get back will go snorkeling and swim with the sharks looking at Royalty facial expression to see if Royalty was scared are not. And all Jacques saw in Royalty face was game on let's go. Jacques knew he had met his match when he meet Royalty ass. And just like that without warning Royalty took off on her jet ski leaving Jacques in the dust. Jacques knew then he didn't need to worry about Royalty then he took off behind her. Jacques admired Royalty adventurous side. Royalty knew how to have a good time. They rode on the jet skis for hours racing and splashing water on each other and almost wrecking into one another at one point but overall having a great time enjoying each other's company bonding more than just sharing each other's saliva and body fluids. Royalty and Jacques had become friends and lovers.

Flying around a turn Royalty jet ski turned over and Royalty fell into the water going under momentarily and coming back up shaking her hair and wiping her eyes and started laughing at herself threading water. Jacques turned his jet ski around when he noticed that Royalty had fallen over and came to Royalty rescue and and jumped in to help her. Royalty started laughing at Jacques calling him captain save a hoe and Jacques started splashing water in Royalty face. They had a water fight for about 5 mins then Jacques went under water and Royalty followed right behind him. They both swam underwater looking at the fish and enjoying the warmth of the water until Jacques signaled to Royalty with his hands pointing up like let's go swimming back up towards the jet ski.

Coming up for air Jacques says. Let's Go I have to pee.

Then Royalty says why didn't you just pee in the water? Looking confused.

Laughing a little bit Jacques replies you're really nasty I hope you didn't pee in this ocean Royalty I mean Ms jackson if you're nasty laughing. Come on let me help you get back on your jet ski holding Royalty jet ski steady, so Royalty could get on.
And once again when Royalty got on her jet ski Royalty shook her hair and got her jet ski started and Royalty took off and left Jacques again.

Fuck the help huh? Jacques says starting his jet ski taking off laughing behind Royalty. Reaching the yacht Royalty had already parked her jet ski and had gotten herself a drink and was waiting on Jacques to arrive.

Babe why you keep leaving me? Jacques says walking up on Royalty.

Look Jacques don't make me square up with you Royalty replies bucking up like what laughing.

Jacques grabs Royalty and pulls her close to him and kisses Royalty and says. Let's take a shower and get some massages on the upper deck then we can have a romantic dinner kissing Royalty again.

I'm with it babe plus I peed in the water, so I need to shower laughing sipping her drink.

Pushing Royalty away from Him Jacques laughs and says your nasty babe get away from me. I'm going to take a shower walking away heading in doors this time leaving Royalty standing in the dust.

Royalty stood there laughing because she made that story up about peeing in the ocean just to see Jacques reaction and Jacques reacted exactly the way Royalty predicted. Men are so predictable Royalty thinking walking in doors to the bar to make herself another drink.

Stepping out the shower Jacques thinking this girl better be heading towards this shower with her pissy ass shaking his head I can't believe she actually did that polluting the water like that No respect Laughing.

What you Laughing at Royalty says walking into the bathroom butt naked.

Looking at Royalty from head to toe Jacques was thinking this girl is perfect but her attitude though. I was laughing at you actually Jacques says walking past Royalty bumping into her.

Excuse you fool Royalty says laughing thinking that boy needs to work on his some timey attitude getting in the shower. The shower felt so good to Royalty she almost didn't want to get out the water was nice and hot just like Royalty liked it with a high pressure shower head that did wonders. Stepping out the shower reaching for her towel Royalty touches Jacques body instead. Jumping oh boy you scared me Royalty says staring Jacques in his face because Jacques was standing there blocking Royalty movement.

Jacques grabbed Royalty face and started kissing Royalty rubbing their bodies together. Royalty put her arms around Jacques neck and Jacques picked Royalty up pinning her back against the shower door and wrapped her legs around his waist and slid inside her. It happened so fast Royalty couldn't catch her breath. Kissing and moaning with Jacques going in and out of her took Royalty to ecstasy making her cum immediately. Jacques came inside Royalty then pulled out and started washing up in the sink. Jump back in the shower babe real quick are masseuse is waiting on the upper deck for us laughing and don't get dressed just put on your robe.

Sticking her head out the shower Royalty asks Jacques what was that about babe?

A nigga was horney that's all now hurry up Laughing Jacques says.

Wait you attack me when I was getting out the shower to fuck now you rushing me ? The audacity boy laughing Royalty says finishing her shower.

Babe you should be grateful a nigga attacked you laughing that means you got some good pussy walking out the bathroom to get ready for his massage yelling at Royalty to hurry up.
Ok I'm ready Royalty says walking out the bathroom. Looking her over Royalty was ready alright Jacques loved how Royalty looked even without any makeup on. Royalty had on her Versace terry cloth robe that matched his robe with matching slippers. Royalty tied her wavy hair in a bun at the

top of her head and had a fresh face look. Jacques believed he was falling in love with Royalty but Jacques wasn't quite sure. Jacques never felt like this before for any woman not even for his wife. Jacques didn't know if it was the sex or was he actually falling in love but either way it felt good. Ok bet let's go we're hella late Jacques says grabbing Royalty hand going up the stairwell to the upper deck were the massage tables were set up waiting for them to arrive. Once they got to the upper deck their masseuses wasted no time diving into their deep tissue massages after they both un robed and laid down on their perspective his and hers side by side tables. Jacques fell asleep during his massage and Royalty felt relaxed.

This was exactly what Royalty needed. A massage in the sun on the upper deck of a luxury yacht with the man Royalty was falling hard for to get Royalty mind off the reality of her life back at home. Royalty loss, her pain and her suffering. This trip took Royalty mind off everything except Jacques. Jacques was the only thing that mattered at this moment. The masseuse instructed Royalty to turn over on lay on her back, so Royalty could get a facial. The esthetician gave Royalty a microdermabrasion facial and changed Royalty nail color per Royalty request. Jacques was supposed to have gotten a facial also, but Royalty said to let him rest. But before Royalty knew it Royalty had dozed off herself also after getting her facial and having the warm towel placed over her face. And thank God The esthetician left the towel over Royalty face because Royalty slept out in that heat for about an hour. Royalty and Jacques both had sun burns on their bodies when they woke up. Royalty body was a shade darker than her face and Jacques back looked like burnt toast. Jacques woke up first from the sunburn then Jacques woke up Royalty shaking her saying Royalty babe get up before you get skin cancer panicking.

Waking up like what Royalty looked around her surroundings because Royalty had completely forgotten she had fallen asleep on the upper deck after their massages. Calm down babe we're ok laughing. You scared me Royalty says getting up. That damn massage knocked us the fuck out. That shit felt so good thanks babe I needed that stretching Royalty said.

Your welcome I just wish the damn captain would have woke us up. That sun is deadly I don't play with the heat babe plus I'm dark enough. Let's go downstairs putting on his robe and slippers irritated. Once they were downstairs Jacques sat on the couch and got his weed out his bag and started smoking and Royalty made herself a drink acting like she was a bartender asking Jacques did he want one. Yes, babe Hennessy no ice Jacques says hitting his blunt. Royalty handed Jacques his drink and sat down opposite him putting her feet on Jacques lap. Thanks babe Jacques says sipping his drink and rubbing Royalty feet. You enjoying yourself? looking at Royalty blowing smoke in her face.

Of course, babe you're the best Royalty replies I appreciate you. This vaca is the best I'm going to squeeze your balls tonight using my pussy muscles laughing. I've been doing my kegel exercises telling Jacques her secret.

You been doing your kegel exercises huh? That's your secret weapon babe that shit really work too. You should teach a class on that shit it's a lot of loose pussy bitches walking around not knowing there's help out there for them laughing Jacques says.

Well that's sucks for them I'm not teaching them hoes shit Royalty says sipping on her drink. They should know anyways because they can't keep a man laughing.

True Jacques says in agreement but the other piece to that is their dick sucking skills be worse.

Damn bad head and bad in bed that's a bad combo babe. It has to suck to be them Royalty says laughing. Shit I know a few pretty bitches that never been in long term relationships or even been married before. I mean if you can't get a nigga to want to marry you something gotta be wrong right babe?

Well babe blowing out smoke from his blunt. Seriously speaking not all women are wifey material. A lot of bitches forfeit that straight out the gate. For one don't no man want no headache straight up and for the rest of his life he'll no! Then a lot of pretty women think they the prize laughing well cutie you're not. You're the runner up to the prize. They be cute and all but what else do you have to offer besides that? Did you graduate high school because most haven't, did you go to college and if so, what was your major? And please don't say no nail tech or some shit like that laughing. Unless you plan on owning the nail salon then that's different. See if they were smart since they went to college and all they would get their license and be a Mobile nail technician and sew up that bag. Because Rich people you should know babe have their nail people come to them. So, whoever in that business got it on lock.

What does that have to do with marriage Jacques you high Royalty says laughing.

Oh, we were talking about marriage laughing Jacques says my bad. But anyways babe a man just wants a woman that gives him peace and good sex. We don't require much babe.

Well why is it so many women that's peaceful can't get married then? Royalty says waiting to hear Jacques answer.

Their probably horrible in bed babe laughing. Don't nobody want to marry a woman that's stiff in bed and that don't suck dick that means he'll have to cheat your forcing him too and if you can't put your legs up because you always saying it hurt guess what? some other bitch taking that dick like a pro elsewhere. And all that complaining everyday. It's a No for me dog sorry laughing. Men deal with enough shit during the day to have to come home to some bullshit that doesn't even matter. I don't want to hear about what your girlfriend and her man got going on I just don't. And I hate a begging bitch. That's my pet peeve like bitch what I look like? I don't mind giving nobody nothing. I give to the homeless all day everyday but I don't owe a mother fucker shit. Especially if we fuck and we both cum bitch that's all you getting don't be looking for no money after a good time. And Bitch realistically should be paying me Jacques says seriously. But I've given lots of bitch's money but it's because I chose to no bitch didn't charge me or got over on me if that's what she was thinking she played herself if anything. But you babe you can have it all codes to the safe, bank account numbers whatever you want you can have whatever you like Laughing. Have a baby by me baby and you'll be a billionaire. Squeezing Royalty feet.

Jacques you never answered my question tho Royalty said Laughing. About why men don't marry certain women.

Because they don't want too babe laughing Jacques says. She probably ain't shit or something she probably ain't worth marrying. Some women is fun and all, but you don't want to spend the rest of your life with they ass. I don't know but for me babe being a lazy ass bitch I won't even date your ass you better be doing something all day besides calling me and you better throw that ass back in bed or you'll never hear from me again. It's like test driving a car babe it only takes one time for me then it's curtains. So, you better give it your best shot the first go round or you can forget a second chance I don't care how cute you are. It's a lot of other cute bitches out there ready to make a nigga toes curls and leg shake and put me to sleep Laughing.

Is that right? Royalty says. I must got that bomb pussy then because I'm still around and I'm good looking whew a bitch winning laughing.

Yeah babe you do rubbing Royalty legs Jacques says. You got that pussy that put a nigga to sleep right after babe laughing not every woman has that. Some women pussy after you done you can get dressed and leave immediately. But yours babe make a nigga sleepy.

Awe thank you babe for the compliment Royalty says learning over giving Jacques a kiss. And you got that Cookie Monster Head Laughing. You eat it up right babe and your deep stroke is a beast too. That's why I like your ugly ass laughing.

I'm not ugly am I babe? Damn Jacques says.

I'm kidding I don't want to blow your head up with all these compliments and shit you look alright but not as good as me Royalty says laughing.

True dat laughing Jacques says pushing Royalty feet off him getting up. Let's go for a night swim babe and come back and make love so you can do your kegel exercises on me Laughing.

Ok let's go I'm ready Royalty says taking off her robe standing there butt naked with her hand on her hip.

Shaking his head Jacques says skinny dipping it is then let's go.
After a night swim and a few drinks and making love twice Royalty and Jacques was dead tired and was snuggled up together butt naked with no covers over them plus the night heat wasn't no joke even at night it was still very warm. A few of the crew was watching the video on their phones they had taken watching Jacques and Royalty make love without them knowing they were being recorded. Royalty was moaning and yelling so loud the whole entire ship heard her and a few of the crew came down to watch them in the act like watching porn being shot. Jacques and Royalty forgot everything around them was wide open with little to no privacy, but they didn't even care. They got down like this was their last night on earth sucking and fucking like their lives depended on each other's soul for survival. This was the most entertainment that the crew had seen in a while. And twice in one night was a bonus for them.

The following morning when Jacques and Royalty went to have their breakfast on the upper deck the crew were all smiling at Royalty and the way the chef said Good morning Miss Royalty made Royalty feel like everyone was staring at her.

Babe you think the crew heard us last night? Because it seems like everyone is looking at me smiling this morning Royalty said biting her wheat toast scared to look around acting paranoid.

Laughing sipping on his orange juice Jacques replies you were loud ma but naw I don't think they heard us still laughing turning to look at one of the crew members who was walking past and gave

Jacques the thumbs up like you the man. Even if they did hear us babe they just know now that you're a freak laughing.

That's not funny Jacques Royalty says I don't want these people looking at me like that getting irritated.

Calm down Royalty it's not that serious babe it's a part of life. I'm sure they're all fucking somebody too Laughing.

Rolling her eyes Royalty says whatever this breakfast is good though babe. This chef is everything. Royalty and Jacques breakfast consisted of mushroom and tomato and pepper jack cheese omelette with sour cream and red sauce, bagel, and fresh fruit and blueberry muffins. And of course, for Royalty a mimosa. They were heading back to the Island to go do a wildlife tour and parasailing today and Royalty wanted to go do yoga and Pilates also. Royalty needed to keep her workout regimen going even while on vacation.

Jacques was reading the newspaper on his iPad thinking about what he had to take care of once they got back home. Jacques had a lot of loose ends to tie up. Jacques wouldn't have too much time to spend with Royalty when they got back so Jacques was thinking how could he make it up to Royalty because Jacques knew that Royalty was going to be tripping. Plan ahead was Jacques motto. Plan for the what if's because Jacques knew eventually the what ifs were coming.

Babe you didn't hear a word I just said Royalty said to Jacques who was in his own zone.

Huh babe what you say I was reading the paper what's up? Jacques says lying.

I asked you was there anywhere to go shopping on the island? Royalty said

That's all women want to do is shop Jacques was thinking No babe only local. But if you want to shop go online and order whatever you want at my expense and have it sent to the house it'll be there when we get back. Jacques thanked God for hearing his prayer. Because Jacques was just thinking about what to do to please Royalty and that was the answer. Babe you want to go horseback riding when we get on the island? Jacques asked Royalty.

Yes, I'll like that on the beach, right? Royalty asks.

Yes, we can ride around the island there's a couple trails then you can go do your yoga and I'll take a nap. Jacques says. Plus, I'm about to get high so I'm not going to want to do too much after that honestly speaking. A chill day was what Jacques wanted and nothing else. Jacques needed to make some phone calls but decided to do that while Royalty was at yoga that way, he could have complete privacy. Babe hurry up and finish eating so I can go smoke Jacques said needed to hit his weed because his nerves were getting bad. Looking over some new inventory for the boutique Jacques knew he had started slacking since meeting Royalty, but Jacques didn't care but Jacques did need to handle his business more Jacques couldn't keep putting all the pressure on his moms even though she didn't mind. Jacques planned on expanding the business and knew he had to get focused for that and his other extra curriculum businesses needed attending to also. And Jacques was the only person who could handle that. Getting back on the island was refreshing for both Royalty and Jacques. They rode horses, went parasailing did an island tour and some local shopping and made love all

over the island for the next couple of days they had left before returning home. Jacques was wearing the fuck out and couldn't wait to get back home and sleep in his own bed. But for Royalty it was just the opposite. Royalty wasn't ready to leave the island at all. Royalty could have stayed forever if it was up to her. Royalty felt like she had found a little bit of heaven right there on earth.
Returning home Jacques driver dropped Royalty off at home and Jacques helped bring Royalty bags inside. Cornering Royalty in the foyer Jacques stands over Royalty and kisses her. Ok babe it's back to business for me for a couple weeks. I'm expanding the boutique and I got some other stuff I have to take care of, but I'll be dropping by here and there so don't you go off being no bad girl you hear me? Looking Royalty in the eyes hating to leave Royalty now but Jacques had no choice.

Royalty Grabbed Jacques by his neck planting kisses on him after every word she said. I'm going to miss you, but I understand. The two just stared at each other for a moment before letting go.

Giving Royalty one last kiss baby I have to go, or I'll be stuck here forever laughing Jacques says.

Forever sounds good Royalty said smiling.

I know right winking his eye. Walking backwards towards the door I'm going to call you babe be good blowing Royalty a kiss and Royalty caught it. Then Jacques was out the door.

Tilting her head Back Royalty hated being back home alone. Looking around Royalty thought maybe she would call Bianca and go over there. But after reading all Bianca texts about her drama Royalty decided against it. Walking into the kitchen to pour herself a drink Royalty noticed her housekeeper had left her a card on the kitchen counter top and Royalty opened it and read it.

I missed you while you were gone senorita Royalty, I cleaned the house and started boxing up senor Amirs things like you asked. I put the boxes in the garage there's still a few items upstairs I'll get to them when I come back from my vacation with my family. I hope you had a good time on your trip. I'll see you soon senorita love Jade aka Mija.

Awe how sweet Royalty was thinking but Royalty was also thinking that not once had she thought about Amir while she was on her trip. Opening the refrigerator Royalty gets an open bottle of wine out and heads to the theater room so she could sit down and watch some old videos of her and Amir they had made for when they gotten old to reminisce about. But now Royalty was the only one reminiscing about Amir at her young age. Watching the videos brought back so many memories for Royalty things Royalty almost forgotten. Royalty didn't even know how Amir kept up with so many pictures of them over the years. Birthdays, holidays, trips they had taken even the passing of both their moms. After watching the video over again twice and finishing the bottle and laughing and crying Royalty called it a night. Royalty was tired from the long flight and the busy week she just spent with Jacques. Taking a long hot bubble bath helped Royalty pass out.
The following morning Royalty went to her salon to check on the girls and to see how business was going Everything was in smooth operation. Royalty even went by the Royalty Express to check on the new manager and assistant she hired. Everything was everything as far as Royalty was concerned. All her business was intact. No problems had been reported which was good and, on the surface,, everything was running smoothly. So, the next couple days back Royalty handled her business with her businesses and got herself together also getting her hair washed and flat iron went and got a body wax and mani and pedicure and even got her eyebrows touched up. Grabbing a bite to eat

Royalty phones rings from an unknown number after looking at her phone ring a couple times Royalty decided to answer it. Hello

Hi Royalty, This Liberty is it a bad time?

No Liberty it's never a bad time for you is Everything ok? I've been meaning to call and check up on you and Angel how are y'all doing?

We're great thanks for asking but that's why I'm calling you Angel wanted me to remind you about her birthday party coming up laughing. Liberty says.

Oh yeah, I did promise her I'll be there when is it? Royalty asks.

Well change of plans I've gotten so big and swollen I can't get out much only for doctor's appointments and I scheduled them early right after I drop Angel off to school because the bus ride takes an hour there and back sounding like she was breathing heavy. So, I'm just going to do ice cream and cake at the house in two weeks on a Saturday. I hope you can make it Liberty solemnly says.

Where are you now Liberty, I want to come see you? Royalty asks

I'm at home looking like a big ass pig laughing Liberty says feeling like one just Big and uncomfortable

I doubt that Royalty says give me a minute then I'll stop by ok?

Ok I'll see you in a little while Liberty says hanging up.

Royalty looked at her call log to see if she was tripping because Royalty knew she hadn't heard from Jacques since they've been back. Jacques hadn't called and said No good mornings or how are you nothing. Hum that's different Royalty was thinking but figuring Jacques must be really busy. So, Royalty decided that she'll get her food to go and ordered Jacques some lunch and would bring it by the boutique because Royalty was sure Jacques was too busy to get out and grab something to eat. Driving over to Jacques boutique Royalty felt butterflies and couldn't stop smiling. Royalty looked cute today with her multi colored wrap around skirt and matching top with thigh high boots on so surprising Jacques was perfect. Checking her lipstick before getting out the car and spraying on more perfume that Royalty kept in her car for a little enticement Royalty was ready. Grabbing Jacques shrimp tacos Royalty gets out of her freshly detailed Car all smiles and crosses the street and walks into the boutique but to Royalty surprise Jacques wasn't there. Walking in the boutique the welcome bell rang to announce a customer and this tall, thin absolutely beautiful dark skin woman looking like the supermodel Iman but much younger with the same West Indies features walks up to Royalty and introduces herself dressed impeccable in an all white satin romper with long hair to her waist and silver Giuseppe heels with perfect teeth and matching smile but it was her skin tone and beauty that Royalty couldn't get over. This woman was absolutely beautiful. Royalty smile immediately turned into a frown.

Welcome to the Heiress Boutique I'm Serenity Jacques wife how may I help you?

Standing frozen Royalty was thinking did she just say wife? Wait what she say her name was? Serenity? didn't we just get off a yacht named Serenity?

You ok Miss? The supermodel looking lady says.

Taking a deep breath counting to ten because Royalty felt her blood pressure rising quickly. Ok Royalty calm down don't do nothing stupid play it cool. Royalty keep telling herself over and over again.

Jacques wife touched Royalty shoulder to see if Royalty was ok. Yanking her shoulder away. Royalty says don't touch me and drops the tacos on the floor and turns around and walks out the boutique hella irritated. Looking up and down the street Royalty hoped Jacques would magically walk up at any moment but of course Jacques never did. Getting in her car Royalty starts beating the steering wheel yelling at herself for being so stupid. People were walking by looking scared because it looked like Royalty was having a nervous breakdown in her driver's seat. One bold person knocked on the driver's side window with hopes of helping Royalty, but Royalty gave her the business.
Rolling her window down yelling What you want bitch? Don't knock on my mother fucking window hoe, you better get the fuck away from my car before I beat your ass!! Sending the poor Good Samaritan woman off running. Royalty sat in her car boiling hot hoping Jacques would walk up so she could go off on his ass but after a few minutes Royalty starting thinking. Fuck him you knew Jacques was married the whole entire time so that's what's I get. Royalty you did this to yourself. Pulling off throwing her food out the window on the ground because she lost her appetite at this point. Driving to Liberty house Royalty started crying and couldn't stop. Royalty couldn't believe this shit. The nigga she was fucking wife was in town and now she was driving to her dead niggas side chick house who was pregnant by him. Life was so fucked Up Royalty thinking.
While Liberty and Angel went into The Baby Gap Store to spend the thousand dollars Royalty gave them but knowing Liberty being frugal Liberty wasn't going to spend that much. Royalty planned on telling her to keep the change because once Royalty gave Liberty the money Royalty gave it to Liberty to keep it. Royalty called the Tesla dealership and made arrangements over the phone to purchase a car and asked that they have it ready when she arrived. Returning to the car all smiles Angel and Liberty both thanked Royalty again for the hundredth time. Liberty tried to hand Royalty a few hundred dollars back that she didn't spend but Royalty told Liberty to keep it and to go open bank accounts for the kids. Royalty suggested that they go get something to eat because Royalty knew they had to be hungry because Royalty definitely was, and she wasn't even the pregnant one.

I want a hamburger Angel said.

Ok let's go to the Cheesecake Factory Royalty said you can have a hamburger and I can have a drink Laughing Royalty says. To the Cheesecake Factory it is Royalty says driving there as fast as she could because they were all starving. After eating and drinking and Angel and Liberty having some cheesecake Royalty was feeling good after having a shot of Hennessy and was ready to surprise Liberty again. Ok ladies I really enjoyed You'll company today we have to do this more often smiling.

Getting down off her chair Angel gives Royalty a big hug and says. Thank you, Miss Royalty, for being so nice to me and my mommy I love you.

This brought tears to Royalty eyes. This little innocent girl who didn't deserve to struggle or experience any pain as a child brought back so many memories Royalty tried to forget. Hugging Angel back Royalty replies I love you too sweetheart and I'll buy you that pink car that you want.

Omg Miss Royalty Thank You Angel says. And Liberty and Royalty both starts crying.

Liberty never thought this day would come when her blessings would be answered.

Why you'll crying Angel says looking confused.

Oh, because we're just so happy baby that's all Liberty says wiping her tears away.

Oh, ok Angel says not convinced but accepting her mom's answer.

In the car everyone rode in silence actually Angel had fallen asleep in the back because she had a long day of walking and shopping plus Angel just finished eating a huge hamburger and fries and had a slice of cheesecake, so Angel was stuffed. Pulling into the Tesla car lot Liberty grabbed her chest in disbelief. When you thought the day couldn't get any better Royalty said looking at Liberty who started crying again. Surprise Royalty said.

Liberty grabbed Royalty and gave her a hug as best she could with her big belly and all and thanked Royalty repeatedly.

Your welcome Liberty I told you I was buying you a car, didn't I?

Yes, wiping away the tears Liberty said.

I'm a woman of my word smiling Royalty said.

I know wiping her tears Liberty responded. I thought it was going to be a used car Liberty says still crying.

Laughing Royalty replies Tesla dealerships don't sale used cars. Come on wake up Angel so you can go see you'll new car.

Liberty woke Angel up who wasn't too happy about that plus her mommy was crying. What's the matter mommy did I do something? Angel asks waking up.

No baby these are happy tears Miss Royalty brought us a car.

Looking at Royalty like you did Angel says Thank you Miss Royalty me and mommy don't have to catch the bus to go grocery shopping anymore? She wanted to make sure this car was really for them.

Laughing Royalty says Nope your mommy can drive your new car to the store now come on let's go look at it Royalty said getting out.

Angel jumped out the back super excited. Holding Angel hand Liberty followed Royalty to a Black Tesla X that had a red bow on it. This your push present from me and Amir Royalty said giving Liberty a hug.

The tears came streaming down Liberty face again. Hugging Royalty back they both cried for a minute until Angel says ok ok enough crying happy tears, I want to get in our new car mommy pulling on her mommy clothes trying to pull her towards the car. Letting go of Royalty Liberty started laughing a little at Angel. Ok let's go see walking to the car opening the door. Putting her hand over her mouth for a moment in complete shock. Royalty this is crazy looking at the luxury interior of her car. The black leather seats with peanut butter trim, the large touch screen navigation screen and Angel had gotten in the back and fastened her seatbelt and pulled out the backseat tray and was trying to turn on the tv that was mounted into the headrest. The look on their faces was priceless and Royalty loved it Royalty didn't even care that she just dropped 60k on a car that wasn't for herself. It just felt right to make someone else happy for a change. No need for everyone to suffer if they didn't have to. Plus, Amir would have probably brought the poor girl a Bentley are something. Amir first child hell his only child it wouldn't have been no limit to what Amir would have done. Except Amir probably wouldn't have cashed Liberty out. Amir would have just brought everything himself and gave it to Liberty. But Liberty must def could have played Amir if Liberty knew how Royalty was thinking. Shit Liberty could play her too her and Angel Royalty was thinking they had already tugged on Royalty heartstring. They made Royalty feel better just being around them today. Royalty wanted to buy them whatever they wanted. Royalty just hated seeing kids suffer because their parents wasn't shit like her mother did her. As long as Royalty was alive Liberty and Angel would never want for anything again.

The dealer gave Liberty the keys and congratulated her and Liberty started up her car still in disbelief. I'm nervous Liberty said to Royalty who was standing at the driver's door waiting to go to her car and have Liberty Follow her.

Why you know how to drive don't you? Royalty asked.

Yes, I've driven before my ex boyfriend use to let me drive his car, but this car is brand new and it's so nice I don't want nothing to happen sounding nervous. Liberty said

Your fine Royalty says it's fully insured I added it to my policy and put the car in both our names until you get your license just in case anything happened your covered. I got you smiling Royalty says now follow me ok we have one stop to make.

Ok I'll follow you Liberty says excitedly.

Driving as slowly as possible Royalty wanted to make sure Liberty was keeping up which Liberty was. Liberty was driving good using all her signals and staying closely behind Royalty. Royalty took the streets to West Beverly Hills instead of taking the freeway which would have been faster, but Royalty didn't know how Liberty would do on the freeway. Pulling up to the townhouse Royalty hit the garage opener and let the garage up. Royalty forgot Amir had a BMW in the garage damn Royalty was thinking what else had she forgotten about. Pulling up behind Royalty Liberty asked where she could park at. Pull inside your car is newer Royalty said. I'll park on the street. Pulling out letting Liberty pull inside the garage. Go slow but there's plenty of room it's a three car garage Royalty yells out her window. Liberty parked nicely besides the BMW. Liberty could actually drive pretty good Royalty was thinking grateful. After parking in the garage and getting Angel out the car Liberty asks Royalty could she go inside and use the restroom. Absolutely let's go in I have to get something from here opening up the door.

Is this where you live at? Angel asks Royalty.

No not anymore Royalty says Unlocking the door and opening it. The house was pitch black. Stay right here Royalty said to Liberty and Angel as she walked inside to the living room to turned on a light it had been a while since Royalty had been there. Turning on the light ok y'all can come in now Royalty yells outs.

Walking in Liberty closes the door behind her and asks where the bathroom was at.

Down the hallway to your right Royalty says. Walking as fast as she could Liberty headed in the direction Royalty gave her directions to.

Sitting down on the cold leather couches Angel says it's cold in here Miss Royalty can you put the heater on please.

The townhouse was cold nobody had been there in months not even to clean up and the place was Hella dusty. Royalty planned on calling the cleaning service tomorrow to have this place cleaned up. Ok baby girl getting up to turn on the heater it is cold huh? Royalty says walking to the thermostat turning it on full blast, so the house could warm up fast. Coming out the restroom Liberty comes and sit down next to Angel giving her a hug. How you like your new car? Royalty asks Liberty.

I love it thanks again Liberty says.

Me too Angel says. I have a tv in the back I was watching cartoons smiling. I like our car we're going to take it home right mommy? Angel asked praying they didn't have the give the car back. Liberty looked at Royalty and paused a moment because Liberty was praying the same thing. Royalty shook her head yes and Liberty turned and looked at Angel and says yes baby we're keeping the car. It's going home with us smiling.

This was me and Amir's first place. We moved here when we were teenagers Royalty said. We were renting at first then a few years later the owner died, and he had one daughter that lived out of state and she didn't want anything to do this this place, so she sold it to us. Thankfully we had the money to buy it. We didn't live here too long about four years or five I think before we brought the house, we live in now we'll me since Amir passed. Royalty says.

Looking around Liberty felt a little awkward being in Amir's and Royalty House that held so much sentimental value Liberty was starting to wonder why Royalty had brought her there.

I'm glad you like your new car but that's not the only surprise I have for you Royalty says tossing Liberty the house keys. Wait what is this Liberty says confused catching the keys looking at them.

It means that you're the new owner of this property. Tomorrow I'm going to the title company and put this house in you and Angel name Royalty said grinning.

Wait Royalty your giving me this house that you and Amir lived in and you brought me a car I'm getting nervous Royalty what is it you need me to do lie to the police or something for you?

Laughing Royalty says no that's not it. I'm just trying to right some of my wrongs in life that's all. Plus, you're an amazing mother to Angel who had fallen asleep on the couch balled up in a knot. I admire your strength and the love you have for your daughter. I didn't have that growing up. My mother never showed me any love but that's another story for another time. I was going to sell this place but by you being pregnant by Amir I feel it's only right that you have it. I know it's not brand new or upgraded but it's nice and it's paid for. I hardly ever came back here after we moved out, but Amir came here for business reasons. There's a safe in the bedroom and I think it's about 50,000 in there I want you to have that also. Put 10,000 in a bank account for yourself, 10,000 for Angel and 10,000 for the baby. The feds can't touch you as long as you put under 10,000 in the bank at a time. So, don't open the accounts at the same time ok?

Liberty was speechless she didn't know what to say. This was too overwhelming for her. Her life had changed completely in 24 hrs. Thank you Royalty I don't know what else to say clenching the house keys in her hands tightly to stop them from shaking.

Giving Liberty a hug Royalty says gladly welcome home let me show you around the house standing up taken Liberty by the hand.
Royalty showed Liberty around the three bedroom two bath townhouse and told Liberty she could keep all the furniture if she wanted to or that she could buy some more it was clearly up to her. Liberty loved everything about the place, but Liberty wanted to make one room into the nursery for the baby and the second room a big girl room for Angel and decorate the room in strawberry shortcake because that was Angel favorite. Royalty told Liberty that she gave her the money to do as she pleased. Plus, Royalty was going to give Liberty an extra $1500 a month from Amir's business account for child support when the baby was born. Liberty was literally on cloud nine. Royalty also told Liberty that she wouldn't be monitoring her so Liberty didn't have to worry about that, but Royalty would stop by from time to time. Liberty didn't mind at all because Liberty really didn't have any friends just her one best friend Tamika, but Tamika was with her boyfriend most of the time. Liberty couldn't wait to share her good news with Tamika tomorrow. After the tour of the house Royalty needed a drink and Liberty was hungry again. Going downstairs to the kitchen Royalty didn't know if there was any food in the house but what Royalty did know was there was something to drink meaning alcohol because one thing Royalty did know was that Amir loved to drink so Royalty was positive there was some bottles in the house. And to Royalty surprise there was a few groceries in the fridge, but Royalty didn't know how old the stuff was. It had to be at least over 90 days. Amir's boy also had a key to the townhouse because they brought their hoes here when they were tricking off this was their honeycomb hideout. Amir didn't know Royalty knew that part, but Royalty knew everything. Royalty would have to call a locksmith tomorrow and get the locks changed and let Amir's day one know that she gave the house to Amir's sidechick. Laughing at that thought pouring herself a drink. You can eat at your own risk Royalty said to Liberty. I'm not sure what's good or should be thrown out but tomorrow you can get rid of of everything and go grocery shopping. I know Angel going to like that in you'll new car laughing.

Right I think Angel more excited about the car than I am Liberty says looking in the refrigerator picking stuff up and putting it back down after reading the date on it.

Look in the cabinet it might be something good in their Royalty says.

Finding a can of chili Liberty says I found something Laughing.

The pots are under the sink over their Royalty says pointing to the cabinets next to the stove. When we moved out, we left everything and started brand new. That's why the house is fully furnished sipping her Moët. You can have everything in the the house except the wine Royalty says laughing. I'll keep the bottles here for when I come over. Plus, my house has a wine cellar fully stocked. Making her chili and sitting down at the kitchen table next to Royalty who had finished damn near the whole bottle of Moët and was staring at a picture of her and Amir that was on a wall next to the kitchen.

That's a nice picture of you two how old were you guys? Liberty asked You'll looked really young.

We were. That was the first professional pictures we had ever taken together it's when I first got out of the hospital from my accident.

It's a beautiful picture Liberty says.

Thank you, Royalty says in a low voice. I'll take the picture when I leave tomorrow. I'm too drunk to drive getting up taking the picture of the wall heading to the bedroom. I'm going to lay down Liberty Royalty says with her head down looking sad. I'm tired. You and Angel can sleep in the other rooms if you need extra blankets there's some in the hall closet. Make yourself at home. Goodnight I'm drunk, and tired Royalty said walking into the bedroom closing the door.

Liberty didn't know what to think at this point. Royalty went from super charged to deflated after looking at that picture of her and Amir. Liberty didn't know if it was that Royalty just missed Amir and seeing that picture brought it all back or mentioning some accident from her past sent her into a depressed state. But whatever it was it wasn't good. Because Royalty didn't even look like herself after taking the picture off the wall and walking into the bedroom. Liberty picked Angel up off the couch and carried her upstairs into the bedroom and laid Angel on the bed. Liberty didn't want to undo the bed that was so nicely made up, so Liberty went back downstairs and got two blankets out the closet and laid one over Angel and one over herself and laid next to Angel hugging her tight and said her prayers and Thank God for the blessings he had given her and Angel today. And Liberty Prayed that Royalty would find peace because Liberty knew that Royalty wasn't as happy as she wanted her to believe. Royalty was dealing with something that only Royalty knew about, and it seemed like it was haunting Royalty and holding her captive and Liberty prayed that Royalty would be freed from whatever it was then Liberty fell asleep.
Royalty woke up with a slight headache from mixing her liquor which Royalty hardly ever did. Looking over on what would have been Amir's side of the bed their picture layed there. Damn I was tripping last night Royalty says to herself getting up laughing at the fact that she had slept in her clothes and shoes. Royalty hadn't done that in a while. Looking around the room Royalty missed this place this is where Royalty and Amir had some long conversations and Big fights at. This was their first official home together where Amir brought Royalty to after her accident and cared for Royalty and treated Royalty like a princess. This is where they first made love for the first time right here in this room in this bed. Damn shit can change quickly Royalty was thinking. For the best or for the worse walking into the closet to see if she had anything in there worth taking. Nope nothing but Amir had a few pieces of clothing that Royalty would leave just in case Liberty wanted something of his for the baby. Royalty checks the safe and counts the money and like Royalty

predicted $50 racks exactly. Royalty remembered Amir telling her he had put some money up over here right before Amir passed. Liberty should be straight with that for a while. Plus, this was money Amir took from a connect during a robbery that went bad and Royalty didn't want no parts of it also Royalty didn't need it. Royalty wished that all the wrong shit her and Amir had done could be reversed that she could take it all back. They never intended to hurt anyone, but they did. And Royalty started to believe that Karma had caught up with her somehow. Suddenly Royalty felt like she needed to throw up running to the bathroom. After throwing up Royalty felt a little better until Royalty noticed the empty box of Trojans in the garbage can. Picking up the box and looking at it for a minute and dropping it back in the trash Royalty felt defeated in life. Washing her face and rinsing her mouth out and looking in the mirror Royalty hated the women she was staring at. Shit is fucked Up Royalty get your shit together don't fall into no depression Royalty told herself. Royalty was ready to get out this house too many memories this house held all her secrets and demons and Royalty wasn't about to give in to this negative energy. Walking out the bedroom forgetting to grab the picture Royalty doesn't see Liberty or Angel. Calling Liberty name no answer. Checking the garage Royalty sees Liberty Car was gone. Good for her Royalty thinking Liberty probably went to take Angel to school smiling. Yeah, this house will be good for them but it's no good for me I'm outta here leaving out the front door locking it not sure when she would ever return. Starting up her truck Royalty sat there for a minute checking her phone. Fourteen missed calls from Jacques hmmm that's interesting. Hella voicemail and a text from Bianca that read:

(Oh, bitch you can't answer your phone now?? You back on your bullshit I see. Anyways Bitch I'm sure you'll call because I have some tea on Jacques. Yeah, I bet that got your attention!!!!! Call me ASAP)

Some tea Royalty wondered what had Bianca

found out. Royalty Listened to Jacques voicemail rolling her eyes.

1st message "I understand your being upset but you have to let me explain my side of the story first. I know what you're thinking but it's not that. Call me back "

2nd message "So you not texting me back now really? You being childish Royalty call a nigga back, so we can talk about this "

3rd message "I'm sitting outside your house and I'm not leaving stop playing with me Royalty I'm trying to explain myself "

4th message "Don't make me fuck you up for playing with me Royalty it's 2am where the fuck you at not answering your phone?"

This nigga crazy or what? Fuck me up the fuck! It was his wife at his shit and he mad at me? Niggas sure know how to switch some shit around to make everything your fault. Laughing. Fuck him and that bitch. Keep calling nigga and keep getting sent to voicemail Royalty said to herself driving off smiling headed to Bianca house to get the tea on Jacques ass.

Listening to Cardi B on full blast had Royalty feeling some type of way and put Royalty in a better mood. As Royalty pulls up to Bianca house Bianca was walking out her house to leave. Rolling her window down Royalty yells out her window. No, you're not leaving bitch we need to talk.

Walking getting in her car Bianca replies laughing Oh now you want to talk, and Bianca closes her car door and started her car up.

Royalty pulls her truck in front of Bianca Car blocking Bianca in then Royalty turned her truck off and jumped out. Hit my shit bitch if you want to and we fighting Royalty said walking to Bianca front door pulling her keys out to open the door.

Getting out her car slamming her car door Bianca started screaming. What the fuck is your problem bitch? Move your fucking car now Walking up on Royalty.

Bitch what's up Royalty says bucking up like she was ready to fight. You know you don't want these problems bitch Royalty says balling her fists up like what.

Bianca says I wish you would hit me bitch i'll shoot your ass in your leg. Going in her purse pulling out her gun.

Oh, bitch we pulling out guns now huh? Like I'm not strapped too bitch. Royalty says pulling her gun out pointing her gun at Bianca face and does the shooting motion like pow bitch. Bitch I does this in real life for a living bitch I'm from the projects hoe what's up? Royalty says standing in attention like she was about to be in a shootout.

Putting her gun back in her purse Bianca says you win bitch I don't have the energy for this shit it's too damn early.

Putting her gun to her mouth and acting like she was blowing smoke Royalty says I knew you didn't want this smoke bitch laughing.

The neighbor that was peeking out his window was in complete shock he just knew Royalty and Bianca was about to start shooting at each other. He wanted to see who was going to shoot first. He thought Bianca had finally got caught up for fucking with everybody's man because Bianca had different men coming and going like Bianca was running a whore house. There was so many foreign cars always parked in Bianca driveway you would have thought she was a celebrity or something. Closing his blinds. The neighbor was thinking ok if not today the day is coming because that girl that lives across the street is a wild one.

Whatever Royalty Bianca says walking behind Royalty as she was opening her front door going into her house punking her Bianca was thinking. Sitting down in the kitchen Bianca says so you read my text, but you couldn't call back?

No bitch making herself some tea. Royalty says I need the tea laughing and I'm making tea that's funny huh?

Bianca didn't find anything funny.

Royalty put her cup in the microwave and when it beeped took it out and added her tea bag to the water and sat down at the kitchen table next to Bianca. Ok tell me the goods Royalty said sipping her hot tea.

Well for starters bitch Jacques is crazier than you Bianca says looking at her phone. My client just canceled. She's not getting her deposit back either.

Why she cancel? Royalty asks sipping her tea.

Um reading her texts she says she was just in a car accident and she's waiting for the tow truck and wants to come a little later.

You got any openings? Royalty asks.

Um I need to check with my receptionist, but I think I do Bianca says looking from her phone to Royalty. Ok back to Jacques. My friend knows someone who dealt with Jacques on a business level. Did you know Jacques was the connect?

The connect to what Royalty asks.

You know what bitch stop acting like you slow all of a sudden. He's the man bitch like Amir was the man. They're both in the same business. Illegal business with store fronts Laughing.

Ain't shit funny Bianca Royalty says. You know I went to Amir boutique yesterday and his wife was there.

Bitch what? And what you do? Bianca inquired.

I didn't do shit I walked out Royalty replied

And? Bianca says.

And nothing bitch laughing Royalty says

No way that ain't even like you? Bianca said you didn't even say nothing to Jacques?

Amir wasn't there Royalty says thinking about the situation.

We're was Amir? Bianca asks

I don't know bitch I'm not his babysitter Royalty says angrily.

Oh, so you left mad laughing Bianca said I'm surprised you didn't come over here and take it out on me Bianca says still laughing.

Ain't shit funny bitch. Royalty says getting up putting her cup in the dishwasher. Bitch I brought Liberty a car yesterday too.

Who's Liberty? Thinking about it for a minute oh that Liberty. You brought her a what? Why you do that? You got that mad that you went and bought the side chick bitch a car? Bianca says confused You must have fell and bumped your head bitch you sound Hella stupid right now.

Getting up to pour herself a drink. You want a drink Bianca asked Royalty holding up a bottle of Moët.

Yes, pour me one but add some orange juice I haven't ate nothing this morning Royalty says.

Getting the orange juice out the refrigerator and making Royalty a drink and handing it to her Bianca asks Royalty and what kind of car did you buy that bitch anyways?

Downing her drink Royalty says a Tesla.

A what bitch? Are you serious right now? Royalty why? What happens if that's not even Amir's baby then what?

That's Amir's baby Royalty says.

Ok maybe it is but damn a Tesla brand new. But they do be catching on fire and shit so maybe the bitch will get into an accident and burn the fuck Up sipping her drink not bothered by what she just said.

Did you really just say that Bianca? You're going to hell for that I'm serious. Royalty says in disbelief Shaking her head.

Well Liberty going with me and plus Liberty going to shell already be on fire laughing.

I can't with you damn Bianca. I thought I was bad Royalty says seriously. Anyways what else did they say about Jacques ass Royalty asks.

Oh, Him yes they said Jacques is will kill you while you'll sitting down eating at the same table and finish his food like nothing ever happened. They said Jacques the number one hitter out here and Jacques flies back and forth to his country to escape extradition.

Royalty couldn't believe what she was hearing. This wasn't the Jacques Royalty knew. But then again Royalty really didn't know Jacques that well. All they did was fuck that's all. Wow Royalty says I need another drink and it's not even 10 am. Right Bianca says pouring them both Another drink.

So, Royalty what you going to do adopt this baby or something? Bianca wanted to know.

Adopt the baby no the baby has a mother, but I plan on being a part of their lives. Royalty says sincerely.

Their who? You plan on being friends with this bitch that was fucking your husband? Why would you do that? We should be planning on beating her ass after Liberty drop that baby that's all the planning you should be doing nothing else. Bianca says not believing her best friend was being so soft with this bitch who was pregnant by her dead man.

I took Liberty and her daughter Angel shopping yesterday too Royalty says sipping her drink.

Pulling her gun out her purse pointing at Royalty Bianca says where the fuck is my best friend at? This feels like some invasion of the body snatchers type shit bitch. Give me my best friend back.

Laughing Royalty says you might as well shoot me then because I'm not done.

Putting her gun back in her purse walking to the wine cabinet pulling out another bottle popping the cork and turning the bottle up drinking straight from it. Bianca says what else is there? Shrugging her shoulders. Please don't tell me you fucked this bitch too Royalty? Damn Jacques got you that fucked up bitch? That's some very dangerous dick sipping from the bottle again. I want some Bianca says seriously. As soon as Bianca said she wanted some Jacques dick he called.

Holding her phone up Royalty says this Him laughing. You talked him up. Be quiet bitch while I answer and I'm a put Jacques on speaker answering her phone. Putting her fingers to her lips like shhh to Bianca.

What Royalty says answering.

What you mean what? That's not how you answer a phone Royalty Jacques says.

Don't tell me how to answer my fucking phone nigga.

Nigga? Who you talking to Royalty that's not how you talk to me Jacques says. I know you're mad thinking I played with you but that's not the case.

Cutting Jacques off Royalty says I can talk to you any fucking way I want to nigga like I said before you ain't my fucking husband nigga that's your wife that owes you some respect not me.

Laughing Jacques says. Ok Royalty look I'm going to say this one more time. I understand your mad or whatever but what you're not going to do is talk disrespectful to me mad or not!! I'm not talking disrespectful to you Royalty and truthfully, I don't have to even explain myself but I'm not that type of man to not let you know what's going on with me. Now yes, I should have told you my wife.

Click. Royalty hung up. Fuck him and his wife. Looking at her phone. Fuck you bitch ass nigga Royalty yelled at her phone laughing.

Royalty be careful they say that nigga ain't no joke don't be playing with Jacques ass like that Bianca said seriously. Jacques might blow your car up or something getting scared Bianca says.

Calling back Royalty sends Jacques to voicemail. Fuck him. Royalty says. And you acting like Jacques is Scarface or something Laughing fuck Jacques ass. I don't know why Jacques feels the need to explain shit to me anyways. I'm just his side piece laughing.

Well side chicks are clearly winning right now Bianca says. For example, Amir's baby mama laughing. Bitch just hit the lotto with your ass getting Tesla's and shit. So, calm down with the side chick title laughing.

Fuck You Royalty says thinking damn I probably can't even go home. What if Jacques was waiting outside her house. Damn what was Royalty going to do now. Bianca I can't go home now what should I do? Royalty asked.

Call that nigga back and apologize because you're not staying here, I don't want no parts of your shit bitch. They say that nigga ain't cool if you cross him. I'm good homie Bianca says.

Shut your scary ass up Royalty says. All the shit you put me in without my approval bitch you got your nerves. Royalty says. You're in it wither you want to be or not now Royalty says trying to figure out what to do. Royalty didn't think about that when she was talking shit to Jacques now Royalty was stuck trying to figure out what the fuck to do next.
Well bitch let's go eat since this might be our last meal Laughing before that nigga Jacques kills us both. Let's go to the Fountain Coffee Room I'm starving Bianca says to Royalty.

The one on Sunset Blvd in Beverly Hills? Royalty asks.

Yes, that one it's close to work then I can go check in and see if I have any openings for today Bianca says getting up from the table checking the locks on her kitchen door and checking the windows.

What your scary ass checking shit for Royalty says laughing. If somebody wanted to do something to your punk ass, I'm almost positive they not trying to break in through no windows. Plus, you know you got neighborhood watch all over this noisy ass block. All these old, retired mother fuckers all they do is stay in people business Royalty said Laughing.

I know right Bianca said but still I feel more comfortable checking bitch is that alright with you? Bianca says walking checking everything.

Ok let's go getting up Royalty says walking to the front door turning around and says oh and don't forget to put your alarm on Laughing walking out to her truck.

After double checking everything Bianca locked up the house and put her alarm on something she rarely did.

I'll meet you there Royalty says driving off.

Bianca waved at her noisy neighbor who was peeking out the window and didn't even know that Bianca saw him looking. Bianca was grateful someone was watching out for her because you just never knew what could jump off especially with Bianca or Royalty. Because the way they were living was real dangerous. They were both young and reckless. Driving to the restaurant Bianca got a call that some guy had stopped by her shop but wouldn't leave his name he only said he'll come back later. Now Bianca was really tripping thinking Jacques was after her too Bianca was getting paranoid. Bianca arrived before Royalty to the restaurant somehow and went inside and got them a table. A few minutes later Royalty walks in smiling. What you smiling at Bianca asks? And what took you so long you left before me?

Oh, I needed some gas and this rapper dude was at the gas station and we talked for a minute and exchanged numbers.

What rapper? What's his name bitch Bianca asks excitedly wanting to know. You always coming up with somebody bitch smiling Bianca says.

And I look a hot mess Royalty says. Anyways he's a up and coming rapper with hella mixtapes out right now you probably don't even know him he's from New Orleans but he's signing with a major label out here sitting down Royalty says. I'm starving looking around for the waitress.

Was he fine bitch? What was he driving Bianca asks curiously?

Laughing Royalty says he was alright. Then the waitress comes over to take their orders. Pancakes and chicken apple sausages and a cup of coffee French vanilla Please Royalty says. I'm going to need it.

Same thing for me please but no coffee but I'll take some hot chocolate with whip cream and add some scrambled eggs with cheese also. Bianca says. As the waitress walks away Bianca starts up again. Ok ok tell me exactly what he looks like did he have on hella chains and shit all excited. Before Royalty could answer in walks Jacques and Serenity. Bianca back was to them, so Bianca didn't see them coming but the look on Royalty face said it all. What the fuck you looking like that for Bianca said turning around and almost stumbled out her seat. What the fuck Bianca said while Serenity walked passed them and went and sat down at a booth.

Jacques came straight to the their table and stood over Royalty. Good morning ladies Jacques says being sarcastic. Royalty sat there rolling her eyes. Bianca was so nervous she almost peed on herself.

What you got a gps tracker on me or something Royalty asked Jacques who was staring Royalty down.

Naw nothing like that. Why you hang up in my face shortie? Jacques asked Royalty.

Boy bye Royalty said waving her hand like move. Your wife over there waiting on you get away from me please trying to act like she didn't want Jacques around her.

See that's what happens when you mess around with hood rats Serenity says walking up behind Jacques with no warning.

And without even turning around Jacques says Serenity please go sit back down this doesn't concern you.

Did that bitch just call me a hoodrat Royalty says getting up?

Yes, I did Serenity said only hoodrats wears the same clothing from yesterday laughing.

Looking at herself momentarily Royalty forgot she did still on the same clothing from yesterday because Royalty hadn't made it home to change yet.

Serenity was Shaking her head laughing This is what happens Jacques when you try and make these types of women relevant.

These types of women what the fuck Royalty says trying to get around Jacques to beat Serenity ass. But Jacques was blocking Royalty from moving. Bitch I've been relevant Royalty says still trying to get around Jacques.

Oh, is that right? Serenity asked what kind of relevant? Group chat relevant or blogs relevant Laughing. Royalty was on fire now and was trying to get to Serenity, but Jacques had scooped Royalty up and was taking Royalty outside. But Serenity was still taunting Royalty while Jacques was taking Royalty out. Are you Hype magazine relevant or Vogue magazine relevant still laughing Serenity said while Royalty was screaming all types of vulgarity at Serenity.

The waitress was standing there with Royalty and Bianca food frozen not believing this was happening at their establishment, but it was. Bianca was scared not knowing what Jacques was going to do to Royalty, but Bianca was also ready to help her best friend.

You type of women always interfering with someone marriage Serenity said towards Bianca walking back to her seat.

Who the fuck you talking to bitch like that? Bianca says jumping up grabbing a plate off the waitress tray and smashing it in Serenity face. My type of people don't play like that bitch Bianca said waiting for Serenity to jump up, but Serenity never did. Instead Serenity wiped her face and started screaming.

Bianca got scared and ran out the restaurant as soon as Jacques came in the whole scene was chaotic. Some customers had even called the police. Royalty was sitting in Jacques car where they had been talking briefly and Jacques ordered Royalty to stay put while he got out to see what was was going on inside the restaurant because a few people started running out. But when Bianca came running out the restaurant flying pass Jacques Car Royalty got out to see what was wrong with her best friend. Royalty couldn't get to Bianca in time because Bianca had jumped in her car and had taken off.

Royalty tried to go back inside the restaurant, but Jacques had came out and told Royalty to go home and he'll call her later this shit had gotten out of control. Hoping in her truck driving to Bianca shop Royalty tried calling Bianca several times but it keep going to voicemail. When Royalty pulled up at her salon Royalty didn't see Bianca car parked outside. Royalty parked in her parking spot reserved especially for Royalty in front of Royalty salon Pretty Please and went inside to see if Bianca had stopped by there.

Hey Royalty girl you coming in today one of the stylists asks.

No, I'm just looking for Bianca looking around the salon everything good here? Royalty asks.

Yeah, we straight the stylist says we just had our Costco run yesterday so we're good on supplies and the floors got done this weekend and all bills are paid Laughing so we straight the stylist says.

Ok good because I'm not shit is going down, I'll call you later to feel you in Royalty said walking out.

You better Royalty stylist yelled back.

Royalty goes next door to Bianca place of business to see if Bianca had stopped by there, but her receptionist said no she hadn't seen Bianca. Where the fuck was Bianca at Royalty was thinking. Calling Bianca Phone again still no answer. Where is this bitch Royalty thinking then it occurred to Royalty where Bianca might be?
Royalty wasn't sure if Bianca would be there, but Royalty decided to give it a shot anyways going to Bianca parents house. And sure, enough Bianca Car was parked outside. Pulling into the driveway Royalty parks next to Bianca Bentley and went inside. The front door was unlocked as usual this family didn't believe in locking their front door for some reason it was strange to Royalty especially since this family was one of the biggest drug dealers in Los Angeles. But despite that their home was always open to anyone. Bianca parents believed in helping everyone they could they were always willing to help somebody out. Where you at Bianca? Royalty yells throughout the house checking all the bedrooms. Bianca wasn't in the house nobody was at home. Royalty went out back and Bianca was in the backyard talking to her cousin Spanky who had just got out of jail.

What's up Royalty giving Royalty a hug it's been a while you still look the same Spanky says.

You too besides getting all buff and shit welcome home. Royalty says checking Spanky out.

Spanky was a devoted Mexican gangbanger with the teardrops tattooed on his face and everything Spanky even had his gang tattooed on his neck for full display and of course he was dressed in his gang banging khaki uniform. You'll never catch him not wearing it and he had his red bandanna hanging out his back pocket.

Why your scary ass run out of the restaurant? Royalty asks turning her attention to Bianca now.

Because bitch I hit Jacques wife in the face with a plate of food Bianca said nervously.

Smiling Royalty says good job raising her hand for high five.

Bianca slapped Royalty hand to high five her back. Bitch I thought Jacques was going to kill me Bianca says. I didn't sign up for the death penalty bitch fucking around with you and your nigga frowning her face up. But Amir's wife talk too much shit I don't care how cute that stallion bitch is she asked for it taking the blunt from Spanky Bianca said hitting the weed.

What happened Spanky asked high as a kite. We got beef?

No Spanky we pointing from him to her we don't have beef laughing I got beef Royalty said. Royalty didn't want to involve Spanky in her shit because Spanky didn't fight fair. Spanky was a straight gangster been like that his whole entire life. All Spanky wanted to see from a person was red blood pouring out from a nigga or a bitch. Spanky was notorious with a machete. Calm down killer patting his shoulder if we need you, I'll let you know.

Ok Lil Sis because you know me, I'll be all over whatever like flies on shit!! I'm knocking niggas down like bowling pins around this bitch hitting the blunt. Spanky probably just got a hard on just thinking about knocking a nigga down. Spanky lived for that shit.

Bianca you always running over here with your scary ass Royalty said sitting down on the lounge chair stretching out like she was at the beach. Damn I haven't been back here in a minute. I remember when we were younger, we would have some crazy pool parties back here. We should do that again. Royalty suggested.

For what? Bianca said irritated. I'm not inviting nobody to the M's house now that we're grown bitch. Plus, the M's don't speak to my ass half the time anyways Laughing Bianca says. The only reason I came over here was because I knew they were out of town and I knew Spanky had just got out. I wanted to see his crazy ass before he went back in because it's only a matter of time Laughing.

Spanky laughed too.

That's not funny man Royalty said. Spanky you not trying to stay out this time?

Hell yeah Lil Sis I'm taking my meds and I'm getting a job driving Uber.

They all burst out laughing. Uber nigga is you crazy? Bianca said. All you going to do is kidnapped some bitch you supposed to be giving a ride.

It's not kidnapping if they requested my services in his Spanish voice Spanky says laughing.

Remind me to cancel my Uber services Royalty said Laughing.

Me too Bianca said blowing out smoke these criminals are finding new ways to do shit legal now damn homie.

Royalty phone started ringing looking at it Royalty says Bianca it's Jacques Laughing. Bianca scary ass jump behind Spanky like Jacques was there or something. I'm not answering it fuck him.

No no Royalty answer it and see what Jacques has to say. He could be looking for me Bianca says nervously.

Girl please if Jacques wanted to do something to you Jacques would have at the restaurant. Royalty says sending Jacques to voicemail. I'm not fucking with his ass no more I'm over it already getting up to leave. I'm going home to wash my ass and take a nap. I'll call you later be careful Laughing Royalty says to Bianca and bye Spanky don't catch a life sentence nigga fucking around with Uber nigga I know your ass you ain't cool blood.

I ain't going back Lil Sis they going to have to kill me this time Spanky says seriously.

Bye Bye you crazy fools I'm out throwing up the deuces walking into the house thinking Bianca whole family was crazy. From her parents who sold major dope for a living flying back and forth from Mexico themselves with the dope because they didn't trust nobody to transport it for them. They were old school and had never been caught. Royalty remembered when they were younger

Bianca parents letting fifteen family members live in their house at once any and everybody was welcome. And Bianca parents also let kids drink alcohol they said they didn't care it wasn't their problem. That's why Bianca was the way she was now because they didn't care about shit. They had no cares in the world besides each other. Walking out the front door Royalty locked it before shutting the door just because you never knew who might try and run up in your shit nowadays people was real thirsty these days. Driving home Royalty was hella tired for some reason and wanted to take a nap before heading out again. When Royalty got in the house Royalty took a hot bubble bath and was about to lay down when the doorbell rang. Thinking it was Bianca Royalty put on her robe and ran downstairs without even putting her slippers on.

Opening the door in walks Jacques. Don't fucking play with me man pointing his finger in Royalty face.

Backing up Royalty responded Get the fuck out my house Jacques with that bullshit didn't nobody tell you to come over here anyways where's your wife at?

She's where the fuck she's at. Why do you keep asking about her? She ain't your business Royalty like I told you before. Poking Royalty in the noise with his finger. I told your Lil ass stop fucking with me like that stop playing with me Royalty.

Royalty turned her back on Jacques trying to run up the stairs but wasn't quick enough and Jacques grabbed Royalty hair and pulled her backwards towards him.

Stop Jacques let me go!! Royalty said trying to yank away but couldn't. Picking Royalty up Jacques carried Royalty up the stairs to her bedroom and threw Royalty on the bed. Take that robe off Jacques said undressing.

No fuck You Royalty said angrily.

That's exactly what your about to do Jacques replied laughing. Get on top and ride this dick nice and slow Jacques demanded.

Are you stupid or retarted boy? I ain't fucking with you like that no more. Royalty said trying to get up, but Jacques grabbed Royalty leg and pulled her down and started kissing Royalty hard. After a minute Royalty reciprocated and stuck her tongue in Jacques mouth and Jacques bite her tongue. Awe Royalty yelled out why you do that? Royalty asked Jacques.

That's what you get for playing hard to get laughing. Now suck My dick baby and get Daddy rock Hard Jacques says laying his back up against a few throw pillows.

Royalty just looked at Jacques like you're playing, right? Sitting on top of Jacques with her titties hard and her pussy wet Royalty robe had come wide open showing Jacques all her goodies. As bad as Royalty wanted Jacques inside her Royalty didn't want Jacques to know it though. Negro please closing her robe let your wife suck Your dick she's in town Royalty said trying to get up, but Jacques sat up and grabbed Royalty ass.

She doesn't suck dick Jacques says trying to kiss Royalty again, but Royalty kept moving her face from side to side preventing Jacques from kissing her.

What you mean she don't suck dick? Why what's wrong with her? Royalty inquired wanting to know.

Your fucking up the vibe babe with all these questions Jacques says laying back again. Look I don't fuck with her like that babe, we're only married by paper only. She has a man and I got you slapping Royalty ass laughing.

Now Royalty didn't know if Jacques was lying or not but for some reason Royalty believed Jacques and even if Jacques was lying Royalty wanted to prove to herself that Jacques wanted her more than Jacques wanted his wife. Royalty wanted to sex Jacques so good that Jacques didn't think about his wife anymore. You know how all the women that cheats with a married man feels when their together. Like Jacques must don't want to be with that bitch he's here with me. Feeding herself all those negative lies and delusional thoughts to make herself feel inferior at that moment. Like what she was doing was ok and it has to be the wife that's doing something wrong not Royalty that's why Jacques was with her right now and not at home in the first place. That's how Royalty was feeling giving her whole soul to Jacques stripping her dignity and morals away. But it wasn't entirely Royalty fault. Royalty wasn't taught any better all Royalty knew was how to snatch souls and dispose of them. Wasn't no love lost with Royalty it even crossed Royalty mind to ask Jacques could her and his wife and Jacques all have a threesome.
Where we going? Royalty asks Bianca who called Royalty and said she needed to talk to her about something important be ready when she pulled up.

Where going to the gun range, I need to get some shit off my chest bitches keep trying me. Bianca says nonchalantly. Looking over at Royalty Bianca says you look cute girly with that glow you got going on what's good with you bitch? Somebody's been getting dicked down and don't deny it either Bianca says smiling.

Staring out the window not wanting to make any eye contact just thinking about the last few months Royalty felt like she let Amir down and herself Royalty hadn't accomplished nothing or moved forward in life if anything Royalty felt like she moved backwards. That's a fake glow it's Vaseline from the brown tube Royalty said turning her attention now to Bianca. And yes, I've gotten some dick. I fucked Jacques last night sighing. I feel so stupid Royalty said caught up in her feelings.

After all the shit went down yesterday girl, I knew you was going to fuck back with Jacques ass Bianca said laughing. And don't you start feeling sorry for yourself bitch shit happens its life Bianca said hitting her blunt. Just imagine there's a woman somewhere probably in the projects but not even in the projects maybe a fucking condo sitting in the dark because her lights are cut off and she has No Pge or maybe there's some bitch that's about to run out of gas because she don't have no gas money or no money Period but they're both fucking with a ballin ass nigga that won't give them a dime but he's just fucking them. Now that's what you call stupid ass bitch laughing that's not you girl. Bianca says laughing.

Royalty started laughing too. That's why I love you Bianca you're going to keep me on my toes at all times. I wish a nigga would be fucking with me and I'm sitting at home broke. The fuck I look like Royalty said getting pumped. Even when Jacques left this morning while I was knocked the fuck out that nigga still left a rack sitting on my dresser Royalty said laughing.

He did let's go shopping bitch Bianca said excitedly.

Frowning up her face Royalty said No! You always think my money supposed to be split 50/50 bitch with your ass. You didn't suck nan ball last night bitch why should I share my trick money with you? laughing Royalty asks Bianca

Well for one bitch you don't know for sure that I didn't suck no balls last night it wasn't Jacques balls, but I did suck some balls laughing and for two bitch I'm your mother fucking counselor hoe, so you rather pay me a little fee than pay them high ass charging by the hour ass counselors laughing pulling into Lax Firing Range.

Oh, you wasn't playing when you said let off some steam huh? Royalty asks. I'm with it I need this kind of relaxation getting out the car Royalty says. But if I would have known where we were going, I wouldn't have worn this freaking dress, but I do have on tennis shoes so I'm Good giving Bianca the thumbs up.

He'll look how I'm dressed Bianca says walking besides Royalty wearing a Gucci hoodie dress with thigh high boots and had her Gucci fanny pack wrapped around her shoulders.

Bitch you always fly Royalty said walking in the gun range excited and couldn't wait to test her skills because it had been a while since Royalty actually shot her gun.

Let's imagine these hating bitches as are targets Bianca says showing her id to the clerk to check out a gun. I always picture a bitch face I can't stand like this morning this punk ass bitch called my phone talking bout you fucking with my man. I said correction bitch Our man Laughing.

Only you Royalty said ok finish.

Yeah then I told the bitch I'm only fucking with him until my man get out.

Wait what man you referring to Royalty asks puzzled.

Laughing Bianca said I just said that shit to fuck her up. I wanted the bitch to think her nigga was my side nigga laughing. You do know most niggas are side chicks their damn selves.

Royalty started laughing too. Right most of them are.

Then the bitch gone tell me to find my own man. So, I had to shut that bitch down I told that raggedy hoe bitch as long as your man putting his tongue in places it don't belong, I'm fucking with him laughing. The bitch hung up in my face and didn't call back.

That was a good One Royalty said Laughing.

Ok ladies your all set the gentlemen says handing Royalty and Bianca their goggles and 9mm and told them their allotted area. Have fun ladies he said laughing from listening to their conversation shaking his head.

Bianca said to Royalty take my picture for the gram, so I can let these hoes know I'm not playing with they assess holding her gun aiming to shoot Laughing. Taking Hella pictures trying to get Bianca angles right finally Royalty and Bianca did there thing at the shooting range and they both did pretty good. I need more practice Bianca said holding her target paper up all my shots were to the left. I didn't even get a headshot Bianca said disappointed.

But Royalty had a head and heart shot she didn't miss a beat. Royalty knew how to definitely shoot her 9mm because she had plenty of experience from her past.

I'm hanging my target up in my guest room as a reminder for me to get better at shooting Bianca said Laughing. You know how people do vision boards and hang then up well this one is mine rolling it up putting it in the backseat of her car. Let's go eat I'm starving Bianca said.

Me too Royalty agreed I need a drink after that shot. Your turning into a baby alcoholic Bianca says seriously you better slow down before you kill your liver looking over at Royalty. Yeah yeah, I'll slow down when you slow down on smoking that weed Royalty says back to Bianca. You always got some slick shit to say my nigga rolling her eyes. Well don't stop then because I ain't never gone stop smoking Bianca says. Singing when I die bury me inside the cannabis store laughing. Royalty laughed too and said you're so crazy. We're are we going to eat I have a taste for some Benihana Royalty says. Ok Benihana it is then Bianca says busting an illegal u turn. Is your license even valid? Royalty asks Bianca who just looked at Royalty and turned Tupac I ain't no killer but don't push me up loud and said that's going to be my caption for my picture when I post it laughing flying down the street like she owned the damn city and was untouchable.

I'm so glad we decided to come here Bianca says sitting down at a table of twelve at Benihana with Royalty. I love the show the chef does it wows me every time Bianca says.

Me too Royalty agrees with Bianca plus their drinks are so bomb Royalty says.

Bianca mouths quietly in Royalty face baby alcoholic laughing.

Fuck You Royalty mouthed back looking over the menu but already knew everything on it and had it memorized. Royalty always ordered the same thing every time she came here. Hibachi Salmon with shrimp with rice with extra garlic and soup. It never changed even if Royalty added an appetizer. After ordering their drinks and food. Bianca phone started ringing off the hook and Bianca kept sending whoever it was to voicemail. Damn who's blowing you up? Royalty inquired.

Nobody important Bianca says brushing it off.

Ok Royalty replies wondering who it was and what was so important to keep calling.

Here's your Mai Tai ladies the server says handing Royalty and Bianca their drinks.

Tapping mugs toasting Here's to the good life and much Success in life and finding true love Bianca says smiling.

Touché Royalty says smiling back. You know Bianca I truly believe that I do deserve to be happy and find true love after Amir hopefully I'll find that again Royalty says solemnly.

You will best friend Bianca says you're so pretty with a good heart even though you act like a bitch sometimes laughing. But you always mean well. Look what you did for Amir's baby mama I would have never even remotely thought about doing no shit like that for a bitch having my husband baby and you don't even have a baby with him. Getting mad just thinking about it. You genuinely love helping people. My mom's always says she wish you were her daughter instead of me Bianca says sipping her drink. And I always remind her that you are laughing shit I was her son first before I was her daughter laughing.

You so stupid Bianca you were never her son with your feminine ass Laughing with Bianca Royalty says.

No, but seriously, sis we will both find real love one day when we're supposed to, I guarantee it but until then let's fuck who we want to and get this money Bianca says downing her drink.

Royalty said I'll drink to that and downed her drink also. While the chef did his little tricks at the table with their food Royalty and Bianca laughed and giggled with each other talking about old times and taking down three more drinks each. Royalty phone rang, and Royalty answered it on the first ring slightly tipsy. What's up with you Player? Royalty said.

You been drinking I can hear it all in your voice where you at? Jacques asks.

I'm somewhere you're not Royalty says laughing.

What's all that noise I hear in the background? Jacques asks.

Why you so noisy fool? I'm out with my friend I'll talk to you later hanging up in Jacques face. Jacques too mother fucking noisy to have a bitch at home Royalty says to Bianca laughing.

Don't get your ass beat Royalty Bianca says laughing.

What, Jacques better beat Serenity ass not mines I'm cool off him for a minute. I'm about to call my new little friend I meet scrolling her phone call log hitting her friend up.

Hello who dis? The caller asks.

Hey, boo it's the girl you meet at the gas station in the G5 smiling.

Oh, hey pretty girl Miss Royalty right? Laughing. I didn't think I would hear from you what's up tho? What you doing tonight? I'm having a show you want to slide thru?

Looking at Bianca Royalty mouths he has a show tonight you want to go?

Hell yes we in that bitch Bianca said getting excited.

Hello Royalty, you there? The caller asks

Oh, sorry I was asking my best friend if she wanted to come hang with me tonight is it ok if she comes along?

Absolutely the more the merrier. I'll put your names on the guest list. Text me your names and it's done. I gotta run gorgeous but I'll see ya later the show is at the House of blues at 9pm don't be late the caller says Hanging up.

Smiling from ear to ear Royalty says where in that bitch to Bianca who was already thinking about what she was going to wear.

I have to look cute and comfortable for a rap concert plus I'm trying to come up with me a rapper too Bianca says seriously. You're not going to be the only one out here dating a rapper bitch laughing. After we eat let's go to the mall Bianca says not even hungry no more because Bianca was too excited about tonight. Royalty and Bianca hurried up and finished their food and drinks and headed to Beverly Center to hit up a few of their favorite stores. Walking into Gucci Bianca saw a pair of Gucci socks that inspired her look for tonight. I want to look like a Gucci goddess Bianca said buying three pairs of Gucci socks in every color and a Gucci headband and a Gucci jumbo size fanny pack. I'm going to wear a one piece bodysuit with a crop Gucci hoodie and fuck it up tonight standing at the register twerking paying for her stuff. What you wearing boo? Bianca asks Royalty

Not Gucci that's for sure Laughing Royalty said. They won't call us the Gucci twins tonight. I'll see what the Versace store hitting for if not probably some skinny jeans and a tank top you know I leave all that over the top shit to you Royalty says. But I am going to buy this Gucci Ny baseball cap trying it on Royalty says.

Yeah get that Bianca says it's so you winking.

After they pay for their goods in Gucci they head to Versace where Royalty buys a Versace print blouse Royalty was thinking about wearing as a dress or maybe with some jean shorts. They hit a few more of their favorite stores Bloomingdales was one of Royalty favorites and Louis Vuitton. Royalty also brought two pairs of vans tennis shoes from the van store. Ok drop me off so I can start getting ready Royalty tells Bianca and come early so you can do my face please Royalty begs with praying hands.

Sighing Bianca says to Royalty you know how to do a soft beat on your own face why you always need me to do it?

Because you're my personal makeup artist that's why Royalty said letting Bianca know what time it was.

Stop taking everything personal bitch Bianca says laughing I'll do your makeup for you this time only because it's a concert and we have to shit in these hoes laughing. And don't tell me how you want your face beat either. Let me do me on this one ok? Bianca says knowing she was about to beat both her and Royalty faces up severely with all types of color popping especially since Bianca just copped all that Fenty makeup by Rihanna Bianca couldn't wait to play in.

Dropping Royalty off Bianca went and got her car detailed because it had been a minute and plus Bianca couldn't pull up in no dusty Bentley in front of no rappers. Everything had to be on point even including Bianca car. Bianca looked at her nails that could have been redone but they were still cool because they were gel polish plus Bianca didn't have time to sit and wait for on nails tonight. But Bianca was ready for a new color because the color Bianca was currently rocking Bianca had went thru three dudes in three weeks with this same color polish on. It was time to start fresh again in every area of her life Bianca was thinking. I might even get my car painted because too many people know my car from this color time to switch it up on these hoes. Bianca was contemplating.

When Royalty got inside the house Royalty took a hot bath and a quick cat nap for an hour to rest her mind that was wondering all over the place. Royalty had to shut down and recharge for tonight. When Royalty woke up, she felt refreshed and vibrant. Royalty felt brand new. It's nothing like a power nap Royalty was thinking looking thru her closet for something to put on thinking Royalty wanted to be comfortable but cute. Royalty had so many clothes that Royalty didn't have to ever buy another piece of clothing in her lifetime if Royalty didn't want to. Royalty and Amir had an addiction to shopping and ordering something online. Royalty patronage a lot of the Instagram online boutiques. Royalty gave everyone a shot at least once until a person fucked themselves out of her business like taking hella long to ship the merchandise or double charging her card or just not sending the shit Royalty ordered to Royalty period and playing with communicating with Royalty. Then it was absolutely curtains for your business with Royalty. No if and or buts about it. Royalty felt like you're not Saks fifth so don't have a Saks Fifth attitude stay humble and return my fifty, sixty dollars back and stop playing with me. It's not even about the money it's the principle. When people start to realize it's the principle behind shit they should act accordingly. But some people never got it and some shit went right over their heads. Pulling the stuff out the bags Royalty just brought Royalty was trying to figure out what to wear to look real cute but still be comfortable at the same time. Royalty wanted to turn heads tonight but also move around without her feet hurting and dance because Royalty knew it was going to be lit. Laying several outfits on her bed with shoes on the floor that matched to see what looked good with what. Finally, Royalty decided to just wear a pair of denim jean shorts with a wife beater and a Hermès scarf around her neck with Hermès accessories and her new Gucci Ny baseball cap because Royalty hair was recently flat ironed bone straight with her Louis Vuitton military boots and orange Hermès cross body. And to complement her look Royalty would wear her Gucci diamond studded glasses that was Royalty favorite go to's at the moment. Jacques had left two text messages that Royalty didn't respond to. Royalty just wasn't in the mood tonight to entertain Jacques bullshit. It was all fun and games until it wasn't anymore. Royalty knew she could find her own damn man and that she didn't have to share a nigga unless she choose to. But what wasn't going to happen was Jacques forcing Royalty into some shit Royalty hadn't signed up for. Like accepting him being married and coming and going as he pleased. Royalty didn't care how good his dick game was. Royalty wasn't the one. Royalty motto was if she couldn't be at the head of the class to simple drop the fuck out period. Royalty wasn't going back and forth with Jacques ass and his shenanigans no more. Royalty turned some music on in her room to set her mood. Alexa play Beyoncé.

Alexa responded which album?

Royalty said Dangerously in Love album.

Alexa said Bet Great choice and that set the mood while Royalty was getting ready for tonight.

Bianca came over and did her thing as usual with both their faces. Your makeup bitch is Every fucking thing Royalty said to Bianca looking at Bianca face when she walked in admiring Bianca skills.

Right bitch I ain't playing with these hoes at all tonight Bianca said blinking her eyes showing off her dramatic eyelashes with her rhinestone eyeshadow.

What made you think of that Royalty asked Bianca? The rhinestones Hella cute and different.

Smiling Bianca says I know right something different boo to set my mood. I'm Gucci Goddess remember? Laughing now sit down it's your turn. Royalty sat down at her vanity, so she could get one of Bianca famous beat down not knowing what to expect from Bianca tonight. Bianca did Royalty face with blue eyeshadows and blue eyeliner that was Hella cute plus Royalty lash extensions was already long and popping. Bianca took it a little further and did Royalty lipstick blue also with a hint of silver sparkly gloss. Bianca called the look I got the blues in a good way Laughing. You ready B let's go get em Bianca said ready to roll.

Bianca always had to be the designated driver because Bianca drove a Bentley is what Bianca told Royalty the day, she purchased it. And Royalty was ok with that because Royalty hated driving looking for parks and all the confusion plus Royalty always wanted to drink and have a good time when they went out, so it worked out perfectly for Royalty that she didn't have to drive. When Bianca and Royalty arrived at the House of Blues it was jammed back with police cars circling the area just in case something jumped off and all sorts of foreign cars everywhere, celebrities galore, big white lights in the air announcing the event and the entrance way even had the red carpet leading inside the club. The scenery was something like a movie premiere the vibe was at a high level that was intoxicating. And Royalty and Bianca was glad they were going to be a part of it.
Walking into the House of Blues was bananas paparazzi was everywhere snapping pictures at anyone who was somebody who was out tonight at this event. It was big. Even the TMZ camera crew was there. Royalty and Bianca felt like celebrities and they looked like some that was for sure. They fit right in posing for pictures walking the red carpet smiling. Approaching the door, the security asked their names and check the list and gave them back stage passes. Jumping up and down Bianca says Hell yes that's what I'm talking about Royalty just shook her head and grabbed her best friend by her hand and went inside the club.

Let's go to the bar first Royalty says leading Bianca to the bar on the first level. This place was packed like sardines it was so lit. The atmosphere was on fire and the dj had it jumping. Royalty needed a drink to calm her nerves and Bianca was already high Bianca smoked her blunt on the way to the club, so Bianca was feeling real breezy. Getting a double shot of Hennessy Royalty takes it down with one swallow and was ready now for whatever. Pushing thru the crowd saying hello to a few people Royalty and Bianca made it backstage where it was packed also not as the actual club was but still a lot of activities was going on. There was a bar backstage and several dressing rooms a lot of security guards and a whole lot of celebrities walking around. Bianca could hardly contain herself. It's like Bianca had died and made it to all men go to Heaven. There were way too many fine balling men with long money back stage and Bianca wanted one hell she'll take two if Bianca thought she could pull it off. Let's go find Taj Royalty said asking any and everyone did they know which dressing room was his. One of Taj Boys was just about to holler at Royalty when Royalty asked him did, he know which dressing room was Taj.

Looking Royalty up and down he said. Oh, you're the shortie Taj was talking about extending his hand to shake Royalty hand. It's a pleasure to meet you. Then he turned to Bianca and said what's up you cute too what's your name?

Bianca wasn't really interested because he didn't look like he was nobody, but the help probably was, and Bianca was tired of fooling with the second stream she wanted a starter. Bianca was polite and respectful but a little standoffish.

Follow me the friend says leading Royalty and Bianca into a private room full of men smoking and drinking. The atmosphere reminded Royalty of a strip club. Taj entourage was thick. Taj was waving his hand like come over here to Royalty once he spotted Royalty and Bianca walking in the room. Royalty was feeling a little uncomfortable, but Bianca felt right at home. Walking pass all these dudes with matching tees on that read Mask Off Production with Hella gold chains around their necks and long ass dreads favoring the rap group Migos. They all parted the way like the Red Sea to let Royalty and Bianca pass them by but not without the oohs and awes and of course the damn they fine comments. Reaching Taj who was tucked in a corner smoking and getting ready for his set was happy to see that Royalty had actually made it. Taking Royalty hand pulling her on his lap Taj introduced Royalty to his crew. Everyone said hello and Royalty introduced Bianca to everyone. Taj asked Royalty did she want to hit the blunt which Royalty declined of course but Bianca hit about three different dudes blunt, poured herself a drink and got loose walking around talking to everyone like old friends. Royalty even saw Bianca get a number Bianca was putting it in her phone Royalty just smiled and shook her head because Royalty just knew it was a matter of time before Bianca cut loose.

What's up with you ma? Thanks for coming Taj said to Royalty touching Royalty hair.

Smiling Royalty said thanks for inviting me looking around. You sure do have a large posse Royalty says laughing.

These are all my niggas I grew up with. My day ones If I eat, they all gone eat smiling showing a mouthful of diamonds. Royalty didn't remember Taj having diamonds in his mouth when she first meet Taj but obviously, he did. Someone knock on the door and said Taj had 10 mins before he was to go on stage.

Lifting Royalty up and kissing her cheek I'll see you later cutie after the show smiling Taj said to Royalty unless you want to come on stage and hang out with my boys.

Shrugging ok Royalty said. I'll come.

Ok I'll see you out there Taj said then Taj and his manager walked out the dressing room leaving about 10 of Taj homeboys who was putting their stuff up and checking themselves out to make sure they were straight and one of them said let's go turn this bitch up. Then they all headed to the stage.

One of Taj homeboys said to Royalty and Bianca come on you'll can stand on stage with us and catch this vibe.

And he wasn't lying either once Royalty and Bianca were on stage and Taj started performing the crowd went crazy. And Taj boys did too. They partied with their bottles and blunts and turn the fuck up. Bianca was grinding on a few of Taj homeboys with her hands in the air kicking it. Royalty was was just standing there bouncing by herself cheering Taj on looking at the sold out club that was packed to capacity rapping right along with Taj who apparently was a hot up and coming rapper that was about to blow up. But little did Royalty know that Jacques was also in attendance at the club and had spotted Royalty on stage and was just nonchalantly watching Royalty smoking his cigar from his table in VIP section. Jacques was invited by Taj manager who was from La who worked with Jacques in a different line of business on the side. Jacques was wondering how Royalty knew Taj because they were from two different worlds. Jacques assumed it had to have something to do with Bianca trick ass but wasn't sure, but Jacques would definitely find out before it was all said and done but for now Jacques was just going to let Royalty enjoy herself and see how far Royalty was going to go with this hanging out on stage with wanna be celebrities.

Laughing to himself Jacques was thinking women are so predictable when they get mad the first thing, they do is go out to try to get over a nigga. But at the end of the night they wishing they were with the nigga they trying to get over. A few groupies come and sat at Jacques table admiring his gray sweater with neon green LV sign on it and his several bling chains to complete his attire Jacques had on his neon green Nike Vapor max sneakers looking like the man that he was. Jacques laughed to himself that women are all alike chasing the nigga with the biggest bag or, so they think. Jacques couldn't blame them though he was a bitch magnet and always has been. That was one of Jacques biggest problems in life. Jacques always looked like a bag of money. It wasn't these women's fault so to speak. Women saw money and power when they saw Jacques and they wanted in any way they could get in. Women didn't care if Jacques had fifty bitches as long as they could be one of them that's all that mattered to them. Jacques had meet so many thirsty women over the years with low self esteem that a few women Jacques meet even offered to give him their money knowing that Jacques already had his own. Them thirsty women was who Jacques was trying to stay away from they were bad news from the jump. But that's what Jacques liked about Royalty she was different. Royalty didn't give a fuck about nothing but her damn self. Royalty spoke her mind, did her own thing and rode her own wave. Plus, Royalty didn't need no handouts. Royalty was self sufficient, and Jacques loved that about Royalty even though Jacques would have given Royalty the world Royalty wouldn't ask for it because Royalty was living among the stars. Taking his focus off Royalty for a moment and talking to the two girls with the tiniest skirts on Jacques had ever seen before. It wasn't flattering to Jacques it was light way prostitution in his book.

Is it ok if we sit here and drink with you one of the ladies asked Jacques who had bottle service but wasn't drinking tonight at all Jacques just wasn't in the mood, so Jacques could care less if they drank all the bottles if they chose to? Sure, I don't mind Jacques said not really paying the two women any mind. Jacques was interested in something else and it wasn't with no broad that just wanted to give up her ass without no cash. Not that Jacques needed the money but the chicks at his table was the ones that needed it you could tell, and Jacques wasn't the one that they would be getting it from tonight. Jacques wasn't interested in any other woman tonight but one and that one woman wasn't interested in him tonight.

You looking for a after party after the party? One of the women said to Jacques smiling looking like she needed a deep teeth cleaning. And the second woman was playing in her weave that looked like a fake fur coat slapped on top of her head and plus she had a lot of dark marks on her face just disgusting Jacques was thinking why didn't she at least put some makeup on? But hey it wasn't Jacques job to judge.

Smiling Jacques replies ladies I'm married in a polite way.

I'm married to the one who was in need of a dental hygienist said still smiling.

Is that right is all Jacques could say in disbelief. Wow married women were at the club now trying to sell themselves to the highest bidder is what Jacques was thinking but Jacques didn't say it. Maybe their poor husbands was pimping them out. Naw say it isn't so. Jacques was still thinking. Looking the women over from head to toe and not impressed at all. Too cheap looking for his liking Jacques was thinking maybe just maybe they could get a nigga that was horney ass fuck that didn't have alot of money but a few dollars to spare or maybe they could get a nigga that got high ass fuck that was too high to realize what type of women they were actually getting but for a real nigga with real money on the line these two women was not suitable. If Jacques was going to trick his money on a bitch, she better be a bad one high priced and worth every dime. Jacques wasn't paying for no dentist, titties no ass you had to come already assembled for Jacques to fuck with you. Not in the preparation phase. Jacques wasn't no Go fund me type of dude and Jacques wasn't about to start being one with these two leeches sitting at his VIP table who sat down uninvited.

After Taj finished his show him and his gang headed back to his dressing room pumped.

That shit was fire my nigga you had the crowd lit one of Taj boys says excitedly.

That shit was crazy loud out there Taj replied juiced looking around at everyone's enthusiasm when he spotted Royalty walking alone in the back. Hold up Taj said to his boys walking up on Royalty.

You did good tonight smiling Royalty says. So, you really can rap? Laughing.

Just staring at Royalty beauty Taj wanted to kiss Royalty but wasn't sure if Royalty was with it or not. Royalty wasn't like the other groupies Taj meet on the road. They were damn near stalkers and too clingy for his taste. But it was something about Royalty that had Taj intrigued besides her beauty. Laughing with Royalty Taj says I guess so the crowd thinks I can still laughing. What you think? Was you feeling it Taj asks Royalty out of curiosity?

Of course, your dope Royalty replied. Your set was bananas. Your headed places for sure Royalty said.

Wrapping his arm around Royalty waist walking inside his dressing room. Taj whispered in Royalty ear. I want to take you with me to all the places I'm headed making Royalty smile.

But Royalty wasn't really feeling Taj like that. Taj was cute, career popping but Royalty knew how this rap game went. Just like the ballplayers. Different girl in every city, different night repeat with a wife at home taking care of the kids getting styled for an instagram photo shoot proving she was the one getting all of the benefits when she miserable ass fuck and at home lonely with another bitch riding her mans dick trying to become his side chick. No Royalty said she'll pass. Royalty was good dealing with the bullshit she was already dealing with. Royalty just wanted to have a good time that's it and that's all. No strings attached. Whispering back in Taj ear Royalty says how big is your dick? And do you like threesomes? And pulls away and starts switching walking towards the bar where Bianca was standing with a few dudes pouring herself a drink.

Taj was left standing there with his mouth wide open in amazement. No woman had ever gotten at him like that until now.

Bianca was living her best life tonight chilling with Taj crew until Bianca it a joint that was laced with something that made Bianca start going the fuck off. Bianca started sweating profusely and trying to come out her clothes talking about she was hot as fuck. Then Bianca grabbed a bottle of Ace of Spades of a table and downed that. Royalty knew that was their cue to exit stage left. Royalty got Bianca keys out her purse and asked the closet guy next to Bianca to help take Bianca to the car. Taj came over to say his goodbyes and told Royalty to hit him to let him know that she made it safely. But what Taj really wanted to say was hit me later, so we can talk about that three way Royalty mentioned that Taj couldn't stop thinking about.

Ok I will Royalty said damn near dragging Bianca with assistance from Taj friend to the door taking Bianca to the car and then taking her home not exactly sure how she would get Bianca out the car once they got there. While Royalty was leaving out the back entrance Jacques was walking in the dressing room with a few of his boys just missing Royalty by a few minutes.

What's up boy giving dap to Taj Jacques says and says what's up to everyone in the room looking around to see you if Royalty was in there but there was no sign of Royalty or Bianca. Taj manager always arranged for the pharmaceutical dealer in every city they frequent to come back stage of all the shows to bring the entourage a party packet that consisted of Epills, coke and cough syrup and weed. Whatever anyone in the clique wanted or needed they had the hookup in whatever city they were in. Kinda like being discreet with your personal business and Taj manager even had the hookup on groupies in every city if that's what his mans wanted. Everything they needed was just one phone call away.

You was nice tonight boy Jacques says to Taj sitting down next to him. You blowing up son I might have to invest in some of your stock Laughing.

You better jump on now nigga before I become the man Taj says hitting a blunt laughing. So, what's good? It's been a minute. What have you been up to? Taj asks Jacques.

Expanding my business and trying to keep my ass out of jail. Jacques replies Laughing.

I heard ya same here shit my tour bus got raided two weeks ago and they found a few guns thank God no bodies was on them feel me hitting the blunt again blowing out smoke. Plus, the pigs couldn't pin them on me even though they wanted too it was way too many people on the bus and the heat wasn't nowhere near me Taj said. So now I'm flying until shit calms down. My niggas still on the bus tho but I can't take that kinda heat shit a nigga just got his major deal. The ink ain't even dry yet Taj said laughing.

Awe congrats my brother what they break you off? What your percentage? Jacques asksed Taj.

It's not much yet only about 6 percent on the dollar but it's touring that we're the real money comes from that's all profit, but I still hustle not in the streets, but you know what's up. I'm opening up a barber shop in a few months also in my hood you have to come to the grand opening Taj says to Jacques.

Bet I'm there giving Taj dap getting up to leave. You'll, straight right? Jacques asks Taj and his manager.

We good folks thanks for looking out and we'll be in touch returning dap Taj manager says.

Jacques walks out the room wondering where the Hell Royalty went so quickly. Jacques had watched a little more of the show of another up and coming rapper after Taj performed then Jacques came directly backstage, but Royalty was gone. Jacques was thinking that he should ride by Royalty house, but he'll give Royalty break tonight plus Jacques was riding with his boys who had work on them and Jacques knew they were anxious to go dump that shit nobody liked riding dirty. Jacques texted Royalty saying Goodnight baby sleep well and alone lol. Royalty never replied back to Jacques text.

When Royalty gets to her house just like Royalty thought Royalty couldn't get Bianca out of the car. So, Royalty pulls into her garage and closes the garage door. And rolls down all the windows on the car and lays Bianca seat all the way back and leaves Bianca asleep in the car. Royalty went inside the house to get a blanket and came back inside the garage placed the blanket over Bianca and said goodnight to Bianca. You have your nerve bitch calling me an alcoholic Laughing Royalty said closing the garage door behind her leaving Bianca sleeping in her car. Royalty took a quick shower and washed the makeup off her face and went to bed. Before Royalty went to sleep Royalty read her text messages one from Jacques and one from Taj. Royalty didn't reply to neither one she thought fuck both them and feel asleep Royalty was too tired from dealing with Bianca ass and her shenanigans tonight to even entertain what these fools was talking about plus neither one deserved Royalty attention tonight anyways. Royalty last thought before she fell asleep was go play with another bitch, I'm tired. Royalty woke up feeling like she had a hangover why Royalty didn't know but Tylenol was screaming her name. Getting out of bed going into the bathroom Royalty heard her phone ring and wonders who it could be this early. Shit they would have to wait plus nothing could be that important at 7 in the morning. Using the bathroom and brushing her teeth Royalty takes 3 Tylenol just in case and heads downstairs to check on Bianca drunk ass. To Royalty surprise Bianca car was gone. Hummm wonder when Bianca woke up and decided to leave Royalty was thinking heading into the kitchen looking inside the refrigerator to see what she could make to eat. Royalty spotted some mix fruit in a bowel and decided to eat that. Going up the stairs Royalty could hear her phone ringing again. What the fuck Royalty said to herself. Who the fuck keeps calling this early? It better not be Jacques pesky ass Royalty was thinking. Royalty didn't even feel like cussing Jacques ass out this early, but Royalty would if she had to. Climbing back in bed Royalty picks up her phone and sure enough a missed call from Jacques. It's too early for this shit Royalty was thinking pulling the covers over her head wanting to go back to sleep for at least another hour or two. Then her phone rings again. Screaming what in the phone without even looking at the phone to see who it was calling.

Liberty says hi Royalty good morning I hope I didn't wake you up.

Oh, hi Liberty my bad I thought you were Jacques ass he keeps calling you ok over there?

Yes, we're fine just getting use to everything that's all. I'm sorry to call you so early I keep forgetting that everyone doesn't get up as early as me and Angel Laughing.

That's ok I was woke I was just trying to go back to sleep for a few minutes that's all. What's up tho? Royalty asks

I was calling to ask you is it ok to move the bed that's in Angel room out I ordered her a big girl bed for her birthday next week and I just wanted to know what you wanted me to do with it the bed that's in the room? Oh, and Angel going to have a party next Saturday at the Jungle she's so excited and you have to be there, or Angel have a fit Laughing.

Royalty had totally forgotten about the furniture at the old house and what she would do with it if Liberty didn't want it. Royalty was thinking what she wanted to do with the furniture. Let me think about the furniture situation Liberty. When the people come to deliver Angel, bed ask them if they can break that bed down and put it in the garage until I can figure out what I want to do with it. How's everything over there? You'll good? You'll don't need anything do you? Royalty asks Liberty

No, we're perfect thanks to you. Me and Angel went shopping for the baby room the furniture comes next week also you have to come over and see it. I did a few little changes around the house nothing major but we're enjoying our new home Thank you again Royalty Liberty sincerely says. We went to church to pray for you last weekend because we're just so thankful.

That made Royalty heart melt. Royalty felt great that she was able to help them in any way she could. And yes of course I'll be at the party. I wouldn't miss it. I'm glad you called me to remind me you know my mind is gone Laughing I'll stop by one day this week to visit you'll also.

Yes, please Angel will love that. I'll like to see you too. Liberty says wholeheartedly

Ok I'll see you soon Royalty says hanging up because her door bell was ringing. Getting up again to go downstairs Royalty hopes it was a Jehovah witness, so she could just say I'm Baptist Thank You and they'll go away pleasantly. But of course, Royalty luck wouldn't be that good now would it. Looking in her peep hole Royalty sees Jacques Royalty immediately started sighing and rolling her eyes. Royalty was thinking isn't this mother fucker married opening the door. What's up Jacques? Royalty said standing in the doorway not inviting Jacques in.

Your being rude early in the morning Royalty you're not going to invite me in? Jacques says holding up a bag of donuts and two cups of Starbucks coffee that smelled so good and was just what Royalty needed at that moment.

Royalty was Standing there thinking should I let Jacques in or should I lie and tell him I have company Royalty was thinking when Jacques pushed Royalty out the way and walked in. Look Jacques it's too early and my head hurts I'm not in the mood for no Bullshit.

Excuse you Jacques said. What you mean bullshit what is that? Pulling out a chair Sitting down at the marble kitchen island getting his breakfast donut out the bag and sipping on his coffee.

Sitting down next to Jacques Royalty asks Jacques what is it that you want from me Jacques? Where is this headed Jacques?

Looking at Royalty who was just so beautiful to him even in the morning Jacques was like huh? Look Royalty I like you and you know this man there's no reason for us to be going back and forth playing games when we can keep going full steam ahead with this relationship why do you feel we need a break?

Because we do Jacques you lied about the situation with your wife. I feel stupid even having this conversation with you about your wife anyways. Royalty yells feeling her blood pressure rising.

Why when I call or text you you don't respond? Jacques asks Royalty waiting for her answer.

I was tired last night I took a bath and went to bed early lying Royalty says.

Really how early Royalty? Jacques asks.

Why damn all these questions like I'm under investigation or something who the fuck sent you over here to be all up in my business this morning? And where the fuck is your wife at? Is She still asleep like I wish I was or could be still if you didn't bring your noisy ass over here asking me a million questions? Crossing her arms irritated Royalty said.

Ok I get it you're done with me Jacques says getting up pushing his chair in getting ready to go. Call me when you're ready to talk Jacques says walking to the door and walking out knowing Royalty wasn't having his shit with his wife being back in town even though him and Serenity wasn't even on them types of terms. But Jacques didn't know how to explain it to Royalty, but he just hoped that sooner or later Royalty would come around if not fuck it he tried. Plus, Jacques didn't like the fact that Royalty just blatantly lied to his face about being sleep last night. Jacques laughed like this girl is a trip getting into his car pulling off not sure if he would ever be back.

Royalty sat down at the island in her kitchen and called to check on Bianca.

Hello Bianca, said

Ooh girl you sound wounded over there Royalty said to Bianca.

I am I had to cancel all my appointments for today I keep going to the bathroom everything coming out from both ends. I'm throwing up and shitting at the same time Bianca said

Damn girl you Hella messed up over there Royalty says. I'll bring you some ginger ale when I get dressed.

No, it's ok my friend is here. Bianca said.

Your what is where? Who the fuck is over there with you when your shitting everywhere? And when did he get there? Royalty inquired

I picked him up when I left your house. He just made me breakfast, but I threw it up tho. Bianca said sounding like she had to throw up again.

Shaking her head Royalty thought he's a good one. Ok well I'm going shopping I'll call and check in on you later I guess Royalty said.

Pick me something up Bianca says sounding pitiful.

No bitch I'm not Royalty says hanging up in Bianca face not believing that Bianca had the audacity to bring someone home in her condition. Royalty gets dressed putting on sweats and a wife beater and her new Gucci baseball hat which Royalty knew was about to be her favorite and decided to go do a little shopping for Angel birthday and buy herself another comforter because every time she looked at her current one, she pictured Jacques lying in her bed. So, Royalty wanted to change that image to something new. So off to the mall Royalty went all by her lonesome. After hitting a few stores and winding up on Wilshire Blvd Royalty got hungry Royalty was about to leave Neiman Marcus but remembered that there was a restaurant on the third level, so Royalty decided to just grab something to eat from there. It didn't take Royalty long to be seated since it was just her thank goodness because Royalty was starving. Looking over the menu not paying attention Serenity walked up to Royalty table without Royalty even noticing she was there. When Royalty finally looked up thinking the waitress had come over Royalty saw who was standing in front of her with her hands on her hips.

We need to talk Serenity said pulling out a chair and sitting down without being asked to.

Royalty was just watching Serenity every move just in case she had to jump up and beat her ass real quick. Serenity sat there for a minute without saying anything just looking at Royalty.

Ok bitch what's up? What you want to talk about Royalty said real smart with her lip turned up.

I want to apologize for the way I acted the other day Serenity said. I was totally out of character I never act like that. My emotions got the best of me.

Royalty wasn't buying that shit, nor did it matter now but Serenity did save herself from an ass whooping because Royalty was ready to take off on her instantly but wanted to hear Serenity out.

Every since me and Jacques moved to the states are marriage has been rocky. That was five years ago. We started a business and Jacques started meeting all sorts of different women and going out I just couldn't handle it so I moved back to Jamaica thinking Jacques would come Chase after me but after one year of being separated Jacques never came. Then when I came back to the states there was this woman who Jacques was seeing that was so rude and obnoxious to me, I realized Jacques was losing his love for me to allow such a woman to come between our marriage. So, I left again. And each time I left it got worse. Jacques never came back to Jamaica to stay or to try to work on our marriage Jacques just came to visit a few times.

The waitress came to take Royalty order, but Royalty asked the waitress to please give her a moment. Ok what was you saying Royalty said to Serenity.

Yes, the last time Jacques came back home to Jamaica I had gotten involved with my CPA It happened so spontaneous I couldn't control it. I was lonely, and I thought my husband didn't love me anymore, so I sought comfort in someone else arms. Almost crying saying it. I missed my husband and I never meant to step outside my marriage but after 5 years of desolation I didn't know what to do so I cheated on Jacques.

Royalty was looking like where's the popcorn at this movie is hella good. Royalty didn't know what the fuck to say this wasn't really her problem.

But now that I've come back to the states this time Jacques has completely shut me out of his life even telling me he has feelings for you starting to cry Serenity says. I've lost my husband completely thanks to you.

Wait what? Royalty was in a state of shock. Feeling for me. Royalty couldn't believe what she was hearing. Jacques never said anything like that to her. This shit was getting wild now. Umm Serenity I don't know what you're talking about. Me and Jacques are just friends. And since you've been back, we haven't really seen that much of each other. Royalty didn't know what to really say. Royalty was caught off guard.

That's not completely true Miss Royalty because I've followed Jacques to your house several times.

Oh, hell no Royalty thinking not one of these types of bitches. Taking a deep breath counting to ten. Ok ok hold up Serenity this conversation just went all the way left now. You did what? And why you do that? I'm curious. I know Jacques is your husband and all but following him to my house is a no no sweetie. Royalty felt herself getting mad balling up her fist underneath the table.

No Miss Royalty when I followed Jacques I didn't know where Jacques was going at first until I saw you open the door. And both times Jacques left out I had no idea where Jacques was headed until he got to your house. Then when Jacques got back the second time, I told him I Followed him, and I knew he went to see you and that's when Jacques told me he wasn't in love with me anymore but he cared deeply for me and wanted me to be happy with whoever I chose to be happy with. Then Jacques told me he had strong feelings for you.

Royalty didn't know what to think or say at this moment Royalty relaxed her hands because Royalty didn't want to fuck Serenity up Royalty actually wanted to give Serenity a hug because Royalty started feeling sorry for Serenity now.

Royalty I dug into your life a little and learned that you recently lost your husband I'm sorry for your lost. I told Jacques that you were just using him to get over your grief that you really didn't care about Jacques like how Jacques thinks he feels about you. I'm praying you're not in love with my husband Royalty. I want to try to make my marriage work with Jacques I love him, and I know we can get past this. You're such a beautiful girl Royalty you can have any man you want. Can you please stop messing with my husband please I want to try and save my marriage that's why I've come back to the states? Are you in love with my husband Royalty? Please tell me you don't have strong feelings for Jacques?

And with that question Royalty lost her appetite instantly.
Royalty and Serenity sat at the table just looking at each other but neither one of them said a word. Royalty was thinking this bitch is really tripping I wonder if this bitch followed me here, I might have to pop this hoe reaching in her purse taking the safety off her glock.

Serenity was sitting there praying that Royalty was just using her husband and that it was just a fling and nothing serious between Jacques and Royalty and that Royalty could just walk away with no hard feelings because if Royalty was in love with Jacques Serenity didn't know what she would do. Serenity was feeling like her life was over if Jacques didn't want her anymore there was really no reason for her to live without Jacques. Serenity mental health was at stake and her mind was playing tricks on her and Serenity didn't know what to do. Serenity last resort was to pray that Royalty obliged her request to walk away from this relationship in peace.

Royalty finally broke the silence and told Serenity she didn't want any parts of this bullshit. Royalty said I don't want your husband and I don't know why Jacques told you that he has feelings for me. Maybe Jacques does maybe Jacques doesn't, but I don't feel the same way as Jacques does Royalty says outright. But we are friends and you can't stop that Royalty says getting up grabbing all her bags. Look Serenity I didn't sign up for none of this. I have my own problems to worry about. All this extra shit I'm cool off. Getting irritated. But good luck with your marriage Royalty said walking away still irritated Glad she didn't have to kill Serenity in the Neiman Marcus restaurant in front of all these witnesses. Royalty could just see herself on the news where they would be hyping it up Homicide over a love triangle wife gets killed by his lover whose husband was just slain a few months ago. The motive of the homicide is still under investigation. Shaking her head. Royalty was looking around her surroundings while walking out the store heading to her car. This bitch is a fucking stalker. I definitely can't fuck with Jacques ass no more. Jacques ass going to make me catch a fucking case getting in her car Royalty was thinking not realizing Serenity was standing by the exit door watching Royalty pull off. Royalty drove to Jinx house to fill Jinx in on the latest news.

Jinx was so happy to see Royalty Jinx keep kissing and hugging on Royalty. Royalty told Jinx about buying Liberty a car and giving her the townhouse and all about her and Jacques Lil rendezvous and of course about Serenity. Jinx listened without commenting because what Royalty didn't have a clue about was that the other women Serenity was referring to as being rude and obnoxious towards her was Jinx. Jinx left the part out about her and Jacques fucking around when they first meet and how Jinx feel hard for Jacques, but Jacques didn't feel the same way because they were both married and because Jacques wasn't feeling Jinx like he's feeling Royalty. Jinx also didn't purposely tell Royalty that Jacques had recently came to see her to tell Jinx he was in love with Royalty and Jacques wanted to tell Royalty that they fucked around but Jinx begged Jacques not too. Jinx didn't want her husband to know she stepped outside of her marriage and Jinx also didn't know how Royalty would react. So, Jacques agreed to not say anything yet. But Jacques wouldn't make any promises that he would never say anything Jacques didn't see what the big deal was anyways. Jinx sat there while Royalty told her all about her and Jacques like Jinx was happy for Royalty but in reality, Jinx was a little jealous that it wasn't her Jacques was in love with. Jinx believed her, and Jacques had a connection and if she would have known that Jacques would have been attracted to Royalty on sight Jinx wouldn't have even brought Royalty and Bianca to Jacques boutique. So, what are you going to do Royalty about Jacques and his wife? Jinx asked. Because that's a real situation right there. Plus, Jacques isn't going to leave his wife they have been together for years Jinx said hating.

I know right Royalty responded. I never thought it would even get this far. It was just something fun to do at first but now it's spiraling out of control Royalty says. I feel like I'm a bad luck magnet Royalty said seriously. Taking a deep breath. I don't know what to do anymore. Maybe I should move out of state Royalty said contemplating.

Where would you go Royalty, Jinx asked. You can't leave me laughing Jinx says.

I know sis I don't know what I'm going to do looking at her phone because it just buzzed from a text message.

Is that Jacques Jinx asked curious.

No smiling it's my new friend the one I was telling you about the rapper.

Ok lil Sis Get it, your bounce back strong Jinx says smiling.

No, it's not I'm just playing around it's nothing serious Royalty says texting Taj back. Well sis it was so good to be able to vent to someone giving Jinx a hug, but I have to run. I'm going to meet my friend at the studio Royalty says. I want to get freshened up before I meet him.

Ok sis please stay in touch and you know your brother mad you haven't been up there to visit him. Jinx says

I know I know please tell Jaheem not next weekend but the following weekend I promise. It's Angel birthday party next weekend you want to go with me Royalty asked Jinx?

Sure, why not I'll go and meet the lil cutie why not. Jinx says excitedly.

Ok so it's a date hugging Jinx again Royalty says opening the front door getting ready to leave. Yeah, I would say me you and Bianca, but Bianca can't stand them even the baby Royalty says laughing Bianca the devil please pray for her Royalty says walking out to her car.

I sure will Jinx says blowing Royalty a kiss shutting the door locking it.

Royalty stopped by her hair salon to check on the girls and they had a full house full of clients. The salon was packed. Hey everyone, waving walking in the salon Royalty says heading to the bathroom. When Royalty finished in the bathroom Royalty went into her office and texted one of her stylists to come into her office. Come in and shut the door Royalty says to her stylist Lisa.

Shutting the door behind her Lisa says what's good Royalty you ok?

Yes, I'm good I just wanted to know if you can put my hair up in a bun with the back down real quick, I have a date smiling.

Oh, is that all you wanted Lisa asked. Of course, wait a minute let me grab my stuff and tell my client to hold up a minute I'll be right back walking out Royalty office shutting the door behind her. Five minutes later Lisa returned with her supplies and curling iron. Turning Royalty around in her chair at her desk Lisa went to work on Royalty Hair real quick hooking Royalty up. When Lisa finished curling Royalty hair, she handed Royalty a mirror.

Sticking her tongue out smiling Royalty says thanks babe for the short notice I'm cute dancing in her seat.

Who's your new boo? Lisa asked.

Looking at Lisa like should I tell her or not even though Lisa was the baddest hairdresser in town Lisa was a little messy too Royalty was thinking humm. He's a rapper it's nothing serious I'll let you know if we make it to the next level Laughing.

A rapper huh? Bitch you ain't no joke, you stay pulling the right niggas I ain't mad at you bitch. Lisa says trying to figure out which rapper it was. Live your best life Lisa said gathering her stuff up heading back to the salon to her waiting clients.

Thanks again girl Royalty says handing Lisa a few hundred dollar bills.

What's this for? Lisa asks surprised.

It's your tip Royalty says.

Tip bitch please all I'm going to do is give it right back to you for my booth rent Laughing Lisa said not accepting the money.

Well Lisa did have a point Royalty was thinking but still Lisa deserved a tip. Lisa always stopped what she was doing to take care of Royalty no matter what and Royalty wasn't taking no for an answer tonight.

Lisa left out Royalty office with all her belongings smiling just knowing her boss appreciated her work.

But when Royalty got herself together and left her office locking the door to leave out Royalty stop by Lisa station and dropped a wad of cash on lisa counter hitting Lisa on her ass like the basketball players do and Royalty said to Lisa I'm not taking no for an answer and winked at Lisa and walked out the salon swinging her hair satisfied. Royalty really liked Lisa a lot Lisa was cool with mad swag and was a straight hustler always getting to the bag and Lisa was sexy ass fuck to Royalty too, but Lisa had a tendency of talking too much at times so Royalty never even acted on her desire to take Lisa down. But Lisa was always looking like a snack to Royalty it was a shame Lisa talked too much though.

When Royalty got home, Royalty wanted to take a quick shower and change clothes, so she could look cute going into the studio. While taking a quick 10 minute shower Royalty was thinking what to put on that would leave a lasting impression on Taj and his boys. Royalty didn't just want to impress Taj Royalty wanted to leave a lasting impression on his whole crew. Fuck it they all gave Royalty that side eye so in return Royalty was thinking she'll get them all excited. It would be funny seeing all these niggas trying to hold their composure around her. Tonight, should be interesting Royalty was thinking. Stepping out the shower Royalty looked down at her feet that needed to be done so open toes shoes was out the question even though Royalty probably could have pulled it off but naw a close toe heel or sneaker would be it tonight. So, with that being said Royalty was thinking maybe jeans and boots or maybe skirt and sneakers. Removing her bonnet letting her curls fall down her back Royalty thought awe ha backless shirt with some skinny jeans and ankle boot. Going in her closet finding the right outfit to turn heads. Pulling her Fashion Nova jeans over her curves barely able to button them Royalty thinking perfect I just can't eat shit tonight laughing to herself Thinking it's a damn shame you're going over to this studio trying to seduce all these men. Royalty couldn't help laughing at herself thinking Amir created a monster with her especially when Amir passed. I miss you baby Royalty said out loud referring to Amir. Royalty grabbed her black suede Christian louboutin boots and her black and red open back off the shoulder sweater. It snapped in the back right at the bra strap and the rest of the back was open. Royalty was Thinking perfect. All I need now is the right perfume which Royalty over sprayed her Bond #9 limited edition perfume and a little blush and gloss on these lips and I'm ready looking in the mirror at the finishing touch. Royalty felt magazine worthy looking at herself. Girl you cute, cute Royalty said to herself with confidence. Grabbing her same bag from earlier because Royalty didn't feel like changing purses. Running downstairs going to her car. Royalty gave herself another look over in the mirror in her foyer blowing a kiss at herself. Then Royalty headed to the studio to chill with the boys. At a red light Royalty found herself smiling just thinking about how this experience was going to go. Royalty had never been to a rap studio before Royalty was a little excited about it. Royalty believed she could rap a little because Royalty and Amir use to battle rap against each other and diss each other in rapping. Royalty thought she was pretty good at it too. Maybe Royalty will get a chance to show off her skills tonight Royalty was thinking. But what if they thought she was trash. As the light turned green Royalty got on the freeway and started practicing her rap game just in case, she was asked to battle one of them at the studio. Royalty was always ready for whatever and going to the studio wasn't going to be any different. Pulling up in the studio parking lot all Royalty saw was foreign cars everywhere. So, Royalty thought she may have been at the wrong location for a minute until Royalty spotted one of Taj boys that had just pulled up. Royalty was thinking it has to be more to this music thing than they're letting on. Mask off production must have a whole different meaning Royalty was thinking. And Royalty could bet money on it that she knew what it was. Royalty had been around a lot of ballers throughout her life and Royalty knew the signs when Royalty saw them, and foreign cars was one of them. Especially if you didn't have a real job. Getting out her car walking thru the parking lot Royalty double checked her outfit then rang the buzzer to be let in. Introducing herself when the person came on the intercom. It's Miss Royalty she said not about to disclose her last name. Royalty didn't know these people like that. Buzzing the door for Royalty to enter Royalty walked thru the door into a dark hallway with a light shining thru a window from a room a ways down. Royalty was thinking why was it so dark but once Royalty reached the studio it was lit up literally. Everybody was in the studio smoking and drinking and laughing and kicking it. The atmosphere was chill, and everyone was vibing listening to the music that was blasting. Taj was in the booth and smiled at Royalty and and did his head like what's up. Royalty smiled back and sat down on a black leather couch that was the only available seat in the room. What's up Royalty? hey cutie, you smoke? this is what Royalty got from everyone as she sat there looking around the room. Royalty sat there on her phone looking thru Instagram something Royalty hadn't done in a minute but since Royalty had this down time on her hands Royalty could catch up. After a few minutes Taj came out the booth and came over to Royalty looking Royalty up and down.

You stay fly cutie Taj said giving Royalty the one over.

Thanks boo Royalty said back laughing.

Sorry for all the smoke all we do is get high and vibe to this music I'm here making these hits that about to take over the radio stations Taj says smiling.

Is that right? You confident of that huh? Royalty asks Taj let me hear a hit then Royalty says.

Ok hold Up Taj says walking over to the engineering board telling his producer to play Blackout his new single. Once the song comes on Taj started bobbing his head to the music his boys got hyped too. Taj started rapping his song feeling it.

Royalty was feeling it to. This song was a hot club banger Royalty was thinking.

Taj started crip walking towards Royalty rapping his song pulling Royalty up out her seat to dance with him. Royalty just bounced a little bit where she stood Royalty didn't want to really let loose in a room full of people she really didn't know. After the song finished playing Taj asked Royalty what she thought about the song. Royalty told Taj that it was hot and definitely was a club banger and that she was feeling it. That's exactly what Taj wanted to hear. Taj loved all the positive feedback especially from females that was the hook Taj used that got all the females wet. Once Taj played his hit song for them Taj most definitely was getting some loving from any female he wanted. But Taj never meet a female like Royalty before. Taj offered Royalty a drink that Royalty politely declined because Royalty wasn't about to get caught up in that bullshit Bianca got caught up in last night. Royalty wasn't 100 percent sure someone put something in Bianca's drink but then again Royalty was sure Royalty gut said be careful and Royalty trusted her gut. A room full of niggas and one woman equals trouble if you was not diligent Royalty was Everybody in the room started freestyling rapping to a beat the engineer was playing, and Royalty was sitting there rapping quietly to herself. Taj was watching Royalty like a hawk noticing Royalty was mouthing something, but Taj couldn't hear what Royalty was saying. Taj touched Royalty leg and asked Royalty did she rap.

Smiling putting her hand in top of Taj hand on her leg Royalty said yeah, a little not professional or nothing but I play around.

Kissing Royalty hand then getting up walking to the booth Taj tells Royalty to follow him. Royalty does as she was told and heads to the booth. Taj hands Royalty some headphones and tells Royalty to sit on the booth chair and Taj walks out the booth and closes the door behind him and walks over to his engineer and tells him to drop a beat. Taj instructs the room to pay attention for a minute and listen up while Royalty raps.

One of Taj boys says oh girl thinks she can rap huh laughing.

And Taj says in return we're about to see turning his attention towards Royalty her in the booth. They were use to girls coming into the studio thinking they could rap but was really trash but sometimes you just never know Taj was thinking. The engineer played a beat and Royalty wasn't really feeling it. Knocking on the glass window Royalty tells Taj to come here. Taj goes over to the booth door and opens it up.

What's up cutie? Taj asks Royalty.

Ask your engineer if he could play your Blackout beat without the words, I want to rap over that Royalty says laughing.

Taj smiled like you really want to rap over my hit joint ok. Let's see what you're made of closing the door instructing his engineer to play his hit joint. When the beat started playing the room was juiced to see what Royalty could do. Royalty started bouncing to the beat holding her headphones feeling it and then Royalty let loose.

YOU BITCHES DIDN'T KNOW I WAS MULTI TALENTED THO!

BUT I'VE COME TO THE CONCLUSION THAT YOU BITCHES ARE SLOW.

LIKE YOU CHASING AFTER THESE BROKE NIGGAS INSTEAD OF A REAL NIGGA THATS BEEN GETTING HIS DOUGH.

I JUST MIGHT MAKE YOU DO A KAPERNICK AND GET ON YOUR KNEES ON THIS CLIT.
BEFORE I CONSIDER LETTING MY MAN EVEN HIT YOUR SHIT.

AND IF YOUR GOOD ENOUGH FOR ME SON YOUR GOOD ENOUGH FOR A THREESOME PUTTING MY LEGS UP IN THE AIR LIKE BITCH MAKE ME CUM.

AND PLEASE DON'T ACT SURPRISED THIS IS A FYI

FOR ALL YOU BAD BITCHES WHICH EQUALS TO YOU MAD BITCHES, IN REALITY YOU SAD BITCHES THAT ALWAYS GO WITH THE FLOW BITCHES THAT DONT HAVE A MIND OF YOUR OWN BITCHES.

YOU FACE BEAT UP BY MAC BITCHES
BUT CAN'T SECURE THE BAG IF HE ASKED BITCHES.

AND FOR ALL YOU MY FRIEND DONT LIKE HER SO I DON'T LIKE HER BITCHES THAT'S WHY YOUR MAN PLAYING YOUR ASS PSYCHE BITCHES!!

AND HERE'S A LITTLE ADVICE FOR ALL YOU NIGGAS THATS CHASING THAT BAG,

YOU SHOULD DO A CREDIT CHECK BEFORE YOU TAP THESE HOES ASS.

BECAUSE THESE HOES AINT LOYAL, THEIR THROATS AINT LOYAL, THEIR ASS AINT LOYAL AND THEIR GONNA LEAVE YOUR ASS IN TURMOIL.

And Royalty drops the mic while the whole room was going crazy slapping high fives and the engineer was in complete shock. They were not ready for Royalty to freestyle and kill shit like that. When Royalty walks out the booth everybody bombarded her with hugs and dap. Royalty felt like Cardi B at that moment. Taj was just standing there shaking his head like girl your full of surprises. Taj engineer said he recorded it and asked Royalty permission to keep it. Royalty said yes but Royalty would have to sign off on it and be paid. Taj went and got his Louie backpack that was sitting on the counter and pulled out three bands and handed it to Royalty. You deserve it cutie damn you killed my track that shit was bomb as fuck. I'm ready to sign you.

Royalty just laughed and said No thanks I'm really not no rapper I just be playing around.

Let's go get something to eat Taj said to Royalty who was hungry, so Royalty was with it. I'm in the mood for some Mastro's Taj said.

One of Taj boys said hell yeah let's go to the one in Beverly Hills the penthouse it's lit up there the views is off the hook.

Not wanting to tell his boys they weren't really invited. Taj just shook his head in agreement and said yeah ok. Somebody call and make a reservation for 10 I guess Laughing.

Royalty said she would meet them there because afterwards Royalty was going home and Royalty lived close by there so there was no need for her to drive all the way back to the studio when Royalty lived only 15 minutes away from the restaurant.

That kinda bummed Taj out some because Taj was hoping to spend some more time with Royalty tonight. Plus, Taj was going to be in the studio doing an all nighter he hoped Royalty had planned on staying with him but Taj guess not. Taj just gave up a few bands and wasn't getting no ass in return. Taj said to himself one way or another he was hitting that ass eventually. Royalty wasn't getting away that easily Taj had never been told no and Royalty wasn't going to be the first. Taj would just have to try a little harder to take Royalty down but when it was all said and done Taj knew that he would.
thinking. They wouldn't catch Royalty slipping tho absolutely no drinking tonight for her. Pulling into Mastro's parking lot Royalty parked and called and checked on Bianca and told Bianca about the studio session. Are you feeling any better now Royalty asked Bianca?

Much better girl there's nothing left inside me I shitted everything out. Only clear shit was coming out of me in the end. Bianca says

Ok ok that's too much information bitch I'm about to go eat damn Royalty says laughing.

Where you at and who you with Bianca asks.

I told you who I was with at the studio you never pay attention Royalty says to Bianca Laughing.

Oh, Taj little, cute, chocolate self. So, you went to his studio session and killed it huh? Only a bitch like you would go and shut a session down. See me if I was there with you while you was rapping, I would have been twerking Bianca says laughing but dead serious. We should start a group you and me. You be the rapper and I'm your hype girl. Shit would be lit Bianca says laughing.

Girl bye I'm hanging up on you on that note. You and I both know that will never happen Laughing hanging up Royalty says. A few minutes later Taj and his crew pulls up in a mercedes Benz caravan with tinted windows and mask off entertainment with a guy with a ski mask resting on his head painted on the side of the van with the music blasting announcing they arrived. Royalty gets out her truck and walks over to the van. When the doors open all, you see is smoke and smell weed. Damn like that Royalty says fanning away the smoke that hit her face immediately. Taj and his boys all got of the van laughing and dancing clowning around.

Let's eat my nigga one of Taj boys says. Everyone was high ass fuck and hungry. Walking in the restaurant niggas was loud and laughing playing too much and the restaurant patrons was looking like oh my Gosh who are these people. Royalty was so embarrassed, but Royalty kept her composure and keep walking with the group to the elevator. Everybody couldn't fit on the first elevator, so Royalty decided to take the stairs instead and of course the remaining few guys followed right behind Royalty. Somebody even touched Royalty ass while they were going up the stairwell, but Royalty didn't even bother to look back to see who it was. They all were laughing and being obnoxious so what was the point. Finally reaching the rooftop pushing the door open the fresh air seemed to change everyone's mood. They all seemed to calm down and relax a bit and take it all in. Royalty sat at the head of the table it just worked out like that sitting next to Taj who was on his phone not even paying attention to Royalty or anyone else for that matter like all the rest of them was doing. The whole squad were all on their phones. Royalty snapped a picture of the guys on their phones with all their heads down preoccupied with Instagram.

This reminded her so much of Amir. This was one of the things Royalty missed arguing about with Amir ass daily. Royalty would say to Amir Get off your damn phone before I break it. And Amir would look up and respond do it I dare you and I can promise you I'll break your fucking hand and go back to looking at his phone. The only time Amir really gave Royalty all of his attention was on date night. Amir made a vow to always be attentive on date night no matter what and most of the time Amir kept his promise.

The waitress finally came, and these fools acted like they were escape convicts that had been locked up for years. Royalty was thinking. They ordered everything on the menu. And hella drinks. Royalty just ordered a glass of red wine and a Dungeness crab cocktail and clear lobster rolls with a side order of asparagus, but Taj and his crew ordered a damn feast. And when the food arrived, they acted like savages Royalty couldn't believe what she was witnessing at this moment. Some people were eating with their hands no utensils throwing food at each other. Disrespecting the poor waitress Royalty felt sorry for her. After the second round of drinks Royalty had enough of their shit and was ready to go. That's when the waitress said they were closing soon and brought the bill and handed it to Royalty. Why Royalty didn't know maybe because Royalty was the only civil acting person or maybe Royalty looked like money either way Royalty wasn't having it and Royalty handed the check to Taj. The bill came up to $2800 Royalty just laughed like these niggas are dumb as fuck to herself Royalty stuck around a little bit longer just to see who was going to pay and how. Of course, Taj dug into his backpack once again and handed the waitress $4000. A thousand plus dollars tip I wouldn't be mad at it if I was the waitress Royalty was thinkin tear this mother fucker up if you want to would have been my attitude if I was the waitress. Royalty wasn't sure if Taj was too fucked up to actually count how much he gave the waitress, or it was intentional, but the waitress got a blessing this night without having to shake her ass. Royalty knew at that moment that Taj supported all his friends and Royalty was cool off Taj at that point. If Taj went broke tomorrow Royalty wondered how many of them niggas would still be walking around rocking them Mask Off tee shirts. Definitely not all twelve of them niggas that's for sure. Taj was probably paying some of these niggas child support payments Royalty was sure of it. It just fit into the dynamic of their friendship to Royalty. Acting like she had to go to the bathroom and excusing herself Royalty dipped out the restaurant and went home grateful she dodged a bullet with Taj ass. And at least Royalty got paid for her little verse on Taj track and that might put Royalty on with another rapper. Laughing thinking about how her day and night went. Completely bananas Royalty was thinking exhausted laying across her bed too tired to even wipe her makeup off and said fuck it and feel asleep with her clothes on. Taj texted Royalty a couple drunk text messages before Royalty actually feel asleep Royalty saw the messages but Royalty ignored them all because Royalty had no intentions on being bothered with Taj or his crew anymore. Fucking with Taj would've been like being a fucking nanny to his ass. Plus, Taj couldn't do shit by himself anyways. Hell, one of his boys probably had to hold Taj dick while Taj used the bathroom Royalty was thinking shit Royalty didn't have no time for a nigga that couldn't even go on a date by himself was Royalty last thought before falling asleep thinking fuck Taj im cool.
Royalty woke up to her door bell ringing and looked at the clock it said 6:26 am What the fuck Royalty was thinking this better not be Jacques ass or his bitch on their let's talk about shit because if so I'm shooting them both Royalty said getting up getting her 9 out her purse cocking it walking

down the stairs opening up her door mad as fuck. What the fuck happened to you Royalty said to Bianca who clothes was full of blood and Bianca face was all scratched up.

I just had a fight with this nigga and his bitch Bianca said out of breath and looked beat up.

Did you win? Royalty asked wanting to laugh from the sight of Bianca whose hair looked like she just fought with a hurricane.

No bitch I didn't win that's why I'm here bitch they jumped me.

Royalty fell out laughing. That's what your ass get always fucking with somebody's nigga and talking shit to the bitch still laughing. Who was it? Royalty asked Laughing The nigga that was taking care of your ass?

Bianca fell out on Royalty living room floor crying.

Awe I'm sorry friend you want me to go bust a cap in their ass Royalty said still laughing.

Yes, Bianca said defeated.

Royalty couldn't stop laughing looking at Bianca who had on one Giuseppe shoe and her pants were ripped and blood on her shirt that was tore and her face and hair told the whole story Bianca lost that battle, but Bianca still had her Chanel bag tho. That bitch was securing that bag at any means necessary. Well best friend at least they didn't get your Chanel bag Royalty said still laughing.

Bitch she tried Bianca said sitting up a little on her elbows. The bitch was trying to grab my bag out the car.

Wait a minute you was in your car fighting? I'm confused Royalty said.

So, what had happened was I was dropping the nurse nigga off at his house and we were sitting in the car talking then his wife pulled up behind us with her friends talking Hella shit. So, I told the nigga to check his bitch. He was just sitting there looking hella dumb and shit. Then this bitch grabbed my hair when I wasn't looking talking to him from the back and tried to drag me out the car.

Oh, my Royalty said sitting down on the couch putting her gun back on safety listening.

Then I turned around and bit the bitch hand, so she would let me go and when I tried to get out to fight the bitch the nigga started grabbing me like no don't fight my girl. I'm like nigga what this weak ass bitch just pulled my Brazilian weave nigga is you crazy. So, I started fighting his ass. Then the bitch came back and started hitting me from behind. I got loose somehow and put my shit in drive and hit that bitch.

You did what? Royalty yelled. You mean with your car Royalty asked

Yeah with my car Bianca said like duh! But I barely hit her but fuck that bitch. Then the nigga jumps out the car to see if his bitch was ok the shit Just was wild ass fuck like a fucking horror movie.

Ok then what happened Royalty asked curious

The bitch jumped up and started chasing after my car and I was trying to back up because they live on a dead end street that's when the bitch was trying to snatch my purse out the car because the windows were down.

Wow Bianca all this happened tonight? Royalty asked with her mouth wide open in complete shock. You always in some shit damn. I'm surprised you didn't shoot them mother fuckers.

I tried to after all that I started bussing at they asses Bianca says laying back down exhausted from telling the story.

Omg I'm so glad I wasn't with your ass. Royalty says seriously. You going to mother fucking jail bitch. And this time I'm not bailing your ass out Royalty says getting up going in the kitchen to get some water. I thought my day and night was crazy my shit was nothing compared to yours Royalty says walking in the kitchen. Here Royalty says to Bianca handing her a water.

I don't want that shit fanning her hand like move Bianca says. I just want to soak in some epsom salt Bianca says. You have any?

Laughing Royalty says
 I do I'll run you some bath water but leave all your evidence downstairs don't bring them clothes upstairs in my bathroom walking upstairs to the bathroom to run Bianca some bath water. After Bianca takes a bath and Royalty took a shower downstairs, they both fell asleep in Royalty bed and didn't wake up until three in the afternoon. When they both got up and got dressed Royalty and Bianca went to get something to eat.

Bianca had a black eye, so she had to wear a pair of Royalty big sunglasses and a hat and Royalty laughed at Bianca the whole entire day. Bianca swore she was going to get her revenge on her assailants both of them if it was the last thing she did before she died. Bianca wasn't letting them get away with jumping her she didn't care if she was in the wrong for messing with someone else man. Oh well Bianca was thinking her man shouldn't be fucking around on her ass fight the nigga not her, but it was cool for now until Bianca figured out what she wanted to do. Bianca was plotting while she ate throwing scenarios out there to Royalty who just keep laughing saying she wish she could have seen them jumping Bianca.

Royalty said she probably would have been dying laughing so hard and couldn't even help Bianca. Because Royalty knew Bianca was doing too much and being hella dramatic like bitch don't touch my 600 dollars weave you ugly, jealous, broke bitch Royalty said Laughing and I could just imagine how you looked when you saw that your nails were broke. Royalty slapped both her legs laughing. Bitch I know you wanted to kill both they asses then Royalty said crying laughing. The people in the restaurant was laughing at Royalty laughing.

It's not funny Bianca said looking at her nails. I'm going to the nail salon right after we eat and I'm going to get a massage Bianca said Hella irritated.

Royalty couldn't even eat her food for Laughing so hard. I'm sorry Bianca but the look on your face is priceless right now Royalty said, let's call him and see what he has to say Royalty asked still laughing.

Fuck You Royalty and his bitch ass. I'm not calling him Bianca said angrily. Rolling her eyes underneath the glasses she was wearing. I hate you so much right now Bianca said ready to go. Come drop me off to my car I don't even want to be around your ass right now you make me sick getting up walking out the restaurant Bianca says.

Royalty was still sitting there crying laughing at her friend every time Royalty thought about it Royalty laughed. The shit was Hella funny to Royalty she couldn't believe Bianca went out like that. But Royalty knew this wouldn't be the last time Bianca got into with someone over their man. Bianca was notorious for messing with somebody's man and getting into with their woman. On the car ride back to the house Bianca rode in silence. Even when Royalty said something to Bianca Bianca just ignored Royalty. And when they pulled up at Royalty House Bianca got out and went and jumped in her car which now since it was day time you could see that it was scratched up a little. Bianca got in her car and started it up and never even looked in Royalty direction. Royalty yelled out what you want me to do with your crime scene clothing laughing and Bianca held up her middle finger at Royalty and drove off Hella mad. Royalty went inside her house still laughing at Bianca because this wasn't the first time, they had been through something like this. With Bianca you just never knew what to expect because Bianca was always into something. Royalty looked at her phone again because Taj keep blowing it up with text messages. This nigga got to be on them pills Royalty was thinking. Taj keep texting me this bullshit talking about he wants to eat my ass. Nasty ass groupie nigga. I should go take a shit and go let him eat my ass forreal Laughing Royalty was thinking but Royalty wasn't that scandalous that was some shit Bianca would do matter of fact Royalty remembered Bianca doing just that to a nigga before when they were in high school. This one dude tried to play Bianca telling Bianca he wasn't dating this other girl when he actually was. Bianca was so hurt that she told Royalty watch how I get him back. So, one day Bianca used the bathroom and didn't wipe good on purpose because Bianca knew he was coming over and was going to want to suck and fuck. Bianca told Royalty when he came over, she was laying on her bed in her robe and spread her legs to let him get to work between her legs and bingo he went straight to the spot Bianca said when he finished and tried to get on top off her Bianca told him to get his potty mouth ass off her. He looked like huh? And Bianca told him yeah nigga I just shitted and didn't wipe my ass on purpose laughing and I'm videotaping your dumb ass for proof for your bitch now get the fuck out my house. Putting him out. He never return to their high school Bianca said he transferred and Bianca saw him once in the mall with another girl and tried to act like he didn't remember Bianca and Bianca told him you remember me nigga all right I'm the one who's ass you ate and before she could finish what she was about to say he had walked away furious. Bianca and Royalty had some stories Royalty was reminiscing about her, Bianca and Amir. They had done some unforgivable things growing up. Some shit they would have to take to the grave and never repeat to a soul some things Royalty was thinking might not get her through the pearly gates. Royalty started thinking it was time to go visit Amir again it was well overdue. Maybe tomorrow Royalty said to herself because Royalty was mentally drained and wanted to take a nap. Once Royalty woke up, she was so hungry but was tired of eating out and decided to make herself something to eat at home instead of ordering food. Stretching before getting out of bed Royalty was hoping that she even had something to cook because it had been a minute since Royalty had made groceries. Going downstairs walking into the kitchen opening up the cabinets they were fully stocked and looking in the fridge there was food in there also. Look at God is what Royalty was thinking to herself. Because

her housekeeper did some grocery shopping for the house Royalty assumed for the nights she slept over or maybe just because she was a very sweet lady. Royalty had to remind herself to leave a little tip out for her housekeeper because buying groceries wasn't a part of her job. Royalty had a taste for some smothered potatoes and grilled chicken and a salad with a hot apple pie with some whip cream or maybe ice cream. Royalty would decide that later. After making her meal and sitting down and eating it in the living room catching up on Power mad at that little mother fucker Tyerik ass for doing dumb shit. Royalty forgot that she could cook a little bit if she wanted too. Putting her plate in the dishwasher and taking the hot apple pie out the oven Royalty couldn't wait to dive into the pie with some good ole whip cream on top and drink a glass of wine to wash it down. Bringing her plate with her apple pie and whip cream on top into the living room getting cozy Royalty doorbell rings. Looking at the door Royalty thinking not again Bianca two days in a row is too much for anybody to be in some drama but to keep coming over here with it is even worse. So, Royalty just turned the volume up on the tv and ignored the doorbell completely until it stop ringing. Finally, Royalty was thinking when it finally stopped like Shit Bianca worse than the Jehovah Witness sheesh leave me alone already Royalty said to herself getting up to take her plate in the kitchen when she saw someone peeking in her patio window with a hoodie on. In shock Royalty drops the porcelain plate on the floor breaking it snapping her out of her disbelief and Royalty immediately runs upstairs to get her gun grabbing it off the dresser running back downstairs turning on all the lights in the backyard Amir had football stadium lights installed for this very reason and turning on her security system alerting the police. But before the police could arrive Royalty was doing her own detective work playing a little game of hide and seek walking around the backyard checking everything the pool, the shed even looking behind trees because if anything didn't seem right it was getting shot on site. Royalty wasn't asking no questions it was just going to be Say Hello to my lil friend!! Was Royalty mood. Fifteen minutes later when the police did arrive Royalty was thinking thanks for coming but I could have been killed by now You'll can leave fucking assholes. The police looked around and didn't find anything or anyone and said if Royalty needed them again to just give them another call and to make sure she locked all her doors and windows. Royalty thanked them for coming but in her head, Royalty was saying Fuck the police in her Ice cube voice. Royalty knew she would never call their slow to come to a black person rescue again asses even if her life did depend on it. Royalty knew how to protect herself plus it wasn't her that needed protecting it was the intruder. Anyways Royalty just needed them to have a record of her calling just in case. Because Royalty wasn't playing about helping a mother fucker to meet their maker. Royalty actually guaranteed it, but Royalty nerves was rattled a bit. The audacity to come looking in her living room window like a peeping Tom gave Royalty the jitters.
Royalty thought about texting Jacques ass to see what he was as up to, but Royalty had second thoughts about it when Royalty figured that Jacques was probably somewhere entertaining his wife. Royalty didn't even like that she was actually thinking about Jacques ass. Royalty wanted to be over Jacques so badly, but it was something about Jacques that Royalty just couldn't shake. Yeah Jacques was cute and all but that wasn't it. Great in bed but that wasn't it either. Royalty thought maybe it was the mystery of not really knowing too much about Jacques and the thought of what her perception of him was. But whatever the fuck it was Jacques occupied Royalty thoughts most of the time. Royalty was irritated now because Royalty was thinking about Jacques when Royalty was thinking Jacques probably wasn't thinking about her and the fact that someone was looking thru windows and shit on her property like Royalty was a punk or something.

Royalty actually wished that whoever it was would come back and try her again. But this time Royalty would even allow them to get it. Royalty was ready for whatever at this point with whoever. Royalty grabbed some blankets and made herself a little fort downstairs, but this time Royalty had both her guns ready locked and loaded sitting nicely under the covers at hands reach. Screaming at the television at Tarik lil ass telling Ghost to slap the fuck out of Tarik. Royalty finally got caught up with all the episodes and was anticipating the next season. Royalty was thinking poor Angela damn why she had to die but shit somebody had to go and it sure as hell couldn't be Ghost fine ass. Royalty pictured herself taking Ghost down in the bedroom. Royalty knew every other woman in the world did too. Ghost could definitely get the business laughing at herself for that thought thinking that his old Og ass probably would do some tricks Royalty had never even knew existed on her ass laughing at the thought. Royalty keep looking out the window wishing a mother fucker would. Royalty had trigger fingers at this point.

Growing up Amir had taught Royalty how to shoot in self-defense because the projects they grew up in wasn't no joke. So, Amir would take Royalty out by the Railroad tracks and show Royalty how to shoot using soda cans as targets. Amir would set the cans on an empty oil barrel that was situated throughout the old railway yard and tell Royalty to shoot all the cans down giving Royalty a Target then telling Royalty to shoot. It took a while for Royalty to get her aim but eventually Royalty got good at it. Then Amir advanced Royalty to shotguns. They would go to the mountains in Pasadena in the summertime and hunt deers. It was full of wildlife even though it was illegal to shoot and kill deers, but Amir and Royalty didn't care. Nothing Amir and Royalty did back then was legal anyways. Amir had a Ford Explorer at sixteen and they would load up the truck with rifles and shotguns which were all stolen from houses Amir broke into during his B&E days and Amir and Royalty would go shoot the shit out of some deers. And no, they didn't keep no deer antler for trophies either. Amir would always say that's white people shit laughing. Royalty remembered the first time she actually shot a deer. Amir and Royalty snuck up on a deer sipping water at a lake and Amir tiptoed away from the tree and hand signaled Royalty to shoot the deer in the back of the head Royalty was so nervous that she closed her eyes after taking the shot and when Royalty finally opened her eyes the deer was laying on the ground bleeding from the neck. Amir high five Royalty and they left to deer laying there and went looking for another one. It didn't bother Royalty too much and Amir could care less. Amir and Royalty were teachings themselves how to survive in this cruel world and that meant doing whatever it took to do that. So, if that meant killing a few deers so be it. But over the course of years Amir and Royalty up their game from cans to deers to actual humans.

Royalty and Amir started out as kids breaking into houses and breaking into cars. Amir was so fucking good at getting into a house you almost thought he lived in the houses he broke into. Amir could break into a house with the best security system. Amir knew how to disarm the best system even if it was state of the art courtesy of his older brother Jaheem. Jaheem knew a guy that installed alarms systems for a living so Jaheem also knew how to disarm alarms. The guy had a gig going with Jaheem that mostly every house he installed an alarm in he taught Jaheem how to disarm the alarm and go in and rob the house and him and Jaheem split the cut. Jaheem did this for years before getting caught up in his murder rap. But one time Jaheem partner couldn't help him with a B&E and Jaheem asked Amir to help him and taught Amir how to disarm alarms and the rest was history. Amir started his own crew and was hitting all the houses in the suburbs in Los Angeles at one point. And Royalty was the driver on most of the gigs. The police never suspected a pretty young girl driving a nice car that they stole right before they hit a house to be a part of a B&E burglary plus Amir and his partner would lay down on the the floor backseat with a blanket over them, so it wouldn't look like nobody else was even in the car but the underage driver. That worked for years until they came up on, they're biggest million dollar crime courtesy Of Teresita that placed them in the situation they were in today balling entrepreneurs living their best life. Rip Amir

Royalty phone keep buzzing from a text message that snapped Royalty out of her reminiscing. Looking at her phone Royalty immediately rolled her eyes irritated. This bullshit has got to stop Royalty was thinking reading Taj text message that read:

I want to beat that Pussy up pretty girl lol.

Royalty was thinking that's exactly why I like bitches because these niggas be corny ass fuck. Royalty text Taj back saying:

Find you a young bitch to fuck with I'm busy!!!

Taj immediately text back:

You are the young bitch Lol.

Royalty laughed at Taj text thinking this boy must pop Molly's he has too. Deleting the whole text thread from Taj. Royalty started to block Taj but thought otherwise just in case Royalty had a lonely night or something you just never knew sometimes. But Royalty wasn't responding to any of Taj text messages no time soon. Taj irritated the shit out of Royalty for some reason. Royalty wasn't sure what it was, but it was probably because Taj was a little too childish for Royalty liking Taj just didn't turn Royalty on at all. Surfing through the channels Royalty winded up watching the Law and order reruns until Royalty fell asleep around three in the morning. The next morning Royalty got up and turned off all the lights in the backyard and was thinking she might go buy a dog even though Royalty couldn't stand dogs. At least Royalty knew with a dog on the property a person would think twice about coming into her yard plus Royalty would just hire someone to take care of the dog because Royalty knew she wasn't going to take care of it. Royalty didn't want to have nothing to do with no dog and to be honest Royalty just wanted some extra security at the house. Royalty didn't want a dog as a pet or nothing like that. But Royalty did like those cute little dogs that wore sweaters though. Amir actually brought Royalty one once for a Christmas present, but Royalty forgot to have someone watch the dog when her and Amir went out of town for over a month and it died by the time they came back. Royalty and Amir took the poor little dog to the vet, but it was too late the dog hadn't ate or drank anything in a month and Royalty had it in cage the whole time. Royalty didn't know nothing about taking care of anything but herself. Royalty didn't mean to harm the dog but that's just how Royalty life was set up. Royalty was her only priority and nothing else. It was Royalty against Everybody that's how Royalty saw it anyways.

Getting dressed Royalty went out shopping and bought Angel a pink Jeep truck from Walmart that's the only place Royalty could find a pink car for a girl at. Royalty saw a kids Mercedes truck G550 like here's, but it didn't come in pink. Angel specifically asked for a pink car which was the hardest thing to find except for this pink Jeep. Royalty paid extra for the Jeep to be assembled and Royalty would pick it up tomorrow before the party. Royalty wanted to get Angel a few more gifts so Royalty went to the mall. Royalty winded up buying Angel a gold bracelet with her name engraved in it with a matching necklace with diamonds a pair of diamond earrings, several outfits from Gucci and Burberry with matching headbands. Royalty had Angel a personalized pink backpack and lunchbox made with an angel on them. Royalty had so much fun shopping for Angel seeing all the cute little girl stuff instead of Royalty shopping for a birthday gifts when Royalty got finished shopping it looked more like Christmas shopping instead. Royalty back seat and trunk was completely full of gifts for Angel Royalty just couldn't resist buying. Royalty just hoped Liberty wouldn't be mad she was spoiling her daughter like this. Hell Royalty couldn't wait to go shopping for Amir's baby. Royalty had actually brought a few things today for the baby that Royalty couldn't resist buying. Shopping for the kids had become habit forming Royalty was thinking driving home.

Before Royalty went home, she stopped by her hair salon Pretty Please and had one of her stylist Sterling who was the only stylist that was available to wash and flat iron her hair. After tipping Sterling and saying her goodbyes Royalty went thru the Starbucks drive thru got her daily fix and went home. Royalty was exhausted from running around today. Royalty had to pull inside her garage because she had all those packages in her car and couldn't take any chances leaving her car parked in front of the house like she normally did. Getting out the car Royalty grabbed a few Gucci bags out the car because Royalty didn't know what was in the bags and Royalty had brought a few things for herself, so Royalty would have to go through each of the bags later to get what she bought for herself and put the bags back in the morning because all the other stuff was for Angel.

Walking in the house there was fresh flowers in a vase on the kitchen table. Smelling them Royalty was thinking how nice the housekeeper has been lately going above and beyond. Royalty would have to leave a nice big tip for Mija then Royalty saw the card. Opening the card, it was from Jacques smiling Royalty read the card out loud

I miss you. I miss waking up to your face in the morning, I miss your smile, I miss the way you touch me, I miss our talks, I even miss your smart ass mouth and I miss the way you walk, I miss smelling your hair, and your youthful glow. I miss everything about you!! I can sleep without you, I can't stop thinking about you, I believe that you complete me. Stop acting like a blank and call me. My number still the same Jacques

Royalty couldn't stop smiling reading the card. Royalty read it several times and decided to text Jacques to thank him for the flowers. Thank You is all Royalty texted to Jacques.

Not even a second after her page Jacques text back, I want to see you can I come by? smiley face.

Royalty wanted to see Jacques but didn't want to seem like no punk, so Royalty didn't reply back right away. Royalty went upstairs and went through the Gucci bags and got her stuff out that she had bought for herself and brought the bags back downstairs and set them on the couch, so she wouldn't forget them tomorrow for the party. Then Royalty poured herself a glass of wine and turned on some music to unwind. Royalty called Liberty to double check the time and location.

Liberty confirmed the time and place and said Angel had taken her bath and went to bed early from being so excited. Plus, Angel big girl bed had came today and Angel couldn't wait to sleep in it. Liberty thanked Royalty again for everything and they said their goodbyes.

Royalty was excited about tomorrow also. Royalty had never been to Boomers Royalty had never even heard of it Royalty was thinking. But Royalty googled it and it seemed like a lot of fun with games and a lot of other exciting things to do there. Royalty knew Angel was going to have a good time and that's all that really mattered. Right when Royalty was about to text Jacques back Royalty doorbell starting ringing. Looking at her phone Royalty thought well at least now I don't have to text him Back smiling feeling like she didn't give in. Opening the door sure enough it was as Jacques holding a dozen roses smiling. Thanking Jacques taking the flowers walking into the kitchen smelling them. Why more flowers Royalty turned around and asked Jacques smiling.

Because they're beautiful just like you I couldn't resist Jacques replied and the dude selling them on the corner gave me a deal Jacques said Laughing. You like the first ones? Jacques asked Royalty sitting down admiring them in the vase. I love white roses Jacques says touching the vase.

Me too Royalty said still smiling. What brings you by Royalty asked Jacques curious to know why Jacques was there.

Taking a deep breath Jacques says because I wanted to see you. Texting you and not getting no response that's why. Jacques replies seriously.

I was just about to text you back Royalty said Laughing.

Oh really it's funny huh? Jacques says looking at Royalty wanting to fuck her right then and there on the kitchen counter that Royalty was leaning on.

No, no still Laughing I really was Royalty said look walking towards Jacques bending down to show Jacques her phone where she was just about to respond to his text. But you came over before I got a chance. Getting up rubbing her hair against Jacques face.

Jacques grabbed Royalty by her waist and pulled her down on his lap and started kissing her. Kissing him back Royalty knew she missed Jacques.

Royalty stopped kissing Jacques and pulled back sitting on Jacques lap and just looked at Jacques for a minute.

What's wrong Jacques asked confused.

Look Jacques I miss you and all but I'm not for all the lies and games Royalty says not wanting to go back and forth with Jacques about his wife. I don't have time to be getting into it with your wife over her husband. Royalty said seriously. Plus, I don't believe you have been very truthful with me Jacques about everything pointing her finger in Jacques face. You been lying nigga Royalty said.

Laughing at Royalty who was tying her best to be tough and act mad Jacques says the only thing I lied to you about was liking you when I actually love you then Jacques grabbed Royalty face pulling her towards him sticking his tongue in Royalty mouth while rubbing on her breast. Then Jacques Stop kissing Royalty and started sucking on her breast one at a time taking his time.

Moaning and grinding on Jacques Royalty whispered in Jacques ear I missed you then started sucking on Jacques ear and neck.

Undressing Royalty ripping her blouse off and undoing her bra Jacques sat Royalty on the kitchen table and lifted up Royalty skirt and slid her panties to the side and started sucking on her soaking wet pussy that he missed so much. Royalty had Jacques sprung and they both knew it at this point.

But who also knew it was Jacques wife Serenity who was in Royalty backyard looking thru the window watching them having passionate sex taking turns kissing and sucking on each other. Serenity chest started hurting and her eyes welled up with tears Serenity couldn't believe what she was actually seeing. Jacques her husband making love to another woman the woman Jacques was actually in love with that wasn't her. The previous night when Serenity came snooping around Royalty house Jacques didn't show up but when Serenity got back home Jacques was in the shower and Serenity found out later that Jacques had been at the gym because his gym bag was next to his bed. Serenity was grateful that Jacques wasn't there with Royalty but tonight Serenity saw it with her own eyes Serenity didn't have to wonder or guess Serenity knew exactly where Jacques was and who Jacques was with. Serenity couldn't believe that Jacques was kissing another women right in front of her. Serenity felt like she couldn't breathe like someone had a boot on her chest. Getting up from kneeling looking thru a side window that Serenity could see into Royalty kitchen Serenity ran to her car. Serenity couldn't take watching them anymore. Crying uncontrollably and not being able to catch her breath like Serenity was having an asthma attack Serenity couldn't focus while driving trying to escape what she had just seen her husband Jacques and his mistress Royalty engaging in. Serenity lost control of her car and hit another car Head on throwing Serenity out her car almost 20 feet and left Serenity fighting for her life.

Meanwhile Jacques and Royalty was getting their freak on exchanging body fluids and dna all night. Jacques rubbed his dick up against Royalty ass as soon as the sun rose the next morning at 6 am ready for another round. Royalty still slightly asleep but awake enough to feel Jacques girth spread her legs open wide to welcome Jacques penis inside her. Morning makeup sex was the best for the both of them coming together in each other's arm. Jacques and Royalty fell back to sleep for a few more hours after their morning sexing and woke up around 10 am both smiling. So, I guess we're back cool Jacques asked Royalty.

Yeah as long as my hair is still straight Royalty said Laughing.

Looking at Royalty hair that looked like she had static in it Jacques replied well babe I guess we're still beefing because your shit is fucked Up. Jacques said Laughing.

Hitting Jacques with a pillow Royalty says yeah because you keep pulling my hair hitting Jacques again with the pillow.

Grabbing the pillow from Royalty putting it over Royalty face like he was smothering her Jacques says. Babe I'm sorry but it felt so good coming inside you I had to hold onto something releasing the pillow from Royalty face because Royalty was tapping out like she couldn't breathe. Kissing Royalty forehead Jacques says Ok babe what are we doing today Jacques asked laying back on his pillow grabbing the remote turning on the tv.

Well today's Amir's baby mama's daughter birthday party at Boomers you want to come with me? Royalty asks Jacques forgetting she invited Jinx to go also.

Yep I'll go why not I don't have nothing else planned hitting Royalty on her ass while Royalty was getting out of the bed. It's jiggling baby Jacques said referring to Royalty ass. Laughing Royalty did a little twerk move for Jacques real quick. Shake that shit then. I need some ones to throw at that ass Jacques said Laughing.

One's boy bye try a few more zeros behind that big faces only Royalty said Laughing walking into the bathroom getting in the shower.

No invite babe Jacques yelled out you ain't cool Jacques said surfing channels.

Smiling feeling good Royalty lathered up thinking how much she was actually feeling Jacques. But what now how were they going to move forward with Jacques still being married? Royalty wanted to ask Jacques was he planning on divorcing his wife any time soon, but Royalty already knew how that conversation was going to go. It's complicated. I have to work some things our first. I want to but it's always a but at the end of the sentence with a nigga Royalty was thinking well at least today they would enjoy each other's company Royalty wasn't going to worry about it today washing her hair even though Royalty just gotten her hair done yesterday. Royalty hair had sweated out last night from all the love making they had done so now Royalty was just going to wear her hair wet and wavy with a cute headband or scarf depending on what Royalty decided to put on for the day. Washing the shampoo out and putting in some leave in conditioner Royalty got out and looked at herself in the mirror and said. Mirror mirror on the wall who is the baddest of them all?

And Jacques yelled out your looking at her babe. The girl in the mirror she the baddest she won.

Royalty bust out laughing because Royalty didn't know Jacques could hear her talking to herself Royalty was glad she didn't say no foul shit. Thanks babe Royalty replied knowing she was about to make Jacques leave his wife because Royalty didn't want to share Jacques anymore with nobody Royalty didn't care who it was Jacques was hers now and if someone was willing to try and take Jacques from Royalty it would be over Royalty dead body.
Royalty was looking in her closet for something to wear while Jacques was taking a shower. The party started at three and Royalty still had to swing by Walmart to pick up Angel Jeep. Royalty didn't want to be late to her very first kid party. Hearing her phone ring Royalty walked out her closet and answered her phone without even looking at it.

Hello Royalty, said Hey Royalty good morning how are you? Jinx asked

Oh, hey Jinx I'm good just trying to find something to put on that's comfortable. Royalty says

You always look cute Royalty no matter what you put on with that perfect shape and cute butt of yours I'm so jealous over here having to work out every day or else laughing. Jinx says seriously speaking

Jinx please your perfect too Royalty says looking through racks of clothing not sure what to wear.

I'm calling to see what time the birthday party starts you still going right?

Yes, I'm still going I forgot about you Laughing Royalty said. But it's at Boomers it starts at three can you meet me there because I have to pick up a Jeep, I bought Angel from Walmart I had them assembled it for me.

Sure, I'll meet you there I have to stop and pick up my gift also. I brought Angel a cute robe and slippers set, and I had her name engraved on the robe it will be ready in a hour.

Awe that sounds so cute I can't wait to see it Royalty said. Ok I'll see you there at 3pm Jinx

Ok Royalty see you later baby Jinx says hanging up.

Babe you not ready yet Jacques says walking to the closet entrance with a towel wrapped around him still wet because Jacques didn't completely dry off looking like a snack.

Licking her lips Royalty says not yet baby you so fine and chocolate touching Jacques chest.

Thank you baby your fine too now get dressed so we can go Lil horny thing you don't want to be late to the party, do you? Jacques asks Laughing turning around and walking away to get dressed.

Royalty put on a jean short romper with a baseball cap and let her hair air dry with big curls hanging and wore her red Chanel sandals and her Chanel boy bag to match.

Jacques had his overnight bag pack and ready to stay for a couple days something Jacques had planned even before Jacques even arrived last night. Jacques knew that he would get Royalty back no matter what it took even though it didn't take much. Jacques was just Happy he didn't have to resort to his plan B to get her back. After Jacques got dressed, he came downstairs we're Royalty was waiting for him ready to go to Walmart.

Awe life is Gucci I see ya!! Royalty said to Jacques who was wearing
 and Gucci signature sneakers and had on Gucci sunglasses and also a Gucci Ny baseball cap. I love your hat I just bought one of those Royalty said.

Oh yeah go put it on Jacques says to Royalty who ran upstairs and switched her cap real quick. Coming back downstairs Jacques says now we're officially a couple when you start dressing alike laughing.

Royalty laughed too at the thought of them dressing alike and being a couple. Then Royalty immediately start thinking was it too soon to be in a relationship because Amir hadn't even been dead a year yet. But Royalty couldn't turn back the hand of time now plus Royalty and Jacques had been messing around for a minute now. Royalty could consider them as a couple. But how would Royalty explain it to everyone Royalty was thinking. Fuck them is how Royalty would explain it. Royalty was happy and that's all that mattered at this point. Grabbing the bags, she left on the couch and headed to the garage.

Jacques asked how is a Jeep going to fit in your car with all those bags and it's most definitely not going to fit in your trunk looking at Royalty back seat full of bags.

My trunk is full also Royalty mumbled embarrassed.

Looking at Royalty crazy Jacques said What you mean your trunk is full also? Why is your trunk and backseat full Royalty I'm curious? Standing there waiting on Royalty answer.

Shrugging her shoulders Royalty said I don't know.

Well where is a Jeep going to fit Sherlock? You didn't think about that part Jacques says knowing he would have to drive also and put the Jeep in his car. I'll follow you to Walmart and put it in my car.

Giving Jacques a hug and kiss Royalty said Thank you babe you're a lifesaver.

Yeah, yeah you better be glad I'm not in no two seater car today smiling Jacques says seriously

Oh yeah, I didn't even think about that Royalty said relieved. What you driving? Royalty asked Jacques.

I'm driving a Bentley Jacques said with authority.

Ok!! Royalty replied giving Jacques the thumbs up. Big baller Royalty said Laughing I want to be like you when I grow up. Switching cars whenever I want, and shit Laughing Royalty says.

If you want a Bentley, I'll buy you one Jacques says seriously.

Naw I'm good thanks tho Bianca has one and she would die twice if I got one laughing. Bianca would swear I'm trying to out shine her or something Royalty says. Plus, I don't need no more cars I have to figure out what to do with all Amir's cars that I'm not going to drive Royalty says solemnly.

I might know someone who might take them off your hands Jacques says.

That would be nice Royalty says we'll talk about it later getting in her car letting up the garage to back out and watching Jacques fine ass walk to an all black Bentley with red leather seats. Royalty always wanted a car with red leather seats, so Royalty knew she would have to drive Jacques Bentley one time. Pulling up at Walmart Royalty went inside and a nice young man who worked for Walmart brought Angel Jeep out and placed it in Jacques car. Royalty had purchased a red bow to put on the car once they got to the party. Following behind Royalty they were finally on their way to the party and it was 3pm already. When Royalty and Jacques arrived the parking, lot was almost full for a kid's party that's crazy Jacques was thinking. But neither Jacques or Royalty had ever been to a kid's birthday party before. Jacques had no clue what Boomers was or that it was a public place for anyone who wanted to attend and that it wasn't a private party just for Angel. Walking in with all the gifts for Angel Royalty spotted Liberty sitting at a reserved table and sat the presents down.

You didn't Liberty said in shock from all the bags Royalty had shaking her head. Royalty No!! You already spoiled Angel Liberty said not believing what she was seeing.

Then here comes Jacques with the pink Jeep. Liberty this is Jacques the guy I was telling you about Royalty says smiling.

Extending his hand out to Liberty Jacques says it's a pleasure to meet you. I've heard a lot of good things about you. Oh, and congratulations on your baby blessing.

Liberty shook Jacques hand but couldn't stop looking at Jacques because Jacques was very handsome and polite and that was not a common combination for most men these days. Thanks for Coming Liberty said Angel going to be so happy with her gifts switching her focus on the gifts and the Jeep instead of Jacques because Liberty knew she was staring at Jacques a little longer than she should have been.

Jacques chuckled to himself when Liberty turned from looking at him Jacques caught that look from Liberty that Jacques saw in so many women's eyes before that lustful look Jacques knew he had that sex appeal that was hard to resist.

Walking in with a gigantic box wrapped in pink Cinderella paper Jinx came over to the table smiling waving at everyone. Royalty introduced Jinx to Liberty and told Liberty that Jinx was the new baby's aunt. That Jinx is Amir's brother's wife. After giving each other hugs Jinx sat her gift down and asked where was the birthday girl at. Jinx waved at Jacques but wouldn't engage in any conversation with Jacques Jinx kept it brief. Jinx was also surprised to see Jacques there at a kid's party.

Liberty sent one of her little cousins to retrieve Angel who was somewhere playing with the rest of the kids. Angel came over to the table with no shoes on and ran right up to Royalty screaming Hi Miss Royalty you didn't forget thank you for coming giving Royalty a kiss on the cheek. Spotting her Jeep Angel yelled Oh my gosh I got a truck like yours Miss Royalty so excited getting in it. Mommie take my picture Angel said. Everyone pulled their phones out taking pictures of Angel in her new pink Jeep. Thank you Miss Royalty I love you you're my favorite person Angel said looking at the gadgets in the Jeep.

Royalty said Angel I have some people here I want you to meet.

Ok Angel said getting out her Jeep going over to Royalty.

Royalty introduced Angel to Jacques first because Jacques was sitting right next to Royalty. Angel this is Jacques.

He's cute Angel said smiling. Are you Miss Royalty boyfriend? Angel asked Jacques.

Jacques looked at Royalty and then back at Angel and said yes, I am pretty girl Happy Birthday handing Angel a stack of one hundred dollars bills.

Running and jumping in Jacques arm Angel says Thank you smiling. Jacques can you be my boyfriend too? Angel asked seriously.

Laughing Jacques said I'm way too old for you Angel, but I can be your best friend for life how about that? We can be Bff

Angel smiled real big and said I like that. Telling her mom. Mommy this is my new best friend for life showing her mom her money.

Liberty apologized for Angel bombarding herself on, Jacques But Jacques says it's ok Angel is my new best friend smiling.

Royalty said to Angel she wanted Angel to meet her new auntie Jinx who was sitting there in disbelief of Jacques and Royalty saying they were a couple. Jinx tried her hardest to hide her frustration hoping no one noticed. Waving hi to Jinx Angel says hi Auntie Jinx getting down of Jacques lap and going over to Jinx and giving her a hug and smiling. You're so pretty Angel said to Jinx and that kinda made Jinx feel a little better. Thank you, sweetheart Jinx, replied. Your adorable I love your outfit. Twirling around showing off her tutu skirt with her Minnie Mouse sweater and rainbow colored tights. Angel was the cutest thing Jinx had ever seen. Jinx couldn't believe how chocolate Angel was with those long ponytails that hung down her back with those cute brown button eyes and to top it off she was the sweetest little thing.

I'll be back Auntie Jinx I want to go play now Angel said grabbing Jacques by the hand come on best friend let's go play.

Getting up Jacques waves bye to everyone and him and Angel played every game rode every ride and danced and ate cake until Angel passed out and Jacques carried Angel to the car and put Angel in the backseat of her mom's Tesla when the party was over. Jacques told Liberty to put his number in her phone and to not hesitate to call him for anything Angel needed.

Liberty smiled and said thank you she would and gave Jacques a hug. Liberty hugged Royalty and Jinx also and thanked them for coming along with the other guests.

Royalty told Liberty she would stop by in a couple days, so they could go shopping for the baby who was due real soon. Jinx said her goodbyes and got in her car and left.

Jacques walked Royalty to her car and waited for her to get in then Jacques said to Royalty. Thanks babe for inviting me I had such a good time smiling. I feel in love with Angel the moment I saw her. If we have a baby our baby probably would look just like Angel.

Royalty was speechless at this point. A baby where did that come from Royalty was thinking. Wow how do you respond to that Royalty was thinking. Smiling back at Jacques Royalty says maybe but for now let's just act like Angels our daughter maybe her mom will let us be her Godparents Laughing What You think about that? Royalty asked Jacques.

I like that Jacques says kissing Royalty and telling her he'll see her at the house and to drive safely. Royalty and Jacques pulled up at the house just around the same time and Royalty blew her horn and rolled down her window telling Jacques to pull his car in her garage and that she would park in her driveway. Pulling into the garage Jacques sat in his car on his phone. Royalty walked passed Jacques going into the house when Jacques held up his finger like he was in church and mouthed I'll be a minute. Royalty went into the house and poured herself a glass of wine and turned some music on and took her shoes and tossed her hat off getting comfortable. Turning on the lights in the backyard looking at the night sky thinking how peaceful it was tonight contemplating on taking a swim in the pool if Jacques was up to it something different to do. Even though it wasn't officially summer yet. Royalty pool was heated year round for occasions like this just in case they wanted to swim all year.

Jacques came into the house sweating and holding his head sitting down on the couch. Babe you're not going to believe this, but Serenity is in the hospital fighting for her life.

What? Royalty asked what happened?

I don't know all the details but apparently Serenity was in a serious car accident that left one person dead and Serenity fighting for her life. Serenity is in a coma and on a breathing machine. The nurse said they couldn't reach anyone until about an hour ago when they got in contact with my mom and my mom gave them my number. Shaking his head looking wounded Royalty didn't know what to say. I have to go to the hospital babe getting up. I'll call you when I get there kissing Royalty forehead walking to the garage going to his car.

Royalty just stood there and watched Jacques leave not believing what she just heard. Royalty turned on the television to the news channels to see if anything about the accident was on there, but nothing was on the news about it. Royalty went upstairs and got her laptop and came back downstairs and sat on the floor Indian style and googled car accidents in Los Angeles recently and that's when it popped up. Unidentifiable African American women driving a 2018 Black Audi A-5 which was completely totaled from the impact that an unidentifiable woman was threw from the vehicle 20 feet. The victim had no identification so if anyone knows anyone who drives a Vehicle fitting this description please contact Cedars Sinai Medical Center to help notify the next of kin. Royalty keep looking at the mangled car and wondered how anyone could survive such a wreck. Wow is all Royalty keep thinking. Royalty wanted to know so badly the details, but Royalty knew she wouldn't find anything out until Jacques was ready to talk about it and who knows if Jacques would ever be ready to have that conversation about Serenity and the accident. Royalty knew eventually she would find out what happened Royalty just would have to wait patiently until the tea leaked out Royalty hoped it would be sooner than later. Royalty got up to get herself another drink because after this Royalty definitely needed a drink. Thinking it's crazy how shit just be happening. Royalty opened another bottle and downed it and felt like she wanted to smoke some weed. Royalty smoked weed occasionally especially when Royalty was stressing, and tonight Royalty was stressing not knowing if Jacques was going to stop messing with her to help nurse his wife back to health or was Jacques going to support his wife throughout Serenity situation no matter how long it took because Serenity was his wife after all. All these thoughts ran through Royalty mind that Royalty needed to put a pause on. So, Royalty went in her secret stash that she keep in her drawer by the bed. It was actually Amir's but now it's Royalty since Amir's gone. Royalty and Amir would occasionally smoke and laugh about certain things and people and Royalty liked how weed made her feel when she was around Amir because Amir keep Royalty laughing. But when Royalty smoked with anyone else Royalty felt paranoid. Weird right that's what Royalty thought also but that's what happened every time Royalty smoked. But tonight, at home by herself was different. Royalty needed a buzz to take the edge off. Royalty went upstairs and rolled herself a joint a nice fat one and inhaled it and held the smoke in for a minute before exhaling. Sitting on her bed looking around the room smiling Royalty imagined Amir being there laughing at her getting high. Royalty could hear Amir voice.

You a punk you can't even hold it in that long hold your breath when you inhale then let it out slow.

Royalty tried it hitting the weed again. But this time Royalty held it in longer choking a little patting her chest like Royalty was putting out a fire laughing at herself for trying to act like she was a pro at smoking. Then Royalty heard Amir's voice again.

Look babe you have to take it all in or your wasting my weed. Hit the weed and hold your breath for a few minutes then blow it out your noise.

Royalty tried it and this time Royalty didn't choke as much. Blowing the smoke out her nose feeling high as hell now. Royalty finished smoking the whole joint and started thinking about Hella shit. Stuff that didn't even make no sense to her laughing. Royalty was so high she felt like playing on people phones. Royalty didn't know why, and Royalty didn't even care. Royalty just felt like doing it. Getting up going downstairs to get her phone Royalty got the munchies also. So, first Royalty went

into the kitchen and raided her snack cabinet grabbing a bag of hot chips and some Oreo cookies and fruit roll ups. Royalty started laughing thinking damn bitch
high high right now and bust out laughing. Getting her phone Royalty turned on the backyard lights and went and sat outside by the pool because Royalty felt claustrophobic in the house and needed some air. Sitting down on the pool chair placing all her snacks between her legs Royalty just stared at the sky thinking how pretty it was. Amir, I know you're up there somewhere Royalty said then Royalty started waving hi. I'm fucked up down here without you boo I miss you Royalty said looking at her phone scrolling thru her call log. Royalty found Bianca number and called Bianca first laughing putting hella chips in her mouth chewing on them.

Hello what you want Bianca said answering the phone.

Chewing her chips hella loud in Bianca ear Royalty started laughing.

Bitch what's wrong with you? Bianca said. Is this Royalty?

Royalty laughed and said Bitch it might be, bitch it might be! And then hung up dying laughing hitting her leg in amusement. Then Royalty started throwing Oreos into the pool to see how far she could throw. Challenging herself how far she could throw a cookie. I bet you can't throw it pass the 6ft or 8ft Royalty said to herself I bet I can she replied to herself trying to throw the Oreos as far as she could cracking up at herself for not making it pass the 4ft. Royalty phone rang, and Royalty jumped because it scared her. Answering nervous and whispering Hello.

Bitch don't play on my mother fucking phone this late you stupid ass hoe Bianca yelled in the receiver at Royalty.

Royalty bust out laughing again. Fuck you you're the hoe bitch I'm over here super fucked up I smoked some of Amir's best weed bitch I'm Litty right now Royalty said Laughing.

Damn that's some powerful ass weed Amir has I need some more Bianca said don't smoke it all save some for me laughing. You by yourself? Bianca asked Royalty.

Looking around Royalty says looks like it unless the boogeyman here hiding behind some bushes or something maybe I need to get my gat and pop a nigga if he hiding in my yard Royalty said surveillancing the area now really tripping.

Girl your over there high as fuck I wish it was me Bianca said laughing. Where's Jacques at? Bianca asked.

Looking at the pool Royalty thought for a moment. Oh, his wife got ran over by a car Royalty says nonchalantly because she was high.

His what? Got hit by a what? Bianca asked not understanding what Royalty was talking about Bianca just thought Royalty was high and tripping. What happened to Jacques wife Royalty drink some water, so you can come down off your high baby because your over there fucked up Bianca said wanting to know what happened to Serenity now.

Putting a hand full of chips in her mouth crunching Royalty said Jacques wife got into a car accident and Serenity in the hospital bitch and Jacques there with her and I don't know what to do crunching on the chips in her mouth in between every word.

Wait I saw a accident on the news last night where somebody got thrown from their car and another person died was that Serenity? Bianca asked hoping it was just a coincidence.

Yep putting another chip in her mouth Royalty said.

Damn that's fucked Up that was a bad accident it was right by your house too Bianca said.

That caught Royalty attention and Royalty high felt like it came down instantly. It was by my house Royalty said wondering if Serenity had followed Jacques over there hoping that wasn't the case.

Jacques probably did something to Serenity car Bianca said seriously.

No Jacques didn't Royalty said still wondering if Serenity had followed Jacques last night. Jacques didn't even know something happened to Serenity until about an hour ago.

How Jacques didn't know something happened to his wife? Bianca inquired.

Because Jacques was here with me Royalty said trying to put two and two together.

Oh well that explains it Bianca said. Maybe Serenity tried to commit suicide Bianca said.

Maybe Royalty replied. I'm going to call you back Royalty said to Bianca and hung up in Bianca face. Royalty laid back on the patio chair and looked up at the sky and tried to count the stars but couldn't get past twenty. I'm high Royalty said to herself, but Royalty high was coming down a little. Royalty couldn't stop thinking about could Serenity really have tried to commit suicide because Jacques was with her? That's crazy if Serenity did. Serenity couldn't be that distraught over it could she? Serenity knew what it was Serenity knew what was up. Royalty had more questions than answers at this point and being high just made Royalty think more. Damn I wish I hadn't smoked this damn weed Royalty was thinking then Royalty started laughing at herself for being high tripping. Royalty stayed in her backyard just thinking about shit for hours until Royalty got sleepy and went in the house and went to bed still high. That weed Amir had was the truth. Even after sitting for months. Amir had so much weed around the house Royalty could start her own dispensary if Royalty wanted to, but Royalty would just keep it for her personal use for whenever Royalty needed it and given Bianca some occasionally as Bianca requested some.

The following morning when Royalty woke up Royalty immediately checked her phone. No call or text from Jacques. Hummm Royalty was thinking that's weird I thought we were in a relationship that's what Jacques said not me Royalty was thinking getting frustrated. Ok Royalty it's too early in the morning to be mad get over it Royalty keep telling herself but in reality, Royalty was mad as fuck Jacques didn't even have the audacity to call even if it was just to say I'm still here at the hospital. Royalty got in the shower and decided not to let Jacques not calling ruin her day. Royalty was at least going to try not to let Jacques ruin it hopefully. Getting out the shower Royalty called Jinx and asked Jinx to meet her for lunch at the mall, so they could talk. Jinx agreed and said she'll meet Royalty at Saks at 2pm. Royalty got dressed and stopped by Pretty please even though it was a Sunday to see if anyone was in the salon working. And sure, enough someone was or so Royalty thought because the lights were on in the salon but when Royalty went inside it wasn't a stylist but Bianca getting her hair done by some random chick. What's good? Royalty asked Bianca as Royalty walked in looking like what the fuck is going on in my salon.

Hey, boo you still high? Bianca asked Laughing.

No, I'm not are you? Royalty asked trying to still figure out why Bianca was in her salon on a Sunday getting her hair done by some chick Royalty knew nothing about.

Hi, my name is Regina the girl doing Bianca hair said to Royalty, but Royalty ignored her and walked right up to Bianca sitting in one of Royalty stylist chair getting her weave put in. You want me to punch you in your throat bitch? Royalty asks Bianca. Why the fuck you at My salon getting a weave put in when you have your own salon next door please enlighten me? Royalty says crossing her arms.

Well first of all I needed hair products not makeup products and I needed my hair washed and dried so I needed the sink and the hair dryer if that's alright with you Miss I own this shop and why are you using the keys I gave you to use my products and run up my PG and E on a Sunday ? Bianca said sarcastically looking at Royalty like bitch I always have a clap back for your ass.

Royalty just rolled her eyes and walked to the door to leave and turned around and said to Bianca make sure you turn the alarm on when you leave and walked out while Bianca said Yes Ma'am Laughing.

Getting in her car Royalty was thinking I hate that bitch sometimes referring to Bianca. Royalty had forgotten what she even stopped by the salon for since Bianca had gotten on her nerves. Shopping should relax me Royalty was thinking pulling into valet parking handing her keys to the parking attendant. Thank you, sir Royalty, said getting out walking inside Saks heading to the shoe department where Royalty had no business being at. Picking up a Giuseppe bootie Royalty Spot's Jinx looking at a Red bottom heel that looked like the heel would break your ankle it was so high. Smiling at Jinx Royalty told the clerk her size and handed her the shoe and walked over to where Jinx was at. Hey girlie giving Jinx a hug thanks for meeting me on short notice you know you're my go to person when I need to vent Royalty said Laughing.

It's fine I love seeing you your always good company Jinx says hugging Royalty back. Saying yes to the clerk about her shoes Jinx says girl Lord knows I don't need another pair of shoes but. laughing Right same here Royalty replies but. laughing also. I want to go upstairs and get some new underwear Jinx says it's that time of the year again. You know when you're sick of looking at all your old undies and lingerie. Royalty knew exactly what Jinx meant but from the looks of things Royalty wasn't going to have anyone to wear anything like that for no time soon. Tapping Royalty on the shoulder you need some freshening up young lady fake smiling. I heard Jacques yesterday say you two were an item Jinx said opening the door for Royalty to walk in with the tea.

Putting her head down briefly Royalty says. Well shit changes suddenly in life especially mines.

What happened Jinx asks all ears praying silently that their relationship fell apart and Royalty was done with Jacques.

We'll talk at the restaurant let's get our shoes and go panty shopping then we'll girl chat Royalty said trying on her shoes the clerk just brought her and walked around in them to see how comfortable they were. Jinx did the same. Both paying for their shoes and finishing up their shopping.
After doing a little damage in Saks both Royalty and Jinx they both brought all the underwear they saw that was cute and then some plus three pair of shoes each at eight hundred a pop. Jinx recommended a small little restaurant within walking distance that had pretty decent food and bomb drinks which was right up Royalty alley considering her circumstances. Sitting down ordering their meals and drinks Royalty let loose. Ok girl so you know Jacques wife is back in town remember I told you? That's more of a rhetorical question Royalty says laughing

Yes, Jinx says.

Anyways last night after we got home from the party before we even got into the house Jacques got a call telling him that his wife using her hands like per say was in a car accident and is in a coma.

Wait what you just say to me Jinx says. When did this happen?

Um two days ago I think but I'm not really sure because Jacques left and went to the hospital and I haven't heard from him since.

Wait I'm still stuck on the fact that his wife was in a car accident and is in a coma that's serious Royalty Jinx says still in shock.

I know right Royalty replied. I wish I knew what happened exactly, but I did google the accident and someone got killed also.

Wait a minute I saw that accident on the news the other night Jinx says. That was Serenity wow.

Yep Bianca said she saw it on the news also. What did the news say Royalty asked Jinx?

That an unidentifiable black female ran a light I think and hit another car head on and the driver was threw out of the car something like that.

Yes, that's what I read to I wonder what happened Royalty said. The news said Serenity ran a light? Royalty asked Jinx

Yes, I believe so Jinx said. Man, I hope Serenity pulls thru Jinx says solemnly concerned. Well Royalty you might not hear from Jacques for a while this is really serious about his wife. Just imagine if that was Amir fighting for his life you got to understand what Jacques must be going thru.

Royalty did try to put herself in Jacques shoes, but Royalty would have called and said something to Jacques.Their food and drinks arrived so Royalty and Jinx briefly took a break from talking about the subject while eating. How's Jaheem? Royalty asked.

Jaheem good he's been in better spirits lately. Jaheem can't wait to meet the baby Jinx said.

I know me too Royalty said slightly irritated by how everyone was so accepting of Amir having a bastard child but whatever. Royalty was excited also.

Does Liberty know what she's having Jinx asked.

No Liberty said she wanted it to be a surprise, but I think it's a boy because she's so big Royalty says.

Awe that's a myth Jink replied. I wasn't big at all with Lil Jaheem remember I gained a lot of weight after he was born from stressing over my case and I blew up.

How's is lil Jaheem doing anyways? I haven't seen him in a minute Royalty replies.

Me either Jinx says laughing. He's good though he's in Aruba with my parents.

Must be nice Royalty says.

Yes, they travel somewhere foreign every year and of course they take Jaheem spoiled butt right along with them laughing.

Yeah that's their baby Royalty says.

That he is Jinx says. So how is Liberty liking her new house I know Liberty excited about moving out the projects.

Yeah, she is, I think. Liberty brought some new furniture and stuff I'm just glad I could help her out. I know if Amir was alive Amir probably would have brought Liberty a mansion Laughing Royalty says seriously.

Laughing also Jinx says your probably right. Amir did have a big heart. Do you think you would have been ok with Amir having a baby Royalty? Jinx asks seriously.

Royalty thought about it and said probably not but what can you do once the person is already pregnant and wants to keep it? I mean I'm not sure we're me and Amir's relationship would have went after that but I'm good now about it so whatever. All I know is bet no other bitch pop up saying she's having no mother fucking baby by Amir's ass laughing. Because she's on her own.

Right Jinx says agreeing with Royalty. There is no more babies you don't have to worry about that Jinx says confidently.

Better not be Royalty says finishing her drink. Royalty got a text hoping it was Jacques but looking at her phone it wasn't it was Bianca.

Locked up the shop and turned on the alarm lol. Bianca text

Royalty text back Fuck You!!!

Jinx asked Royalty was that Jacques texting you?

No that was Bianca annoying ass.

Oh, tell Bianca I said hello Jinx says smiling.

I will next time I see her Royalty says putting her phone down on the table looking at the bill. I got this Royalty says after all I invited you. Royalty says putting her credit card on the table with the bill and leaving a twenty dollar tip.

Thanks girl I got you the next time Jinx says grabbing all her bags. Let's plan a spa day next week Jinx says to Royalty.

I need one badly any day you want I'm down Royalty says grabbing all her bags to getting her credit card from the waitress ready to go home and relax. Oh, and please tell Jaheem I swear I'm coming to visit him soon Royalty says.

He understands Royalty that you have a life but just don't forget about him Jaheem loves you Jinx says.

I know I love Jaheem too Royalty says giving Jinx a goodbye hug and they walk to their cars and go their separate ways. Royalty got home and took a nice hot bath and had another glass of wine to help her fall asleep. Royalty was so tired she missed Jacques text message saying

"Hey babe sorry didn't call sooner I was tired from being at the hospital all night signing paperwork and talking to doctors I'll try and stop by tomorrow been fighting with Serenity family give you update when I see you. Love you be good Jacques".

When Royalty woke up because Royalty keep hearing her phone buzz from a text message Royalty started smiling. Royalty boo was thinking about her so now Royalty could go back to sleep and rest peacefully. Jacques surprised Royalty the next morning with Starbucks and donuts putting the biggest smile on Royalty face. Jacques looked tired and worn out.

Babe I'm sorry for my lack of communication but it's been a hectic couple of days Jacques says sitting down at the kitchen table.

How is Serenity doing? Royalty asked.

Well they say Serenity will possibly be a vegetable Serenity has a lot of swelling on the brain and she's really swollen from the injuries so we just have to wait and see when the swelling goes down, but Serenity parents wants to have her transferred to Jamaica which the doctors don't believe is a good idea especially not right now while Serenity still swollen everywhere.

I'm sorry Jacques you have to go through this Royalty said.

I'm good thank you It's Serenity that's going through it not me. I just pray Serenity makes it out alive. Nobody deserves what Serenity going through Jacques says feeling sorry for his wife. Serenity for the most part is a very sweet, genuine woman that wishes everyone well and love to see people succeed but I've hurt Serenity so badly that her spirit has shifted to anger and aggression. I just pray that I wasn't the cause of this fatality with Serenity because I can't live with myself knowing that.

So, what is Jacques going to do kill himself Royalty was thinking. It's not your fault Royalty said trying to console Jacques.

Well I should have handled some matters differently Jacques says. And I know
that honesty saves everyone's time so I'm being honest by telling you Royalty I love you and I care deeply for you but I'm going to have to fallback for a minute I have to be there for Serenity and Under the circumstances I hope you can understand that Jacques says.

Leaving Royalty heart racing and Royalty nerves bad.

And I know what you're thinking Jacques said how can a man be in love with two women at the same time right? Royalty didn't respond. Well I love you both and yes, it's humanly possible to actually love two people at the same time like you love your mom and dad equally you can love two women equally. But that's not my case Royalty. I'm in love with you but I love Serenity she's my wife and Serenity been my friend my whole entire life. You understand what I mean Royalty? You understand Jacques asked Royalty

Royalty did kinda get it. Because that was the case with her and Amir Royalty never knew how to explain it like that but how Jacques explained it made sense. Yes, I understand Jacques and I believe it's the right thing to do Royalty said but what Royalty really wanted to say was what the fuck are you talking about falling back on me? Me Royalty no nigga you're going to go visit your little wife during the day and fuck with me at night. But Royalty couldn't bring herself to be that gangster with Jacques.

I don't want you to think I'm giving up on us Royalty it's just that as a man and being Serenity husband, I have a obligation to support Serenity thru this until it's all said and done. My main focus is making sure Serenity recovers. I owe Serenity that.

Ok Royalty said feelings defeated and Royalty was also ready for Jacques to leave because Royalty was tired of him repeating that he was Serenity husband over and over again.

Jacques stood up over Royalty and said give me some sugar kissing Royalty long and hard. Then Jacques just looked at Royalty and said when you get horny hit me this doesn't mean you can be out here acting like you single and giving my pussy away either looking Royalty in her eyes.

Royalty responded boy please I'm about to put this pussy on Backpage anybody that wants this pussy can get it laughing.

That made Jacques laugh too. What you know about backpage? Jacques asked Royalty Laughing.

Hummm Royalty replies still laughing.

Bianca must have told you about Backpage Jacques said seriously.

Oh, that's fucked up you think my Bff knows about backpage Jacques get out Laughing pointing to the door.

Ok ok maybe Bianca didn't tell you about it, but I know for a fact Bianca knows about it Laughing Jacques says walking to the door opening it. I'll text you later ok Jacques says standing in the doorway. Because if I stay any longer, I'll probably never leave Jacques says winking his eye blowing Royalty a kiss. Royalty caught it and waved bye then Jacques walked out. And Royalty sat there feeling like she just got kicked in her stomach once again.

The next few days Royalty threw herself into her new business venture that had just went through that Royalty had been waiting to see if she was going to get approved for the business loan or not. Royalty business meeting went well with her investors and Royalty was ready to move forward with her life. Once Royalty knew that she was approved now it was time to work. Royalty started getting the building renovated and started shopping for her new business a hair boutique called Bargain Bundles Hair Boutique and it was exactly across the street from Royalty Hair salon Pretty Please. The previous owner was a little Chinese lady who owned a dry cleaner for over Forty something years but after her husband died recently Mrs Wang didn't have any interest in the business anymore and they didn't have any children so Mrs Wang the little Chinese lady wanted to move back to her county to be with her family. Royalty had known Ms Wang for many years and hated to see her leave, but a new business venture was a goal for Royalty. Royalty wanted to expand her business or start another one, but Royalty just didn't know what kind of business she wanted until the Dry cleaners became available. Royalty got the idea of a Hair Boutique when Royalty was at Pretty Please one day and a client was saying she was having trouble with ordering hair and said she wished she could just buy some decent bundles without all the hassles. Then bingo the light turned on in Royalty head and Royalty knew she needed to capitalize on the hair game after all Royalty did own a hair salon it just made sense. And when Royalty neighbor was closing her business Royalty knew that was a sign to go ahead and start another business. But the process was hard and tedious. The bank wanted all this information background checks Royalty needed another business license all these things had to be done before Royalty was given the green light but now all that was behind Royalty and Royalty was ready to open up shop in six weeks after all the renovations were done. The building was small but had plenty of potential Royalty help draw out the layout with the contractor and architect. Royalty wanted it to be like a real boutique with bundles hanging from hangers on different aisle with pretty packaging with cute mirrors and brush murals on the walls and nice chandeliers throughout the isles. The contractors said between 4- 6 weeks, so Royalty was handling business as fast as she could with marketing and networking getting samples ready and Royalty even did a small commercial budget to reach a broader audience of clientele. Royalty was really getting into this and couldn't wait until the grand opening. Royalty stylists each had a very large clientele, so the grand opening should be really nice. The Bargain Bundle Hair Boutique keep Royalty very busy for weeks that some days Royalty didn't even eat until late and Royalty didn't have time to think about Jacques as much as Royalty would have if Royalty wasn't keeping herself busy all day.

One day when Royalty was at the building about thirty something days into renovations waiting for the painter to come Royalty was walking around with her hard hat on going over dimensions with her contractor and Jacques popped up.

Hey stranger you're looking like the boss around here Jacques said standing in the doorway.

Royalty took off running and jumped into Jacques arms almost knocking Jacques down kissing him for dear life. After a long kiss Jacques put Royalty down and Royalty said thanks for stopping by but how did you know about this place curious?

I saw the commercial and I heard about it on the radio smiling Congratulations Jacques said standing there taking a look around. This is going to be big Royalty I'm glad you're keeping yourself busy Jacques said smiling.

Yeah, I didn't have no other choice Royalty replied referring to Jacques being M I A for weeks at a time. How's Serenity? Royalty asked.

Serenity woke up about a week ago, but she doesn't have any memory of the accident yet or anything else for that matter but Serenity doing ok Serenity not a vegetable and Serenity alive, so I guess Serenity doing better than some people Jacques said.

That's good Royalty said. Does Serenity remember you? Royalty asked Jacques.

No not yet Serenity just laying there without any recollection of anything yet, but the doctors says that normal at first. Serenity might regain her memory and become herself again and then again maybe not. It's still too soon to tell. But enough about Serenity for now let's talk about you Miss businesswoman Jacques says give me a tour and help me visualize the boutique tell me your layout taking Royalty hand allowing Royalty to explain her vision.

After Royalty showed Jacques around the salon Royalty took Jacques to her makeshift office and told Jacques this is where her office will be at. Sitting down on the one chair Royalty had in the office Jacques sat down and Royalty sat on Jacques lap facing him. Holding Royalty ass Jacques said I miss you mean lady squeezing Royalty ass.

No, you don't you miss my bootie Royalty said feeling herself getting moist between her legs just looking at Jacques who had let his mustache grow out a little.

I missed that too Jacques said smirking. But seriously I really do miss you Jacques says grabbing Royalty face kissing her sticking his tongue in her mouth. Rubbing Jacques head running her fingers thru Jacques hair made Jacques hard as fuck. Jacques pulled back and told Royalty to lock the door and started undoing his pants. Royalty tried to lock the door, but it wouldn't lock Royalty said fuck it oh well then Royalty wasted no time getting on her knees and pleasing Jacques. It felt so good Royalty sucking on Jacques dick, but Jacques didn't want to bust in Royalty mouth Jacques wanted to cum inside of Royalty. Jacques wanted to feel Royalty wetness against him. Pulling Royalty up Jacques said take them off pointing to Royalty leggings. Royalty quickly undressed and slid on top of Jacques. Nice and tight baby just like I like it Jacques says moving in and out if Royalty real slow. Laying her head on Jacques neck nibbling on it Jacques whispers in Royalty ear I missed you baby. The warmth of Jacques breath in Royalty's ear made Royalty cum instantly picking up her speed making Jacques match her pumping in and out of Royalty a few minutes later Jacques came too. Jacques held Royalty in his arms and whispered in her ear. Babe sorry about the quickie it's been a while and started laughing.

Royalty said yeah same here. And they both started laughing but they both could hear footsteps walking away from the door. Lifting up off Jacques shoulder Royalty looked at Jacques and said babe looked like we had some company somebody enjoyed the show Laughing.

Jacques said yeah right does the bathroom work in here?

Royalty said no and bust out laughing.

Jacques said get up little nasty girl we need some wet ones or paper towels.

But I don't have any here Royalty said. If I have to use the bathroom, I go across the street but thank you for blessing my new business I know business is going to be booming now Royalty said looking around for a napkin or something and spotted a six pack of paper towels she had brought and forgotten about. Look babe paper towels hopping over to the paper towels by her desk opening them up throwing a roll at Jacques who caught it and wiped himself clean.

This some back alley homeless people fucking babe Jacques said Laughing. I wonder how the homeless really get down babe Jacques inquired.

They don't wipe themselves clean I betcha that babe Royalty said Laughing.

Well you know what I'm going to buy a shit load of paper towels and give it out to the homeless babe Jacques says. You want to help me pass them out Jacques asked Royalty.

Yes, that oughta be fun Royalty said getting dressed.

Thanks for the relief babe how much I owe you? Jacques asked Royalty Laughing.

Let me think about it and I'll let you know Laughing Royalty said.

I want to wake up to you babe Jacques says sincerely I miss that.

Awe hugging Jacques I miss you too babe we have to figure it out. Royalty says happily

I'm coming over this weekend and staying I'm tired of sleeping on the hospital couch and eating hospital food.

Royalty didn't respond because Royalty didn't know Jacques was staying over with Serenity. Royalty said to herself oh

I'm going to have to put it on Jacques this weekend to get him away from that damn hospital smiling. Walking back inside the hair boutique two workers were in there acting like they wasn't just being noisy listening to Royalty and Jacques just get down. And Royalty acted like she didn't care because Royalty didn't.

Giving Jacques another kiss goodbye. Jacques said I'll hit you later and left.

Royalty left for the day also with a huge smile on her face. Royalty was so happy to see Jacques. When Royalty got home, she got a text from from Liberty that she was in labor and going to the hospital and to meet her at Mlk Hospital. Royalty got so nervous Royalty started calling everybody like it was her going into labor. When Royalty called Bianca, Bianca said she wanted to go to the hospital to make sure the baby was Amir's Royalty told Bianca yo just meet her at the hospital she was on her way. Jinx didn't answer so Royalty sent Jinx a text message and told her to call her back ASAP. And Royalty text Jaheem also and told him she would send pictures of the baby as soon as she could because of course Jaheem had several phones because Jaheem was still bossed up despite being incarcerated that didn't stop Jaheem swag though. Royalty wanted to text Jacques but thought otherwise Royalty would just tell Jacques over the weekend Royalty knew Jacques would be exited. Pulling into Mlk hospital parking lot Royalty saw Bianca walking to the entrance and told Bianca to get in the car while she found a park. You got here quickly Royalty said to Bianca while Bianca was getting in the truck.

I know I was close by when you called. How many centimeters is Liberty you know? Bianca asked.

No, I don't know anything but that Liberty in labor finding a park pulling in Excited to meet the baby. Royalty grabbed her overnight bag just in case she was going to stay the night.

Bianca looked at Royalty and laughed. Your way too excited for me Bianca said. I'm like Maury Povich right now bitch Like You are Not The Father Bitch!!! Laughing.

Royalty laughed too I am now since Amir's gone, I'm taking Amir's place Royalty said Laughing. And don't go inside this hospital being disrespectful to Liberty either or I'm going to put your ass out Bianca I'm not playing either.

I'm not going to be disrespectful to your lil baby mama boo, but she better not say no slick shit, or I will put that sidepiece without the biscuit ass in her place snapping her fingers like the queen Bianca was.

I can't with you shaking her head Royalty said.

Wait a minute hold the fuck Up Bianca said holding her chest standing with her legs wide open with her hand on one hip. Is that them mother fuckers right there? Bianca said looking at two people kiss goodbye and the women was walking towards them, but she was a little ways away. Bianca grabbed Royalty and pulled her on the side of a car.

What the fuck is wrong with you? Royalty said trying to get loose.

Shhh Bianca said. Peep game that's the bitch and the nigga that jumped me Bianca said whispering. Peeping thru the cars to see how close the woman was. She's about to be right here Bianca said getting herself ready we're taking off on this bitch but before Royalty could say No it's not the place. Bianca jumped from behind the car they were hiding behind and jumped out and scared the shit out of the women who didn't see this coming at all. Surprise bitch bam bam Bianca said taking off on the woman hitting her in her face twice. The woman fell back because she had lost her balance when Bianca jumped out at her and she tripped over the sidewalk, but it was too late because Bianca was all over her now.

Royalty was trying to get Bianca off the lady, but Royalty did slip a punch or two in accidentally. That's enough Royalty said to Bianca pulling Bianca off the girl who was bleeding from her mouth and her eye was starting to swell up.

Getting up off the ground the woman says. You bitches done fucked up now jumping me.

Royalty was looking like wait what. Then Royalty said nobody jumped you Sis Bianca beat your ass by herself Not We beat your ass because if I would have jumped in you definitely wouldn't be talking Period!! Royalty says getting mad now. Bitch don't start that We shit before We really do beat your ass Royalty said standing over the woman now.

Fuck this bitch Bianca said and kicked the women in her face knocking the woman head into the ground. Take that bitch and run tell that Bianca said grabbing Royalty arm let's go walking away. The bitch is at the right place to get looked at by a doctor Laughing. The mother fucking hospital laughing Bianca said. Let her lil RN husband come nurse her laughing Bianca said feeling vindicated.

Royalty didn't know who to be mad at the most at this point Bianca for putting her in this situation or the woman for saying they jumped her lying. Didn't matter Royalty was mad but glad that it didn't come down to someone really getting hurt to where the police would be involved.

Bianca couldn't stop laughing. Did you see the look on that bitch face when I jumped out on her ass Bianca said walking into the hospital?

Royalty just rolled her eyes and asked the information desk where to go for labor and delivery.

Bianca saw her friend the Rn guy running towards her but Bianca didn't know if he was running towards her or outside to help his wife but either way Bianca wasn't letting him off the hook so easily .Bianca knew his wife must have called him but before he could reach Bianca she stuck her foot out and tripped him making him fall into a row of chairs with people sitting down waiting to be seen. Jumping out the way Bianca said oh excuse me and started laughing.

Royalty turned around to see the commotion and saw the dude on the ground trying to get up from being entangled among a few people. Royalty just shook her head and grabbed Bianca and told her to knock it off they were in a hospital to welcome the baby being born it wasn't the time or the place for this. Yanking Bianca arm.

They started it Bianca said still laughing as the elevator doors closed taking Them up to the 6th floor to Liberty delivery room.
Looking nervous walking in Liberty room Royalty waves hi to Liberty. The nurse was hooking Liberty up to a machine to check the baby's heartbeat and Liberty looked like she was pain. Sitting on the couch in the room Royalty and Bianca sat down quietly and just watched the nurse get Liberty situated and comfortable. When the nurse was done Liberty introduced Royalty and Bianca. Liberty explained that Royalty was the baby's father wife and Royalty was supporting her throughout her pregnancy since the father past away.

That's really mature of you and respectful honoring the father being here the nurse said to Royalty.

Smiling Royalty said thank you feeling some type of way at this point. Because it had finally hit Royalty that Amir was about to have a child at any moment. And Royalty couldn't help but think that if Amir was alive Amir would have been there sitting on the couch not her. Royalty felt a lump in her throat. Clearing her throat Royalty asked the nurse for some water.

Of course, I'll bring you both some water back the nurse said walking out.

How you feeling Liberty? Royalty asked.

Well I'm ok right now but when the contractions hit there brutal Liberty said. I asked for a epidural I'm just waiting for the doctor to come in. Thank you for coming Royalty I appreciate that Liberty said looking like she was about to have another contraction. Holding onto the side of the bed rails squeezing it until it passed.

Royalty got nervous.

Of course, Bianca crazy ass asked Liberty what a contraction feel like and to describe it to her.

Well the best description I can give you Bianca is it feels like someone squeezing you around your neck and you gasping for air. Liberty said

Damn that doesn't sound fun Bianca said I'm glad it only last for a few seconds. You're getting medicine, so you can't feel it right Bianca asked.

Yes, hopefully soon Liberty said.

Where's Angel Royalty asked.

She's with my cousin. My cousin will bring her up here tomorrow my cousin staying at the house with Angel.

Oh, ok Royalty said looking around the room. There was a bassinet in the room with a light over it Royalty didn't know what that was about, but Royalty was sure she would find out soon.

The nurse came back in the room with their waters and told Liberty the doctors was on their way and then she walked out.

A few minutes later two young men doctors came in who informed Liberty that they would be giving her a shot in her back to relieve the pain. One doctor had Liberty turn on her side while the other one put some brown stuff on Liberty back then put this big as needle in Liberty back and five minutes later, he was done. Ok Liberty all set congratulations on your baby he said and the other one check Liberty to see how far along Liberty had dilated and when he finished, he said well Liberty you should be a new mom in a few hours hopefully smiling. I'll be back to check on you he said and then both doctors walked out and said goodbye.

Royalty was watching the machine and said Liberty looks like you're having another contraction you can't feel it?

Liberty said no smiling I can't thank God.

Jinx texted Royalty back and Royalty text Jinx and told her Liberty was in labor and to come up to Mlk hospital and the room. An hour later Jinx walked in with a teddy bear and some balloons. Hey everybody I'm here to crash the party Jinx says walking in giving Liberty a kiss on the forehead. Liberty was taking a nap but woke up when Jinx came.

The nurse came back and checked Liberty and said it shouldn't be much longer now Liberty was 7 centimeters. Liberty was ready Liberty couldn't wait to meet her baby. Royalty was so nervous Royalty keep having to go to the bathroom. Jaheem had FaceTime Jinx and Jaheem meet Liberty for the first time it was an exciting time. The atmosphere and energy in the room was on a high level. Everyone was anxious. But shit got real a few hours later when the nurse checked Liberty and Liberty was fully dilated at 10 centimeters. A whole team came into the room and Royalty and Bianca didn't know what to expect they were sitting on the couch with their knees in their chest biting on their nails looking paranoid, but Jinx was standing next to Liberty rubbing Liberty hair telling Liberty it was going to be ok.

The doctor had Liberty spread her legs apart and told Liberty to push. Liberty was pushing but looked like nothing was happening. Then the doctor said push again. Liberty was straining trying to push. At this point Royalty and Bianca was hugging each other in fear. This transition to becoming a parent for Liberty had Royalty emotional. To actually see a birth, take place touched on all Royalty emotions. To see what woman had to go through to bring a child into the world was frightening and joyful at the same time. Finally, the doctor said he saw the head and Royalty peeked and Royalty could see the head also. Ok Liberty one more good push the doctor said then Liberty grabbed Jinx hand and squeezed real hard and out came the baby. Liberty started crying tears of joy. Royalty started crying Bianca had already been crying. Congratulations the doctor said laying the baby on Liberty chest while the baby took its first breath. You have a healthy baby boy.

At that moment Royalty imagined Amir being there crying and excited grateful he had a son. Then Royalty thought about her own mother that had given birth to her but didn't develop that bond and Royalty really got emotional and the tears started to flow. Royalty started feeling sorry for herself. Why didn't her own mother love her? Why did Amir have a son with another woman?

Royalty do you want to cut the umbilical cord? Liberty asked.

The whole room was staring at Royalty and Royalty got light headed then Royalty passed out. When Royalty woke up a few minutes later laying down on the couch with the doctor standing over her Everyone was relieved. You scared us young lady. But we understand the doctor said. Most of the time it's the father's that passes out the doctor says laughing. How you feel? The doctor asked Royalty.

Looking around Royalty said hot.

Ok well just lay here for a minute the doctors says we brought you some water handing Royalty a cup of water.

After drinking the water Royalty felt better. Thank you I'm ok Royalty said getting up. I want to see him. Walking over to to Jinx who was holding the baby. Looking at him all Royalty saw was Amir's face. He looks just like Amir Royalty said reaching down kissing his forehead. Hi lil Guy welcome we've been waiting on you. I'm Royalty your step mother your dad would have loved you so much Royalty said getting emotional again. Wiping away her tears Royalty said but I'll love you for the both of us. Making everyone cry in the room including the nurse. She wiped away a tear.

Then Liberty said You want to name him Royalty?

Me Royalty said. Are you serious Liberty? I mean he's your son.

No, he's our son Liberty said sincerely.

Let me name him I want to be his Godmother Bianca said smiling.

You can be his godmother Liberty said honored.

That's sweet thank you Bianca said ready to go shopping for the baby because Bianca feel in love with him the moment, she saw him. He looked identical to Amir he was just a lighter version. Bianca hated that she ever even doubted the baby was Amir's.

Can we name him King? Royalty said because he's going to be the king to Amir's throne. He'll inherit everything him and Angel. Liberty said I love the name King. King Spencer Royalty said smiling I'll let you give him his middle name Liberty. Liberty said Bianca you can give him his middle name if you want since you're his godmother. Bianca started crying again. Really omg I'm so happy getting up giving Liberty a hug. I'm sorry I was so mean to you I'm such a bitch Bianca said. The whole room started laughing. I understand your such a good friend to Royalty I wish I had friends like that. Liberty said sincerely well you don't need friends you got us we're family Jinx said smiling. That made Liberty heart warm. You got babysitters now Jinx said. I'll keep my nephew anytime kissing Baby King. Thank you, Liberty, said happy she finally had a family for her and her kids. Everyone started taking pictures of baby King before Jinx laid him down in his crib and Liberty feel asleep too. Royalty and Bianca and Jinx left to go get something to eat at Catch La even though none of them were dressed and they all had on sneakers. But they were celebrating King, so it didn't matter. Ordering their food and drinks laughing and talking about how spoiled King was about to be a few celebrities' guys walked in and sat right next to them. Even though none of them was dressed up they were all still baddies. The guys sitting next to Royalty and her crew were trying to holler at them. Royalty who was nice and tipsy at this point told one of the guys were out celebrating my dead husband's new baby boy. The guys at the table was so inquisitive about Royalty situation they listened to Royalty tell her story then the guys all said their congratulations and said dinner and drinks were on them. By the end of the night Royalty had secured a trust fund for baby King from the guys plus dinner not bad considering none of the girls were dressed up with no makeup on. They could still pull niggas on their worst days Royalty was thinking. Exchanging numbers and Bianca started following each of the guys on social media everyone said their goodbyes. Royalty and Bianca went back up to the hospital and brought Liberty some food in case Liberty was hungry and Jinx went home but said she'll return tomorrow. When Royalty and Bianca returned back to the hospital Liberty was still sleep and the baby also. Royalty and Bianca said they would take turns with Baby King tonight and let Liberty get some sleep and since Liberty wasn't going to breastfeed Liberty had declined because she said her breast was to heavy and sore. Royalty asked the nurse for some bottles and diapers even though this would be Royalty first time ever taking care of a newborn baby or any baby for that matter. The nurse said she would help them when they needed her. But

Royalty and Bianca caught on right away. They both fell in love with the baby. Especially Royalty she was in love with King because he was Amir's baby, Amir's first born child, Good morning Jinx says walking in the hospital room with Starbucks and bagels waking everyone up.

Yawning Bianca says yes sis thank you I need some coffee I was up with King throughout the night. I had no clue that babies woke up that much. I'm not even sure if King is a newborn Bianca said erupting the room into laughter.

Royalty was glad to have some coffee also because Royalty was tired also. I need to take a shower Royalty said where's the guest bathroom at?

Everyone looked at Royalty like what? There's no guest bathroom Royalty Jinx said smiling. This isn't a hotel it's a hospital Laughing.

So where does the fathers get changed at? Royalty asked perplexed.

Liberty said. You can use my bathroom Royalty it has a shower in it.

But most fathers go home and change Jinx said Laughing. I know it's a lot to take in having a baby and all. But when it's your turn Royalty you're going to be a pro Jinx said seriously speaking.

Will see about that Royalty said. I don't know when that will be maybe in another lifetime but for now, I have King as my baby. I didn't even have to push him out Laughing Royalty said. Plus, I'm not sure if I'm built for that and the pain. Naw I think I'll pass I'm good.

Me too Bianca said still replaying the events in her head of Liberty having contractions and pushing King out.

Duh we know about you fool Royalty said to Bianca.

What you mean duh? Bitch I might be pregnant right now Bianca said sipping her coffee laughing.

And I'm the first woman to ever walk on the moon Royalty said responding to Bianca walking into the bathroom shutting the door to take a shower.

Liberty and Jinx had no clue what those two were talking about but found the conversation funny.

You two are truly meant to have been best Friends Liberty says sitting up looking at King sleeping in his hospital crib. Thank you Jinx for breakfast I appreciate all your support Liberty says drinking her coffee and eating her bagel.

So, Bianca how many times did King wake up last night? Jinx asked.

Too many Bianca said seriously. I thought babies especially newborns slept all night.

Some do, some don't Jinx says laughing. Now he's going to sleep all day. When are they releasing you Liberty? Jinx asked.

I think today they don't keep you long anymore they kick you out if you had a successful childbirth. Plus, I rather be home than here. I hate hospitals Liberty said. Not my favorite place to be.

Me too Bianca said. Let's bring the party to your house I'm going to start coming over your house visiting the kids Bianca said.

Well like that Liberty said.

Well let them get some rest first Jinx says to Bianca Liberty needs to rest for a couple days but we're all here to help you Liberty if you need it.

I know Liberty says. I'm grateful.

The nurse comes in and says I see the gangs all here smiling. Good morning everyone I'm your nurse this morning Miss Liberty and reading your chart looks like your scheduled to be released this afternoon.

See told ya Liberty said to no one in particular.

You feel good enough to go home? The nurse asks Liberty.

Yes, I feel great I'm ready to go home. I know my daughter is waiting by the door for her little brother laughing.

Ok that's great. After the doctor comes and check on you and signs off on your paperwork, you'll be free to go. I'll be back in before then do you need anything before, I leave? The nurse says checking King out making sure he was ok. Baby looks perfect Congratulations he's a cutie.

Thank you and no I'm ok Liberty replies. Ok I'll see you later the nurse says walking out to leave.

Dang only one day in the hospital that's offly short Jinx says offended. I stayed in the hospital I think for about four or five days I believe Jinx says I could be wrong, but I know it was more than two. Things has really changed.

Yes, they told me ahead of time I wouldn't be in the hospital longer than two days if everything went well. With Angel I was in the hospital three days. Liberty says. It also depends on your insurance also, I think.

Oh, that might be it Jinx was thinking maybe that's why.

A nurse came in with papers for Liberty to sign to be released. Walking in the room the nurse saw Bianca and thought oh shit but before he could leave out Bianca spotted him. What the fuck are you doing coming in here? Bianca said seeing her guy nurse Friend she was beefing with.

Look Bianca just let me do my job and I'm outta here the nurse said nervously not wanting no problems but knew he had just walked into one.

Really your job nigga was it your job to jump me? You punk ass nigga Bianca said yelling now.

Royalty was coming out the bathroom when she heard the commotion and peeked out the door and saw it was the male nurse Bianca was messing with. Also, the same nurse Bianca was beefing with too. So, Royalty didn't want no parts of this so Royalty quietly closed the bathroom door and sat on the toilet and thought she would wait this one out and just wait there and listen because Royalty already knew it was going to be bad.

The nurse tried to give Liberty her papers to sign but Bianca had jumped up and mushed him in his face. Bianca stop putting your hands in my face he said trying to walk out the room, but Bianca kicked him in his back sending him flying into the door.

Now get out you bitch ass nigga!! Bianca said standing there waiting to see what he was going to do.

Trying to get up from the floor and regain his balance and pick all the papers up off the floor because they went everywhere the nurse finally stood up and got his composure and turned around and looked at Bianca and said you're an evil bitch you know that I hope you burn in Hell then walked out.

You gone join me bitch. Bianca was able to say before the nurse actually walked out.

Jinx and Liberty was just looking at Bianca like what just happened, but nobody said I word.

Royalty came out the bathroom shaking her head. Can't take you nowhere Royalty said to Bianca embarrassed. Damn you couldn't even let the nigga do his job Royalty said. They gonna jump your ass again Royalty said Laughing.

Who got jumped? Jinx asked.

Bianca Royalty said. Bianca was messing with that nurse guy and he's married and him and his wife jumped Bianca ass now Bianca on some get back type shit every time she see them. This shit Is getting out of hand now tho. Royalty said seriously What would have happened if he would have tried to fight you with the baby in the room huh Bianca? Royalty asked. You didn't think about that with your messy ass.

Bianca wasn't listening to Royalty nor did Bianca ccare. Fuck him and that bitch it's on every time I see them fools Bianca said seriously. He better be glad I didn't shoot his bitch ass. Bianca said mad.

Whatever Royalty said walking over to King who was waking up now. Hi baby picking King up handing him to his mother.

Hi son Liberty said smiling at her handsome baby boy. You ready to go home giving him a kiss.

Your cousin coming to pick you up Liberty? Royalty asked.

Yes, she's on her way now. Liberty said still smiling looking at the baby.

Ok cool I'm getting ready to go before some more shit jump off looking at Bianca. Let's go Bianca I'm going to walk you to your car just in case somebody outside waiting on your ass Royalty said.

I'm coming too Jinx said. Hell were all going to be fighting Jinx said ready for whatever.

You see that Bianca you done went and put Jinx in your business. Damn shame. Innocent people all up in your shit behind a nigga you fucking not us. Fighting and shit Royalty said disappointed in Bianca.

Liberty laughed and said you guys are a reality show in real life.

I know right Royalty said. Bianca is her own show Royalty said.

Fuck You Bianca said getting up ready to leave.

Ok I'll stop by tomorrow, but I'll call you later Royalty said to Liberty ready to leave.

I'll stop by tomorrow also Jinx said following Royalty and Bianca Out.

Ok ladies thank you for everything Liberty said as the ladies walked out to leave.

Once everybody got in their cars safely Royalty went home Royalty wanted to take a nap because Royalty didn't sleep that well last night at the hospital. When Royalty got home before she could even make it upstairs to her bed.

Jacques called hello babe you at home?

Yes, Royalty replied.

You sitting down? Jacques asked

Huh what you mean sitting down? what happened Jacques you making me nervous. Is everything ok?

Yeah, it's nothing that can't be fixed. Jacques said

what's wrong? Royalty asked nervously

Serenity regained her memory. Jacques replied

Awe that's good I thought You was about to say something else that's good I'm glad Serenity ok. Royalty said

Well that's it Royalty Serenity Isn't ok. I mean she is but. Jacques said

But what Jacques? What is it your trying to tell me? Royalty said sitting down in her living room now trying to figure out what Jacques was trying to say. Was Serenity fucked Up or something? Did Serenity take a turn for the worst what? Royalty said to Jacques.

I don't know how to tell you this Royalty, but Serenity got her memory back and Serenity had her parents call her attorney.

Cutting Jacques off Royalty said Attorney? Serenity wants a divorce Jacques already? Royalty asked thinking that's what Jacques was about to say.

No Royalty let me finish please. Serenity doesn't want a divorce or at least not yet. Serenity suing you!

Wait did I hear you correctly Jacques? Serenity suing me why what I do? Royalty asked so confused.

Serenity saying that it's your fault that she had the car accident. That you caused her mental anguish for messing with me and I'm her husband.

Royalty almost laughed not believing what she was hearing. Suing me is that even legal? Royalty Asked. This has to be some kinda joke.

It's no joke Royalty I'll be over there later we can talk more about it then. But contact your lawyer and give him a heads up Jacques says then hangs up.

Royalty sat there for a minute just looking at the phone like what the fuck is this world coming to? This bitch not even grateful she woke up from a coma now this bitch wants to sue me. What the fuck type of lawsuit is that anyways? Royalty was thinking. Crazy bitch hit her head to hard Royalty was thinking. Blaming me for what? Bitch blame your husband. The wife always wants to blame the other woman but what about that nigga Royalty was thinking. They're never wrong getting up to go into the kitchen to pour herself a drink. Not believing Serenity ass was seriously trying to sue her. After pouring herself a drink Royalty sat down at the kitchen table thinking this shit had to be some kind of Karma or something. This some sci fi movie type shit pouring herself another drink. Sue me for what bitch Royalty kept saying to herself. What the fuck you want my life bitch. Because I'm living my best life and I ain't going back and forth with you bitches Period! Ha this is some bullshit. Sue me for what? That's exactly why you can't be nice to these bitches Royalty was thinking, these hoes be really mad out here. Royalty called Jinx to tell her the latest news because Royalty needed to hear someone else opinion about this nonsense Royalty was in straight denial about this one. It was almost hilarious, but Royalty wanted to see if this was even possible and Royalty knew Jinx would have the answer. After all Jinx was a third of a babymama to a man doing a life sentence that got three women pregnant at the same time and they were all correctional officers. Sounds crazy right well so did this to Royalty. Straight unbelievable. This was some straight bullshit Serenity was on and Royalty didn't want no parts of it. Fucking bitch just couldn't take her L in piece Royalty was thinking.
Amir's son and Amir's King.
Calling Jinx and telling Jinx what Jacques said Jinx couldn't believe what Royalty just told her. That's horrible Jinx said feeling terrible for Royalty. I wonder what Made Serenity take that extreme measures Jinx said. You're not the first woman Jacques cheated with Jinx said. Maybe it's because Serenity got into the car accident but wow suing you that's a bit extreme.

Right the nerve of that bitch Royalty said pissed. Is that even legal? Can Serenity actually sue me and for what? Royalty wanted to know.

Well technically yes Royalty Serenity can sue you unfortunately but how it works exactly I'm not sure. But I have heard about a wife suing a girlfriend before and winning 9 million dollars.

What Royalty said. I'm not giving that bitch one dollar. Serenity got me fucked Up if she thinking that. Millions of dollars for fucking her husband. Bitch please. The dick ain't worth no millions of dollars that's for sure Royalty said.

Jinx wanted to disagree, but she kept quiet. So, Royalty I think you should contact your attorney and see what your options are with this. It's probably nothing too serious but you never know. I'm sorry you have to go through this though Jinx said seriously. I'm praying for you girl.

Thanks sis Royalty said but I'm not too worried because I'll counter sue that bitch. I'm not playing with that hoe Serenity don't know who she's fucking with Royalty said seriously. If I was the old Royalty, I'll send someone to the hospital and finish that hoe off. Royalty said Laughing.

You know what Royalty with that being said I'm hanging up. Call your attorney I'll talk to you later Jinx said hanging up. Wanting no parts of the conversation any longer.

Royalty called and left a message for her attorney because he wasn't in the office. And then Royalty went and took a bath to relax and of course the doorbell would ring that's just how life was going for Royalty right now. But Royalty anticipated this would happen, so she left the door unlocked for Jacques. And Royalty had her phone sitting on the floor next to the tub because Royalty knew at any moment Jacques would call. And like on que Royalty phone rings. Hello babe the door is unlocked I'm in the tub come upstairs. Royalty said before hanging up hearing Jacques come into the house going into the kitchen. Walking into the bathroom with two glasses of wine Jacques handed Royalty a glass and pulled the toilet seat down and sat on it and sipped his glasses of wine before speaking.

Hi babe Jacques finally said.

Hi Jacques Royalty, said relaxing in the tub sippin on her glasses of wine Jacques just handed her.

I'm sorry about all of this but.

Its ok Jacques I don't even want to talk about it no more. I'll just let my attorney handle it.

I love your attitude babe because I wouldn't be this calm. Jacques said seriously. I wanted to cuss Serenity ass out but under the circumstances. Plus, Me and her parents have been beefing since they got here. You know I understand Serenity being upset and all and needing to vent about it but me and Serenity have been technical separated for years now living our separate lives. I felt like for years of marriage I was the only one inside the boat rowing, so I jumped ship. We just never really got along that well as husband and wife. We were better off as friends. I think that high school crush shit had us both thinking we were soulmates but that just wasn't the case. And years later neither one of us just wanted the hassle of a divorce. We had business and acquired inheritance it just got to complicated and I know for me it was just cheaper to keep her I guess. Jacques says needing to get that off his chest. Get out the tub babe so we can have a little talk Jacques says handing Royalty a towel to dry off.

Getting out the tub Royalty says ok I just need to get dressed first walking into her bedroom.

Don't get dressed babe just put on your robe Jacques says walking up behind Royalty nibbling on Royalty ear. No clothes on makes it easier for me babe easy access Jacques says slapping Royalty on her ass walking out the room going down stairs to refill his drink.

Royalty dropped her towel to the floor and thought about what Jacques had just said smiling laughing to herself. Jacques knows he's the man, but he better not be playing with my feelings Royalty was thinking putting on her robe and furry slipper with the heels. Royalty sprayed on her favorite perfume that she had been wearing lately Dolce and Gabbana light blue all over her body even her hair and feet. Royalty other go to fragrance was Tom Ford in the black bottle but she wore Jacques out with that one. It was time to switch it up. The same with Royalty white nail polish. Royalty wore white nail polish all winter it was entering summer now so it was time for a summer color Royalty was thinking looking at her feet. But it was so hard to let go of. Her toes looked so cute with white polish on them. Royalty was thinking but oh well they'll look cute with a hot pink polish in sandals too wiggling her toes heading downstairs where Jacques was on the couch stretched out in his wife beater and jeans with his feet up chilling smoking a cigar and drinking a glass of liquor.

I thought you forgot about me Jacques said smiling blowing out smoke. Come here Jacques said reaching for Royalty. Sitting on the floor next to Jacques laying her head on his lap Jacques says to Royalty we need to figure out where we stand and how your feeling right now Jacques said blowing out smoke from his cigar again

Ok but why now? Royalty asked not really understanding where Jacques was going with this conversation. I need a drink before you start getting all serious on me Royalty said.

Like reading your mind I brought you a bottle Jacques said handing Royalty a bottle of Louis thirteen from his personal collection from home.

Not the Louie babe Laughing Royalty said. What's the occasion getting up to get some shot glasses walking into the kitchen getting they fancy Versace shot glasses since they were drinking Louie. Pouring herself a shot and downing it then another one Royalty heads back into the living room and pours Jacques a shot and hands it to him and watch him down it. You want another one Royalty asked.

Looking down at Royalty sitting on the floor looking so pretty Jacques said. I'm a mess around and get into a lot of trouble fucking with you.

Smiling Royalty said no you're not.

Jacques said I already have. Give me another shot baby keep them shots coming it's about to be a long night I can tell just by the way you said that I'm not going to get into no trouble fucking with you way too confident for me. You really don't fear nothing Royalty and that scares me Jacques says seriously. I was raised that there's always something that someone fears and that's what you use against them play on their weakness. But with you Royalty I can't find your weaknesses and that concerns me downing another shot Royalty just poured him.

Why do you want me to be fearful of anything or why would you try to use it against me? Royalty asked Jacques seriously.

I didn't say I wanted to use it against you it's to strengthen you were your weak at it's a difference babe. I'm here to build you up not tear you down kissing Royalty briefly. But it's going to take a lot of trust from you for us to make it thru this staring at Royalty.

Ok babe Royalty said taking another shot. What's good? Royalty asked.

That pussy you got for one Jacques said and that bomb as head for two.

Royalty bust out laughing. No not that babe what's really good?

Oh yeah baby it's really good Jacques said smiling. Now give me another shot. Jacques said ready to have this conversation. Royalty and Jacques both took another shot, but this time Jacques switched positions. Instead of laying down on the couch Jacques sat up and pulled Royalty between his legs facing him. And ran his fingers thru Royalty hair and kissed her. Babe you ready to have this conversation because there's no turning back now Jacques says seriously.

Looking at Jacques Royalty didn't know why they were having such a serious conversation but maybe Royalty could understand better why Jacques wife wanted to sue her and were the breakdown of his marriage went left at. Royalty thought she was about to get all her questions answered until Jacques threw a curve ball in the conversation at Royalty that Royalty never saw coming. Jacques asked Royalty to tell him how she first knew she was in love with Amir and to start from the beginning. Royalty looked puzzled at first then Royalty got nervous Royalty started getting hot and sweaty and felt like she needed some air. Why did Jacques want to know about Amir? And why right now? Royalty had tried to forget so much about her past that she almost forgot when her and Amir became an actual couple. It wasn't how most people thought or how most people got into a relationship. Royalty hands were soaking wet now and Royalty felt like she couldn't breath and got up off the floor and walked to the patio door and opened it up and was gasping for air.

Jacques didn't know what was happening, but he knew it wasn't t good. Babe you alright Jacques asked Royalty who was sucking the night air in her lungs for dear life. Royalty just keep sucking and sucking until Royalty finally felt like she could breathe normally again. Holding her chest Jacques walked up behind Royalty asking babe you ok?

Finally, Royalty turned around with tears in her eyes and said. I think I had an anxiety attack. Wrapping his arms around Royalty holding her tight. Jacques said it's ok babe just breathe just breathe. Your fine babe. If you don't want to talk about Amir, I understand grabbing Royalty face kissing her.

Then Royalty said. Babe it's some things I thought I would never talk about I thought I'll probably take my skeletons to my grave with me. I've never had this conversation before with anyone ever, but I trust that you won't hurt me with my past situation and use it against me. Just thinking about my past makes me nervous I haven't thought about my past in years and back then when I did, I've always been able to block it out. Maybe it's time I faced my demons starting to cry. Babe I think you better sit down for this because after I tell you my life story you won't be able to stand.

Jacques sat down and didn't move Jacques just sat there waiting to hear Royalty tell her story waiting to listen attentively not imagining what could have been so detrimental that had Royalty having panic attacks.

Sitting down on the floor Royalty closed her eyes and tears started running down her face then Royalty says you know life has a funny way of showing us how strong we really are. I wondered for years why God brought me into this world I hated myself for years I've been hurt my whole life, I've been let down and disappointed my whole entire life. But that's the way Life is sometimes. Royalty said. Wiping tears from her eyes. The kind of hurt I experienced as a child no child should ever have to experience Royalty said thinking back to her childhood. As far as I can remember I was treated like an orphan even though I had a mother in the house. But my mother who I always called Teresita because that's what she told me to call her. Teresita never loved me, and Teresita made sure I knew that early on. I never knew who my father was, but it was speculated that my father was my mother's pimp name Sugarman but if Sugarman was my father that would would have made me and Amir brother and sister. My birth certificate says father unknown, so we'll never know. But Sugarman was Amir and Jaheem biological father but Sugarman was also their mother's pimp. So, when people ask me how long have, I loved Amir I can only say my whole entire life because that's how long I've loved him.

Jacques didn't know what to think at this point he was sitting there in a state of shock.

See Me and Amir and Jaheem and our mothers and Sugarman in the beginning plus two other hoes all lived in one house in the projects in a two bedroom apt. Sugarman and all his hoes slept in one room with a king size waterbed. And Jaheem, Amir and I slept in a wooden bunk bed with the top bunk was a twin and the bottom a full and me and Amir shared the bottom bunk until Jaheem moved out when I think he was Fifteen or sixteen years old somewhere around there. Our house was filthy dirty we had roaches and we hardly ever had any food Royalty said shedding a tear and wiping it away thinking about her childhood. Sugarman controlled all the money in the house. The welfare checks the food stamps the hoe money everything. And if that wasn't bad enough Sugarman and all his hoes were on drugs including Teresita Royalty said. Crying now. We never got anything for Christmas, we didn't get new school clothes. And Sugarman use to beat Jaheem and Amir for anything and with anything. Sugarman never beat me but he talk to me like I was a hoe in training. He would say Miss Royalty get your fine little ass over here and take daddy shoes off or lil mama go get big daddy a soda shit like that which was so inappropriate for a father or stepdad to say to his daughter Royalty said still wiping away her tears. Shit was fucked Up for us. We didn't know anything about love in our house. Besides us as siblings loving and protecting each other. Teresita never said she loved me not once. Teresita never gave me baths or combed my hair. Teresita never even took me to a doctor's appointment. I remember I fell and hurt my ankle and Sugarman took me to the hospital but when the doctors saw how dirty I was and how small for my age I was they called Cps on Teresita and Sugarman. The peoples came out and gave Teresita a warning that if they didn't clean the house up and have some food in the house the next time, they came back they would take us. But of course, when they came back the house was kinda clean a little better than when they first came. And Sugarman brought Hella cup of noodles and sodas. The other food was free we got government issued boxes every month. Free cheese and powdered milk and non-name brand cereal. Cps said Teresita and Sugarman was cleared and they never came back.

Wow Jacques couldn't believe what he was hearing.

And this is only the beginning Years it got way worse Royalty said. That was nothing. As we got older crack and heroin became a favorite drug of choice in our household. Sugarman had lost two of his hoes one just left and never came back, and one got took by another pimp. So that just left Teresita and Bee that was Amir's mom her real name was Beatrice, but we called her bee for short. So Sugarman would have them Working nonstop tricking with anybody for a dollar. And when Sugarman couldn't get high he would beat the shit out of the both of them Teresita and Bee until they were black and blue and still make them go out and turn tricks. Teresita and Bee started hoeing on Hollywood Boulevard but eventually they ended up hoeing downtown and on Sepulveda Boulevard when it was all said and done. Jaheem when we were growing up always hustled to get us clothes and shoes. Jaheem and Amir are the ones who made sure I was ok. In the beginning I remember Sugarman's other hoes taking care of me. Bathing us and feeding us but when they left Jaheem and Amir took care of me, Jaheem would make sure I bathe, and Jaheem would wash my hair and have the neighbors braid it and I would keep them braids up sometime for a month. Or sometimes his girlfriend when Jaheem got older would comb my hair and buy me new clothes. Teresita acted like I didn't exist most of the time plus Teresita was always getting high. Jaheem and Amir's mother died from aids when Jaheem was seventeen and Amir was thirteen and I was eleven. So that just left Sugarman with Teresita. Who was starting to look washed up from her hard lifestyle. Teresita was once one of the baddest Filipino hoes out there they said. Teresita had blonde long hair pass her ass thin with a little shape with a bad mouthpiece until crack came along and took her teeth and everything else. And they say Bee was like the black Naomi Campbell back in the days. Tall, dark and bad but of course after Bee got sick, she started to deteriorate quickly. Bee had sores on her face and mouth she lost all her hair. And Bee had long, thick hair once upon a time. Jaheem had stop speaking to Bee before she died, and Jaheem didn't come to Bee burial or funeral either. Jaheem said if it wasn't for me and Amir, he wouldn't come around at all. When Jaheem moved out Amir started hustling doing little shit here and there, so we could eat and have clothes. First Amir started breaking into houses and cars. That keep us with everything we needed. Amir had a crew and they would go out every day and get money. Amir and Jaheem made sure I always went to school no matter what. They didn't play about me not going to school. Jaheem made sure I had whatever I needed for school. Amir was really book smart to so Amir always helped me with homework and stuff. Then two years later after Bee died Sugarman got killed shooting dice in the back of our jet. I'll never forget the day that Sugarman got killed. Me and Amir was in our room Amir was counting his money and Teresita comes bursting in the house crying they killed Sugarman, they killed Sugarman falling out on the floor. I was at the top of the stairs looking at Teresita then I said who the fuck is they? And You should be happy he's dead. You forgot just two days ago Sugarman beat your ass huh? And let's not forget Sugarman turned you into a two dollar hoe. And I walked back in our room and shut the door leaving Teresita alone crying on the floor with her stupid looking ass. At this point Teresita was a straight junkie hooked on heroin and crack. I hated the sight of Teresita and I definitely didn't care that Sugarman was dead. They had all been dead in my eyes years before they actually died. Royalty said. And after Sugarman died Teresita had just given up on life at this point and was a full fledge junkie with no hope. Teresita was turning tricks at the house when I was at school and Amir was out hustling. We told Teresita repeatedly to stop bringing tricks in the house, but Teresita would sneak them in and out before we got home. But this one particular day I was deadly sick with the flu and Amir was out hustling but Amir said he wouldn't be long he would come home and bring me back some soup because I couldn't keep any food down. I was so weak from not eating for days my head was congested I was super fucked up. Teresita was downstairs getting high as usual Teresita never once even came to check up on me. Amir and I had pagers and Amir told me to page him in case of an emergency and to only page him for a emergency because Amir was hitting a house and coming straight back. Well this particular day all our lives changed.

Royalty said starting to cry. Putting her head down crying in her lap. Jacques got up to console Royalty, but Royalty said no it's ok babe I need to get this out. I've never spoken about this before to anyone and I'll never speak on it again. Royalty said in between sobs. Teresita was the worst parent a child could ever have crying wiping away her tears. That day I was laid up sick as a dog Teresita was downstairs and I heard someone at the door. Then I recognized the voice as Teresita let him in. It was Javier the janitor for the housing authority who was also the dope man around our building. Javier was a pervert that all the girls hated. Javier was known for being a big trick. Javier was a nasty old Mexican man that always said inappropriate shit to people. I could hear Teresita asking him for some dope but telling Javier she didn't have any money until the first. Teresita was saying she would turn a trick for some dope while I was sick right upstairs. Royalty said as her voice was starting to get low and shaky now. Then Royalty continued to say I heard Javier say I like your sweet little daughter and I could hear Teresita say she's upstairs if you want her just give me a hit and you can have her. I started paging Amir 911 over and over again I was so scared Royalty said crying and I was looking around the room for something to hit Javier with in case he came upstairs I was trying to get out the bed, but I was so weak I could hardly move. Royalty said crying uncontrollably talking in between sobs but then I heard Javier say to Teresita I'm going to give you a hit and you still owe me on the first then Javier started coming upstairs. I can still hear the squeaky stairs in my head as Javier came up each one. I got so scared and started crying thinking how could Teresita do this to me her only daughter her only child, but Teresita didn't give a fuck about me. Royalty said crying. Jacques started holding Royalty saying he was sorry, but Royalty keep talking in between tears. Javier reaches the top of the staircase and I could smell his cigarette and I crawled to the back of the bed hoping Javier wouldn't come in the room but then Javier came thru the bedroom door and started unbuckling his pants saying you know you want this pretty girl. I've always liked you. I kept saying No but Javier didn't care he beat me and raped me and sodomized me until Amir came running in the house and shot and killed Javier. Amir blew Javier head right off his shoulders and Javier brain membrane went all over me. I passed out and when I woke up, I was in the hospital in ICU for three weeks. With two black eyes and a broken jaw with my mouth wired shut. With twenty eight stitches in my pussy and ass. The doctors said I may never have children. And they were treating me for gonorrhea. And I was only thirteen years old. Royalty was shaking and crying so hard Jacques got nervous.

Baby I'm so sorry I'm sorry that happened to you rubbing Royalty head trying to console Royalty. I'm sorry baby Jacques said feeling so sorry for Royalty. Who had held all that in for years without ever telling anyone. The thought of being molested as a child but even worse your mother selling you to the dope man. Jacques didn't know what to say but he was sorry.

Royalty cried for twenty minutes straight rocking in Jacques arms reliving her horrific ordeal. Then Royalty finally said in between tears looking up at Jacques. Why didn't Teresita love me? Crying putting her head down on Jacques again.

Jacques was heartbroken for Royalty. Jacques didn't have the answer Royalty was looking for. Nobody had the answer that Royalty was looking for. The only person that knew that answer was Teresita and Teresita took the answer with her to her grave.
Jacques took Royalty upstairs to her room and laid Royalty down. Royalty had finally stopped crying and fell asleep in Jacques arms. Holding Royalty tight Jacques kept replaying what Royalty had just told him about being brutally attacked as a child in his mind over and over again. No child should have to go through what Royalty went through Jacques kept thinking. Jacques wished he could have

killed Javier himself. And Teresita. Some people should just not be mothers at all. Especially if they didn't want the child. Jacques swore from that moment on if he ever had children he would be the best father he could be. But Jacques also had great parents that loved him unconditionally. So Jacques didn't believe he would ever be a bad parent. Jacques wondered what happened with Teresita that made Teresita not show no affection to her only daughter. Something must have happen to Teresita when she was a child. Jacques just couldn't understand how anyone couldn't love a child. Jacques eventually feel asleep holding Royalty until Royalty woke up from a nightmare and woke Jacques up.

Sorry to wake you up Royalty said to Jacques.

It's ok are you alright ? Jacques asked Royalty.

No but I will be Royalty said. Can we go get something to eat Royalty asked.

Looking at the clock it read 5:30 am. Royalty nothing open Jacques says.

Let's go to Denny's Royalty replied.

Seriously Jacques asked you want to go to Denny's at 5:30 in the morning looking confused.

Yes is that a problem? Royalty asked Jacques because Royalty was going to go with or without Jacques. Royalty needed to get out of the house and plus Royalty was starving.

Ok babe let's go we're already dressed Jacques said looking at himself and Royalty who fell asleep in their clothes. Babe we're nasty who sleeps in their clothes Jacques says.

We do Royalty said getting up going into the bathroom to freshen up real quick. After Royalty and Jacques get themselves together they headed over to Denny's to grab something to eat. Sitting down at the restaurant Denny's had a few people already there before Royalty and Jacques showed up Jacques was surprised to see people out this early eating. I've never been to a Denny's before babe Jacques confesses looking over the menu. This is considered fast food babe huh ? Jacques asked.

No they cook it after you place your order Royalty said.

Then why is so cheap? You can get a whole breakfast for $4.00 that seems a little suspicious to me Jacques says laughing.

It's just reasonably that's all no suspense there babe relax rich boy Royalty says laughing.

Ok Jacques says I trust you Royalty and I can't help that I was born with a silver spoon in my mouth. Jacques says seriously. Poor people always call rich people rich in a derogatory way. It's not fair. Jacques says laughing but was dead serious.

Whatever Royalty said not paying Jacques no mind. After Royalty and Jacques ate breakfast Royalty asks Jacques are you ready for part two babe?

Huh what's part two? Jacques asks.

There's more to my story I didn't get a chance to finish. Royalty says.

There couldn't possibly be more to the story could there? Jacques was thinking I Hope Royalty isn't about to tell me she use to be a boy in a previous life. I don't know how much more of this story I can take Jacques was thinking. Ok tell me when get back and we get in bed in case I pass out I'll be already laying down Jacques says seriously.

Hitting Jacques arm boy please. You're not going to pass out. I've already told you the worst part.

Oh, ok I wasn't sure Jacques says grateful the worst part was over hopefully. Royalty feel to sleep on the ride back home Jacques looked over at Royalty and was thinking how much Royalty had endured in her young life and Jacques hoped Royalty wouldn't snap one day because that's usually what happens. Pulling up to the house Royalty looked so peaceful almost angelic even Jacques hated that he had to even wake Royalty up. But without even touching Royalty she just woke up on her on.

I was just about to wake you up Jacques said to
Royalty who replied I wasn't sleep babe I was just resting my eyes Royalty said getting out the car.

Jacques was thinking to himself I could have sworn Royalty was asleep that whole time that's some hella mediation technique Royalty was doing Jacques said to himself getting out the car behind Royalty like this girl is full of surprises. Going In the house Royalty and Jacques both took quick showers and got in the bed. Jacques plops himself up on several throw pillows Royalty had on her bed and gets himself prepared for part two of Royalty story as if he was about to watch the second part of a movie.

Royalty laid her head on Jacques lap and started finishing her story. Well babe as you know Amir shot and killed Javier and I was in the hospital for two months because I couldn't walk my in sides had been severard severely that's why the doctors weren't sure if I'll ever be able to have children.

Well can you have them now Jacques asked?

I don't know Jacques I've never been pregnant before Royalty says not sure if she could or couldn't have children time would tell. The police took Amir to juvenile immediately after the shooting but released Amir three days later. The police was originally charging Amir for the gun, but Amir Claim was that It was Javier gun and they fought over it and Amir got control of the gun and that's when Amir shot Javier. The police couldn't prove otherwise so they had to let Amir go.

So, was it Javier gun? Jacques asked wanting to know.

Looking up at Jacques Royalty says. Just know this Javier was on top of me molesting me when he got killed. Royalty said sarcastically. And stop interrupting me please Jacques Royalty said laying her head back down wanting to finish the story while she still had the guts to tell it without having a panic attack. Ok back to the story Royalty said. But when Amir was in juvenile hall, they gave him a private attorney for his case that Amir turned around and hired when Amir got out to sue the housing authority for negligence and assault for me being that Javier was at work during my assault and the housing authority had numerous complaints against him and never did anything about it. And Amir sued the police department because they beat Amir up and broke his jaw when they arrested him saying Amir was a known gang member with a extensive aggressive background which was false. It was Jaheem they were referring to not Amir, but the police knew that Amir and Jaheem were brothers and just thought they could do whatever to Amir Until we both won our lawsuits. I was awarded 4 million dollars for damages and Amir got 2.5 million for defamation. The city didn't appeal or even contest because they didn't want any more publicity for their neglect and two years later after our lawsuits me and Amir were millionaires.

That's what up Jacques said smiling.

Yes, I wasn't allowed access to all the money until I turned eighteen, I had an allowance for a couple years that was in a trust fund, but Amir got his money because he was seventeen in a half. And also within those two years Teresita died from an heroin overdose but Teresita was dying anyways because Teresita had stage four ovarian cancer. But to me Teresita had died many many years ago way before any of that happened. The moment I realized that Teresita never loved me the hurt and pain took over and made me heartless when it came to Teresita. At first, I would cry and be hurt that Teresita didn't love me and when Sugarman use to beat Teresita up after a while I was looking forward to Sugarman beating the shit out of Teresita. I use to secretly want Sugarman to beat her. I know that sounds cruel, but Teresita tormented me for years. Me wishing bad luck on Teresita was my way of getting Teresita back I suppose. Sometimes when Sugarman would beat Amir or Jaheem I would yell out beat Teresita she's the one you're mad at not them crying and Sugarman would stop beating Amir or Jaheem. Sugarman hated us too but we were his check that's the only reason why I think he kept us around.

Jacques was in shock once again from what Royalty was telling him. Royalty life was like a horror movie that was rated R. The only good thing was the compensation, but can you really put a price on years of abuse? Some people never really heal from abuse. Royalty looked up at Jacques and Jacques didn't know what to say. Jacques wasn't normally a guy lost for words but in this case. Well babe since we're being so honest let me be honest with you. I knew Amir I did business with Amir a couple of times.

Oh, really Royalty said wanting to hear more.

I meet Amir thru a business associate that put me on with Amir's trucking company that Amir was smuggling drugs through. Amir was placing large quantities of coke in the trunks of the cars he was taking cross country and delivering it to distributors in different states.

Royalty lifted her head up and looked in Jacques eyes and said you're a drug dealer Jacques?

Laughing briefly Jacques said surprise!!

Wait a minute so all that inheritance shit was a lie? Royalty asked thinking Jacques had been lying the whole time.

No, no I was born rich my family is very wealthy. But I was thrown into the game by default.

What you mean default Royalty asked crossing her arms.

Well it's like this my cousin lived in the states and he was in the game and I was visiting the states and my cousin got caught up, but he told me before they feds got him where his stash house was located and told me if anything happened to him to get rid of everything and make sure he was straight. See my cousin was on the run but I never knew that. Well it was a lot of things I didn't know but that's another story for another time. So, when the feds got my cousin I went and got his stash I didn't know what to do with the dope at first because it was so much but let's just say I learned fast. But it got to Be addicting to me becoming a drug dealer the lifestyle of being a drug dealer the the prestige and respect. I was already a bad boy back home I ran around with killers in Jamaica and killers from home that could kill you with their bare hands. These killers are vicious babe my father made sure I would be able to take care of our family and protect them in case anything ever happened to him because where I'm from poor people don't care who you are, they'll kill you if they ever get the advantage to especially for money. See my father didn't grow up rich he was from a poor village in Jamaica, so my father knew how to protect himself. And when he became a businessman a lot of people was jealous of him, so he made sure I knew how to protect myself at all cost. My father taught me how to shoot to kill and what arteries to stick to kill a person instantly my father was a trained assassin growing up.

Now Royalty was looking at Jacques like she wasn't the only person with a secret past life when Royalty thought she was the only fucking elephant in the room geesh.
So, tell me Jacques since you knew Amir did you know who I was when we first meet? Royalty asked.

No, I didn't Jacques says seriously. I only did business with Amir a couple times and it went thru someone else, but I had heard that Amir had a fine wife that he would kill over. Tell me Royalty I'm curious if you and Amir grew up as brother and sister how did you two get involved you know sexually? Jacques asked.

Well Jacques that's the million dollar question Royalty said. While I was in the hospital Amir never left my side not even to shower Amir showered at the hospital. Amir said he felt like it was his fault what happened to me because he was supposed to have protected me and Amir knew Teresita didn't give a fuck about me. But the day I got my bandages taken off my face and they gave me a mirror I broke down because I didn't look the same anymore. A few of my teeth were missing and broken from Javier slamming my face into the side of the railing on the bed and one of my eyes was completely shut. I just wanted to kill myself Royalty said getting emotional. I thought my life was over that no one loved me, and I was better off dead. But Amir said it didn't matter what I looked like he loved me and always had. That no matter what he would never leave me alone again and from that day on We were kinda together. Amir admitted that he cared for me and not in a brotherly way. That he knew he loved me but held back his feelings because of how we were raised up together but after my incident Amir said he wanted us to be together forever. I had to have reconstructive facial surgery and I had to get my teeth fixed smiling showing a perfect set of veneers and I had to have physical therapy for a whole year to regain strength in my legs from being so weak from the abuse on my torso I had suffered. Remember I was a young girl and I was a virgin. Royalty said. When that pervert brutally abused my body, my mind and body shut down after that. The body has its own way of dealing with trauma like getting hit by a car. Sometimes the body takes longer than the mind to heal or vice a verse. And my body wasn't cooperating it wasn't healing as fast as the doctors would have liked it to. But Amir was there with me every step of the way. Amir had three outfits he wore the whole three months I was in the hospital. The nurses washed his clothes every other day and Amir slept on a pull out couch he never left me ever. And if Amir did leave

Amir had one of his boys sit with me. And that only happened once or twice I believed because Amir had to go to court. Amir would read to me when I couldn't see, and we listened to music at night and when I had my two surgeries Amir was right there. Me and Amir became really close with the doctors and nurses. We actually still kept in touch with most of them. One of the doctors wanted to adopt us but Amir said we were good. But being in the hospital all that time together under those circumstances we bonded in a way we had never before. It was something special between us. And you know the whole time I was in the hospital Teresita not once came to visit or checked on me. Amir said Teresita called the hospital to see how I was doing. But Amir was lying because the nurse told me no one ever called. Amir just didn't want to admit to himself that Teresita didn't give a fuck and that Teresita sold her only child to a drug dealer a child molester who could have killed me if Amir hadn't killed Javier first. Royalty got quiet for a moment before continuing the story. Well the moral of the story is Amir was my everything my whole entire life and Amir meant everything to me. I wish things could have been different and we had our old life back but things happened abruptly and life happens Royalty said then Royalty started rumbling .

Jacques was like what's Royalty talking about Royalty just went off course then Royalty said.

I'm tired of talking about my past. I don't want to keep revisiting it. It's way too painful Royalty said getting up going into the bathroom.

Jacques was tired and had fallen asleep by the time Royalty came out the bathroom. Royalty was relieved Jacques was asleep because Royalty didn't feel like being bothered with no more questions. Going downstairs to get herself something to drink Royalty noticed Jacques had left his car keys and his phone and wallet on the kitchen counter. Royalty wanted so badly to go through Jacques things but thought otherwise instead Royalty made a cup of hot tea, but Royalty keep glancing over at Jacques things. The temptation was so strong that Royalty ran back upstairs and got in the bed and just stared at Jacques thinking damn this nigga really a drug dealer and he doesn't even have to be. Most people with money had desires to run a successful business or become a tycoon but this fool wanted to be a drug dealer out of all the things you can be in life. Royalty guessed that real drug kingpins probably came from money also. Royalty knew if she would have been born rich Royalty for damn sure wouldn't have chosen the life she had lived or the mother that she had. Royalty also dreamed of having two parents who weren't on drugs of course living in a big house in a nice neighborhood with lots of brothers and sisters and family dog even though Royalty hated dogs. Royalty also had that same dream about what Royalty believed a family should look like then the dream turned into a horrific nightmare. Royalty woke up looking around and looked at Jacques and realized she must have fallen asleep but when Royalty was thinking I was just awake a few moments ago Royalty was thinking. Royalty knew she had to be hella tired because she was starting to hallucinate closing her eyes going back to sleep. A few hours later Royalty woke up sweating profusely with a fever then Royalty started shivering that woke Jacques up and Jacques asked Royalty was she ok but Royalty didn't respond she just laid there shivering.

Jacques pulled the covers over Royalty who was now crying and saying help me please rocking back and forth. Jacques didn't know what to do. Jacques didn't know if Royalty was sick and had come down with something or if talking about Royalty past had triggered something else. Jacques held Royalty and stroked her hair while Royalty rocked and cried for a minute then Royalty feel back to sleep. Jacques held Royalty thinking that Royalty childhood trauma was too much for Royalty to bare alone and that Royalty held on to it for quite a long time. Kissing Royalty forehead laying her down Jacques sat up and just watch Royalty sleep turning on the tv to help him occupy the time.

When Royalty finally woke up it was 4:30 in the evening Jacques was smiling at Royalty hoping she felt better. You feel better ? Jacques asked.

Yes, I'm fine Royalty said looking confused. Why you ask me that? Royalty said.

Because you woke up not feeling good earlier, I'm just making sure you're ok Jacques said.

I did? Royalty asked not remembering that part. The last thing Royalty remembered was having a talk with Jacques after breakfast then both of them falling asleep.

Well if you don't remember not feeling well that means you must feel better Jacques said. Let's fly to Vegas and go gambling and do some shopping Jacques said wanting to take Royalty mind off everything that had occurred within the last couple days. Jacques knew Royalty was overwhelmed but damn Jacques didn't know how serious it was until today seeing Royalty damn near have a nervous breakdown is how Jacques diagnosed it.

Ok I'm with it Royalty said jumping up looking in her closet.

Jacques was looking at Royalty like is that the same person from earlier? Royalty was totally fine now. Jacques wasn't sure if he was glad that he got Royalty to tell him about her past or if he should have just left shit well enough alone because now Jacques felt like a physiatrist with no remedy for a cure. Maybe going to Vegas would be good for the both of them. Jacques called and ordered a private plane and booked a suite. Jacques was thinking they both could use some R&R and Jacques was hoping that he had enough money on him. Jacques had about twenty racks in the trunk of his car. So, if they needed more Jacques would have it wired to his room plus they were only going for two days and Jacques did have his black card on him also so Jacques was thinking they were pretty straight.

I'm ready Royalty said coming out the closet with luggage in hand looking fly. Royalty sure knew how to clean up nice. Looking at Royalty with her Nike sports bra and matching leggings with Nike sun visor and off white air max and wearing some Ray Bans looking real cute and comfortable you wouldn't even believe Royalty was the same women that had went thru all that trauma as a child and lived to tell her story and now Royalty was standing there ready to turn up but a few hours ago Royalty was suffering from memory loss and having panic attacks. Shit was crazy to Jacques he definitely needed a few days away from La before he went crazy his damn self. Yep looks like it babe you ready to go win some money and do some shopping.

I was born ready for whatever Royalty replied smiling.

That's what up babe let's go Jacques said getting up going into the bathroom brushing his teeth and taking a quick shower. Jacques walked out the bathroom while Royalty sitting on her bed counting some money. How much money is that babe Jacques asks Royalty catching Royalty off guard because Royalty didn't hear Jacques walking up behind her because Royalty was distracted counting her money.

Fifteen bands it's supposed to be twenty, but I forgot I spent some money the other day when I went shopping. Royalty said It's my emergency money I keep at the house why you need to borrow some money Royalty asked Jacques.

Laughing Jacques says yes all of it.

Royalty handed it to Jacques, but he didn't take it. I'm kidding babe I'm good. You don't need to bring no money we straight. You know whenever you're with me I'll treat you like a queen you'll never need anything when you're with me. Jacques said seriously. I got you always winking at Royalty. Now put that money back up and let's go our plane is waiting. Jacques says heading downstairs, so Royalty can put up her money in peace.
Landing in Vegas at 11pm was exciting. The bright lights everywhere the limo ride to the suite was even fun Royalty hung out the sunroof singing Ain't nothing but a gangsta party every word by Tupac. Jacques just laughed he was glad Royalty was feeling better. Once they got into their suite Jacques asked Royalty what she wanted to do it
Royalty said let's hit the strip club first and we'll figure the rest out from there. What happens in Vegas stays in Vegas right winking Royalty said.

Laughing Jacques said Exactly babe. Let's get dressed and hit the club. Getting dressed Royalty pulled out a blunt and asked Jacques if he wanted to hit it.

Jacques declined saying I didn't know you smoked babe.

Not all the time but occasionally especially if I'm stressing Royalty said.

Jacques just shook his head thinking Royalty was full of surprises. After getting dressed Jacques was like babe forreal you gone kill em like that? Impressed with Royalty attire, Spinning around slowly showing off her outfit Royalty had on a Versace print blouse wearing it as a dress with her shirt open showing her push up bra Royalty had on several gold chains and gold Versace open toe sandals. Red lips with bone straight hair parted down the middle looking like a straight ten. But Jacques was playing fair his damn self with his black Fendi tee and black fitted jeans, Fendi belt and black suede Fendi boots with a brown suede brim and Cartier glasses and a course his Gurkha Black dragon cigar fifteen hundred for one but nobody knew that but him.

Let's go turn up babe Royalty said grabbing her purse walking to the door lit high off her weed. Inside the limo ride Royalty and Jacques had a shot of Hennessy and toast to the good life. Ok babe follow my lead Royalty says pulling up to the gentlemen's club getting out walking pass the line. At the door the bouncer says Welcome back to Royalty hugging her and nods his head what's up to Jacques and lets them inside. Royalty heads to the back VIP area dancing to the music feeling it. It was thick inside the club. Once Royalty reached her table Jacques ordered bottle service and lit up his cigar watching Royalty party by herself off Snoop smile bitch song. Royalty walked to the Dj booth and whispered in the Dj ear then the Dj gave Royalty the mic. I got 5 bands for the baddest bitches at my table I need thick bitches with ass only Royalty said handing the Dj the mic back and went back to her table. Jacques handed Royalty five thousand and their table got flooded with strippers. Royalty picked the baddest two and got a lap dance. When Cardi B money song came on Royalty went off dancing with them giving Jacques a dance twerking for him. Throwing money in the air. Royalty partied hard all night spending around ten thousand in the club. But Jacques didn't care it was nothing to him, but Jacques did have to pay their tab with his black card because Royalty brought the two strippers to the suite with them for the after party. Jacques didn't know what Royalty was up, but Jacques couldn't wait to see. What happened next Jacques wasn't ready for. Royalty had both the broads on their backs with their legs in the air taking turns freaking them both one Royalty sucked her uterus out of her and the other one Royalty fingered. Royalty had both the women shouting Yes like they were in church. Then it was Royalty turn to get broke off. With one sucking on Royalty tittes while the other one ate Royalty out. Royalty acted as if Jacques wasn't even in the same room until she came. Then Royalty told Jacques to fuck both the women. First fuck one of them then pull out and hit the other one. Royalty said giving marching orders. But first Royalty wanted one of the women to suck Jacques dick while the other one jiggled his balls. Jacques got undressed and laid back and let the women handle their business. Royalty enjoyed seeing Jacques come after a long night. The next morning Royalty gave each of the women four bands each and thanked them for their services slapping them on their asses on the way out the door. Jacques was still sleeping when their company left so Royalty got in the shower. When Royalty got out of the shower she went and got in the bed and crawled between Jacques legs and woke him up sucking his dick. Before Jacques could cum Royalty got on top and rode Jacques slow gripping the bed railing. Jacques made Royalty cum by sucking on her breast while Royalty rode him. Then Jacques came too and they both fell back to sleep. When Jacques and Royalty both got up to finally start their day it was evening and they were both starving. Royalty wanted to go to the all you can eat buffet at the MGM.

Sounds good to me Jacques said. I have to go pick up some more cash Jacques said.

No, you don't Royalty said. I had some money deposit into my account at the MGM babe Royalty said I'm a frequent flyer out here I have access to everything Royalty said Laughing. After they showered together and got dressed, they headed to the MGM to eat.

Sitting down with full plates before digging into his food Jacques asks Royalty babe you brought condoms last night laughing you came prepared huh?

Taking a bite of her crab leg Royalty says I was born ready remember winking.

Jacques started laughing. Jacques didn't know what to do with Royalty Jacques never meet anyone like Royalty before. What we doing tonight babe? Jacques asked knowing it wasn't nothing he could possibly imagine especially after last night.

Whatever you want to do babe Royalty said cracking crab legs.

Jacques knew exactly why he liked Royalty at that moment it was because Royalty was easy going and down for whatever plus Royalty could hold her own. But after last night Jacques grew a whole different level of respect for Royalty. Allowing him to fuck not one but two bad bitches and not trip at all was on another level to Jacques. Most women would absolutely have a problem with their man even thinking about fucking someone else but Royalty expected nothing less. Royalty damn near forced Jacques to do it. Royalty got off on it. Royalty sat there and played with her own clit while Jacques broke the two women off. They don't make too many women like Royalty Jacques was thinking. The universe was definitely working in Jacques favor. I want to go play some poker Jacques said ready to gamble.

Ok babe Royalty said let's go get this bag babe. Double our money Royalty said finishing her food.

You were really hungry huh babe ? Jacques asks Royalty .

Yep Royalty says but I would prefer eating some pussy. But crab legs will do Royalty said.

Jacques spit his drink out when Royalty said that. Damn babe Jacques says laughing.

What Royalty replied seriously. I love women sorry babe you had to find out like that. I've been fucking with women for years babe Royalty says laughing. I like bad bitches with pretty feet. I have a foot fetish Royalty said seriously speaking.

Me too Jacques says. It's something about a woman with pretty feet I love it. I imagine what women feet look like inside their shoes Jacques says laughing. That's one reason why I have a women's boutique. I absolutely could not deal with no niggas and their feet.

Right I get it Royalty says in agreement. But I do love a well dressed man though Royalty says. You kill it every time babe Royalty says to Jacques.

Thanks babe you too. But I have a stylist Jacques says.

You do? Why? Royalty asked shocked.

I've always had one my whole life Jacques says. I don't use her all the time but most of the time. I don't have time to shop like that. Plus, she's a fashion whore she keeps me laced with the flyest shit.

Ok Royalty says thinking who was this person.

Yes, babe she the one who ordered all your outfits for our trip. I texted her your picture and sent her your size and she went online and ordered everything for me.

Well she did a good job tell her thank you Royalty said.

I'll introduce you to her one day when she's in La she lives in Atlanta right now. That's where a lot of her clients are. She has all my stuff shipped right to me so it's perfect business relationship plus she's my cousin from Jamaica.

Royalty relaxed a little when Jacques said that she was his cousin. It made sense now. Ok babe you ready to go get money Royalty asked.

Hell yeah babe let's go take the MGM for everything they got getting up from the booth taking Royalty hand leading the way to the money cage.

Royalty had twenty thousand wired to her account and handed Jacques ten thousand and Royalty keep ten and then they went their separate ways. Royalty went and played the crap table that's what Royalty and Amir always played. But Jacques played High roller poker. Royalty lost five thousand real quick and decided to quit and walked around and played slots here and there while Jacques was over at the card table killing them. Jacques was up six thousand and counting. Royalty went to the bar and had a couple drinks then went and found Jacques. Walking over to where Jacques was sitting Royalty gave Jacques a kiss and sat down next to Jacques and watched him play. Jacques used his free hand and started rubbing on Royalty breast and started poking on her pussy. Royalty started grinding Jacques hand in her seat and Jacques knew it was time to go especially while he was up six thousand. Throwing in his hand Jacques was happy with his total win of eight thousand. Not bad for a few hours of fun.

When they got back to their suite Jacques and Royalty were both hot and bothered from touching and feeling on each other in the elevator. So, when they entered their suite Jacques dumped all the money he won and had in his pocket on the bed and fucked Royalty on top of it in every position possible. The next day Jacques and Royalty ate breakfast in bed of course removing all the money and showered and got dressed then flew back home. Did you enjoy yourself Jacques asked Royalty pulling up at house?

A fucking blast thanks babe I appreciated that Royalty said tired as hell.

Ok babe back to reality Jacques says reaching over his seat giving Royalty a kiss. I'm about to go home and rest up for the week and I'll call you later babe be good Jacques says to Royalty.

I will be smiling getting out the limo Royalty says. When am I going to see you again? Royalty asks holding the car door open.

Close your eyes and imagine me being there then I'm always with you Jacques said.

Stop with the pimp shit Royalty said and they both bust up laughing.

I'm no pimp babe Jacques says still laughing.

You could have fooled me nigga limos and shit private jets, stripclubs, bad bitches Royalty said Laughing.

I'll call you Jacques says smiling and you'll see me sooner than you think.

Ok I'm ok with that answer Royalty said closing the car door waving bye blowing kisses. Watching Jacques limo drive off. Going in the house Royalty puts her bag down and calls Liberty to check on the kids and decided to go spend the night over there with them picking her bag back up heading right back out the door. Royalty didn't feel like being alone in that house. Talking about her past to Jacques brought up abandonment issues that Royalty wasn't ready to deal with tonight.
Arriving at Liberty house Royalty was so tired Royalty barely played with Angel before Angel went to bed and was grateful King was a newborn, so Royalty didn't have to play with him. Royalty talked to Liberty briefly telling Liberty about her trip sorta then Royalty went to bed shortly after. Royalty forget how comfortable the guest bed was until she laid down on it. Amir picked out most of the furniture in all their houses. Amir wanted his guest rooms nice and comfortable because you never knew what a person was going through, and they just might have needed some good rest Amir would always say. Most people wouldn't care how comfortable their guest beds were because they didn't want their guest overstaying their welcome, but Amir was just the opposite. Amir wanted everyone to be comfortable at their houses. Didn't matter who you were. So, laying down on the Queen, fluffy, lux mattress was like heaven to Royalty. Royalty never heard the baby cry at night for his feeding or Liberty getting up getting Angel ready for school the next morning. Royalty didn't even hear her phone going off the few times it rung or beeped from a text message. Royalty lawyer had left her several messages to return her call, but Royalty was so tired Royalty slept thru all that until the next afternoon when Liberty came in to check in on Royalty to make sure she was ok.

Shaking Royalty several times until Royalty woke up Liberty was like girl you scared me sleeping this long you haven't even gotten up to use the bathroom once Liberty said concern.

Yawning Royalty said I was tired thanks for checking up on me still not wanting to get up.

You hungry? Liberty asked. I can order you some food.

Royalty thought about what she wanted to eat. Does anybody deliver seafood Royalty asked because Royalty had a taste for some fish? Royalty asked

I don't know but I can order you some seafood and go pick it up Liberty said. Just listen out for King for me. He's asleep and I just feed him so he's good for a few hours Liberty said not worried about King waking up anytime soon. What you want ? Liberty asked.

Snapper, fries and banana pudding. Royalty said

Banana pudding Liberty said looking like seriously Royalty.

I'm hungry Royalty said Laughing.

Anything else? Liberty asked before she left

Oh and a Pepsi Royalty said.

Ok if you want anything else while I'm gone that you forgot just call me. Liberty says walking out the room to leave to go pick up Royalty food.

Royalty was grateful for her new little family and was glad she didn't just say fuck them all together like Royalty intended too at first .Royalty got up to use the bathroom and washed her face because Royalty was trying to wake up. Royalty went to check on King and sure enough King was knocked out looking so perfect. King had his little mittens on so he couldn't scratch his face and King had on a onesie that said King. Royalty smiled admiring him then Royalty picked King up and kissed his small, fat cheeks and laid King back down. Royalty stood there looking at King thinking how Amir would have felt having a son. Royalty knew Amir would have wanted to be with his son as much as possible bonding with King even if that meant leaving Royalty at home alone stressed out. Amir could have cared less about how Royalty was feeling when it came to his seed. King was Amir's flesh and blood and nothing else would have mattered. Royalty remembered Amir once saying having a son is the epitome of life for a man except for Sugarman. So Royalty knew King would have been Amir's whole world. Hearing the front door shut Royalty looked down at King one more time before walking downstairs to eat her food.

I'm back Liberty yelled out.

Thank you Royalty said to Liberty sitting down at the table getting her food out the bag. Did you get you and Angel any food for later ? Royalty asked Liberty.

Yes I got Angel some turkey wings Angel loves them with some macaroni and cheese and me I got some Tilapia with string beans and yams Liberty said sitting down next to Royalty to eat her food. So Royalty you turned up in Vegas Liberty said smiling. I wish I had your life Liberty said.

Royalty was thinking you almost did but didn't say it. Yeah we had fun that's why I'm hella tired now. I was drunk and high as fuck the whole weekend.

I didn't know you smoked Liberty said looking shocked.

Not all the time Royalty said in between bites. Just Sometimes especially when I'm stressing Royalty said tearing her food up.

What you have to stress about? Liberty asked curious.

Royalty was thinking my dead husband just had a baby for starters a fucking son at that by you. But instead Royalty said I have shit that stresses me out laughing. I'm not perfect.

You're the closest thing to perfect Liberty said seriously complimenting Royalty.

Awe thanks Royalty said but no I have issues. Not like you think but trust me I do have issues.

Well I know we just met recently, and I just had your man's baby sorry Liberty says smiling, but I do care about you Royalty and I appreciate all that you've done for me and my kids. So, if you need to talk, I'm here for you Liberty says solemnly.

Royalty just smiled. Royalty was feeling some type of way all of a sudden and Royalty didn't know why. Royalty was looking at Liberty like she wanted to choke the shit out of Liberty. This was the first time Royalty felt this disdain towards Liberty. Royalty started thinking this bitch could have ruined my whole entire life having a baby and she just sitting over there smiling and shit. Taking a deep breath Royalty said. Thanks for the food but I have to go there's something I have to do getting up leaving her food on the table going to get her bag before she said something she would regret later. After getting her stuff Royalty said bye and walked out the door.

Liberty was looking like what just happened maybe Royalty had gotten a phone call before she returned with the food because Liberty knew she didn't say anything offensive. Whatever it was Liberty was sure she'll find out later getting up cleaning up the food off the table putting it in the refrigerator for later, so she could go check on King.

Royalty got in her car still wearing her pajamas not giving a fuck Royalty just needed to get out of that house away from Liberty as quickly as possible before Royalty said something to hurt that girls' feelings. Royalty didn't know where this burst of anger came from, but Royalty wasn't feeling Liberty at the moment and what was best for them both was that Royalty left peacefully for the sake of everyone involved.
Royalty found herself driving straight to Bianca house why Royalty didn't know because Royalty knew Bianca was about to be hella messy. Pulling up Royalty wondered whose car was parked in Bianca driveway Royalty didn't recognize the car. But that wasn't unusual for Bianca of course. Parking on the street Royalty got out her car and took out Bianca house keys to let herself in because now Royalty was curious who Bianca had in the house. Opening the door Royalty heard

moaning and followed the sounds right into the living room. Royalty just stood there in complete shock at what she saw in total disbelief. Bianca and some dude was so into fucking they didn't even hear Royalty come thru the door. Clearing her throat Royalty said really bitch you got rid of your dick to fuck a nigga in the ass with a strap on? Bianca and her lover both jumped when they realized Royalty was standing there watching them. Wait a mother fucking minute Royalty said realizing the dude was her friend Taj the annoying rapper boy. Taj Royalty said looking at this nigga with a strapon in his ass. All that hard shit you be spitting in your verse's nigga Royalty said in disbelief. And you like it in the ass?

Bianca started saying I can explain Royalty throwing her hands up in the air like Royalty was the police.

Taj was trying to grab his clothes embarrassed picking his shit up off the floor knowing he was busted like fuck. Then Taj said what you mean cut her dick off? Looking at Bianca like what the fuck Royalty talking about.

Yes, you heard me right fraud ass nigga. Royalty said Yes Bianca she pointing at Bianca was born a he looking at Bianca who had turned beat red in the face and was about to cry. She-he had that good ol surgery done sweet cakes. Royalty said To Taj and then Royalty turned her focus on Bianca. Oh, this how you do your best friend Royalty says mad as fuck and then Royalty takes off on Bianca and steals on Bianca bam, bam hitting her twice in her eye. Squaring Up telling Bianca I'm not going to forget your no fucking boy either bitch I'm going to overdo your bitch ass ready to beat Bianca ass for disrespecting her for fucking with a nigga Royalty was talking to first.

Taj had managed to get his clothes back on and was standing there in shock at all that just transpired. Look Royalty I don't want no problems and I don't need my personal business out in the streets. Plus, it's not what you think Taj said a little threatening.

Shut you bitch ass up too Royalty said to Taj you don't know what the fuck I'm thinking nigga. Plus I already went live on Instagram Royalty said lying but Royalty wanted Taj to think that she had.

Get the fuck outta here Taj said running out the front door leaving it open.

Punk ass nigga Royalty said.

Bianca fell on the floor crying saying over and over that she was sorry.

You right you scandalous bitch you are sorry supposed to be my best friend Royalty said now crying too feeling bad for hitting Bianca who didn't want to fight Royalty because Bianca was too much of a bitch to fight back. Bianca only fought girls Bianca thought was scared of her over their man Bianca didn't want no real smoke. Royalty kneeled down over Bianca and said I'm sorry too for hitting you like that but damn bitch what if I liked the nigga? You don't want me to have nothing to myself that's fucked Up Royalty said crying now too falling to the ground.

Bianca looks up at Royalty and says in between tears. I'm sorry sis I knew you didn't like his bitch ass he really wasn't your type plus you see what type of nigga he was. I believe the nigga was on the downlow anyways Bianca said.

You think Royalty said sarcastically

Taj said he only got down like this with women but I don't believe his ass the nigga tutted that ass up in the air like way to comfortable for me Bianca said. Taj knew what he was doing he acted like a pro Bianca said still crying. I was going to tell you but I was scared. Bianca said still sniffling.

Scared of what Royalty asked.

This reaction Bianca said pointing to her eye which was swelling up.

Girl please Royalty responded. You deserve that one take that L with pride bitch. I miss Amir ass so much Royalty said thinking about how her life was fucked up and nobody understood but Amir.

I know sis I miss Amir too Bianca said still crying,

So Bianca how long have you two been fucking anyways? Royalty asked I'm so glad I didn't fuck him.

I wouldn't have fucked him if you seriously like him Bianca said.

Yes you would have bitch quit lying Royalty Laughing now.

Bianca laughed a little too. No I wouldn't sis I love you I wouldn't do that.

Well you did just that as we can see. Royalty said Shit what's love got to do with it ? Royalty said.

Nothing Ike Turner Bianca said pointing to her eye again. They both bust out laughing.

Damn Bianca you just got to fuck everybody damn. I'm so glad Jacques Won't fuck with you like that because bitch then I'll have to kill you Royalty says seriously!!

It's not like that Bianca said. I knew for a fact that you didn't like ol boy. The night we went to the concert I saw how you were acting towards Taj like boy whatever Taj knew it too. Taj tried to talk to me then on the low but I was like boy bye. But after you told me you couldn't do him I ran into him and his boys at Neiman Marcus and Taj tried hitting on me again and I was drunk and high so I took his ass down that night. I knew Taj was a mark then. Bianca says. I didn't really like the nigga I was setting his ass up to blackmail his ass.

Whatever Royalty said sarcastically.

No really that's why I didn't fuck him in my room I have my secret camera hidden inside that vase over the fireplace recording us laughing.

Royalty wanted to see if Bianca was lying or not. Getting up off the living room floor Royalty walks over to the fireplace and looks at the porcelain vase and it did have a little light coming from it like it maybe had a candle inside it. But looking closer sure enough a light was coming from the vase. So Royalty picked the vase up and looked inside it and bust out laughing. Bitch you've been recording niggas seeing the video camera inside the vase.

Yep Bianca said proudly. For years you should see my collection.

Bitch you a suicide bomber Royalty said still laughing. Niggas gone kill your ass. That's why I do it videotaping they ass because there's always proof Bianca said.

What if a nigga wants to fuck you in the bedroom ? Royalty asked.

That's cool Bianca said but most of the time it starts right here in the living room them getting some head .

I don't believe you Bianca when I all this time I thought your ass was slow You was smart all this time .

Fuck You Bianca said.

Well bitch let's get some popcorn because we about to watch some porn movies tonight Royalty said Laughing. I still can't believe you were secretly videotaping niggas. Bitch you goals Royalty says laughing. You're the true meaning of goals bitch. Straight hustler bitch it doesn't get no better than this. Straight money cow. Let a nigga try and deny some shit then bam the tape surfaces. You need to get a reality show hoe you bad. Royalty said still laughing. You changed my whole mood bitch you are a mood Royalty said still amazed at Bianca video vixen skills.

We cool again? Bianca asked Royalty getting up looking in her living room mirror at her eye which had shut and needed ice for the swelling and hurt like hell. Don't hit me ever again Bianca said to Royalty walking into the kitchen to get some ice for her eye.

Wait, wait bitch cover up Royalty said. I don't want to see your goodies all in my face like that bitch. I don't care if I am a part time lesbian bitch cover the fuck up. Oh, that reminds me I knew I had something to tell you. Bitch I finally got some pussy this weekend Royalty said Laughing. I just hate I had to pay for it like that Royalty said.

Walking out the kitchen with a bag of ice on her eye Bianca said stopping in the living room before heading in her bedroom to put her robe on. You brought a hooker home? Bianca asked Royalty.

Not really but kinda. Me and Jacques flew to Vegas and I brought two strippers back to the room and we had a after party it was fun it was so lit. I swear but the shit was dope in real life.

And you always talking shit about me Bianca said rolling her one good eye. Ok tell me more about it when I get back walking down the hall to her bedroom to put her robe on Bianca said.

Royalty was to juiced to see how Bianca could ruin a few niggss lives if Bianca really wanted to. Bianca was sitting on a goldmine or a morgue table the cards could fall either way and Bianca didn't even realize it.
After watching a few of these niggas hit Bianca ass raw I'm starting to believe all niggas are nasty now Royalty was thinking just watching Bianca with a few hood niggas they both knew, and a few grew up with them both and knew of top Bianca had the surgery, but it didn't matter. Bianca wasn't no joke Royalty was thinking watching the tapes. Royalty was so grateful she turned a lot of niggas

down when she did. The shit some niggas did late night was ridiculous. Royalty wondered how many other scandalous bitches had tapes of Amir or Jacques being out of pocket. Royalty knew for sure Amir had a secret tape floating around somewhere all the women Amir knew that called Amir brother and cousin but was light way in love with Amir on the low. Royalty had seen enough and was over it already. Looking over at Bianca who was laying her head back laying on the couch with a ice pack over her eye Royalty was contemplating hitting Bianca in the other eye for all the shit Bianca had done to her and Royalty let her get a pass on. Bianca roll up, so we can smoke Royalty said tapping Bianca leg.

Oh, you smoking again Bianca said unfazed.

Yep Royalty said roll up I want to get high and pour me a drink Royalty said.

What the fuck I look like the maid Bianca said not moving. You're the one with two good eyes bitch you roll up the weed underneath my bed and you know where everything else is at Bianca said and pour me a drink. Shit my head Hella hurt. Bianca moaned.

That's what you get Royalty said Laughing getting up walking towards Bianca room to get the weed. Royalty kneeled down to get the weed from underneath Bianca bed and saw that Bianca had several guns underneath her bed and Royalty was thinking why? But all the shit Bianca was doing with these niggas Bianca did need to protect herself in the bedroom and in the bed. Going into the kitchen Royalty got two bottles of wine and opened them both no need for no glasses they could drink straight out the bottle. The hood was coming out of Royalty now.

Handing Bianca a bottle of Moët Bianca looked up and said why you bring the whole damn bottle sipping from it.

Because we're going to wind up drinking the whole bottle anyways so why not? Royalty said taking a sip from hers. And yes, I have my own bottle bitch I am not drinking after your ass Royalty said seriously speaking.

But it's alcohol it kills all germs Bianca said Laughing.

Probably not the type of germs you might have living in your mouth deep throat im cool Royalty said Laughing. Let's watch a movie Royalty said turning on the tv looking through the on demand channels. Roll the weed up Royalty said to Bianca who was already rolling up. Going through the guide Royalty said let's watch Belly that's my favorite movie with Nas fine ass and Dmx.

Firing up the weed Bianca said yeah that movie is hard as fuck my favorite part is when Dmx was fucking Keisha after she called that little thot back that paged Dmx.

Yeah that would be your favorite part Royalty said Laughing. And why do you have all those guns underneath your bed taking the weed from Bianca looking at it like should she hit it or not.

Blowing out smoke from her nose Bianca says for protection what you think? But you're not using zero protection in the bed with these niggas tho. Royalty says deciding to hit the weed taking a pull. Blowing out smoke. Bitch you letting these random ass niggas hit raw, but you got guns for protection. Seems to me your protecting the wrong shit Royalty says hitting the weed again.

Whatever Bianca says getting comfortable on the couch to watch the movie, Royalty and Bianca got high and drunk and watched Belly and talked shit about what they would have done in certain situations and laughed at other situations. This was how Royalty and Bianca was use to kicking it with each other laughing and enjoying one another's company catching up on the latest tea and updating each other on current events happening in each other lives. Royalty didn't know when they got away from that, but they did. It was almost as if they were disconnecting from one another. They had been friend's their whole entire lives well since elementary school. Bianca and Royalty were more like sisters than friends. Royalty and Bianca were both bullied growing up. Royalty because she didn't have clean clothes or parents that came to the school to check up on her and Royalty never brought lunch to school or had a parent for field trips. Royalty was the outcast up until high school and even then, Royalty didn't socialize with the other kids. And Bianca was a boy that wore dresses to school because his parents believed in letting Bianca do whatever he wanted to even back then and Bianca twirled around all day at school and none of the other kids would play with Bianca and made fun of Bianca Until Royalty and Bianca meet and hit it off immediately and became best friends and they've been best friends ever since. But their friendship has been tested and tried several times thanks to Bianca antics. But Royalty loved everything about Bianca even Bianca crazy ways. That's what made Bianca who she was is her crazy personality. Bianca said anything and did anything Bianca gave zero fucks about anything or anyone. Bianca was brutally honest. Too honest at times and very transparent about her life. That's what Royalty loved about Bianca and Royalty wouldn't change nothing about Bianca she loved her just the way Bianca was. Well there were a few things Royalty would change about Bianca but since Royalty couldn't change them shell just keep accepting Bianca the way she was. Crazy, sexy, and obnoxious nymphomaniac that Bianca was. Bianca was the only person in the world that Royalty trusted with her life with her secrets with everything Royalty owned. Bianca was more than Royalty best friend Bianca was like Royalty twin sister, but they were just fraternal and from separate parents. Royalty started reminiscing back when her and Bianca was in high school. Hey Bianca Royalty, said remember in high school when we had beepers and dressed like Aaliyah?

Hell, yeah I love Aaliyah Bianca said I'm going to be her for Halloween this year. I'm glad you brought that up Royalty thank you Bianca said happy Royalty had brought that memory up.

Roll another blunt Royalty said to Bianca.

That was my last black and mild Bianca said. You have to go to the store because I damn sure ain't going out this house until my eye is back to normal, I don't care how long it takes Bianca said. I have to cancel a few appointments but oh well. My older clients can come over here to the house. Shit after all I started in my living room Bianca said reminiscing about her fist years as a makeup artist.

Ok I'll go to the store Royalty says getting up wanting to continue smoking.

Go to AL's liquor store Bianca said. He'll be surprised to see you and grab some Doritos and peanut M&M's oh and a Pepsi Bianca said.

Anything else Royalty said Laughing.

Let me think Bianca said.

Bitch fuck You Royalty said walking out. Going back to their old hood always brought back memories for Royalty. Royalty drove to Al's liquor store on the corner of Grape st. Royalty hadn't been back here in years. Going in the store nothing had changed same old liquor store front that the Arabians owned that sold everything you needed diapers to black and milds and now they had a little chicken joint in the store. This liquor store had been in the hood before Royalty was even born. The Arabs were just like niggas too. Wearing Jordans and hoodies and they were the real plug for most of the guns being flooded in the hood. They sold more than just candy and liquor in this store.

Royalty is that you one of the Arabs brothers said coming from behind the counter to give Royalty a hug. You look good girl sorry to hear about Amir.

Smiling Royalty says thanks.

What brings you back around here ? I never thought I would see you again Malak said.

Well me and Bianca needed a black and mild and this was the closest store so here I am.

Oh, Bianca Malak says Bianca Bianca she's always in here. Why Bianca didn't come herself? Malak asks.

Well Bianca is under the weather she's not feeling too good right now Royalty said, or else Bianca would have came herself. Plus, I wanted to stop by and say what's up to you'll it's been a minute. Royalty said.

I know I know it's good seeing you all grown up Malak says looking Royalty up and down admiring the view.

Then Blue walks in and Royalty looked at him and pictured him naked because Royalty had just watched him on the tape fucking with Bianca. Blue was one of the niggas Bianca had videotaped.

What's up Royalty? What brings you back to the hood? Blue asks. Looking like a rich hood drug dealer that he was. Blue was fine too but after seeing the video tape of him Royalty looked at him differently now. Royalty couldn't help admiring Blue swag tho. Blue had on the big donkey rope chain with the Rolex watch fresh haircut which Blue always had because Blue owned a barbershop in the hood that his father once owned before he passed a few years ago. Blue was a avid weed. smoker always had been Amir use to always get high with Blue back in the days that's why Blue was in the liquor store for the same reason Royalty was to buy some black and milds.

You looking thick Royalty I see you ain't been stressing laughing Blue said About to hit Royalty on her ass, but Royalty stopped Blue in the process.

And then Royalty says to Blue forreal Blue you know I don't rock like that. Me and Bianca are best friends laughing.

What that mean Royalty? It wasn't nothing between me and Bianca Blue said Laughing. That girl is too aggressive for me.

Royalty just looked at Blue and laughed a little but what Royalty really wanted to say was from watching the porno tape of Blue and Bianca that Blue was the aggressor not Bianca. Blue even pulled out of Bianca and nutted all in Bianca face but Royalty didn't say anything Royalty just said is that right and turned around and paid for her black and milds and said to Blue it was nice seeing you take care throwing up the deuces and waved bye to Malak who had slid his number in Royalty bag with Bianca snacks in them shooting his shot hoping Royalty was with it.

When Royalty got back to Bianca house Bianca had rented the Black Panther movie from Netflix and was sitting on the couch eating some popcorn and sipping on her Moët all into the movie. Throwing the bag of snacks that Bianca wanted at her Royalty sits down and take her shoes off and gets comfortable.

Thanks Royalty Bianca said pulling the candy out the bag and finding Malak little love note with his number. Reading the note Bianca says to Royalty handing her the number this must be for you because Malak can't stand my ass laughing .

Royalty took the note and started reading it.

What's up Ma you grew up and your sexy as hell let's go out sometime hit me up Malak.

Royalty balled the paper up and threw it on the floor.

So that's how you feel Bianca said .

Royalty didn't even respond Looking at her phone Royalty said damn I forgot to call my lawyer ass back calling her back.

Hello Royalty make this quick I'm walking into the airport I really can't talk but I got your messages and I looked into the case. And yes your boyfriend wife Is suing you for damages and medical bills and her attorney fees. And yes it's all legal. So I advise you to start liquidating assets and put some money in the cayman island just in case.

Huh? Royalty said getting mad now. How the fuck can it be legal to sue someone for fucking someone's husband? This is some bullshit. I'm not giving that bitch a dime of my money tell her attorney that. I'll have that bitch knocked down before I give her a fucking quarter Royalty said yelling now.

Ok Royalty calm down I'm about to hang up before you make me an accessory to a crime and having firsthand knowledge of it. I'm just telling you hypothetically what can happen I'm not saying it will. I'll be gone for a week we will talk more when I get back. Until then stay calm and don't do anything that will have me flying back sooner. Stay positive Royalty hanging up Royalty attorney says.

Making that what was that all about face Bianca asks that exact question to Royalty curious.

Still looking at her phone Royalty says turning her attention to Bianca now. I didn't tell you this bitch Jacques wife is suing me for fucking her husband. Royalty said furious.

For fucking her husband? Can she sue you for that? Bianca asked because Bianca had never heard anything like that before this was a first.

Apparently so Royalty said. My attorney bitch ass just said I should start liquidating my assets.

The fuck she talking about liquidating Bianca asked not understanding any of this. How much is fucking somebody's husband worth? Bianca asked seriously wanting to know.

The fuck if I know Royalty said. But I'll kill that bitch before I give her a dime. That bitch ain't getting shit from me but her man back. She got me so fucked Up Royalty said. Roll the weed up Royalty said to Bianca, I need to smoke now Royalty said getting up going into the kitchen getting another bottle of Moët.

Hay calm down on my bottles bitch Bianca said to Royalty. Get something else to drink I only have a few bottles left.

I'll buy you some more bitch shut up Royalty said. I'll buy you 5 million dollar's worth of Moët matter fact I'll buy you your own liquor store full of Moët before I give that bitch a penny of my money Royalty said sitting back down on the couch.

Hire a hitman Bianca said Laughing.

A hitman you acting like this some Hollywood ass movie type shit. Why would I hire a fucking hitman Bianca? Royalty asked.

Because you don't want anything to come back on you Bianca said seriously.

I'll hire a nigga from the hood if I was going to hire anyone because I know for a fact it would be done right Royalty said but I don't even have to do that I'll kill that bitch my mother fucking self.

No, you can't do that best friend then who would I have out here on these streets with me? You can't go out like that. Let Jacques poison that bitch Bianca said still laughing.

Jacques isn't going to poison his wife shut your dumbass up and roll the weed you talking too much anyways. I should have punched you in your mouth Royalty said turning up her bottle of Moët.

After Bianca rolls the blunt Bianca and Royalty smoke until their lungs both hurt. Royalty and Bianca was high ass fuck watching the Black Panther movie when Bianca says I wish you had one of those swords like she has referring to the women with the sword from Wakanda. Then you could slice Jacques wife bitch ass up Bianca says laughing.

I wish I had all that high tech shit they have in Wakanda Royalty says I'll be a beast nobody could touch me Laughing Royalty says. I wish I could move to Wakanda right now I would be fucking with one of those niggas from the Lion head crew they wasn't no joke. Royalty said high as hell.

I want the cousin Bianca said the bad boy that wanted to take over the empire and be king.

Royalty looked over at Bianca and said only you would want his ass that's why he got killed. Then they both started laughing.

Oh well then, I would have gotten at his cousin Bianca said Laughing.

Lupita would have beat your ass trying to fuck with her man Royalty said to Bianca Laughing.

Lupita does look like she can fight too Bianca scary ass said Laughing.

Always fucking with somebody's man Royalty said Laughing. You right bitch please keep that arsenal underneath your bed and in the trunk of your car shit in all your purses. You ain't cool Bianca Royalty said Laughing.

I'm just living my best life that's all Bianca said Laughing.

Your dead life you keep moving the way you moving Royalty said Laughing. I don't know how you do it Bianca Royalty said. Your little fake pussy should be destroyed by now all the dicks you done had trying to name all the niggas Bianca had been with.

Bianca started throwing names out there also laughing. There's so many you know nothing about Bianca said.

Oh really is that right Royalty said shaking her head. That's a damn shame. It's time for you to move to another city there's no one left in Los Angeles for you to fuck or suck bitch it's a wrap. Royalty said Laughing. You nasty Miss Jackson if you're nasty Royalty said Laughing.

And bitch you sitting over there laughing at me what about you tho? Bianca said now getting on Royalty line.

Huh ? What about me bitch Royalty said seriously. I've only been with two men in my whole life looking at Bianca stupid.

Yeah but what about all the women hoe! Stop fronting like you ain't no douchebag pussy mouth eating bitch. You had more pussy than a trick in a whore house in Vegas. Bianca said Laughing falling off the couch.

Royalty tried to count how many women she had actually been with over the years and lost count. Royalty had been sleeping with girls since she was young. Her first sexual experience was with a girl when Royalty stayed the night over her neighbor's house at ten years old and they slept in the same bed because the neighbor had a full size bed and Royalty told the little neighbor girl let's do what we seen your mom and dad doing before. Royalty got on top of her neighbor and started grinding her and trying to kiss her until the girl told Royalty that was enough and pushed Royalty off her. But Royalty got the neighbor a few more times when Royalty stayed the night over the neighbor's house throughout the years. But now when Royalty sees her old neighbor Royalty doesn't even speak to her old neighbor because she's a full fledge crackhead. Royalty saw her old neighbor one time in front of her salon Pretty please and gave her a few dollars to move away from the salon, but Royalty doesn't believe that the old neighbor even recognized her which Royalty was grateful for. Royalty thought about the last time she had turned a young girl out when Royalty was fourteen and had the little poor girl biting the sheets when she was thirteen years old while Royalty ate her from the back. Now that girl is a crackhead too. Royalty laughed thinking at the thought that maybe it was her fault that these women got on drugs. Maybe getting turned out at a young age was too much for their little minds to handle. Shit maybe Royalty provoked them into doing drugs and turning them into crackheads. Naw couldn't be the case Royalty was thinking if it was Royalty would be a crackhead, too wouldn't she?

What you over there laughing at potty mouth Bianca said getting up off the living room floor going to the bathroom.

Fuck You was Royalty rebuttal.

If we weren't best friends, I might let you Bianca said walking towards the bathroom.

Ugh you're so nasty Bianca Royalty said. I don't know who's more delusional these days that stupid ass president we got now or you. I wouldn't fuck you if you were the last person left on earth. I'll just be celibate until I die Royalty said Laughing. Fucking around with you would probably give me throat cancer or something worse Royalty said sticking her tongue out like she was gagging.

Whatever Bianca said walking down the hallway unbothered by what Royalty just said.

Royalty looked at her phone and saw that Jacques had text her and that made Royalty smile. But after having the conversation with her attorney Royalty smiled quickly turned into a frown. Royalty just didn't know how loyal Jacques was to her after all they haven't been talking that long and Jacques has been married to his janky ass wife for years. Not wanting to think about it anymore Royalty deleted the text tread with Jacques and ordered a pizza from Roundtable with some hot wings. Bianca comes back into the living room dancing. What you so happy about? Royalty asks Bianca.

I'm just glad I'm alive and free because you know I could be locked up somewhere for some bullshit Bianca says seriously.

Agreed I should be dancing right along with you Royalty said. Because every time you get locked up, I have to bail you out. My accountant said she thought you were on my payroll because of the amount of money I paid out for you last year. You think I can get a third of that money back B? After all I'm the one getting sued. I need as many coins as I can get Royalty said Laughing. But was serious though.
I just ordered a pizza Royalty said to Bianca who had sat down now and placed her ice pack back on her eye. All that dancing and twerking must have made Bianca head start hurting again Royalty was thinking. That's what Bianca gets for always talking shit and doing something. Royalty said to herself sitting down next to Bianca on the couch then Bianca puts her feet on Royalty lap. Look bitch I'm not your man or nor am I a fan of yours. Get your dog's off my lap slapping Bianca feet off of her lap.

You just mad because my feet is cuter than yours Bianca says wiggling her toes that was painted neon yellow bringing her feet up to her chest getting comfortable.

Rolling her eyes Royalty says ok if you say so. Everything about me is cute bitch remember that Royalty said. You got me fucked up like the rest of the 7 Billion other mother fuckers that's in the world Royalty said sarcastically referring to Jacques wife and her attorney. Hearing the doorbell ring Royalty gets up to answer the door because Royalty knows it's the pizza, she just ordered rubbing her hands together excitedly. Opening the door Royalty jumps back about to take off on this nigga saying what the fuck you doing here? Looking at the nurse nigga standing at the door in his nurse uniform.

No- no Royalty I called him over her to check on my eye Bianca said leaning over the couch yelling trying to stop Royalty from jumping on her friend.

Royalty opened the door wider to let the nurse guy in and turned around and looked over at Bianca fuming mad like a hungry wolf and said this nigga and his wife jumped you less than three weeks ago and then you fought his wife at the hospital and put me in that shit were we could have both went to jail bitch and on top of that you attack this stupid ass nigga at his job and now he's here checking up on your eye forreal? He's not a doctor he's a nurse and a scary one at that!! Royalty said yelling. You better hope and pray this nigga wife ain't outside hiding waiting for the signal to run up in this bitch. So, with that being said I'm going to leave because I don't want no parts of it Royalty says walking towards to living room to get her stuff. Putting on her shoes and grabbing her bag and purse Royalty picks up her bottle of Moët mad as fuck. I'm taking this bottle with me just in case his bitch outside waiting in the cuts and I have to hit this bitch over the head to defend myself. Royalty says shaking her head not believing Bianca ass. Royalty Walks out the living room towards the front door hotter than a Hawaiian volcano ready to erupt but before Royalty leaves out Royalty gets to the door and turns around and says to Bianca DO NOT CALL ME BITCH IF YOU NEED SOME BAIL MONEY EITHER YOU DUMB BITCH!! I swear on Amir bitch I'm not answering no calls from you consider yourself permanently blocked walking out the front door slamming it and gripping the Moët bottle in case this nurse nigga wife was outside waiting. Getting in her car Royalty was so mad but Royalty definitely wasn't leaving without her pizza. Royalty damn sure wasn't letting Bianca and nurse dummy eat her pizza and wings. Sitting there mad looking at the nurse car Royalty took a picture of his license plate just in case something jumped off because you never knew with Bianca ass. When Royalty pizza finally arrived, Royalty wasn't even hungry anymore. Driving down the street before getting on the freeway Royalty handed a homeless man the box of pizza and wings.

Royalty wanted to hurry up and get home because Royalty was high as hell and didn't want to get a DUI which because Royalty knew if she was to be tested, she would be way over whatever the limit was. Trying to drive the speed limit Royalty seemed like she was in the twilight zone. Royalty keep laughing feeling like she was moving in slow motion. That was some good weed they had smoked Royalty was thinking. When Royalty got home there were two boxes waiting at her door Royalty was like she didn't remember ordering anything. Pulling in the garage Royalty jumps out and goes around the front to retrieve the packages There was no return address or name on the box. Going inside the house Royalty opens the boxes and it was three dozen yellow roses in each box from Jacques. Awe Royalty thought happy Jacques was thinking about her, but it was going to take more than some roses to get them back on track because Royalty was feeling some type of way about Jacques wife trying to sue her. Royalty placed the flowers in a vase and sat them on the kitchen table and smelled them and smiled. Jacques was really sweet Royalty was thinking but Jacques also had a bad side to him. Seemed almost impossible but Royalty thought anything was possible after seeing Bianca with that crash dummy nurse Bianca was in love with. Turning on some music Royalty goes up stairs to roll up some weed even though Royalty was still high a little bit from earlier, but Royalty's high was coming down now and Royalty wanted to relax so Royalty ran herself some bath water. Royalty smoked her blunt and got undressed and looked at herself in her floor to ceiling mirror thinking she needed to lose some weight. Royalty had picked up a few pounds the last couple of months since dealing with Jacques. Happy weight Royalty predicted. Looking at her thighs Royalty didn't like what she saw. I'm getting to fat Royalty said to herself turning around looking at her ass, but that ass looked nice and plump. Maybe I'll hold on to the weight until after my birthday which was approaching soon Royalty was thinking it was time to plan a trip maybe Africa. Yeah Africa would be nice Royalty thinking walking into the bathroom sticking her foot in the water to check it and make sure it wasn't too hot, but it was perfect. Getting in laying her head back on her tub pillow closing her eyes Royalty let her hands explore her body imaging it was Amir. Opening her legs Royalty found her spot and let the imaginary Amir go to work. Amir always knew how to make Royalty feel good no matter where they were at. They could be sitting in the car when Amir touched Royalty spot it felt like magic or even in the movie theater same effect it even felt better when they were being sneaky doing it. But right now, it felt good in the water. The movement of the water mixed with the sound the water made put Royalty on a sexual high that the weed couldn't give her. Loving yourself was the best feeling. Royalty put one leg up on the tub to tilt her body just right to hit her g spot and make herself cum. Speeding up a bit did the trick and Royalty came like she just finished making love to someone. Removing her hand and relaxing in the still warm water Royalty winded up falling asleep and she didn't wake up for an hour and when Royalty did wake up the water was cold. Royalty got out and brushed her teeth and brushed her hair into a ponytail and put on a face mask and went to bed feeling like she had released all her worries and washed them down the drain. I love you Amir and I miss you Royalty said to herself before falling asleep curled up hugging one of Amir's pillows. Royalty missed being held and kissed good night by Amir Royalty really missed Amir tonight more than she ever did reality had really sunk in that Amir was gone forever and never coming back. Waking up to the smell of pancakes and coffee Royalty knew her housekeeper was in the house. Royalty smiled because it had been a while since they saw each other. Stretching and looking over at the mirror Royalty realized she was naked. I have to stop drinking so much Royalty said to herself laughing knowing she was lying. Royalty could hear the housekeeper coming up the stairs, so Royalty pulled the covers over herself.

Hi Miss Royalty, welcome home Bonita the housekeeper says bringing Royalty a breakfast tray with homemade pancakes and scrambled eggs with chicken apple sausage and a bowl of strawberries and orange juice and coffee. Oh, I forgot the silverware I'll be right back the housekeeper says running down the stairs.

Royalty sat up and drank some of her coffee that was made to perfection. Mija always made everything perfect. Placing the tray to the side of the bed so she could get up and out the bed Royalty goes inside the drawers and grabs one of Amir's wife beaters and puts it own and gets back into bed.

Here Bonita here's your silverware handed Royalty a knife and fork to eat her breakfast. The housekeeper says.

Thank you Mija I'm so happy to see you how was your trip? Royalty asks.

It was nice thank you Miss Royalty my family loved all the stuff you gave me for them. My sister says next time you clean out your closet she's coming to help you laughing.

Anytime tell Maria she's always welcome she knows that Royalty says cutting into her pancakes.

So, Miss Royalty tell me what you've been up to since I've been gone sitting down at the foot of Royalty bed. I see you've been a naughty girl laughing Mija said. Somebody brought you beautiful Roses and it wasn't Senor Amir because he's our Angel now Mija said putting her head down crosses her heart and kissing it up to heaven.

It's nothing serious Mija I promise he's just a friend and he's a nice guy that's all.

Ok Miss Royalty I don't want anyone to break your heart Mija says.

Smiling chewing her food and taking another sip of coffee to wash it down Royalty finally says he won't I promise.

Do you like him Miss Royalty? Mija asked.

Royalty thought about it for a moment before she answered and said yes, I think I do actually.

Well he's not Senor Amir remember that Mija said getting up going back downstairs.

Royalty finished her entire plate because Royalty was hungry and hungover, and this breakfast was right on time. Royalty knew why Mija was a little upset it was because Mija had a soft spot for Amir for being so good to her and her family. Amir brought Mija and her family a home back in Mexico where Mija was from because Mija and her family home was destroyed in a flood and they didn't have the money to rebuild Amir also brought Mija a BMW 325 I for Christmas when Mija first started working for Amir and Royalty four years ago because Mija was taking the bus to work through the brutal winter months. Mija was now like a member of the family. Amir meet Mija at a bus stop on her way to school a few years ago. Amir was at the light and saw Mija standing in the rain without an umbrella or jacket waiting for the bus and Amir said he couldn't watch Mija suffer like that, so he pulled over and asked Mija did she need a ride to wherever she was going. Mija was hesitant at first but finally gave in. Amir learned Mija had just arrived from Mexico her family sent her to stay with her aunt to have a better life but Mija aunt was an old, mean, alcoholic that mentally abused Mija and constantly kicked Mija out with nowhere to go. Mija was going to community college at the time and occasionally stayed with friends when her aunt threw her out until Mija meet Amir. Amir gave Mija a job as the housekeeper because that's what Mija said she was good at plus it worked out with her school schedule and Amir got Mija a apartment and brought Mija a car to get back and forth from work and school Amir didn't want Mija on the bus. Four years later Mija is in nursing school about to graduate all thanks to Amir's generosity. Royalty suspected Amir and Mija were fucking but couldn't prove it but if they were Royalty didn't mind because Mija was a sweetheart and never a threat. Royalty wished she could have gotten Mija herself but Mija was a devoted catholic and Mija wasn't having that lesbian shit. Royalty dropped a few hints before and Mija shut that down. Mija was so beautiful though Royalty was almost positive Amir fucked Mija at least once. And no one could replace Amir in Mija heart no one.

Getting dressed Royalty decided to go visit Amir today. It had been a minute so today was the day. Throwing on a workout outfit and sneakers and sunglasses Royalty planned on working out today also Royalty wanted to go running to sweat the small shit out Royalty was facing in her life at the moment. Mija was washing clothes when Royalty came downstairs and Royalty peeked inside the laundry room and said goodbye. Mija was a little dry with her goodbye but whatever Royalty was thinking she'll get over it eventually. Royalty knows you can't please everyone and that everyone wasn't going to approve of Royalty dating so fast after Amir's death. But it was also Royalty's life and Royalty was going to live her life exactly how she wanted to live it. While getting in her car Royalty got a call from the contractor that they were on schedule and the Bargain Bundles Hair Boutique would open on time. That made Royalty's day. Royalty planned on doing a grand opening right before her birthday in August which was less than 90 days away. Royalty needed to hire a assistant ASAP. Royalty was thinking because Royalty saw this project getting out of hand. Plus, Royalty had a lot on her plate already.

Arriving at the cemetery the sun was beaming down on the cemetery grounds this summer was hotter than it's ever been in June Royalty was thinking. It felt like earthquake weather. Stepping out the truck Royalty looked at her G wagon and decided it was time to switch up her ride. Royalty was just so use to jumping in her truck and going but Royalty did have various options especially now. Amir left several cars behind so many that Royalty even decided to sale a few but hadn't gotten around to it yet but it was Coming it was on Royalty to do list. Walking into the mausoleum Royalty got the chills despite how hot it was outside. Looking at all the plots on the walls and seeing how young some of the people were scared Royalty. Royalty started thinking she better get her shit together or else this could be her sooner than later. Approaching Amir's plot Royalty noticed Amir had fresh flowers and balloons. There was a card attached and Royalty removed it and read it. It was from Mija no wonder Mija was all in her feelings today Royalty was thinking. Reading the card, I miss you so much Senor Amir Rih love always Mija. Awe how sweet Royalty said to herself. Yes, rest in heaven Amir Royalty said touching Amir's plot. Everyone misses you down here my love especially me I missed you so much last night Amir Royalty said laying her head on Amir's plot. I wish I could feel your heart beating against mine and feel you inside me. I wish I could have given you a son or daughter that looked exactly like you that we could have taken to doctor's appointments together, watch take their first step, first tooth, said their first words. I wish you would have been able to look at me and say that's my baby mama stepping away from Amir's plot crying now Royalty continues but you wanted to be all over the place with your love Amir why? Wasn't I enough for you? I loved you more than anyone in this world, but you choose to continue to hurt me why Amir wiping away her tears. You now have a beautiful son that looks exactly like you and I love him, but this is no walk in the park for me. I did right by him and his mom and Angel what I thought was appropriate to honor you because we both know if you were here you would have went overboard Royalty says laughing and sniffling at the same time. Your son name is King the name you loved so much that you said we would name our son if we ever had one. Well you have a King now. Royalty said wiping her tears away I love you Amir Royalty said blowing a kiss and waving goodbye. And I'm holding it down out here but it ain't easy Royalty says walking away heading out the mausoleum going straight to the gym to get on the treadmill to ease her mind. After working out for an hour Royalty goes into the steam room to sweat it out for thirty minutes then showers and then goes and get a facial.

Driving home Royalty passes by a Ferrari dealership and decides to take a look at the latest cars. Pulling into the dealership and getting out her truck a nice, Older well groomed, moisturized man comes over to help Royalty and asks Royalty what exactly she looking for in a car. Royalty explained that this was a spontaneous move and she just wanted a cute new car that was fast to lift her spirits up. The dealer said he knew the exact Ferrari that could do the trick and took Royalty to the showroom floor. There it was the dream car that Royalty didn't need but had to have especially now that Royalty saw it in person. Royalty mouth dropped looking at This beautiful Car. Royalty walked around the car admiring it for a second touching it taking it all in. Royalty never really liked colored cars before it was either black or white for Royalty but this Red two door, tee top little thing was screaming Royalty name and Royalty knew she had to have it. Opening the door touching the steering wheel with the black pony on it and looking at the precision to detail inside the car that looked like a spaceship inside with all its gadgets and that soft black leather interior with red stitching plus the new car smell had Royalty feeling like she died and went to heaven. Getting in sitting in the driver's seat. Rubbing her hands around the steering wheel then gripping it Royalty was sold no matter what the price tag read. Smiling thinking Happy early birthday to me Royalty keep hearing the voice saying in her head. Yes, bitch you only live once ball out. The dealer was smiling knowing he just made a huge commission without Royalty even signing the paperwork yet. Royalty Look said it all.

How do you like it Miss the gentleman said like a proud father very distinguished?

Who said I liked it Royalty said I love it getting out the car and started jumping up and down like she just won the lottery or something. Thank you, Royalty, said hugging the gentleman kissing his cheek making him blush.

It's my pleasure Ma'am I'm glad you love the Ferrari the gentleman said happy Royalty was happy. The dealer didn't get many women that got that excited about buying a Ferrari. Not too many women drove them. The dealer took Royalty into a very big fancy office that looked like it was for a executive with cherry wood furniture and Ferrari car pictures everywhere. Royalty filled out all the paperwork and planned on picking up her new baby up tomorrow. This felt like a milestone for Royalty she was finally making decisions on her own without Amir's approval. This car would be liberation for Royalty and that's exactly what Royalty needed at this time in her life. Because Royalty felt like she was going through a midlife crisis in her twenties. Royalty was ready to stop stressing over things that didn't matter and get focused on things that mattered the most and right now purchasing this vehicle felt like a power move to Royalty. After all the paperwork was done and a copy of Royalty driver's license was taken the dealer wanted to run a credit check Royalty didn't understand why even though Royalty credit was excellent. Do I have to pay with credit Sir? Royalty asked the gentleman.

Looking at Royalty like how else were you planning on paying? The gentleman says well ma'am this car is very expensive it's a 252,800 how else were you planning on paying the gentleman asked looking confused.

In cash Sir I can go to the bank in the morning and then catch a Uber here and pick up my car Royalty says excitedly.

The gentleman swallowed hard even though he hadn't drank anything like he was trying to figure out exactly how to respond. So, you're saying looking at Royalty paperwork Miss Royalty it is Miss isn't it? The gentleman asked trying to see if Royalty had a rich husband or something to pay this much money in cash.

Yes, it's Miss Sir Royalty replied. I can be back as early as nine o'clock if you like.

Still in amazement the gentleman says we don't open until ten.

Ok I'll see you at ten tomorrow Royalty says getting up shaking the gentleman hand.

Before you go Miss Royalty you know it's the law, we are speaking for the Ferrari dealership have a obligation to report this purchase to the IRS the gentleman says in case Royalty was trying to spend some drug money and wasn't aware of the procedure.

Smiling because Royalty knew what the gentleman was trying to imply so Royalty says politely, I'm aware of that Sir this isn't my first large purchase with cash Sir but thank you for the heads up. Royalty says walking out laughing this wasn't Royalty first rodeo Royalty had gotten used to this tone from people and kinda shrugged it off because most people didn't value her presence let alone her finances, but Royalty was ok with it all. Because at the end of the day Royalty knew her worth and even if nobody else acknowledged it Royalty knew she was Intimidating most men and women with splurging cash that was legal. Well most of it was legal mixed in with a little drug money here and there that Amir had washed though his businesses. When Royalty got home, Royalty got on her computer and transferred money from one account to another and checked her stock portfolio something Royalty hadn't done in a while because Royalty never thought that she really needed to until now. Royalty's CPA took care of Royalty finances pretty well. Royalty had a lot at stake now being sued and wanted to make sure all her assets were being protected. Royalty planned on having a meeting with her CPA this week to weigh all her options especially pertaining to her business. Royalty was many things but stupid wasn't one of them. Royalty became business savvy and handled her business when it came to managing her money. Amir taught Royalty how to make a dollar out of fifteen cents. Everything Amir touched turned to gold. Amir said everything had a price tag to it. And Amir didn't indulge in things that didn't make him money also Amir taught Royalty his motto. Make money while we sleep Amir would say day after day. And that's exactly what they both did. Amir trucking business not only transported cars across country Amir's trucking business transported model homes across country and race cars and motorcycles and had an app you could use if you wanted a car picked up and dropped off at a certain location and also Amir's company had a gas delivery app for locals. Who paid for a certain amount of gas to be delivered to you anytime anywhere. Amir also had two of the largest weed dispensaries in Los Angeles and before Amir died Amir was opening one in New York City that's why they were in New York at the time and Amir's business that's still awaiting approval that Royalty would have taken over if it's approved at this point. If it didn't make money it didn't make sense to Amir that's why Royalty hated that Amir was so loose when it came to women because Amir was a sure target for women wanting to get pregnant to secure the bag for eighteen plus years or women trying to set Amir up to be robbed. It was a lot of shady women running around these streets these days. But Royalty didn't have to worry about that part anymore unfortunately now Royalty had to secure her own financial stability due to a women scorn. Royalty had a lot on the line to lose. Not only did Royalty own Pretty Please Hair Salon Royalty owned a makeup line Pretty please cosmetics that was sold through the hair salon and a nonprofit for abused women named A Happy Place which is a six bedroom, three bathrooms house with a daycare for abused women and their children. Royalty always knew she wanted to help abused women but didn't know how exactly until Royalty stumbled on a six bedroom house that was going into foreclosure thing bingo the idea formulated. That's when Royalty took advantage of the opportunity to help abuse women who had nowhere to go or that wanted to leave an abusive relationship. Also, the county hospital referred abused women to A Happy Place. A Happy Place has a 24 hour hotline and a van to pick women up from wherever they were at and picked up women from the hospitals. A Happy Place was having its fourth year Anniversary soon. Royalty was looking into purchasing a second home to open another shelter but was looking for the right location and property that could house more women this time. Royalty never made a lot of noise about her moves or businesses Royalty left that up to everyone else to do but Royalty was handling her business as a young entrepreneur. Amir told Royalty from the beginning if you don't work you don't eat it's your choice. So, Royalty made sure that she stayed on top of everything that brought money into her pockets. So, to just give her money away wasn't a option for Royalty. Royalty worked too hard for her coins to give them to some mad bitch over some dick Royalty started thinking what the fuck all over again. Royalty wasn't going out like that No matter who got hurt in the process. Royalty considered herself as a philanthropist but only at her discretion not being forced to do shit Royalty didn't want to do. After all Royalty suffered the abuse at the hand of a predator for her millions not Serenity so fuck her, and the lawsuit Serenity thought she was going to win against Royalty.

Transferred complete came though Royalty email. Thank God Royalty said she was all set for tomorrow to pick up her new whip. Shutting down her computer walking out her home office Royalty heads straight to the kitchen for a drink of course to celebrate because tomorrow Royalty wouldn't be drinking and driving. Royalty planned on driving up to the Bay Area to spend the weekend and do a little shopping in San Francisco. Royalty always had a great time there the city was beautiful at night even with the homeless population everywhere. Royalty always made sure to bring at least a thousand dollars in ones to give out to the homeless when she visited there because the homeless were everywhere in that city. Opening the fridge Royalty saw that Mija had made fresh tuna yeah Royalty said to herself grabbing the bowl to make herself a sandwich and grabbed some chips out of the cabinet and of course Royalty poured herself a large glass of red wine. Taking her plate and drank into the living room Royalty sits on the Persian rug in front of the fireplace and turns on the big screen to watch a movie. But instead Royalty turned on Martin because he always cracked Royalty up. Martin reruns was everything. Royalty finished her food and drink and took her plate to the kitchen and was about to pour herself another glass of wine when her doorbell rings. Looking at the door from the kitchen knowing who it was Royalty waited a minute to answer it saying to herself a little tipsy never jump when a nigga want you too or be available every time, he's available. Make him sweat a little Royalty said to herself and poured herself another drink and when Royalty finished her drink decided to answer the door and play with Jacques to see where his head was at.

Barely opening the door Royalty peeked out the door with lock on holding a glass of wine. Whispering Jacques, I have company right now it's not a good time can we talk tomorrow?

Jacques looked at Royalty crazy then Jacques said Fuck No open the door before I kick it in and stop playing with me Jacques said serious as fuck.

Still whispering Royalty said I'm not playing call me tomorrow and tried to close the door, but Jacques stuck his foot in the doorway and knocked the glass out Royalty hand trying to unlock the door.

Royalty don't make me shoot this motherfucking lock off the door open the door now!! Jacques said with authority.

Look Jacques you're going to respect my home and respect me or you can leave trying to shut the door again.

Pulling out his gun Jacques shoots the lock off the door and barges his way in the house with Royalty screaming you could have shot me not believing Jacques just shot her lock off the door. Running into the kitchen with Jacques right on her heels.

Where's your little friend at Jacques asks Royalty walking up on her.

What? Royalty says.

Your company Jacques says all up in Royalty face.

He left Royalty says nervously now.

Oh, so when did he leave? when he heard me at the door? Jacques says still in Royalty face. You fucking with scary niggas now Royalty? Jacques says walking into the living room looking around and then runs upstairs to check Royalty room.

Royalty started thinking she couldn't play with this nigga Jacques he wasn't the one to play with.

Coming downstairs walking up on Royalty Jacques says I should beat your ass for playing with me.

Stepping back a little Royalty says oh you the type of nigga that beat bitches up now putting her hands on her hips.

Grabbing Royalty throat Jacques says don't start playing with me Royalty doing childish shit. Pushing her back while releasing her throat. And the answer is no I don't beat bitches up for your information but I'm not going to let you disrespect me either. I will slap the taste out your smart-ass mouth tho and you can label it however you want to Jacques says seriously walking into the living room going to the bar to pour himself a drink. Royalty walked up behind Jacques and Jacques turned around and pointed his gun at Royalty and said Don't walk up behind me unless you want to get shot.

What's wrong with you tonight? Royalty said not remembering ever seeing Jacques like this before.

Your what's wrong with me Royalty it's you Jacques says pouring himself a drink and sitting down on the couch.

Sitting across from Jacques because Royalty didn't want to get to close to the mad man Royalty says Your paying for my door too trying to act mad but knowing she started all this.

Going in his pocket Jacques pulls out a wad of money and throws it at Royalty like a stripper. Here this should be more than enough Jacques says putting his head back on the couch and closing his eyes momentarily.

Royalty was looking at Jacques like what the fuck is wrong with this nigga he must need some pussy or something. Royalty gets up and goes and shuts the front door but couldn't lock it and shook her head. Walking back into the living room Royalty says to Jacques what if someone tries to run up in my house tonight? The door can't be locked standing there with her arms crossed waiting for a answer from Jacques.

Jacques pulls out his phone and texted someone or so Royalty thought and within a few minutes Jacques says a locksmith will be here in thirty minutes. So, before he gets here take all your clothes off and come ride this dick.

Huh? Are you fucking serious right now Royalty says not believing this nigga? You just shot off my lock, ran through my crib and choked me Now you want me to sit on your dick like nothing happened Jacques or you serious?

Yeah, I'm Serious hurry up babe before the locksmith come and catch us. Jacques says sipping on his drink not paying Royalty no attention about that bullshit Royalty was talking about. Jacques starts unblocking his pants and kicking off his shoes. Royalty just stood there contemplating what to do. This is all your fault babe Jacques says for playing with me trying to make me jealous. Now that you know that I am a jealous man don't do that shit again or else it won't be the lock that I shoot Jacques says laughing. And hurry up babe I'm horny Jacques says rubbing his dick. You know you want this dick Jacques says sitting there looking like he belongs on the cover of GQ magazine with a big dick in his hand smiling. Come here babe and give me a kiss Jacques says begging Royalty and sure enough Royalty came and sat on Jacques lap. After sitting on Jacques lap Jacques pulls Royalty's hair and says don't do that shit no more you hear me babe? Royalty didn't answer. Jacques started kissing on Royalty neck and ears. Let's make a baby Jacques said in Royalty ear then kissing Royalty pulling her sweatpants off. I want you to be my baby Mama Jacques said again in Royalty ear. Once Jacques got Royalty pants off, he sticks his finger inside Royalty who was soaking wet fingering Royalty for a minute. So, you wanted this dick and was playing like you didn't babe huh? Jacques says in Royalty ear. Royalty was feeling too good and was laying her head on Jacques shoulder gripping Jacques back. Now since you're in the playing mood today you're not getting no dick Jacques says picking Royalty up and sitting Royalty on the chair next to the couch then turned around and started putting his clothes back on Laughing. Get dressed babe before the locksmith come Jacques says going to the bar to get himself another drink Laughing.

Royalty sat on the chair feeling played now.

Turning around Jacques says holding his drink I bet you won't play with me like that no more huh Miss Royalty? sipping his drink Jacques says laughing.

Royalty was still just sitting there looking at Jacques.

Put your pants back on before the man gets here and sees your ass and then I'll have to shot him Jacques says laughing.

Oh, shit funny now Royalty says getting up picking up her sweat pants and panties. You ain't shit Jacques Royalty says rolling her eyes.

We even now Jacques says sitting down sipping on his drink watching Royalty get dressed mad hurrying up. Fuck You Royalty said irritated.

Nope Jacques replied laughing.

When they heard a knock on the door. Jacques and Royalty both looked at each other knowing who it was. But Jacques wasn't getting the door this wasn't his house. And Royalty felt like it was Jacques fault that a locksmith was at her house in the first place this late at night Jacques should get the door so they both sat there for a minute until the locksmith let himself him saying is anybody home?

And Royalty yells yes, we're here in the living room rolling her eyes at Jacques who was smirking at Royalty thinking about how he couldn't wait to fuck Royalty. Jacques would have earlier, but Jacques knew he wouldn't have enough time to get it in like he wanted to do so instead Jacques decided to make Royalty pay for playing with him. But later tonight it was on. Laying in the bed Jacques asks Royalty did she feel safe now laughing. Royalty turns around and hits Jacques with a pillow. And Jacques says what we're having a pillow fight now? Looking up at Royalty curious. Royalty went to her drawer to put on her pajamas when Jacques says oh no babe come to bed in your birthday suit smiling showing all thirty two of his teeth.

Really Royalty was thinking you're not getting no pussy tonight we already established that earlier when you pulled that little stunt. You had your chance and didn't take it. It's like I threw you a alley oop and you missed your shot. I'm over it buddy try again tomorrow. Royalty laughed to herself because Royalty knew she wasn't giving Jacques none not tonight. Babe I'm tired and drunk morning sex sounds better let's cuddle. Royalty said.

Cuddle this dick Royalty Jacques said Laughing. Ok let's cuddle patting the mattress next to him like come lay down right here.

Ok here I come but I'm thirsty I'm about to go get some water you want something to drink Royalty asked Jacques hoping he'll say yes. And he did.

Bring me a shot of Hennessy babe please Jacques says getting comfortable turning on the tv.

You want a chaser to? Royalty asks Jacques.

Yes Jacques says as Royalty walks out the room going downstairs.

After Royalty makes Jacques a drink of Hennessy and squirts four drops of visine in Jacques drink that Royalty kept in her cabinet to knock Jacques ass out then Royalty gets her water and a coke for Jacques to chase his drink with.

Handing Jacques his Hennessy and coke Thank you babe Jacques said downing his Hennessy.

Bingo Royalty was thinking. Too easy.

Then Jacques drank his coke and sat the can on the nightstand. Jacques started yawning and rubbing his eyes. Babe I'm tired Jacques said hitting his pillow then passing out.

Bingo Royalty said goodnight Mr I did too much tonight it was time for me to go to sleep. Royalty hadn't done this to someone for several years but Jacques asked for it tonight. This was the thing Royalty and Amir did to niggas at the bar back in the days when they were into robbing niggas. Royalty would set them up at the bar and Amir would act like he was helping them to their cars and rob them. It worked for years. You'll be surprised how many niggas be slipping at the bar especially when they trying to show out in front of a woman. They never saw it coming until it was too late then boom. Most marks would wake up not remembering shit. Royalty laughed at the thought and went to brush her teeth and went to bed and laid underneath Jacques. I said I wanted us to cuddle Royalty said wrapping her arms around Jacques and falling asleep herself.

The next morning Jacques woke up feeling like he had been asleep for days. Like that was the best sleep he ever had. Royalty had been up and dressed and was waiting on Jacques to wake up to give her a ride to the bank and the car dealership. Babe how long have you been up Jacques asked Royalty who's was in the closet packing her overnight bag.

Not long about an hour Royalty replied from inside the closet.

You want to go have breakfast ? Jacques asked Royalty getting up going into the bathroom.

No I have to go to the bank and go to the car dealership.

After showering and getting dressed Jacques comes into the room and there's no sign of Royalty. Going downstairs Royalty was in the living room talking to the housekeeper. Mija looked at Jacques and instantly got mad. Jacques this is Mija our housekeeper well my housekeeper now but she's more like family.

How you doing Mija it's a pleasure meeting you extending his hand Jacques says but Mija didn't reciprocate. Mija just looked Jacques up and down.

Mija don't be so rude Royalty said waiting for Mija to apologize but she didn't. Mija walked out the living room and into the den.

What I do? Jacques asked puzzled.

Don't mind her she's probably on her period or something Royalty said.

You ready? Royalty asked Jacques.

Yeah now what was you talking about going to a dealership? What dealership and why we going there? Jacques asked Royalty.

Oh, because I'm buying a new car a early birthday present to myself Royalty says smiling.

Looking at Royalty suspiciously Jacques says ok what kind of car Royalty?

I'm getting a Ferrari wait until you see it and I'm driving up to San Francisco for the weekend to break it in.

I need a cup of coffee before I can digest this news Jacques says seriously. How much is the car Royalty? Jacques asks I would have brought you a car for your birthday babe Jacques says.

You still can Royalty says. I haven't purchased it yet I needed to go to the bank and get the money.

You were going to pay cash for a car ? Jacques asked Royalty Especially that type of car. That's ludacris babe. I know you have it like that but still that's what credit is for it's called credit for a reason Jacques says laughing. Big baller shot caller the boss Miss Royalty Jacques says. I'll buy the Ferrari for you but I damn sure ain't paying cash Jacques said. I'll put it on my black card Jacques says looking in his wallet making sure he had it on him.

Your going to buy me a Ferrari Jacques don't be playing trying to get me back from last night Royalty said getting more excited now that Royalty didn't have to spend her own money for such a large purchase.

Babe I'm a grown ass man and a man Of My word if I say I'm going to do something that's exactly what I'm going to do. No games over here that's all you kid Jacques says seriously.

Wow thank you babe Royalty says giving Jacques a hug and kiss.

Mija was in the other room thinking maybe Jacques wasn't all that bad after all but still Royalty was moving on to fast.

Ok then since your buying me a car for my birthday the least I can do is take you to breakfast and treat you to San Francisco this weekend everything on me Royalty said smiling.

Naw Frisco on me too Jacques said. You can buy me some coffee though grabbing Royalty overnight bag.

Sounds like a plan Royalty said excitedly. Bye Mija Royalty yelled out I'll see you next week and I'll show you my birthday present Jacques buying me walking out the door.

Mija was thinking good riddance slut. Amir had told Mija on several occasions that Royalty was sneaky now Mija knew what Amir was talking about. Mija missed Amir so badly Amir was the love of Mija life that's the only reason Mija still was working for Royalty was to stay attached to something of Amir's. Royalty didn't know that when Mija was telling Royalty that she was getting rid of Amir's things Mija was actually keeping them for herself. Mija also had some of Amir's money a hundred thousand that Amir had put up at Mija place that Royalty knew nothing about. And Mija had recently suffered a miscarriage by Amir also a few months before Amir's passing. Amir was the only man Mija had ever been with and the only man Mija would ever love. Mija didn't care that she had to share Amir with Royalty. Mija knew how Amir felt about her and that what they shared was true love. Amir would tell Mija all the time he wished things could have been different and Amir was really hurt when Mija lost the baby. Amir said maybe it was time he came clean with Royalty about everything, but Amir never got the chance too. Mija lost the baby and Amir got killed. Life has a funny way of giving us experiences Mija was thinking starting to cry thinking about Amir. Here Mija was still grieving and distraught over Amir and Miss Royalty was headed to San Francisco with another man but Royalty was Amir's so called wife. Life isn't fair Mija was thinking I miss you so much Amir Mija said looking at one of Amir's picture in the den. Why you leave me here alone this isn't fair Mija says falling on the floor crying.
Royalty and Jacques went thru the drive through at Starbucks and then headed to the car dealership to pick up Royalty new Ferrari. Looking at her Cartier watch Royalty read eleven o'clock on the nose. Perfect timing. Royalty was so excited Royalty jumped out Jacques car while it was still rolling Royalty didn't even let Jacques park.

Good morning the salesman from last night said to Royalty smiling knowing he was about to secure a hefty commission from the sale.

Extending his hand Jacques says what's up? How are you to the salesman.

This is my boyfriend Royalty says he's actually going to purchase the car for me.

The salesman looked from Jacques to Royalty and said ok it's ready for you. It's been detailed and gassed up and all the paperwork is ready. Walking towards the office with Royalty and Jacques following behind him. Sitting down the salesman hands Royalty the keys and says Congratulations to Royalty. Who was jumping up and down holding her keys. Ok so you're paying for the car the salesman says directing his attention to Jacques now getting straight to the point.

Yes, smiling I am Jacques says going in his wallet handing the gentleman his black card.

Can I get a copy of your driver's license the salesman asks Jacques?

Yes of course Jacques replies taking his driver's license out handing it to salesman. Is the car going in your name Sir the salesman asks?

No, hers pointing at Royalty.

Ok I'll be right back the salesman says walking out to make copies. A few minutes later the salesman comes back in and hands Jacques his driver's license and credit card back and shakes Jacques hand and says thank you for his business and gives Jacques a business card. Enjoy your car Miss Royalty the salesman says. And don't get pulled over for speeding the salesman says as Royalty and Jacques walks out the office to Royalty new car that was waiting for Royalty in front.

Nodding his head Jacques says nice watching Royalty getting in her new car starting it up.

I love the way it purrs Royalty says smiling from ear to ear. Thank you for my birthday present.

Your welcome Jacques says thinking it ain't trickin if you got it right. This was the first time Jacques had spent this much money on a female besides his wife but that's how much Jacques was feeling Royalty. It didn't matter to him what Royalty wanted or how much it cost if Royalty wanted something it was hers. Jacques just wanted Royalty to be happy.

You ready to go to San Francisco Royalty said ready to fly down the highway.

Absolutely but first I need to take care of something real quick Jacques said. Pick me up in a hour at my boutique. Reaching down in the car giving Royalty a kiss. And drive safely lil mama Jacques says walking to his car. Jacques had almost forgotten he had to deliver three kilos to one of his distributors and Jacques had his crew waiting for instructions. Calling his boy telling him to meet him at the spot then hanging up Jacques gets ready to take off but looks back at Royalty who was putting on her lipstick Jacques laughed and shook his head thinking that Royalty was too much laughing. Meeting up with his boys Jacques tells them where the drop off was at and where to deposit the money. Jacques informs them that he'll be out of town for the weekend and everything was to remain the same and if something was to happen to hit him up, he'll fly back if he had to. Then Jacques had his boy drop him off at his boutique to wait for Royalty to pick him up.

When Royalty pulled up, she blew the horn and Jacques came out with his overnight bag and they hit the highway headed to the Bay Area.
Bianca felt like she needed some fresh air from being cooped up in the house for several days and getting air from opening the house windows just wasn't getting it for Bianca. Plus, Bianca was out of wine and needed a black and mild for her weed. After Bianca last client leaves her house Bianca planned on going to the store for a quick minute and coming straight back home. Plus, Bianca friend was stopping by later on to check in on her.

Tonight's going to be so lit Bianca it's too bad you can't come out with us Bianca client says getting her face beat for the occasion.

I know right you can thank Miss Royalty for that Royalty always fucking up my plans Bianca says finishing up her client's face making her go from a five to a ten real quick handing her a mirror.

Bitch you know you bad Bianca clients says loving her look. She keep batting her eyelashes and smiling.

What you wearing? Bianca asked her client wanting to know how her client was going to kill shit tonight especially since it was going to be a concert at the club. I should go and just wear my glasses and do my makeup really good Bianca says wanting to go Hella bad but didn't want to be in the club with shades on all night plus Bianca didn't want to drink and drive with only one good eye after the club that was asking for trouble.

I wish you would come bitch you know you're the life of the party Bianca client says.

Naw I'm good I'm going to have to miss this one but the next party I'm there Bianca says seriously, but what you wearing bitch Bianca asks her client again.

I'm wearing a fitted sweater dress with some knee high boots the client said.

First of all bitch it ain't winter Bianca said and second of all bitch it's going to be all kinds of ballers up in that joint tonight why would you cover up? I'm so confused right now Bianca said seriously. You better dress like a stripper bitch Bianca said and save all that church attire for Sunday Bianca said Laughing. Bianca client laughed too.

I know I know the client said I just don't know how to dress sexy without it looking like I'm trying to hard the client said.

Bitch if you don't go in that mother fucker damn near naked, I'm going to kill you Bianca said ready to turn into a stylist, so her client wouldn't get laughed at but most importantly ignored all night. Bianca saw the girls in the club that nobody ever looked in their direction they didn't get any free drinks nothing nada and Bianca was sad for them. Look bitch you're not paying me 110 plus a tip to not get no action tonight, so I advise you to turn the fuck up bitch Bianca said seriously. Hold up Bianca said walking out the living room into her bedroom and within a few moments Bianca returned with several outfits laid out on the couch. Here's a gift from me to you Bianca said smiling.

I already wore these outfits and I'm not wearing them again there yours Bianca said feelings generous.

Thank you Bianca her client said looking at the outfits. These hella cute the client says holding them up. I really like this see thru jumpsuit but what do I wear underneath it? The client asks curiously.

Matching underwear and nothing else Bianca replies. I wore red lace underwear when I wore it with my red Giuseppe heels and pulled three niggas that night bitch killed shit on purpose. Bianca said Laughing.

Ok ok what about these see thru wide leg pants the client asks holding them up.

Same thing bitch Duh Bianca said. I hooked them up with a wife beater and wore my big Gucci belt and Gucci heels like I said I kills shit on purpose laughing Bianca says.

You do always hands down Bianca clients says in agreement.

So, put your flavor to the outfit and make it hit Bianca said seriously because bitch that beat you got is fire with the Smokey eye and plum lips.

Yes, Hunny it is the client says paying Bianca and giving Bianca a nice tip.

Have fun doll Bianca said. I'm jelly bitch I wish I could go.

You can just ride with us I can pick you up and drop you back off after the club unless you come up on some work bitch you know how you do Laughing the client said.

Ok I'll think about it call me when you get home I'll see how I feel then Bianca says. I'm about to run and get me a black and mild and get high I might feel a little better Bianca said walking out the door behind her client.

I'll call you in a hour Bianca client says getting in her car.

Bianca was thinking if she did decided to go her client would have to drive her Bentley to the club because there was no way on earth Bianca was getting in a Toyota Corolla going to the club. Pulling up at the liquor store it was thick outside everybody was out. The corner was poppin tonight. Getting out her car Bianca says what's up to the homies before going inside the store. Once inside the liquor store Bianca grabs two bottles of Moscato and gets her black and milds.

Malak says you look tired laughing at Bianca.

And you got a small ass dick Bianca replies back to Malak laughing too. And I read your little love note to Royalty laughing Royalty would never give you the time of day. Royalty fucks with real niggas not some wanna be who acts like a nigga Bianca said pissing Malak off.

Pay for your shit bitch Malak said to Bianca irritated now.

Bianca threw ten dollars at Malak and said keep the change shortie and turned around and walked out the store switching her ass laughing. Waving bye to her folks Bianca drove off and went home and rolled herself a blunt and poured herself a glass of wine. After getting faded Bianca decided to go out because Bianca was tired of being in the house and plus Bianca needed some new work. These other niggas Bianca was dealing with was getting on her nerves and Bianca wanted something new and exciting. Life was to be enjoyed not be sitting around being miserable Bianca kept telling herself getting dressed. And Bianca planned on living her life to the fullest and fuck whoever feelings got hurt in the process. It was Bianca world and everybody else was just a squirrel in her world trying to get a nut in her book.

Bianca wanted to make sure she was unforgettable tonight and wanted to make sure she got bitches all in their feelings tonight. Looking through her closet listening to Kash doll on full blast getting pumped. Trying to find the right outfit that turn niggas heads. Bianca was on one tonight. Bianca found the perfect outfit and was about to get in the shower when her client texted her and Bianca text her client back and said yes she was going out with them tonight and to drive to her house and that she'll be ready when her client got there. Bianca jumped in the shower real quick and got out and did her makeup. Bianca eye was a little better now but it was still black and blue but at least it was open now but it was flaming red inside. A blood vessel must have popped and it still hurt like hell. But Bianca did her makeup so good that you really had to be staring in Bianca face to tell her eye was black because all you could see was the redness but that could have been from allergies. But it didn't really matter anyways because Bianca was wearing her Christian Dior sun visor with the red tint and glasses. Bianca pulled her 24 inch blonde mink bundled in a high ponytail that hung down her back and got dressed. Putting on her black biker shorts and black wife beater with no bra and wearing her red supreme LV fanny pack across her breast and red suede Christian Dior signature heels and red lips. Bianca sprayed herself from head to toe with Nyc Bond 9 the signature black bottle now Bianca was ready.

Bianca lit her blunt and smoked until her client pulled up outside with one of her homegirls in her car. Bianca threw her car keys to her client and told her to drive her Bentley. Bianca client was in absolute denial at first until she actually got in the driver's seat and then Bianca client started taking selfie for proof. Bianca told her client to dream big because dreams do come true and if she really wanted a Bentley, she could definitely own a Bentley one day if she believed she could. Bianca got in the back of her own car to let the other two ladies floss while she kicked back and enjoyed the ride. Plus, Bianca brought her blunt and had her drank in her red cup, so Bianca wasn't tripping. Bianca was getting lit in the back seat all by herself. Once they arrived at the club the place was packed as usual and the vibe was crazy. Bianca was ready to show out tonight. We're in Vip ladies Bianca said and the two ladies with Bianca was ecstatic. Going in you could barely walk it was so crowded, but Bianca and the women pushed their way through to the Vip area where Bianca had a table. Bianca client and her friend sat down at their booth, but Bianca stayed standing bouncing to the music. When the bottle service came Bianca grabbed a bottle all to herself and popped it open and drank from the bottle dancing by herself having a good time. The other two women poured themselves a drink into their glasses and sat there vibing to the music. Drake Kiki song came on and Bianca got lit screaming hey over and over again twerking looking back at it. Bianca was having a blast hella niggas was at Bianca all night coming and going from the table it was like Bianca was a celebrity or something. The two ladies Bianca was with had such a good time watching Bianca have a good time.

This guy came over to the table while Bianca was all over this other dude booed up and started standing over Bianca. At first the two ladies with Bianca didn't think too much about the guy until the guy started saying to Bianca so that's how you gonna do a nigga after I came over your house and checked on you Bianca and made sure you was ok?

Bianca didn't even notice no one standing over her at first because Bianca was so high and drunk and kissing all over the dude, she was with sitting on his lap making love in the club with.

Bianca client stood up and said excuse me can you please move away from Bianca trying to push the guy back.

The dude said mind your fucking business angrily and drunk

That's when Bianca turned around after hearing the arguing back and forth. Looking up at the nurse dude Bianca said oh what's up? I didn't know you went out where's your wife at? Laughing. The dude Bianca was sitting on his lap started laughing too.

Can we talk outside? Bianca male nurse friend asked.

And Bianca said No!! And turned back around with ol boy like the nurse dude wasn't even standing behind her. The nurse guy stood there for a minute then walked away furious. Bianca client got nervous and was ready to go. But she knew she couldn't leave Bianca after all she was driving Bianca car, so she just sat there trying to make the best of a bad situation. Bianca and the dude finally stopped making out and sat there drinking and taking pictures. Bianca male nurse friend started walking back towards the Vip section still mad that Bianca wasn't paying him no mind plus he felt disrespected. His wife was following right behind him with her girlfriends and the nurse dude was so upset he didn't even notice they were behind him. Reaching the rope to Vip security wouldn't let the nurse guy by this time.

So, Dude just stood there screaming at Bianca So you're really going to do this huh? Acting like you don't even fucking know me Bianca.

The nurse dude wife walked up to him screaming at him slapping him upside his head. You chasing bitches in the club now Sam? This bitch is a hoe really? You're going to disrespect me like this in front of all these people? He keep saying move pushing her hand out his face.

Bianca had turned her nose up at the nurse dude once Bianca saw the commotion like ugh, he's drunk and belligerent he needs to go home with his wife. Bianca wanted no parts of his bullshit tonight. Ignoring the commotion, the nurse dude was causing Bianca and the guy she was partying with exchanged numbers with their phones and Bianca promised to call him later after she got home and dropped her passengers off. The dude said he'll walk them outside to their car because he knew the other guy whoever he was to Bianca was tripping and he just wanted to make sure they all got to the car safely. Bianca thanked her new bodyguard once they arrived at her car safely with a long kiss and rubbing of his testicles promising him a good time later. The ladies got in the Bentley and headed to Bianca house Laughing and talking about the night at hand and how some nigga are bitches too. They be having a whole wife at home well in this case the club and still be tripping off the side chick, unbelievable but hey shit happens like that some time when you got that good good Bianca said Laughing with the ladies both laughing in agreement.

Thank God we made it safe Bianca client said getting out the car handing Bianca her Bentley car keys. I had a good time thanks for coming out with us sis it's always an adventure with you Bianca the client says laughing.

I know right it's always something Bianca says getting out the back seat into the driver's seat. Drive home safely ladies' text me when you get home Bianca said waving bye to the two ladies. Bianca sat in her car for a moment and rolled up another blunt and decided to hit her weed before texting her new friend but before Bianca could text her new friend, he texted her What's up babe? Reading his text laughing Bianca texted back what's up tho? I'm sitting in my car getting faded waiting on you to come through lol. Bianca text her new friend her address. He texted back see you in ten minutes. Bianca texted back ok and put her phone down and finished hitting her weed listening to Cardi B money singing every word waiting for her friend to pull up.

But instead the nurse dude pulls up and knocked on Bianca driver's window scaring her. Bianca cracked her window a little and asked him what the fuck he wanted and don't be popping up at her house uninvited and without calling then rolled her window back up. The nurse dude knocked on the window again, but Bianca ignored him turning her music up acting like the nurse dude wasn't even standing there. Then Bianca new friend who she was actually waiting for pulls up looking like what the fuck is going on seeing the dude from the club at Bianca house.

When the nurse dude saw the guy Bianca was with booed up from the club pulling up, he got extra mad hamming on Bianca window yelling What's he doing here? You plan on fucking him or something?

Bianca turned around and saw her new friend and instantly got irritated at the whole scenery this wasn't how Bianca operated and this wasn't acceptable to Bianca either. Getting out her car to explain to her new friend this nurse dude was tripping and that she didn't invite him over the nurse dude wife pulled up in front of Bianca house also with a car full of chicks and jumped out with a bat. Get your ugly, twelve year old Chinese boy looking ass away from my fucking house you stupid ass bitch Bianca said mad ass fuck that this bitch and this nigga both came to her house with this bullshit. Running up on Bianca with the bat swinging it Bianca started running around her car yelling bitch I'm going to kill you. The nurse dude tried to take the bat from his wife, but his wife swung and hit him with bat and the nurse dude pulled his hand back and rushed his wife to the ground.

Bianca new friend was sitting in his car like wow Bianca must have some real good pussy if she got this nigga fighting his wife at her house on her yard. I'll wait to find out myself he thought sitting there watching the show.

Bianca ran to her car to try to get her gun out the glove compartment but somehow the nurse dude wife had gotten loose and her friends were out the car now cheering her on to get Bianca and one of them had given her a knife and before Bianca could reach the glove compartment in her car the wife had jumped on top of Bianca back and stabbed Bianca in the neck and keep stabbing Bianca eighteen more times to be exact until her husband was able to get his wife off of Bianca who was bleeding to death across the front seat of her car. Bianca new friend didn't know what was happening all he could see was the wife jumping up and her girlfriends running towards her and then the wife jumping on Bianca back inside the car. He was rolling a blunt and thought they were just going to try and jump Bianca and he would have broken it up after he hit his weed. Because he thought this shit was hella funny. It was too dark for him to see everything that occurred, but he knew something was wrong when he saw the nurse dude drag Bianca body out the car and was yelling somebody call 911 and started doing Cpr on Bianca.

Bianca new friend also heard the nurse dude wife say Let that bitch die that's what she gets.

He jumped out his car and ran over to Bianca who wasn't breathing and was covered with blood. What can I do to help he asked the nurse dude who was still trying to work on Bianca? Call 911 but they could hear the sirens coming in the background. One of Bianca noisy neighbors had already called the police from the beginning and said something terrible was happening and the neighbor had taken down the nurse's wife license plate number because the nurse's wife had gotten in her car and took off. When the firefighters arrived, Bianca was DOA, so they covered up Bianca lifeless body and waited for the police to arrive. The nurse dude passed out and was being treated and Bianca new friend had went and sat in his car and smoked his weed in shock he couldn't believe that Bianca was dead. Bianca neighbor who called the police had came out his house and told the firefighters what happened and said he would tell the police when they arrived. The police arrived pretty quickly because they were able to catch the nurse's wife a few blocks away and arrested her after the neighbor gave them the information. The police had told the nurse dude and Bianca new friend to come down to the police station to give a statement and the police had Bianca car towed for evidence. The neighbor went to the police station also after his daughter came to drive him because he was almost ninety years old and didn't drive anymore. The police had all three of the ladies that were in the car with the nurse's wife under arrest. The wife was being charged with murder and the three Friends was being charged with accessory to murder.
Arriving in San Francisco Royalty was tired from the six hours of driving. Royalty wouldn't let Jacques drive at all Royalty told Jacques maybe on the way back. Their hotel was in the financial district which was in the downtown area and the traffic was straight horrible. But it was worth it because their suite was on the 45th floor with panoramic views of the entire city and it was walking distance to downtown on a nice summer night like tonight, but Royalty was too tired for that. Checking into the Loews Regency on Sansome street Royalty tried to pay for the three thousand dollar a night room but Jacques wouldn't let her. Stopping Royalty before Royalty even gets her wallet out her purse Jacques gives the desk clerk his black card and pays for the room and receives two room keys and thanks the clerk. Thank you, Royalty, said to Jacques going up on the elevator.

Stop thanking me for shit I'm supposed to do babe Jacques said seriously hugging Royalty.

Royalty laid her head on Jacques shoulder tired. Once they got into their suite Royalty took a bath while Jacques showered. Then they sat out on the terrace and took in the fresh air admiring the beautiful city night lights. Its nice out here Royalty says I love this congested city.

Yeah, it's cool I've been here a couple times I couldn't live here though but it's a lot of money here Jacques said. Silicon Valley is booming in the technology world. My sister good with that type of stuff. Building apps and websites she's like a genius or something. I'm really proud of her Jacques says.

Really that is smart Royalty said not really caring but being polite. I'm tired I'm ready to go to bed getting up about to go inside but Jacques grabs Royalty hand and pulls her down to his lap and start kissing her. Royalty kisses Jacques back rubbing his head then stops and looks Jacques in his eyes. Ok let's go to bed kissing Jacques lips getting up taking Jacques by the hand. Royalty got in the bed and laid down and spread her legs open and said go slow make love to me.

Jacques dropped his pajama pants and said yes ma'am climbing on top of Royalty who was soaking wet. They made love over and over again throughout the night with the cool night breeze coming into their room from the terrace door that was open and they both woke up in the morning at the same time to a knock on the door from room service. Neither one of them had ordered room service but that's how the hotel treated their guests in suites with concierge services.

Jacques pulled the covers over his head and said I need a few more hours sleep smiling at Royalty.

But Royalty got up to eat breakfast because Royalty was hungry, so Royalty went in the living room to eat in there and watch some tv. Royalty closed the bedroom door behind her and picked up her breakfast tray and went and sat down to eat her breakfast. Royalty looked at her phone she had three missed calls from Bianca punk ass Royalty was thinking this bitch play too much I'm not calling her dumb ass back tossing her phone on the couch eating her pancakes not paying her phone no mind. Royalty was planning her and Jacques day out in her head. Royalty knew first was shopping downtown San Francisco had all her favorite stores and they could go to the movies which was also downtown. Then maybe they could go to the Pier they could ride the cable car down there and take a ferry to Alcatraz. Royalty knew Jacques hadn't visited the island before because no nigga didn't want to visit a prison facility didn't matter that it had been closed for decades or not it wasn't on no niggas bucket list Royalty knew that for sure. But Alcatraz had so much history Royalty wanted to go. Royalty googled things to do in the Bay Area and found out that there was a Kevin Hart comedy show in town and a old school concert they would most definitely have to do both. Royalty wanted to lay back down for about another hour Royalty was full after she just fucked her whole breakfast up. And Royalty was still tired so Royalty went and climbed back in bed underneath Jacques who was knocked out. When Royalty and Jacques woke up it was noon they got dressed and headed downtown. They went and had lunch at the Westfield mall downstairs next to Bloomingdales then headed to Saks Fifth. Royalty wasn't feeling so good Royalty just thought it was probably something she ate until Royalty passed out walking down Market street. The ambulance came and took Royalty to the San Francisco Zuckerberg General Hospital emergency room the county hospital because Royalty hit her head when she passed out so for precautionary measure the firefighters wanted Royalty to be checked out completely. Jacques waited in the waiting area for Royalty until the doctors approved that Jacques could come back to see Royalty. Jacques wasn't too much worried about Royalty Jacques figured a night of drinking and the long drive from La probably had Royalty dehydrated nothing serious. Holding on to Royalty belongings Royalty phone kept ringing. Jacques didn't want to answer it but Royalty phone wouldn't stop ringing and it was Bianca, so Jacques answered it thinking it had to be an emergency or something.

What's up Bianca this Jacques he said answering the phone. But this distraught sounding man spoke and said his name was Sam Bianca friend and he was looking for Royalty. Jacques explained to Sam that Royalty was unavailable at the moment, but he would take a message and give it to her. Sam told Jacques that he didn't know who else to call that he only knew Royalty he didn't know how to get in touch with Bianca parents because she didn't have mom or dad listed in her phone and that he was at the hospital with Bianca and the doctors was trying to get in touch with the next of kin and asked him to look through Bianca phone to call someone. This Sam person started crying and told Jacques that there had been a terrible accident and Bianca was killed by his wife. Jacques was looking at the phone like was this some sort of sick joke but that was Bianca phone number showing up, so Sam obviously had her phone. Jacques said he'll let Royalty know and he'll call Sam back. But Sam said to call the hospital and speak to the doctors he was giving them back Bianca phone and going home he couldn't be at the hospital any longer he couldn't take it anymore and hung up. Jacques couldn't believe what he had just heard. Bianca dead how why? The nurse came up to Jacques and said he could see Royalty now finally Jacques was thinking it had been three damn hours since they first arrived there. Walking down the long hallway Jacques was thinking how would he tell Royalty the news about Bianca maybe it wasn't the right time since Royalty was laying up in a hospital herself. Maybe Jacques could hold off until tomorrow and tell Royalty then. At this point Jacques was eager to get back to La. Entering Royalty room Royalty was laying on the hospital bed crying but smiled when Jacques walked in. How you feeling ma? Jacques asked out of concern.

My head hurts a little, but the doctor says I'm fine I was dehydrated.

I thought so Jacques was thinking to himself.

And I'm eight weeks pregnant you're going to be a father Royalty said then she bust out crying.

Pregnant those words hit Jacques like a ton of bricks. Wait what you just say to me? Jacques says moving closer to Royalty face wiping her tears then kissing her. Baby were having a baby? Are you serious Royalty are you sure?

Royalty shook her head yes and handed Jacques her discharge papers. That said Royalty was eight weeks pregnant and to follow up with her primary care doctor as soon as possible.

Jacques kissed Royalty forehead and started smiling. Damn I was starting to think a nigga had a low sperm count or something because I've never gotten a woman pregnant before until now Jacques said seriously.

I've never been pregnant either Royalty said the doctors told me I'll probably never have kids after what that monster did to my young body. My insides were completely destroyed and infected but today I can say I'm going to be someone's mommy. Royalty said still crying. Royalty and Jacques hugged each other, and Royalty cried tears of joy and Jacques was ecstatic also but Jacques knew that their joy was about to turn into pain in a matter of days when Royalty found out her best friend was dead. A life was beginning while one had just ended.
Getting out their Uber in front of their hotel Jacques gets out first and opens the car door for Royalty helping her out the car like Royalty was nine months pregnant or something. Peeking in the back-door Jacques tells the driver thanks my brother for the ride much appreciated then closes the car door. Holding Royalty hand walking hand and hand in the hotel Royalty says to Jacques.

I'm feeling better really babe you don't have to worry about me I'm good. Because Royalty was starting to feel like Jacques was about to start babying her and being overprotective Royalty didn't want that.

I know you feel ok babe but remember you just passed out. And I think we should go home so you can get some rest in your own bed and I'm driving back it's not up for discussion either Jacques said while they were getting in the elevator going up to their suite.

Why can't I just relax in San Francisco were already here Royalty said not understanding the urgency to leave.

I know babe, but I don't feel comfortable with you being way out here in your condition I'll rather you be close to home plus I can have my private doctor see you if you need one Jacques said worried about Royalty and the pregnancy. Jacques didn't want nothing to happen to his seed it was bad enough Royalty was about to get the worst news of her life when they got back home.

Jacques I'm pregnant Royalty said not believing she was actually saying that. But it's not like I can't do regular shit like I was before. I just probably need some vitamins that's all Royalty said seriously.

Looking at Royalty Jacques knew this was about to get ugly. Bianca death and the pregnancy. Jacques wife wasn't going to be so understanding and Jacques knew it. Jacques knew Serenity was about to lose her mind fuck a lawsuit Serenity was going to want to see blood. A baby by another woman and by Royalty at that. All bad .

What's the matter with you babe ? Royalty asked Jacques because Jacques was standing there holding his head and didn't even realize it.

Taking a deep breath Jacques says let's just get our stuff and go home, we can come back to the Bay another time. Jacques said walking towards the closet to get his overnight bag.

Royalty started thinking Jacques wasn't happy about her being pregnant because like most men who just got the pregnancy news would have been so excited they would have been calling their boys and kept talking about it but Jacques just wanted to go home. And Jacques was probably going home to that bitch Royalty was thinking. But it's ok fuck Him Royalty was thinking. Jacques doesn't have to be happy I'm happy for the both of us Royalty was thinking. Yes I'm ready to go home to get the fuck away from Jacques bitch ass getting mad. How could a nigga with no kids not be happy about having a baby? Royalty was thinking. Maybe it was because I'm his side chick Royalty was thinking but Jacques was the one who kept coming back Royalty was thinking . I tried to move the fuck on. Royalty started tearing up but didn't want Jacques to see her crying so Royalty walked into the bathroom closing the door. Royalty yelled out I'll be ready to go in a few minutes to Jacques through the door. Then Royalty turned on the sink and ran the water and started crying. Fuck him I don't need Jacques anyways. Thank you for the baby tho go back to your wife nigga who by the way is suing me. But I'll flip this shit and sue Jacques bitch ass for every dime his wife wants to take from me and I'm not sharing custody either. Wiping her face and blowing her nose.

Royalty looked in the mirror and said to herself your stronger than you think. You got this mommy then Royalty looked down at her stomach and touched it and said to her unborn child.

I know what it's like to be unwanted crying again and to be mistreated and not loved but I promise my whole entire life that this will never happen to you. I love you and I've wanted you before you were even conceived I've wanted you my whole entire life. I'm going to love you with everything in me every fiber of my being I'm going to be the best mother to you I can. I promise to love and protect you no matter what. It's me and you kiddo against the world.

Knocking on the bathroom door Jacques asks Royalty is she ok.

Yes damn I'm using the bathroom flushing the toilet like she had just used it. Royalty says.

Hurry up so we can go It's getting late Royalty Jacques says.

Royalty rolled her eyes like this nigga gone make me cuss his ass out. He must be trying to get back and check on his bitch. Royalty said opening up the bathroom door walking pass Jacques bumping into him without saying excuse me getting her bags ready to go. Ok I'm ready Royalty said with her bag in hand thinking she should have come by herself to the city.

Ok let's go Jacques says walking to the door holding it open for Royalty .

Walking pass Jacques Royalty wanted to say you bitch ass nigga but thought twice about it Royalty was already in the hospital earlier today and Royalty wasn't trying to go back no time soon. Royalty decided to just give Jacques the silent treatment until they got back to La then Royalty would block Jacques ass and say fuck him all together Royalty didn't need this shit. The elevator ride they rode in silence both of them consumed in their own thoughts. Royalty thinking Jacques was stressed out that she was pregnant because his wife was going to be mad and Jacques was thinking how Royalty was going to be fucked up about her best friend being killed and that Royalty was so newly pregnant Jacques Prayed it wouldn't affect his baby and how Royalty was going to really need him now and how he had to start divorce proceedings and give half his inheritance to Serenity ass because Serenity wasn't settling for less. It's crazy how some shit can change in 24 hrs. Damn is this what life was really about? Passing the hardest test to see if you deserve true happiness. Well whatever it was Jacques was ok with it either way. Jacques just wanted his baby to be healthy and happy at any cost. So if that meant giving up half of his five hundred million dollar empire so be it. Royalty had no clue that the baby she was carrying was about to be a very wealthy baby that every year the baby father inheritance generated millions of dollars while Jacques doesn't have to do nothing in life but be himself but ran a business to wash dirty money . And yes Jacques was one of the biggest drug lords on the west coast also that nobody would ever even thought about crossing or else they might get a family member tongue or finger through the mail or even worse one of their family members might come up missing. Yeah unfortunately that's who Jacques was but now you could add father to his repertoire. Jacques checked out the hotel while Royalty went and got the car from valet parking.

When they brought the car around Royalty started thinking she should just leave Jacques ass right there Jacques could find his way back home, but Royalty didn't want no extra problems. When Jacques got in the car Royalty closed her eyes and played like she was tired. Jacques drove all the way home listening to Tupac and Royalty slept. This was by far the most stressful ride either of them had ever had.

Before passing through the grapevine Royalty woke up to having to use the bathroom and Royalty wanted to stop and get something to eat. Jacques wasn't hungry at all especially since they were getting closer to La reality was setting in now. Looking at Royalty when Royalty got out the car to walk to the bathroom Jacques was thinking damn that's about to be my baby's mother, I'm about to have a baby. Smiling Jacques couldn't wait to tell his mother who always wanted to be a grandmother that she was about to become one. And Jacques sister was going to be happy about this also Jacques sister loved kids. Jacques wished his dad was alive to meet his grandchild Jacques father made a lot of sacrifices for his family and to make sure that his grandchildren would be financially secure for the rest of their life. Jacques knew his father would be proud. Jacques was thinking that he would probably have to move Royalty and the baby out of Los Angeles this wasn't where Jacques wanted his child to be raised at. Jacques wanted his child to have the same kind of childhood he had. The best education, the best schools, around the clock nannies their own chef and driver and of course the best security. When Royalty came back to the car Royalty only had food for herself. Jacques thought that was odd but whatever Jacques didn't eat fast food anyways and he planned on stopping Royalty from eating it while she was pregnant, but Jacques knew this wasn't the time for an argument, so Jacques didn't say anything. Gasing up for the remainder of the ride Jacques and Royalty rode in silence again until they reached the Los Angeles border. Then Jacques said to Royalty we're making a pit stop before going home. Royalty just looked out the window and said whatever. It was one o'clock in the morning and Royalty couldn't imagine where they were going to be stopping at this hour, but it didn't matter they were back in La and soon enough Royalty wouldn't be fucking with Jacques ass no more good riddance to this fool. Jacques didn't want Royalty to find out about Bianca tonight Jacques would take Royalty up to the hospital tomorrow morning but Jacques wanted to get his car from his boy tonight because Jacques has never let anyone keep any of his cars this long. Pulling up at the spot Jacques parked in front of the house that looked like a bungalow that needed to be torn down but inside it was a million dollar drug operation being conducted daily. Jacques called his boy and told him to bring his car keys outside he was in front. Running out Jacques boy runs up to the car on Royalty side and tries to give Royalty the keys but Jacques says Nigga that's not her car and I didn't tell you to give my girl my keys to my car if you don't come around on my side and place my keys in my hand nigga it's going to be a problem.

My bad Jacques boy says coming around to the driver's side giving Jacques his Aston Martin keys. Thanks bro for trusting me with your baby Jacques friend says laughing.

Speaking of babies my girl pregnant Jacques says looking over at Royalty who was sitting there acting unbothered, but she really was.

Royalty was shocked that Jacques told his boy she was pregnant maybe she misjudged Jacques, but Royalty doubted it.

Congratulations dawg that's big Jacques boy says oh and congratulations to you too lil mama he says leaning in the car window from Jacques side.

Thank you, Royalty, said dryly.

Giving Jacques dap Jacques boy runs back in the house. Ok babe I'm following you to the house Jacques says turning looking at Royalty.

Ok Royalty said but what Royalty really wanted to say was Go to your own house you don't have to come to mine I'm good.

Ok babe drive slow this car got a lot of power Jacques says still admiring Royalty new car.

Yeah ok Royalty replies not wanting to hear shit Jacques has to say at this point. I do know how to drive Royalty says irritated and ready to go home.

I'm right behind you babe Jacques says trying to give Royalty a kiss but Royalty turned her head.

What's wrong with you? Jacques asked Royalty you can't be having a pregnancy mood already it's too soon isn't it? Jacques asked confused. I'm tired Jacques I'll see you at the house Royalty said I'm ready to go home. Alone is what Royalty wanted to say but didn't.

Royalty got to her house before Jacques did and Royalty parked inside her garage and went inside the house leaving the garage open for Jacques to get in. When Royalty went inside the house she walked into the kitchen and saw that her house phone answering service light was blinking that was strange Royalty thought. Going in the refrigerator to get something to drink because Royalty was trying to stay hydrated when Royalty closes the refrigerator door Jacques was standing there and that scared the shit out of Royalty. Damn Jacques you almost gave me a heart attack Royalty said glancing at the phone again.

Placing his arms around Royalty holding her stomach Jacques says I love you in Royalty ear nibbling on it.

Rolling her eyes Royalty says no you don't. Changing the subject Royalty says my answering service light is blinking that's never happened before.

Jacques looked at the light blinking and knew it was a message probably about Bianca and Jacques didn't want Royalty to find out about Bianca tonight because Jacques really didn't know what to do if Royalty did found out. So Jacques turned Royalty around towards him and said the battery probably needs to be replaced I'll do it tomorrow for you and started kissing Royalty who was pushing him away.

Don't kiss me Royalty said walking away.

Whew at least I distracted Royalty Jacques was thinking to himself walking behind Royalty. What's wrong with you Royalty? You're been on some standoffish shit since we left the Bay Area. I know you didn't want to leave but it was the for the best Jacques says.

Best for who Jacques? You? I was ok I had a little fall so what.

A little fall Royalty you passed the fuck out and bumped your head for crying out loud. What would have happened if you lost the baby? Jacques says seriously.

You wouldn't have cared Royalty says.

Why you say some shit like that Royalty? I do care what happens to you and especially my child. You sound ridiculous right now. I sure hope this isn't going be your mood for the next couple months Jacques says getting irritated now. Let's go to bed maybe you'll feel better in the morning Jacques says going to the bar and fixing himself a drink.

Maybe I will maybe I won't Royalty says going upstairs too tired to fight.

I swear this girl better not have this kinda attitude for nine months downing his drink Jacques says to himself I don't know how much of this I can tolerate. Turning off the kitchen lights and heading upstairs to go to bed Jacques knew tomorrow was going to be a far worse day than today was. Knowing the moment Royalty finds out about Bianca was going to change Royalty life. Jacques knew he had to do everything in his power to make sure Royalty was going to be ok. Jacques didn't know what he was going to do but he just knew he had to do something. Getting undressed and getting in the bed Jacques held Royalty tight from behind and kissed her neck and whispered in Royalty ear I love you no matter what and don't you ever forget that.

Royalty wanted to say something but she was playing sleep when Jacques came in the room so Royalty keep quiet thinking maybe Jacques does really love me and he's happy about the baby.

As for Jacques he was hoping that after tomorrow Royalty doesn't have a miscarriage from getting stressed out Jacques planned on calling his private doctor tomorrow to tell him the news and get advice on what to do about the situation at hand. Jacques and Royalty both feel asleep deep in their own thoughts.

Royalty woke up the next day to the water running in the shower. Looking over at the clock it read 9:00 am. Laying her head back Royalty was thinking what could she eat she was starving. Today Mija was off so breakfast in bed was out of the question. Mija had cut back her days to only two maybe three days a week since Amir's death. Walking out the bathroom butt naked going in his overnight bag Royalty was saying to herself how can you be mad at a species this beautifully made laughing to herself.

Hearing Royalty laugh Jacques turned around and said oh hey I didn't know you were woke good morning ma smiling. Jacques was glad Royalty was in a good mood for now, so Jacques decided to make the best of it. I was thinking I want to buy you a new house in the coming months where would you like to live at? Jacques asked knowing Royalty was going to say in some gated community instead of saying a different city or state. Jacques knew he would have to work on that part later.

Royalty sat up a little on her pillow and said I'm not sure I'll have to think about it. But maybe somewhere that it's sunny all the time.

Sunny you mean warm constantly like Florida or an island? Jacques asked.

Yes, maybe Royalty said. Well see getting up out of bed going into the bathroom.

Jacques knew Royalty was probably hungry but didn't want to take the chance on running into anyone at a restaurant who could possibly tell Royalty about Bianca, so Jacques would drive Royalty to the hospital and go through the Starbucks drive through, so he wouldn't have to worry about that. After they got dressed sure enough Royalty said she was hungry, and Jacques told Royalty he had to make an important run and on the way, they could stop at Starbucks Royalty could grab a bite to eat there until later they'll go out to eat. Royalty was ok with that. Getting their coffee and Royalty breakfast sandwich and donut Jacques headed to the hospital and when Jacques pulled up Royalty was like what are we doing here? Parking Jacques says babe Bianca in the hospital she's been in a accident that's why I wanted to come back home I didn't want to tell you while you weren't feeling good.

What you mean accident Jacques? Royalty asks getting nervous.

Babe let's go in and talk to the doctors. Jacques said.

Royalty started shaking getting nervous Royalty thought Bianca could have been in a car accident or something and Bianca was fucked up. Royalty just stared at Jacques for a second. Is Bianca in a coma Jacques? Royalty asked nervously.

Babe let's see what the doctors say I didn't get all the information Jacques says getting out the car going around to Royalty side opening Royalty door helping Royalty get out.

Royalty formed tears in her eyes immediately the not knowing part scared the shit out of Royalty. Waking into the hospital brought back so many memories and none of them were good except for King being born and that even left a bad taste in Royalty mouth because Amir's baby was born to another women not her. Royalty knew that she would not be having her baby at Mlk hospital under no circumstances too many bad vibes for her. Stopping at the information booth and giving them Bianca name the clerk says one moment and picked up the phone and calls someone. A few moments later a doctor and a priest walks up and introduces themselves and shake Royalty hand and asks Royalty to please come with them. Looking at Jacques Royalty was thinking this is bad, but Royalty had no idea how bad it really was until they took the elevator downstairs to the basement and they started walked in a long hallway where morgue this way was on the wall with a arrow pointing in the direction they were headed. Royalty didn't think they were going to the morgue, but Royalty started squeezing Jacques hand nervously wondering where they were going until they stopped at the morgue door and the doctor opened it. Royalty immediately feel to the floor and started screaming no over and over again. Royalty screams was echoing off the basement walls that sent a chill through each person present body. Jacques tried to get Royalty up, but Royalty had curled up in a fetal position and was yelling and crying at the top of her lungs. The pain was too excruciating for Royalty to bare. The three men got Royalty up off the floor and Royalty kept repeating Bianca, Bianca over and over like a chant. The doctor was able to place Royalty in a chair where Royalty started rocking back and forth crying. Jacques hated to see Royalty like this. Jacques told the doctor that they had just found out that Royalty was eight weeks pregnant and he was concerned for Royalty health. The doctor said that he was going to have to sedate Royalty and the baby would be fine. But the condition Royalty was in the doctor was concerned that Royalty was close to having mental breakdown. Royalty was yelling at the top of her lungs Bianca no Bianca that some people on the first floor could hear Royalty. It was a really frightening scene for the people witnessing this. The doctor paged an emergency team and a nurse came in and gave Royalty a shot in her arm without Royalty even being aware of what was happening then Royalty went out like a light and the team put Royalty on a gurney and took Royalty to the isolation room. The doctor told Jacques to come back tomorrow most likely Royalty would be out all night and that they would be monitoring Royalty. And if Jacques wanted to come back tonight, he could but Royalty would probably still be resting peacefully. Jacques said he'll return tomorrow morning. When Jacques got into his car Jacques just sat there picturing Royalty falling on the floor screaming. Jacques knew Royalty was going to be hurt but Jacques had no idea that Royalty would need to be sedated. Jacques didn't know how emotionally fragile Royalty really was that Royalty didn't handle loss and pain the way most people did. Jacques didn't know that Royalty wasn't going to be the same Royalty that Jacques had known before that Royalty life had changed forever at this very moment.

Jacques drove home and when he got there his mom was in the living room watching a lifetime movie happy to see her son.

I've missed you my dear son where have you been? You haven't called are came home in several days I was starting to get worried about you kissing both sides of Jacques cheeks.

Momma we have to talk Jacques says sitting down besides his mother. These past couple months have been crazy for me. I've falling in love with a woman who's about to have my child.

Lighting up Jacques mom smiles and says is it her the women Jinx introduced you to? Jacques mother asks

Yes, momma it's her smiling back at his mom. Remember her name is Royalty.

Yes, Jacques how could I forget such a beautiful name for a beautiful woman Jacques mom says in her Jamaican accent. So, son what are you going to do now that your about to become a father to a child? You know you have to do right by your child and by your wife it's only fair you do right by both Jacques mother said grabbing Jacques face. The time has come my dear son for you to give up all your illegal activities and act like a civilized man. You have too much at stake to lose all this your father worked hard for to make sure we all have a beautiful life. Your father did enough dirt and got away with most of it to make sure you didn't have to kissing Jacques forehead.

Momma what are you talking about Jacques asked his mom unaware that his mother knew what he had been doing all these years.

I know what you've been up to Jacques I'm no dummy kissing Jacques face and releasing it. I've known for years now. I just never said anything I just make sure you was ok. Making sure you always had disposable money in case something was to happen to you. Just like I knew what your father did to make himself rich. Your father had a lot of blood on his hands Jacques before he died, he just wanted his family to be ok forever but that came with a price. Nothing in life is free always remember that my son. So, do what you have to do by you wife and make it right by Serenity son Serenity deserves that. Jacques mother said. Now let me finish watching my movie and I'm so happy to be a grandmother I can't wait to meet this blessing of a child. Then Jacques mother turned away and finished watching her show.

Jacques went into the den and made himself a drink. This was about to be a very long night for Jacques. He was wondering how did his mother know about his dual lifestyle. It wasn't the money so how could she had known. And Jacques was worried about Royalty and his baby.
Jacques woke up early and headed to the hospital to check on Royalty. The doctor told Jacques that Royalty had most likely suffered from some sort of traumatic psychosis and would probably need medication for a couple of weeks. Jacques wasn't too sure about that especially since Royalty was with child. The doctor tried to explain to Jacques that the medication wouldn't harm the fetus. That this particular medication is given to mothers with postpartum syndrome after giving birth and the mothers were still able to breastfeed. Jacques didn't care about those mothers Jacques only cared about the mother of his child and the answer was no for Jacques. Royalty would just have to go through the motions but taking medication while pregnant with his child wasn't an option. Jacques thanked the doctor and asked if Royalty was ready to be released and the doctor said Royalty was still sedated but somewhat alert, they medication had worn off a little that Royalty could be wheelchaired to the car and that Jacques would have to monitor Royalty for the next twenty four hours. The doctor also told Jacques that Bianca body had been picked up by a funeral home and that her parents came and released her body and had left their information for Royalty emergency contact. Jacques asked for Bianca parents' number which the doctor said they had left information for him at the nurse's station and wanted Jacques to call them. Jacques told the doctor he would bring his car around the front and wait for someone to bring Royalty down.

Going to his car Jacques got a text from Jinx Jacques texted Jinx back and said that he would call her in a minute. Once Jacques got in his car Jacques called Jinx and explained everything to her. Jinx was heartbroken about Bianca and said she heard about it through some mutual friends and was checking on Royalty who hadn't been answering her phone in days. Jacques told Jinx they were in San Francisco and Royalty passed out and that's when Royalty found out she was pregnant and how Royalty blanked out when she found out about Bianca and that they were at the hospital currently and that he was going to take Royalty home to rest. Jinx congratulated Jacques on the pregnancy but Jinx feelings were really hurt.

Jinx really had strong feelings for Jacques but hide them well. Jinx told Jacques if he needed anything for Royalty not to hesitate to call her and she would be happy to oblige. Jinx also said she had been in constant contact with Liberty and Angel and that she would let Liberty know what was going on with Royalty and of course her husband also.

Jacques said ok and that he had to go they were bringing Royalty to the car he would keep Jinx informed on any changes with her and they hung up. The nurse put Royalty in Jacques Car. And handed Jacques a bag of medication if needed. Jacques Thank the nurse and strapped Royalty in and took off.

Jacques drove Royalty to his house and put Royalty up in one of the guest room. Jacques removed Royalty clothing and put one of his tee shirts on Royalty and laid Royalty down where Royalty fell asleep like a newborn baby. Jacques mother inquired about what was wrong with Royalty and why Royalty hadn't come out of the room. Jacques explained to his mother what happened and how Royalty just lost her best friend to a violent crime of passion and that's why Royalty wasn't doing too good and that Royalty just needed to rest for a couple of days that's why he brought Royalty there because Jacques didn't want Royalty to be alone. For the next couple days Royalty would wake up out her sleep screaming and Jacques would rock Royalty back to sleep. Jacques personal doctor had come by to check on Royalty and told Jacques that this was going to be a long process of recovery for Royalty and that Royalty pregnancy probably wasn't going to be a easy one. The doctor prescribed some prenatal vitamins and a lite sedative for Royalty to take at night to help her sleep. Four days had passed, and Royalty was still in the same condition. Jacques would wake Royalty up in the mornings and feed her some breakfast then Royalty would go right back to sleep and when Royalty had to use the bathroom Royalty would get up and go and come lay right back down. Jacques didn't like how the medication was doing Royalty, so Jacques stop giving it to Royalty on the fifth day. Royalty was fidgety and shaking but Jacques wanted Royalty to kick the medication out of her system. The following day Royalty woke up looking around the bedroom like where was she at. The big king size mahogany wooden canopy bed was beautiful. The curtains match the comforter and the room had plush carpet with a fireplace in it. Royalty keep looking around like where was she at? Until Royalty saw Jacques walk in the room holding a breakfast tray smiling. How you feeling babe this morning? Jacques asked Royalty.

My head really hurts like I have a migraine Royalty said. Where am I?

You're at my house you're been here for almost a week Jacques replied.

Royalty still looking around asked why am I here and not at at my own house? Royalty wanted to know. Jacques sat down next to Royalty and asked Royalty what was the last thing she remembered, and Royalty said being in San Francisco and finding out she was pregnant and going to the hospital to see Bianca. Then Royalty started crying and laid her head on Jacques shoulder. My best friend is gone isn't she Jacques Royalty asked.

Yes, babe I'm sorry they buried Bianca two days ago.

Lifting her head up Royalty says I missed her funeral babe how?

Jacques explained that Bianca parents wanted to wait for Royalty to get better but also was ready for this nightmare to be over. So they decided to go ahead with the funeral because they didn't know how long it would be until Royalty recovered. Babe you had a little breakdown and wouldn't talk or eat you just shut down babe that's why your here. Holding Royalty who was crying uncontrollably.

I want to go home Jacques Royalty said I want to go home please take me home trying to get out the bed but was too weak to move without assistance. Royalty just keep saying please take me home. Jacques told Royalty after she at least tried to eat a little breakfast he would take her home. Royalty ate all her breakfast and Jacques took Royalty home like he said he would. Jacques ran Royalty a nice hot bubble bath and washed Royalty hair. Royalty asked Jacques to make her something to drink Jacques had to remind Royalty that she was nine weeks pregnant. Royalty had completely blocked her pregnancy out her mind and was just mourning the death of her best friend. Royalty touched her stomach and said Bianca would have been so happy for me laying back down crying again. Royalty cried, herself to sleep and Jacques sat there and watched Royalty not knowing what to do to get Royalty out of this depression it was going on almost two weeks. Jacques couldn't handle none of his business or make money moves but Jacques did arrange for his Attorney's to make Serenity an offer for divorce that Serenity could keep the home they owned in Jamaica they shared worth one point five million and one resort on the island that generated a million a year in tourism all the cars he owned there in Jamaica which was a pretty nice collection worth over one hundred thousand ,half of Jacques inheritance worth 500 million dollar and to stop the lawsuit against Royalty or else they could go back to negotiations and drag this divorce out it was Serenity choice. Jacques was just waiting to hear back from Serenity Attorney's, but this was a hard deal to pass up especially since Serenity had flown back to Jamaica with her parents and was recuperating in a rehabilitation center there. Serenity was in no shape to be calling any shots and Jacques was being generous with his offer. Jacques knew Serenity was going to take his deal.

Bianca parents had flown to Mexico and had spoken to Jacques before they left. They wanted Jacques to let Royalty know they loved her dearly and when she was ready to please come and visit them because Bianca parents were almost positive that they were not coming back to the states. Bianca parents took her death really hard. They wanted Royalty to have all of Bianca possessions. Bianca house, Bianca business and Bianca car if Royalty wanted it after it finished being processed by the homicide investigators. Bianca parents owned a house in Mexico and had a family business over there also, but Bianca mother wanted to be far away from Los Angeles Bianca mom said. When the women who killed my child, trial starts Bianca mom said that's when I'll return. Bianca mom said and not a day before that if she even makes it to a trial date.
Three months had gone by since Bianca death and Royalty hadn't gotten any better. Royalty birthday had passed in August and Royalty didn't want to do anything but visit Bianca gravesite. Royalty opened her Hair boutique but without a grand opening like Royalty anticipated. Royalty only came outside to go to her doctor's appointment because Royalty was now almost six months pregnant and miserable. Royalty went to visit Bianca gravesite at least three times a week and whenever Royalty went to her prenatal appointments. Royalty didn't bother getting dressed anymore nor did Royalty keep her appearance up like she used to. Jacques stayed with Royalty most of the time to make sure Royalty was ok, but Royalty didn't even care that Jacques was there most of the time. Their

relationship was very strain to say the least. But Jacques was determined to make it work for the sake of his child. Jacques wanted to buy Royalty a bigger house before Royalty delivered the baby, but every time Jacques brought the subject up Royalty brushed Jacques off and said ok can we talk about it later. Jacques really wanted a change of scenery for Royalty and also himself. But Royalty wasn't having it yet. Jacques keep asking Royalty to get someone to run her businesses and get a personal assistant for Royalty day to day affairs because Royalty stop caring about everything all together it was like Royalty had no reason to live no more Royalty gave up on everything. Jacques didn't know exactly what Royalty businesses were in detail and the more Jacques asked the more Royalty resisted with giving Jacques the information to even allow Jacques to hire someone to take over Royalty affairs. Royalty was becoming very difficult to deal with and it was becoming very frustrating for Jacques. The only good thing was when Royalty had the kids over for the weekends. Angel and King came over every other weekend. One morning Royalty got a phone call that seemed to snap Royalty out of her funky mood. Royalty said to Jacques after getting off the phone that she was heading to her shop Pretty Please to get her hair done something Royalty hadn't done in months and that she was going to talk to her attorney and Royalty would see Jacques later on. Jacques was happy to see that Royalty was starting to act like herself again Jacques didn't know who had called Royalty to snap Royalty out of it, but Jacques was thankful. Later on, that night Jacques got in kinda late, but Royalty was still up laying across her bed eating some ice cream waiting on Jacques. When Jacques came in the room Royalty said they needed to to talk.

You look nice Jacques said admiring Royalty who had her hair flat iron straight no more curls thank god Jacques was thinking. And Royalty had on a fitted dress with her stomach poking out Royalty got her lashes done and had gotten her feet done and a wax. Royalty looked like a brand new women to Jacques no more baggy sweats and tees or rotating the same few pairs of tennis shoes. I'm all ears Jacques says smiling happy his baby was finally getting her groove back after all these months.

I have some good news Royalty said smiling. Jacques was hoping Royalty was saying she found out she was having a boy that's all the good news Jacques wanted to hear.

Ok what's up? Jacques asked curiously.

I spoke to a realtor who has a client that wants to pay cash for my property in New York.

Jacques was looking like yeah, he guess that was good news, but Jacques also knew that was were Amir had been murdered and didn't want Royalty to slip back into her depressed state of mind. The doctors says any little thing could trigger Royalty to go in and out of depression and Jacques didn't want to chance that once Royalty was out of depression and feeling better. Jacques just wanted to keep it that way. Well babe do you have to be present for the sale? Jacques asked Royalty.

Yes, babe the realtor said they needed me to sign some papers and sign off on the property. The building is very strict about everything being in order or the seller won't be able to occupy the unit. Royalty said. I know what you're thinking I'm not going to the actual condo I said I would meet them at a private restaurant in Manhattan.

Ok when is all this supposed to take place? Jacques asked Royalty.

Tuesday Royalty said.

This Tuesday like in three days Tuesday Jacques asked.

Yes, they want to be in be in the building by Christmas their eager to buy Royalty said excited for a change.

How much is the property worth? Jacques asked.

Two point five million Royalty replied.

And their paying cash? They must be Oriental Jacques says seriously.

They are Royalty said how did you know?

Because they're the only ones who pay cash when buying property, they keep all their money in there houses buried underneath their floors they don't believe in banks Jacques said.

How you know that? Royalty asked wanting to know.

Just know I know Royalty ok. Jacques said But Tuesday is soon I need to call and reserve a plane how many days you want to stay in New York babe? Jacques asked about to make their arrangements.

Maybe a couple days not too long because I have a doctor's appointment the following week you know I can't miss that.

Right ok I'm on it now Jacques said calling his assistant to make him and Royalty some travel arrangements for a private plane and a hotel and car. Jacques hoped this trip wouldn't set Royalty back into a depression and that whoever it was that was purchasing the property was serious. Jacques didn't have no time for games. Jacques was happy that Royalty was taking small steps getting her business in order before the baby was born now Jacques just needed Royalty to decide where she wanted to move to, so they could start their lives together as a family. Serenity had agreed to all Jacques requests for a divorce the only thing Serenity wanted was to keep her last name for business purposes. That didn't bother Jacques at all Jacques could care less about that. Jacques was a free man now free to do whatever he wanted to do without the headache. Jacques had planned on proposing to Royalty on Christmas if Royalty acted right. Not cussing him out or putting him out, telling him to go home to his own damn house like Royalty had been doing lately acting hella crazy and stuff. Jacques knew a lot of it was hormones from the pregnancy, but Jacques came to the conclusion that Royalty really was kinda crazy and Jacques contributed it to Royalty childhood. But Jacques knew Royalty was going to be a great mom because Royalty was spending a lot of time with Angel and King spoiling them and Royalty was great with them every time they came over. Royalty treated them just like they were her own. Very loving. Royalty even went and got the kids sometimes because Royalty missed them. Giving their mom a break and allowing Liberty to go out and chill with her friends. So, Jacques wasn't concerned about Royalty parenting skills it was everything else about Royalty that Jacques was worried about.
Confirming the appointment for Tuesday Royalty made sure everything was taken care of before her and Jacques left for New York tomorrow. Royalty spoke with her attorney to make sure all the paperwork on her end was good and it was. Mejia had hired movers a few months back to move

Royalty and Amir things out and into storage and had the condo professionally cleaned. The condo was as good as the day Royalty and Amir first purchased it. Royalty had made reservations at a few restaurants Royalty wanted to visit while there and booked her and Jacques his and hers spa treatment. Royalty was slowly starting to feel like herself again, but Royalty wasn't one hundred percent just yet. The baby was moving around a lot now and Royalty was getting a little bit excited, but Royalty didn't want to know the sex of the baby until the baby arrived to surprise her and Jacques, knowing the sex of the baby took all the fun out of it to Royalty especially since this was her first baby. Royalty packed her bags and started thinking about Amir. Royalty wondered if Amir was still alive would she had gotten pregnant and if so, would it have been any different since Amir already had a child by someone else. Oh well it didn't matter now anyways Royalty couldn't change the past. Jacques called and said he was on his way and did Royalty need him to stop and pick anything up before coming home. Royalty smiled thinking Jacques was amazing Royalty was happy she meet Jacques when she did. Some things were just meant to be Royalty was thinking. Royalty told Jacques there was nothing that she wanted but him and to hurry home then Royalty hung up. Sex while pregnant was the best lately Royalty couldn't get enough of Jacques. But poor Jacques the first couple months Royalty wouldn't let Jacques touch her now it's just the opposite. Royalty was smiling thinking about how happy she was and that she was in a really good place right now. Royalty was taking the medication to calm her down despite Jacques request for her not to. But Royalty actually needed the medication it helped Royalty with her mood swings. Hearing Jacques walk in the house Jacques had his own key now Royalty started smiling anticipating seeing him. Jacques came in looking rich with a Burberry trench coat on and a Burberry wool sweater with jeans and boots with a brim hat on. Take all that off babe everything Royalty said rubbing her big belly.

Laughing Jacques says hold up babe I got something for you close your eyes Jacques says.

Closing her eyes Royalty says babe what is it?

Hold up Jacques says holding out two paper bags in front of Royalty. Reach inside these two paper bags and pull what's inside them out.

Royalty was thinking paper bags huh? Ok reaching inside the paper bags Royalty pulls out something and asked Jacques what it was.

Put it in your mouth Jacques said.

My mouth Royalty responded.

Just do it and Royalty did it was a candy pacifier Royalty laughed and asked could she open her eyes now. No one more thing reach inside the bag Jacques said. Reaching in the bag Royalty pulled something out but couldn't tell what it was. Now open your eyes Jacques says. When Royalty opened her eyes, Jacques was on one knee and Royalty was holding a little box. Looking at the box then at Jacques Royalty started tearing up. Open it Jacques said. Royalty opened the box and really started crying Jacques had gotten her a eight carat green diamond ring shape like a heart it was Royalty birthstone peridot. I want you to be my wife Jacques said Royalty will you marry me?

Royalty grabbed Jacques by the neck and started screaming yes but Jacques was screaming he couldn't breathe tapping out for Royalty to let him go. Royalty let Jacques go and they started kissing. Let's do it tomorrow Royalty I don't want to wait another day let's go to the courthouse

Jacques said. Just you and me. Wiping the tears from Royalty eyes Royalty said ok but I really would like to wait until the baby comes to be a part of the ceremony Royalty said. And Jacques agreed to wait until they had the baby. Royalty keep looking at her ring in total awe. It was beautiful. Life was so perfect right now nothing could kill their vibe. Royalty was the happiest women on earth. And Jacques was happy that Royalty was happy.

When Tuesday morning came Royalty wasn't feeling well but Royalty was ready to get this deal over with. Royalty made arrangements with her bank to deposit and wire the money to another account because the funds were going into an account with her and Amir's name and Royalty wanted the money in her own personal account Royalty also had a notary coming to notarize the signing of the deed to the condo. The plane ride was cool, but Royalty was ready to get this chapter over with and move forward with her life. Jacques had a black car service pick them up at the plane and take them straight to the famous restaurant Keens Steakhouse in Manhattan to meet the realtor and client who was there waiting on their arrival. When Royalty and Jacques got to the restaurant it was empty besides the realtor. Royalty shook the realtor hand and introduced herself because they had only spoken a few times over the phone but never meet in person. The realtor said she was waiting for her client to come and they were just five minutes away.

Royalty Introduced Jacques who excused himself to the restroom. Once Jacques got into the restroom Jacques checked every stall because something just didn't seem right it felt like a set up to him but why? Jacques or Royalty wasn't carrying large sums of cash on them Royalty was the one supposedly waiting on the money. The bathroom was empty. But for precautionary measures Jacques took his gun out because Jacques never left home without it and that's why Jacques always flew private just for these types of situations. Walking out the bathroom Jacques was meet with a gun to his head from behind him.

Drop your gun I'm with the New York Police dept the officer said kicking Jacques gun after Jacques dropped it. And put your hands behind your back the officer said handcuffing Jacques.

Jacques was wondering what did the New York police dept want with him until the police walked Jacques out the bathroom area and Jacques saw that a whole damn swat team had Royalty surrounded and the person who was supposed to be a realtor had a gun to Royalty head placing Royalty under arrest. What the fuck is going on Jacques was wondering. Detective Maceo was helping Royalty up off the ground and reading Royalty her miranda rights. When detective Maceo finished he said to Royalty I knew you were too good to be true. You're under the arrest for the murder of Amir Spencer. Amir Jacques was thinking this is some sort of big mistake. Why would Royalty kill Amir? and why would they think Royalty killed Amir.

What you want me to do with him boss the officer with Jacques asks detective Maceo.

Let him go he's clean detective Maceo said.

He had a piece on him the officer said.

Tag it and process it but let him go I ran a background check on him already he's squeaky clean detective Maceo said letting Jacques know that he was well aware of who he was.

What the fuck is going on? Jacques said mad as fuck who the fuck are you? Jacques asked Detective Maceo.

I'm your worst fucking nightmare buddy that's who the fuck I am. Ask your little girlfriend when you visit her in prison who I am laughing Detective Maceo said feeling pumped about arresting Royalty after his damn near yearly investigation of the murder of Amir. Get her ass out my face Detective Maceo said to his squad of police officers that had Royalty surrounded like she had just did a school shooting or something. The whole Nypd where there to assist with Royalty arrest. When taking Royalty out the restaurant flashing lights went off taking pictures there were news reporters everywhere waiting outside. Detective Maceo says to Jacques while another police officers was undoing Jacques cuffs. If I was you, I'll get my little baby after it's born in prison and go back to your own fucking county. Because your little girlfriend is never fucking getting out. Royalty is a serial killer with a cute face and a bad body my friend. But make no mistake about it Royalty is a killer and a dangerous one at that. Royalty killed Amir because Amir was planning on leaving her are, so she thought in her little twisted mind of hers. Royalty is a cold hearted killer Jacques and you could've been next on her list of foes. Royalty feed her own mother heroin and watched her overdose with a needle sticking out her arm and never called for help. Amir found Royalty mom and called 911 but Royalty mom had been dead for hours before help arrived. Word on the streets is that Royalty was in the house upstairs packing all her mother's belongings throwing her mother's stuff out in the dumpster outside their unit. Like Good riddance. And they say Royalty never shed a tear for her mother. Imagine that. No remorse at all not even for her own mother. But the Los Angeles police department could never prove it. It was just hearsay, but they knew what really happened. Royalty will kill anyone who brings harm her way. And if Royalty even thinks you're about to hurt her Royalty will finish you first. Royalty is a savage raised in the hood that experienced a lot of pain and you want to know a little secret walking up on Jacques. Royalty tried to kill your ex wife . Yeah you didn't know I knew my shit huh? I've been watching Royalty ever since I first meet her when Royalty first killed Amir something just didn't seem right about his murder. My gut told me it was something more to it. And I be damn it wasn't. Come to find out Amir had a phone stashed in one of his coat pockets that gave me all the information for motive on Royalty. And I had Amir's body exhumed and Amir's head reconfigured, and Amir wasn't shot by someone knocking at the door like the fabricated story Royalty has in her little twisted head. Amir was shot in the back of the head by Royalty. Amir had a hole in the back of his skull the size of a golf ball. That's right in order with Royalty 9mm with hollow point bullets. Detective Maceo said confident he had an open and close case against Royalty. And I've been working with the Lapd on Royalty for Information about Royalty past and on their active case involving your ex wife. You did know your ex wife break line on her car had been cut right? Jacques was standing there listening to Detective Maceo in denial.

We ruled you out because we had someone alibi you for the time of the accident. But the day before your wife unfortunate accident Royalty was seen hiring a jailhouse mechanic to cut the brake lines on your ex wife car. Yeah, my man your little baby mama is a very dangerous women with a dual personality disorder. That started after her brutal rape as a child. Did Royalty tell you about that? Jacques didn't respond.

Well it's very unfortunate but it turned Royalty into a killing machine. Royalty develop dissociative identity disorder which means that Royalty has split personalities that Royalty unaware of and Royalty forgets or blocks out trauma but does serious harm to other people without realizing it. And in Royalty case Royalty was provoked to kill Amir out of fear of losing everything they had accomplished together other over the years. Amir was Royalty whole life until Amir got another woman pregnant and wanted to include the woman and his child in his will. I got a copy of Amir's will that Amir had revised that Royalty knew nothing about from Amir's lawyers. See Amir felt that

Royalty was worth enough money on her own without him having to leave his whole entire fortune to Royalty. So, Amir was leaving his company to his unborn child with a conservative over the estate until the child reached adulthood. And also, Amir was dividing his company shares between three people Royalty was one, his side chick Mija was second and another woman Amir's cousin in his will. But all his possessions went to Royalty and their houses also went to Royalty in the event that something ever happening to him. But here's where the story gets interesting at detective Maceo says. I don't know when exactly Royalty snapped but what I do know is that Amir and Royalty had a conversation about breaking up and Royalty felt like she was about to lose everything that she and Amir had built together. And Royalty felt like how can you just give another woman what's supposed to be rightfully mine so easily and Royalty felt betrayed. And the one thing a man has to be very careful about is betraying a woman and breaking her heart. Some women never recover from that shit and Royalty was one of them. All that Royalty and Amir had gone through throughout the years of growing up and being together the thought of Amir possibly up and leaving Royalty caused Royalty to snap and brutally kill Amir. You can kinda say Amir caused his own death at this point. Either way Royalty snapped into a different personality and took her gun and shot Amir and blew Amir head of his shoulders and walked into her closet and put her gun away. Then Royalty snapped into a different personality and went back and found Amir's body and forgot that she had just killed him. Royalty a very sick and dangerous woman Jacques. And if I were you, I'll get my kid and move far away and forget that Royalty ever existed. Royalty needs help a lifetime of treatment. And the courts will make sure that Royalty gets the help she needs. Sighing Have a nice afternoon and enjoy New York Detective Maceo said and snapped his fingers at the remaining police officers and walked out the restaurant leaving Jacques standing there in shock over what he had just heard.

This sounded like a sci-fi horror movie this couldn't be true could it? Jacques sat down at the bar and ordered himself a drink. Jacques looked around at the empty room and thought Am I in love with a serial killer?

www.ingramcontent.com/pod-product-compliance
Lightning Source LLC
Chambersburg PA
CBHW080322170426
43193CB00017B/2873